SUR SO-AWD-271

You may be reading the wrong way!

It's true: In keeping with the original Japanese comic format, this book reads from right to left—so action, sound effects, and word balloons are completely reversed. This preserves the orientation of the original artwork—plus, it's fun! Check out the diagram shown here to get the hang of things, and then turn to the other side of the book to get started!

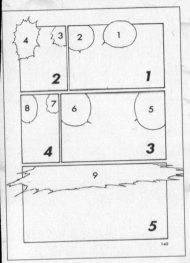

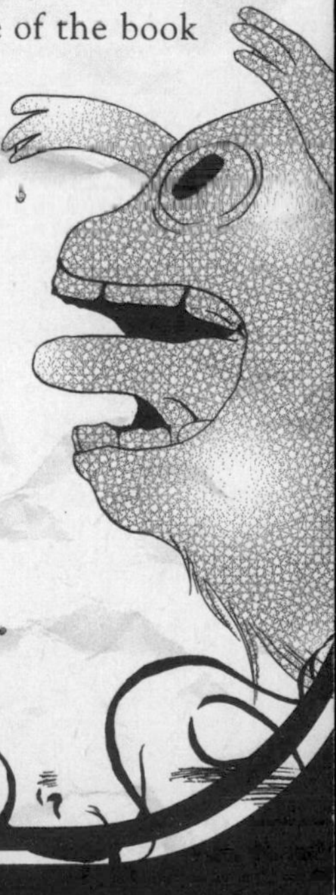

NATSUME'S BOOK OF FRIENDS
Vol. 11
Shojo Beat Edition

STORY AND ART BY *Yuki Midorikawa*

Translation & Adaptation *Lillian Olsen*
Touch-up Art & Lettering *Sabrina Heep*
Design *Fawn Lau*
Editor *Pancha Diaz*

Natsume Yujincho by Yuki Midorikawa
© Yuki Midorikawa 2011
All rights reserved.
First published in Japan in 2011 by HAKUSENSHA, Inc., Tokyo.
English language translation rights arranged with HAKUSENSHA, Inc., Tokyo.

The stories, characters and incidents mentioned in this publication are entirely fictional.

Printed in the U.S.A.

Published by VIZ Media, LLC
P.O. Box 77010
San Francisco, CA 94107

10 9 8 7 6 5 4 3
First printing, February 2012
Third printing, May 2019

Yuki Midorikawa
is the creator of *Natsume's Book of Friends*, which was nominated for the Manga Taisho (Cartoon Grand Prize). Her other titles published in Japan include *Hotarubi no Mori e* (Into the Forest of Fireflies), *Hiiro no Isu* (The Scarlet Chair) and *Akaku Saku Koe* (The Voice That Blooms Red).

Natsume's
BOOK of FRIENDS

Shojo Beat

Natsume's BOOK of FRIENDS

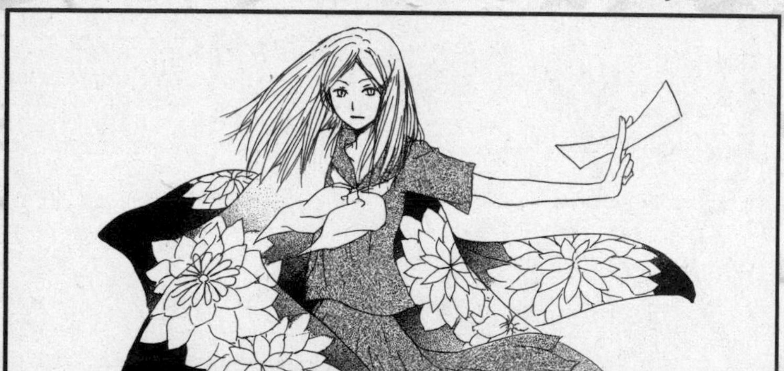

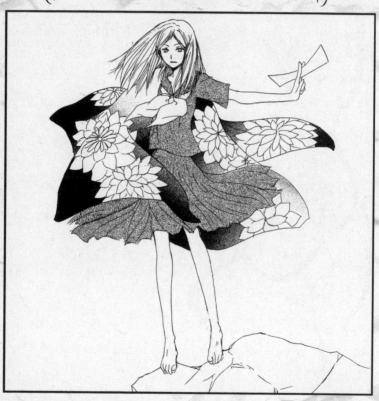

STORY and ART by
Yuki Midorikawa

VOLUME 11

Natsume's
BOOK of FRIENDS

VOLUME 11 CONTENTS

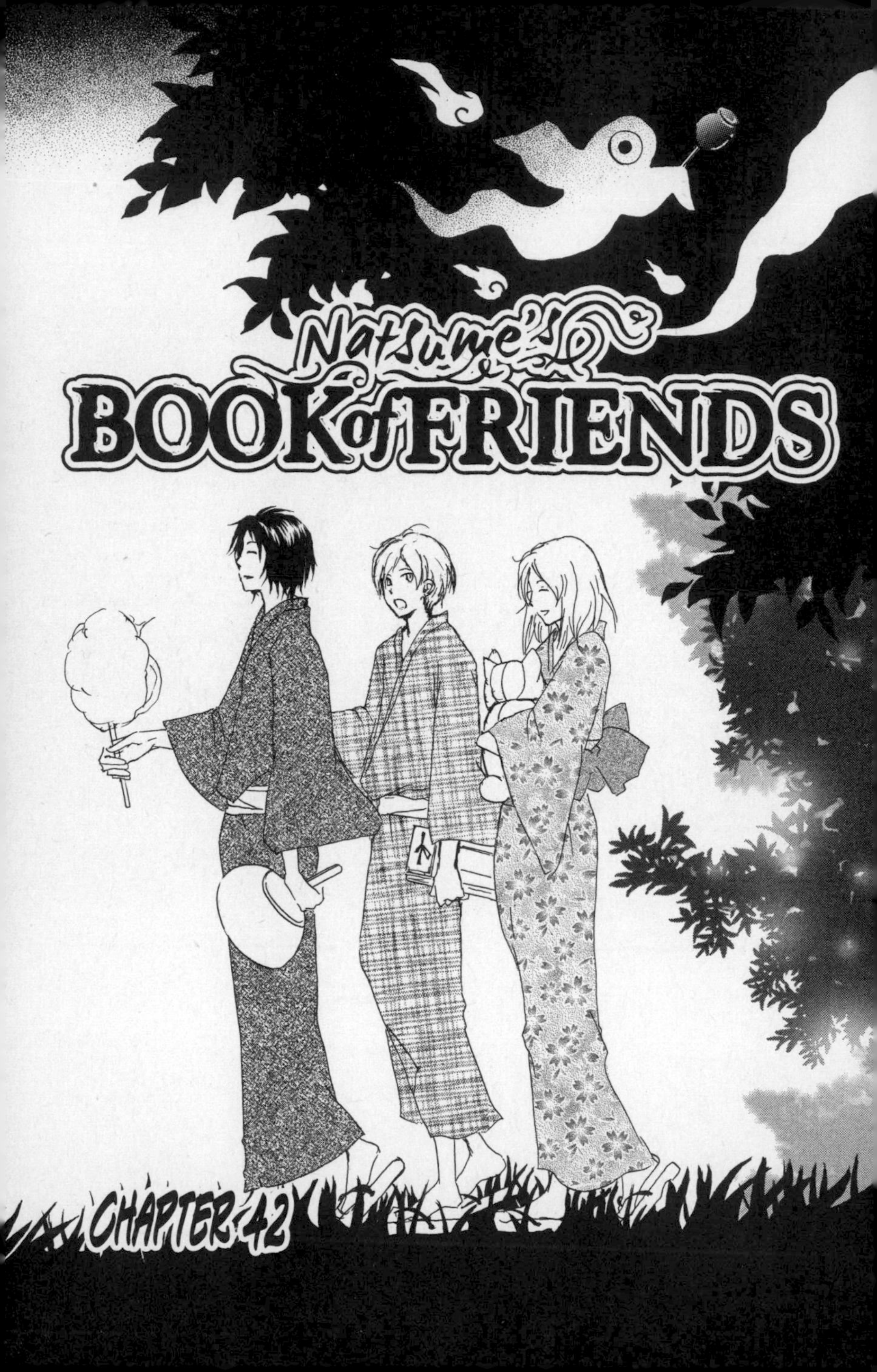
Natsume's
BOOK of FRIENDS
CHAPTER 42

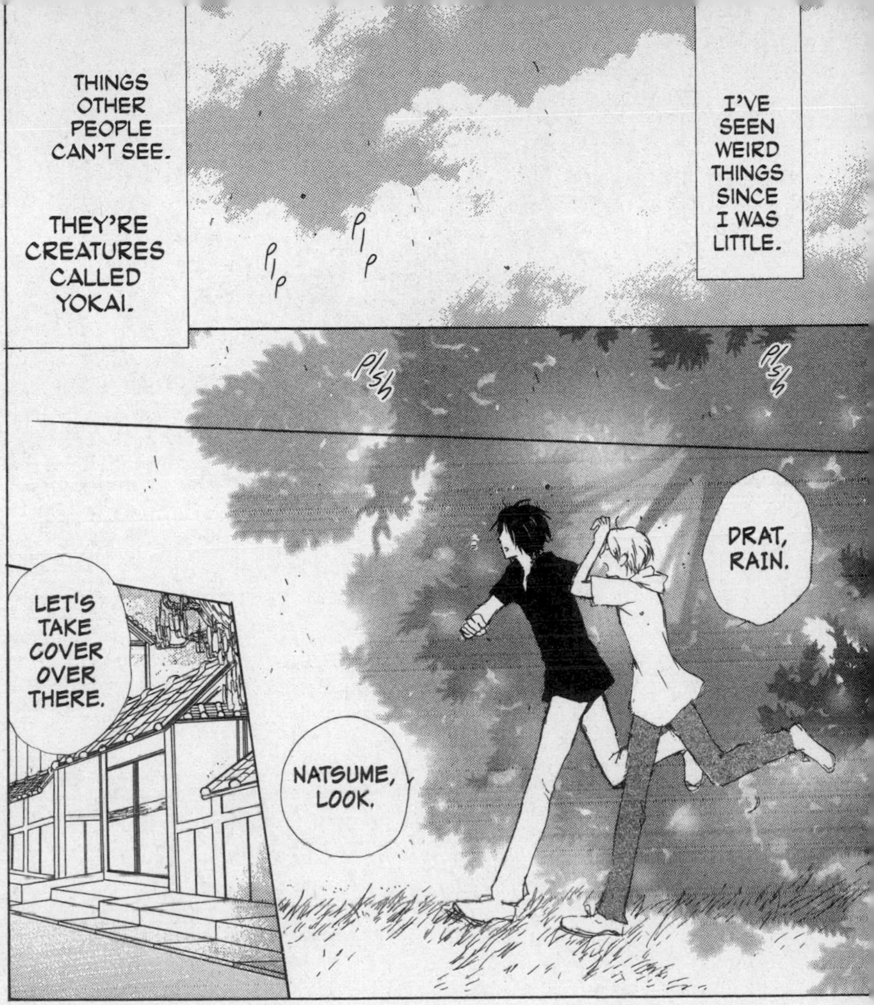
I'VE SEEN WEIRD THINGS SINCE I WAS LITTLE.
THINGS OTHER PEOPLE CAN'T SEE.
THEY'RE CREATURES CALLED YOKAI.
plip
plip
plsh
plsh
DRAT, RAIN.
NATSUME, LOOK.
LET'S TAKE COVER OVER THERE.

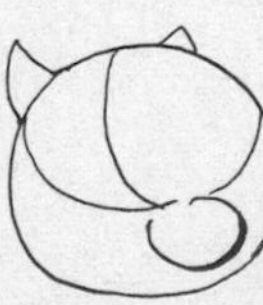

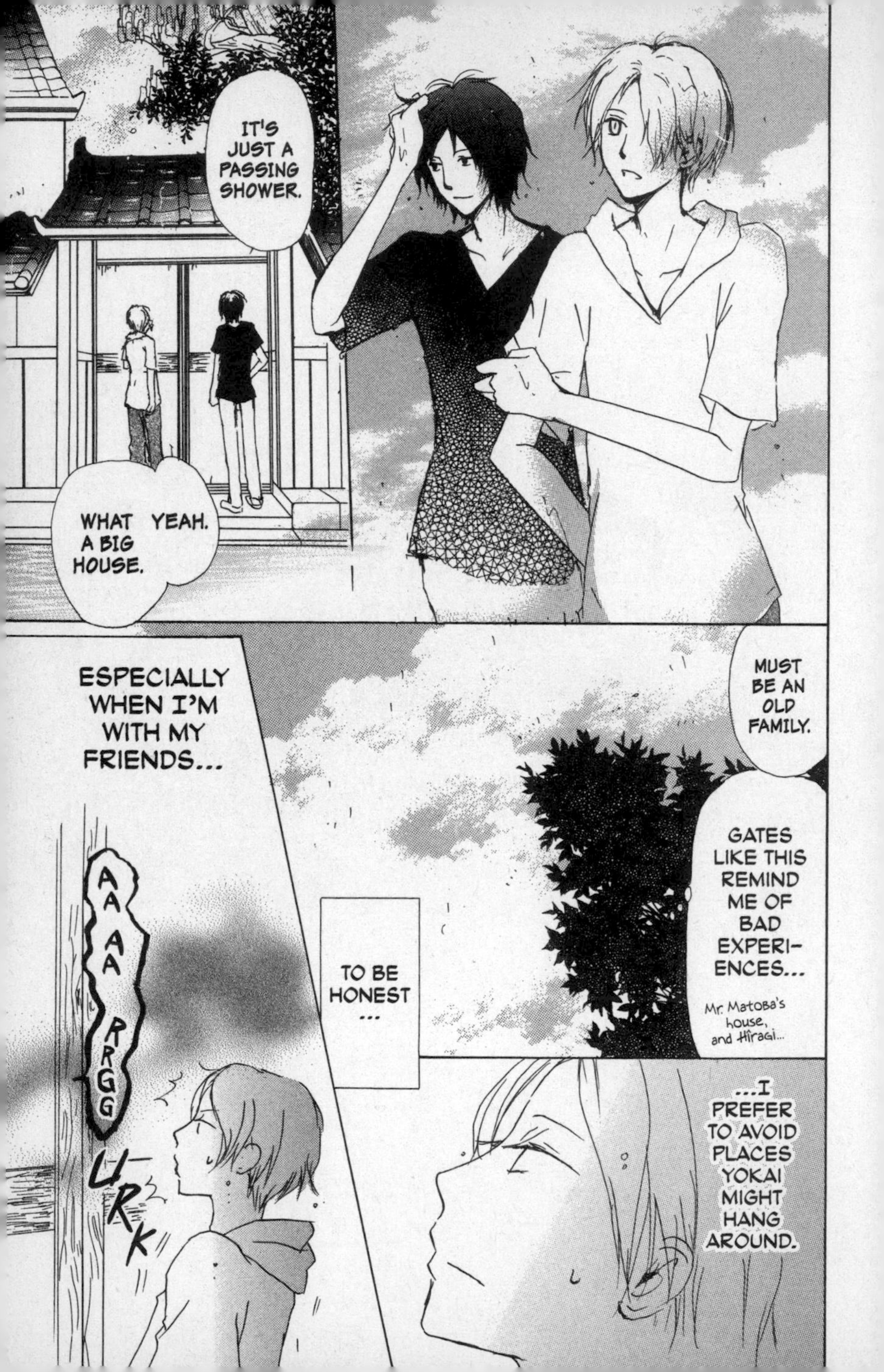
IT'S JUST A PASSING SHOWER.
WHAT A BIG HOUSE.
YEAH.
MUST BE AN OLD FAMILY.
GATES LIKE THIS REMIND ME OF BAD EXPERI-ENCES...
Mr. Matoba's house, and Hîragi...
TO BE HONEST...
...I PREFER TO AVOID PLACES YOKAI MIGHT HANG AROUND.
ESPECIALLY WHEN I'M WITH MY FRIENDS...
AA AA RRGG
URK

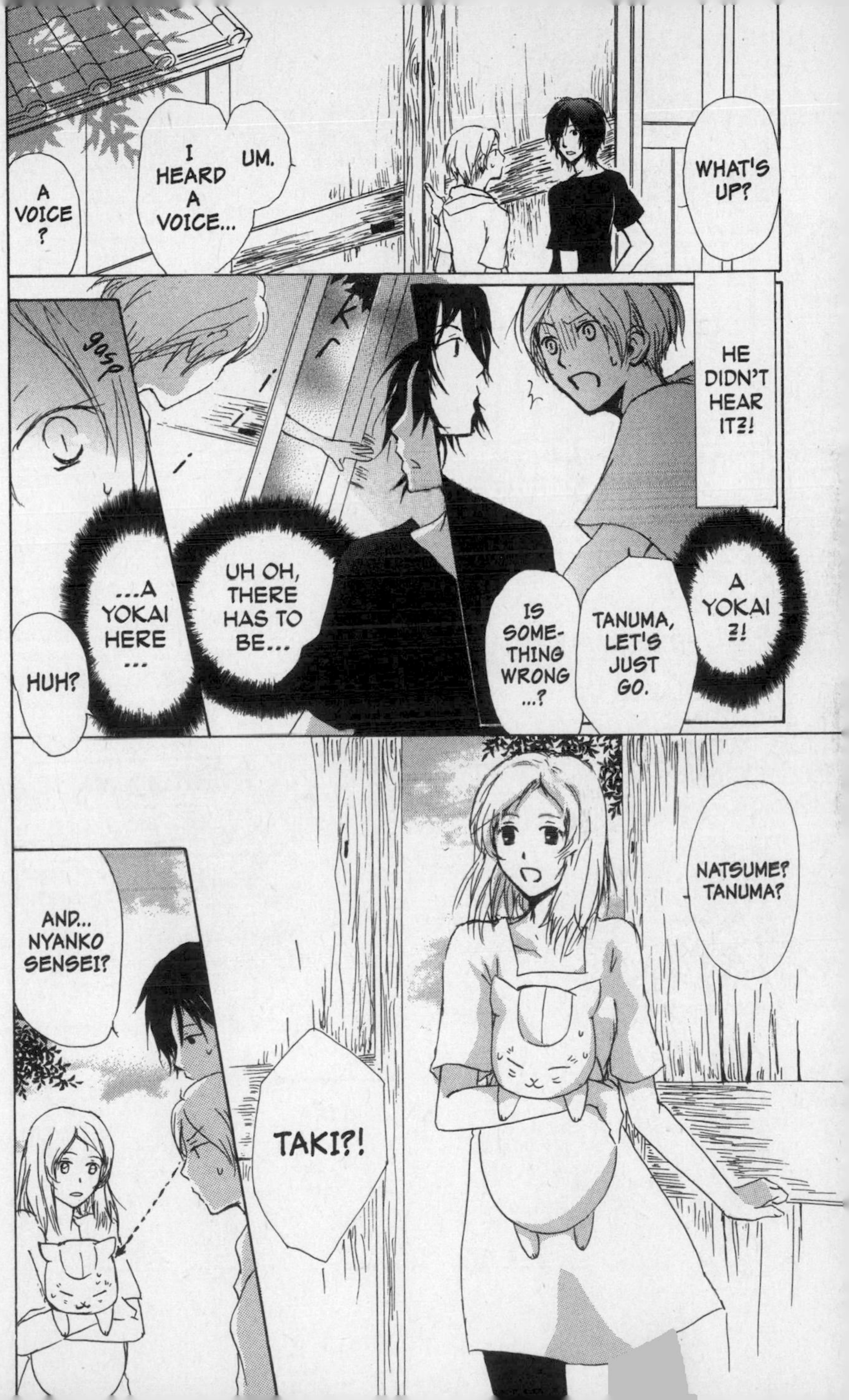
WHAT'S UP?
UM.
I HEARD A VOICE...
A VOICE?
HE DIDN'T HEAR IT?!
A YOKAI?!
TANUMA, LET'S JUST GO.
IS SOME-THING WRONG...?
UH OH, THERE HAS TO BE...
...A YOKAI HERE...
gasp
HUH?
NATSUME? TANUMA?
TAKI?!
AND... NYANKO SENSEI?

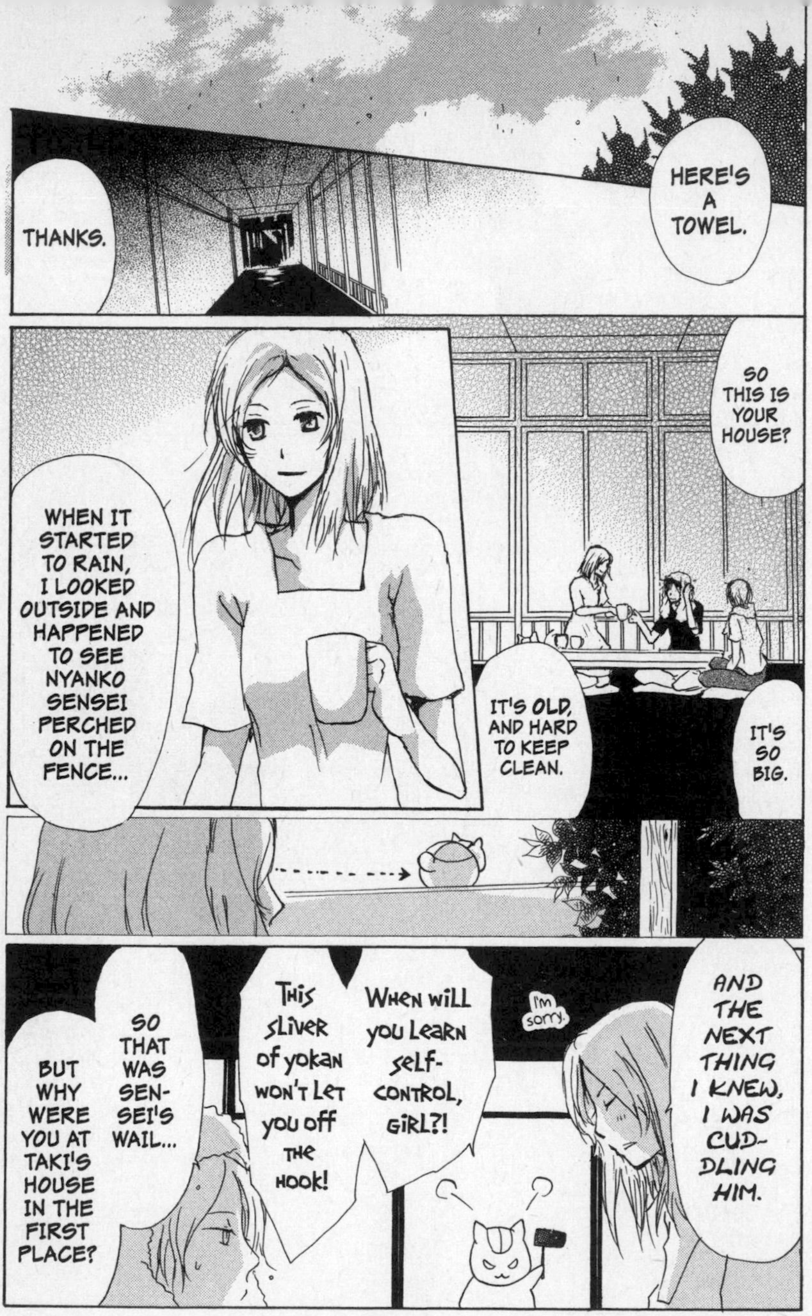
HERE'S A TOWEL.
THANKS.
SO THIS IS YOUR HOUSE?
IT'S SO BIG.
IT'S OLD, AND HARD TO KEEP CLEAN.
WHEN IT STARTED TO RAIN, I LOOKED OUTSIDE AND HAPPENED TO SEE NYANKO SENSEI PERCHED ON THE FENCE...
AND THE NEXT THING I KNEW, I WAS CUD-DLING HIM.
I'm sorry.
When will you learn self-control, girl?!
This sliver of yokan won't let you off the hook!
SO THAT WAS SEN-SEI'S WAIL...
BUT WHY WERE YOU AT TAKI'S HOUSE IN THE FIRST PLACE?

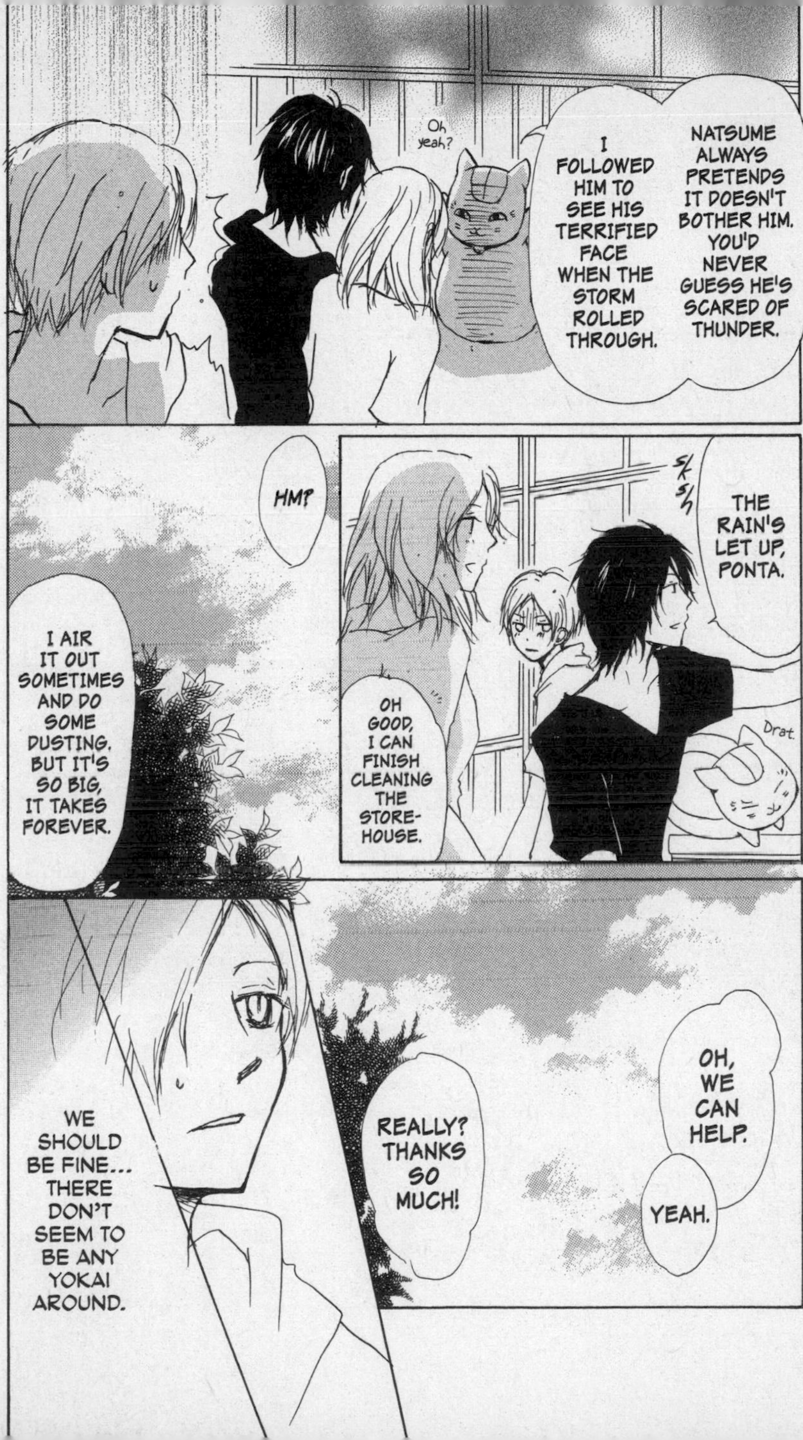
NATSUME ALWAYS PRETENDS IT DOESN'T BOTHER HIM. YOU'D NEVER GUESS HE'S SCARED OF THUNDER.
I FOLLOWED HIM TO SEE HIS TERRIFIED FACE WHEN THE STORM ROLLED THROUGH.
Oh yeah?
THE RAIN'S LET UP, PONTA.
Drat.
OH GOOD, I CAN FINISH CLEANING THE STORE-HOUSE.
HM?
I AIR IT OUT SOMETIMES AND DO SOME DUSTING, BUT IT'S SO BIG, IT TAKES FOREVER.
OH, WE CAN HELP.
YEAH.
REALLY? THANKS SO MUCH!
WE SHOULD BE FINE... THERE DON'T SEEM TO BE ANY YOKAI AROUND.

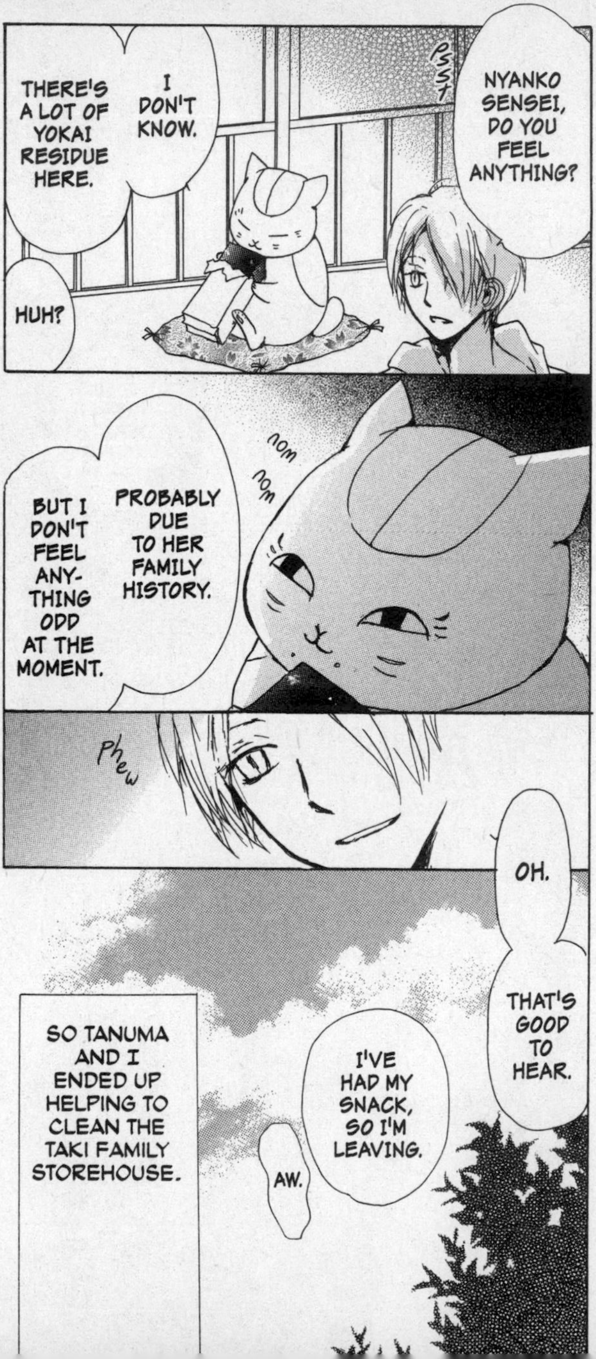
PSST
NYANKO SENSEI, DO YOU FEEL ANYTHING?
I DON'T KNOW.
THERE'S A LOT OF YOKAI RESIDUE HERE.
HUH?
nom nom
PROBABLY DUE TO HER FAMILY HISTORY.
BUT I DON'T FEEL ANYTHING ODD AT THE MOMENT.
Phew
OH.
THAT'S GOOD TO HEAR.
I'VE HAD MY SNACK, SO I'M LEAVING.
AW.
SO TANUMA AND I ENDED UP HELPING TO CLEAN THE TAKI FAMILY STOREHOUSE.

01

Hello, I'm Midorikawa. This is my 19th total graphic novel. I'm so happy I get to keep drawing manga.

Thank you to everyone who has given me a chance.

I'll keep working hard episode by episode to make a manga worthy of your time, so please continue your support.

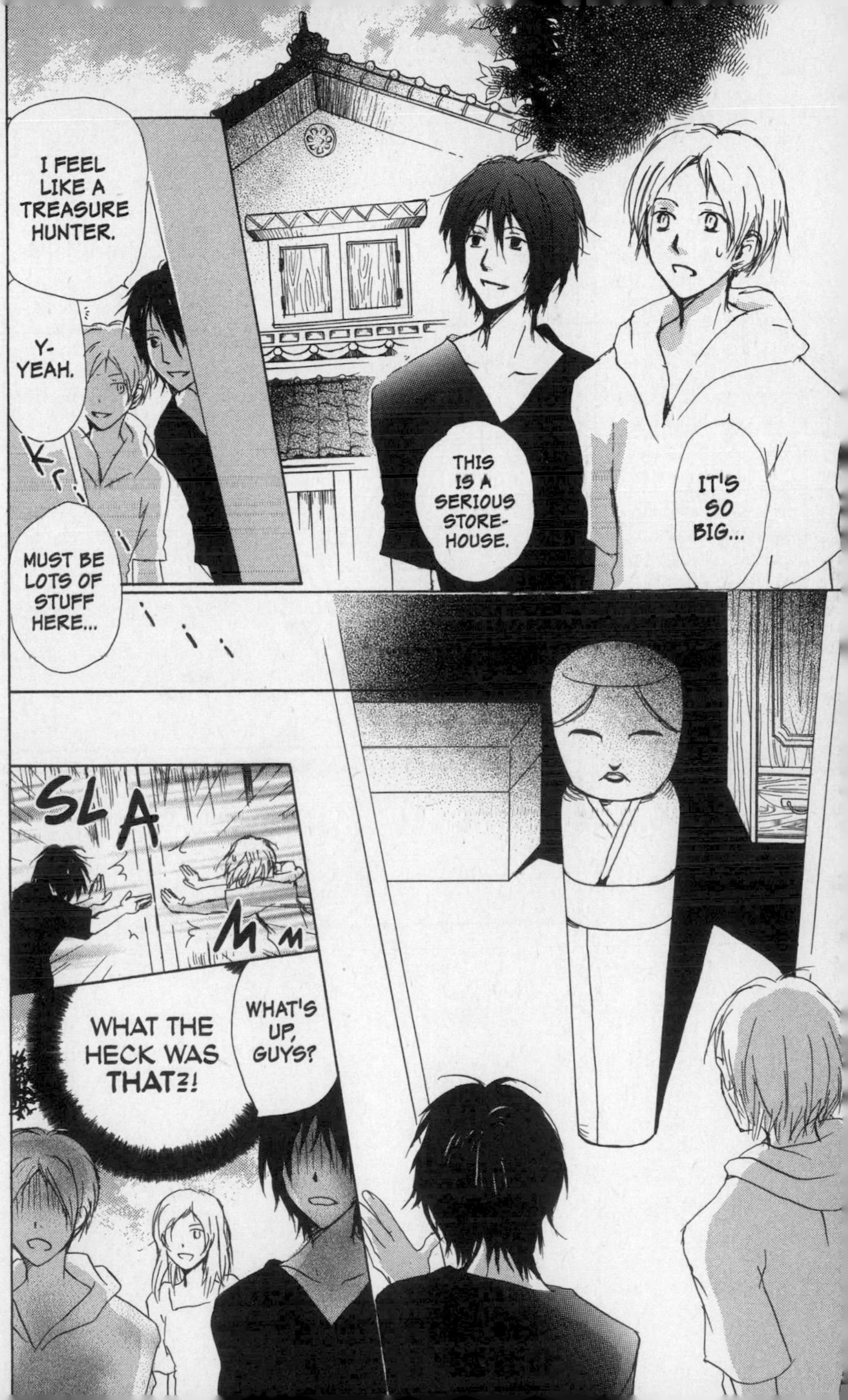
IT'S SO BIG...
THIS IS A SERIOUS STOREHOUSE.
I FEEL LIKE A TREASURE HUNTER.
Y-YEAH.
MUST BE LOTS OF STUFF HERE...
SLAM
WHAT'S UP, GUYS?
WHAT THE HECK WAS THAT?!

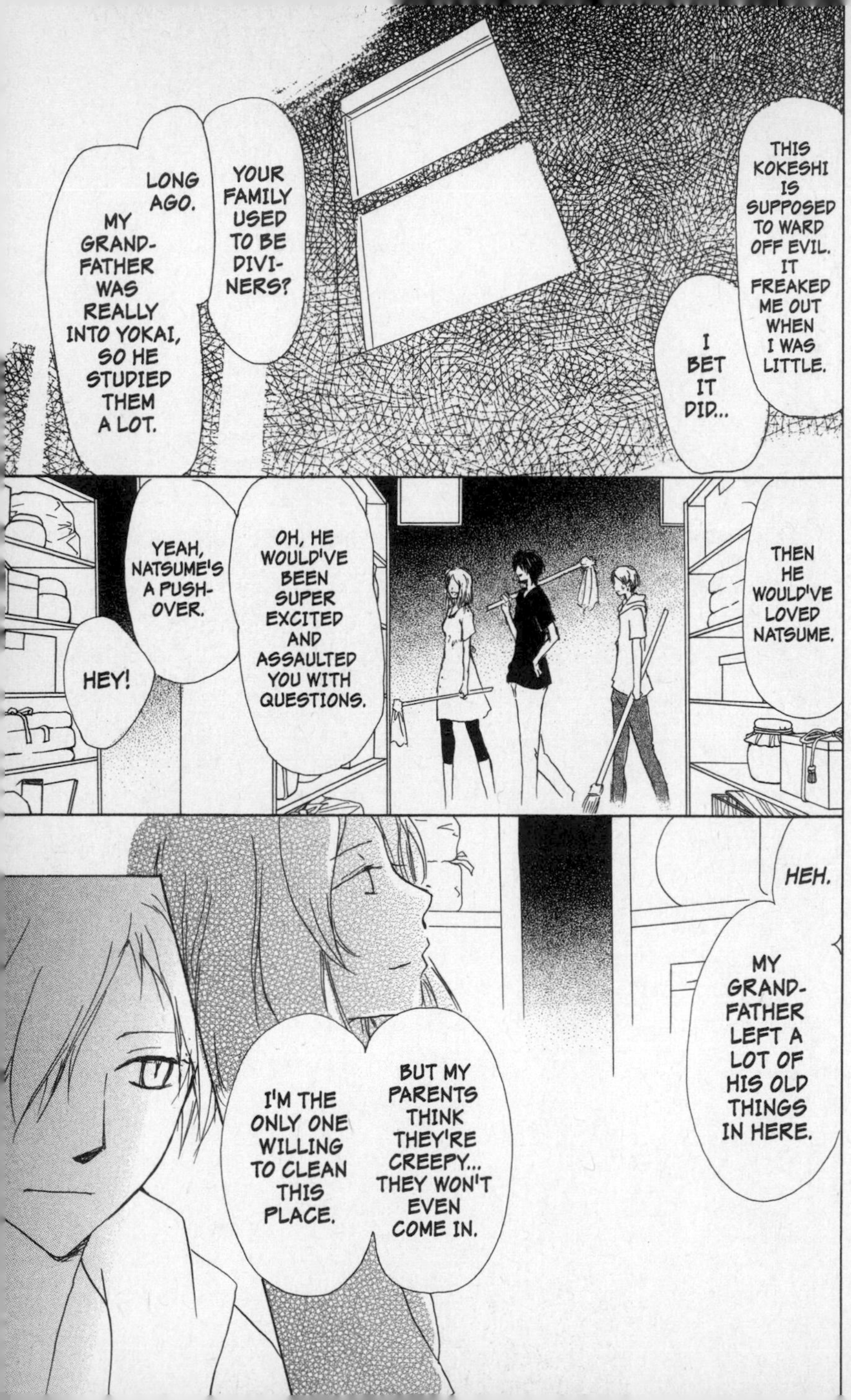
THIS KOKESHI IS SUPPOSED TO WARD OFF EVIL. IT FREAKED ME OUT WHEN I WAS LITTLE.
I BET IT DID...
YOUR FAMILY USED TO BE DIVINERS?
LONG AGO. MY GRANDFATHER WAS REALLY INTO YOKAI, SO HE STUDIED THEM A LOT.
THEN HE WOULD'VE LOVED NATSUME.
OH, HE WOULD'VE BEEN SUPER EXCITED AND ASSAULTED YOU WITH QUESTIONS.
YEAH, NATSUME'S A PUSHOVER.
HEY!
HEH.
MY GRANDFATHER LEFT A LOT OF HIS OLD THINGS IN HERE.
BUT MY PARENTS THINK THEY'RE CREEPY... THEY WON'T EVEN COME IN.
I'M THE ONLY ONE WILLING TO CLEAN THIS PLACE.

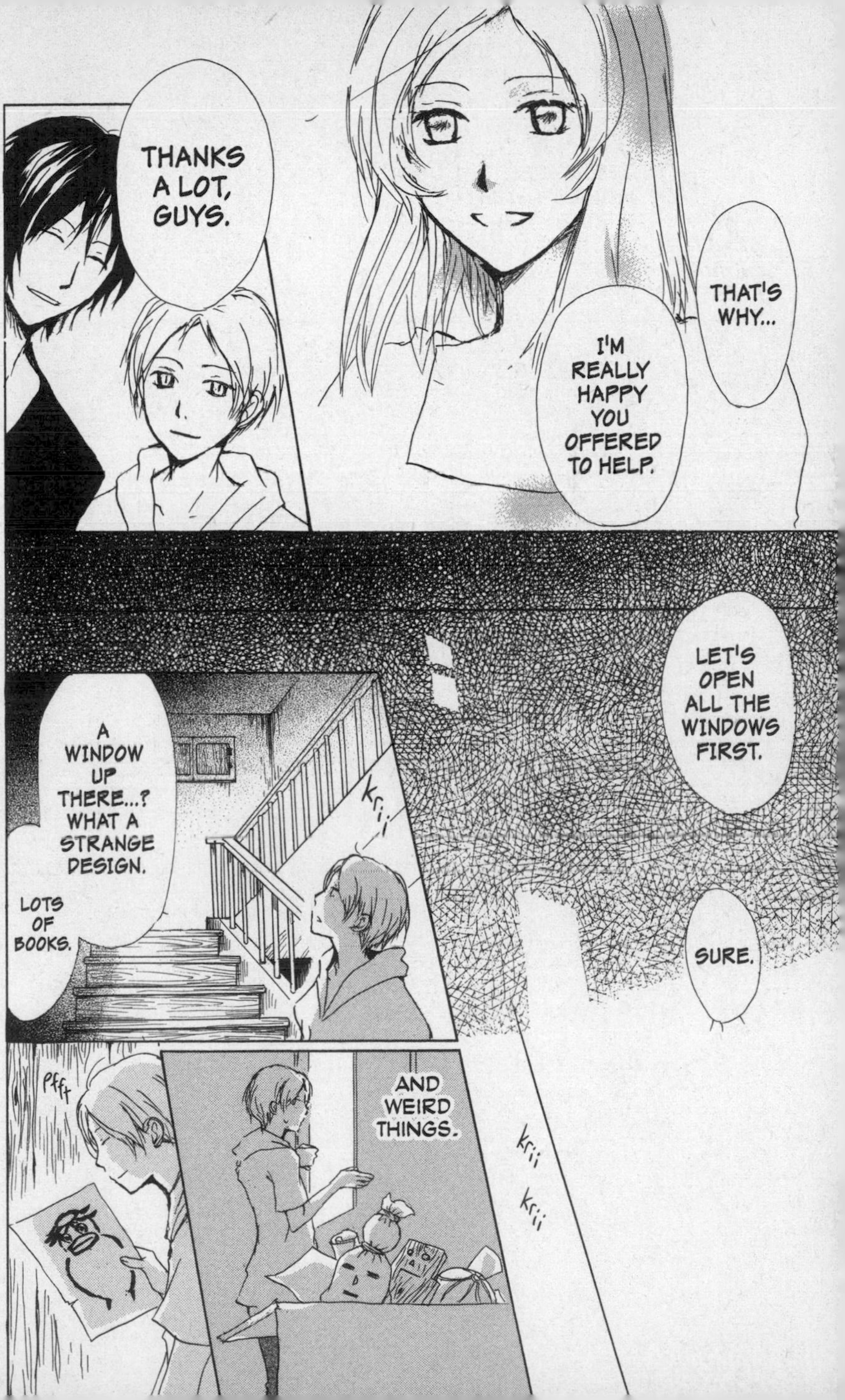
THAT'S WHY...
I'M REALLY HAPPY YOU OFFERED TO HELP.
THANKS A LOT, GUYS.
LET'S OPEN ALL THE WINDOWS FIRST.
SURE.
kri
A WINDOW UP THERE...? WHAT A STRANGE DESIGN.
LOTS OF BOOKS.
krii
krii
AND WEIRD THINGS.
pfft

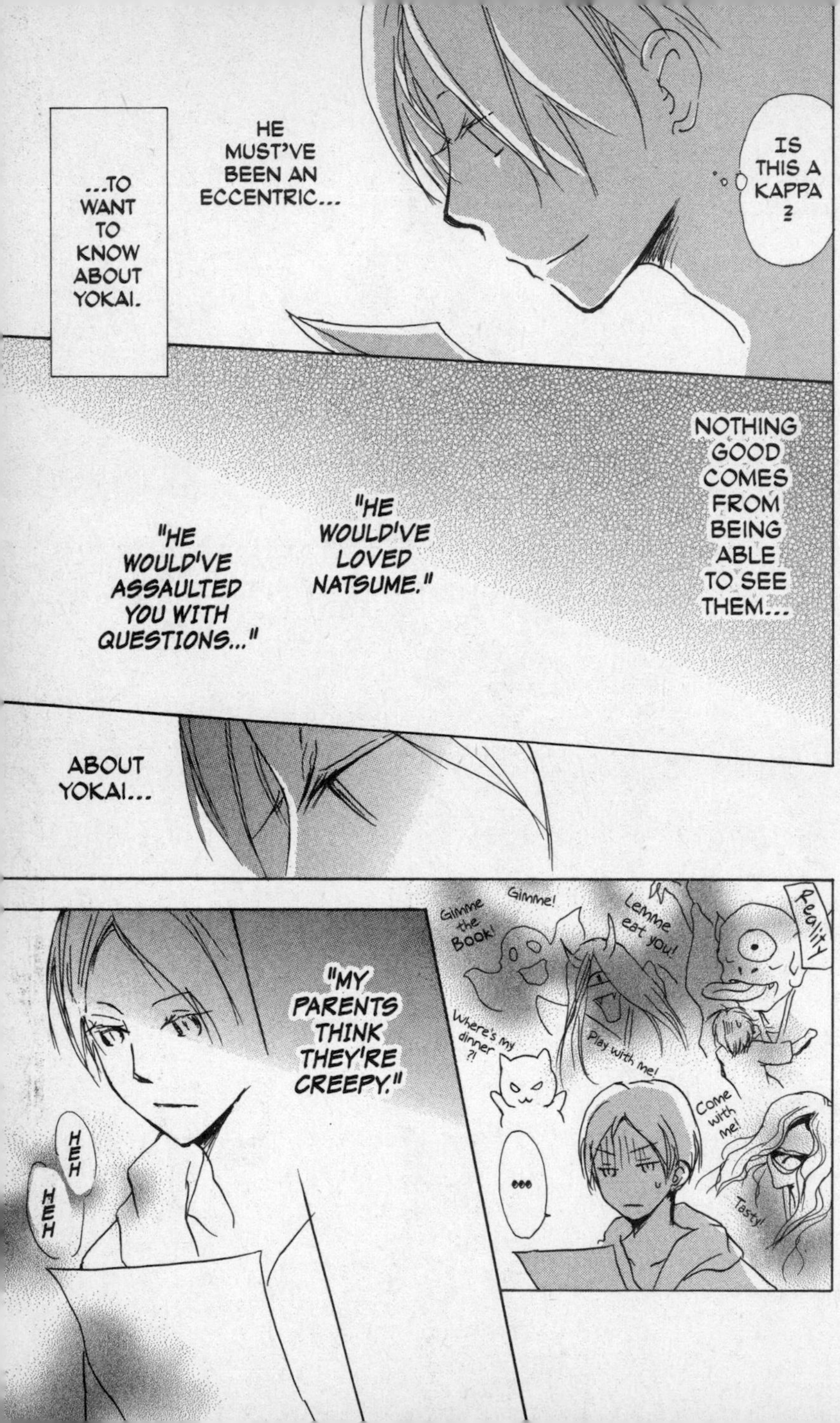
IS THIS A KAPPA?
HE MUST'VE BEEN AN ECCENTRIC...
...TO WANT TO KNOW ABOUT YOKAI.
NOTHING GOOD COMES FROM BEING ABLE TO SEE THEM...
"HE WOULD'VE LOVED NATSUME."
"HE WOULD'VE ASSAULTED YOU WITH QUESTIONS..."
ABOUT YOKAI...
Reality
Lemme eat you!
Gimme!
Gimme the Book!
Where's my dinner?!
Play with me!
Come with me!
Tasty!
...
"MY PARENTS THINK THEY'RE CREEPY."
HEH HEH

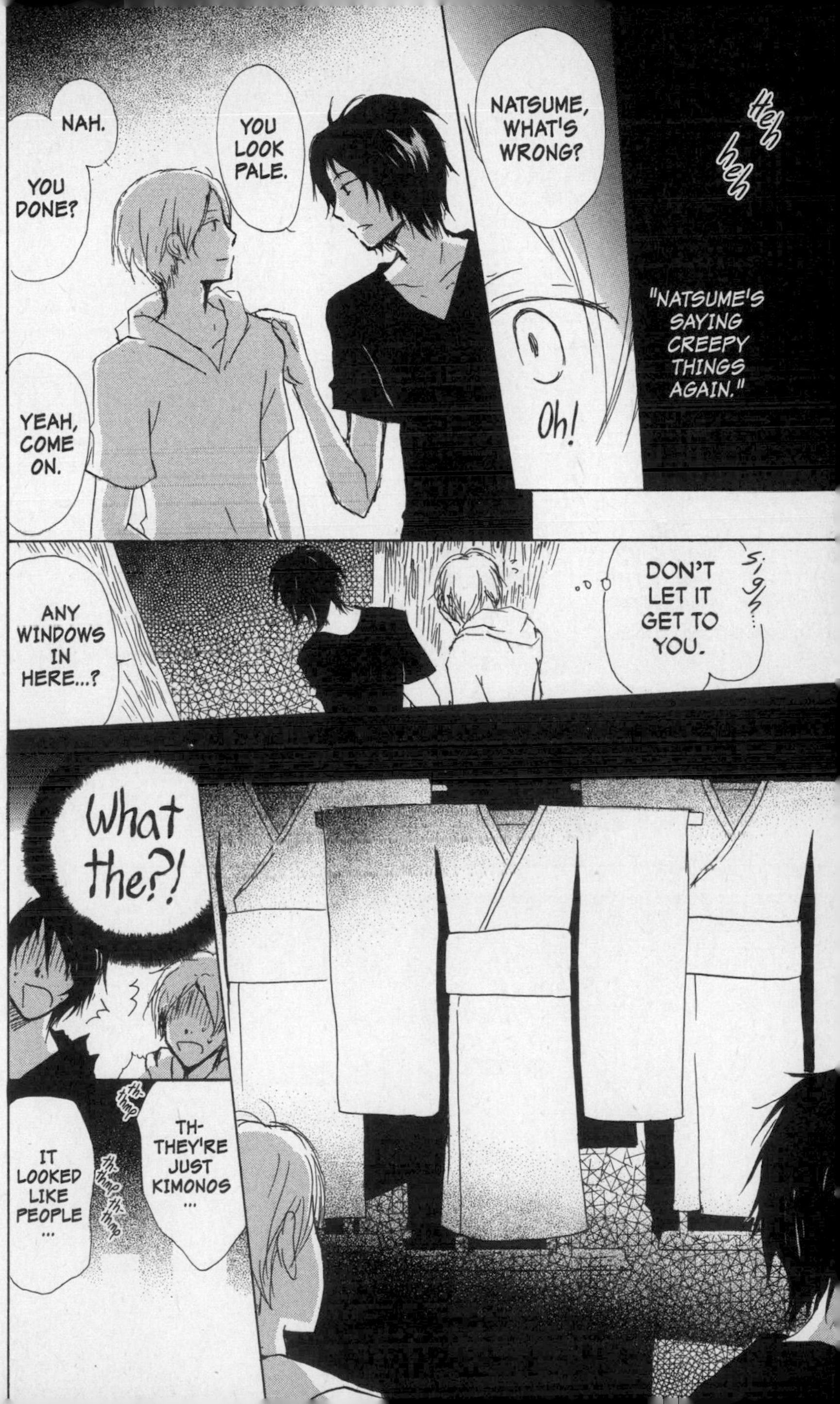
heh heh
NATSUME, WHAT'S WRONG?
"NATSUME'S SAYING CREEPY THINGS AGAIN."
Oh!
YOU LOOK PALE.
NAH.
YOU DONE?
YEAH, COME ON.
DON'T LET IT GET TO YOU.
sigh...
ANY WINDOWS IN HERE...?
What the?!
TH-THEY'RE JUST KIMONOS...
th-thmp
th-thmp th-thmp
IT LOOKED LIKE PEOPLE...

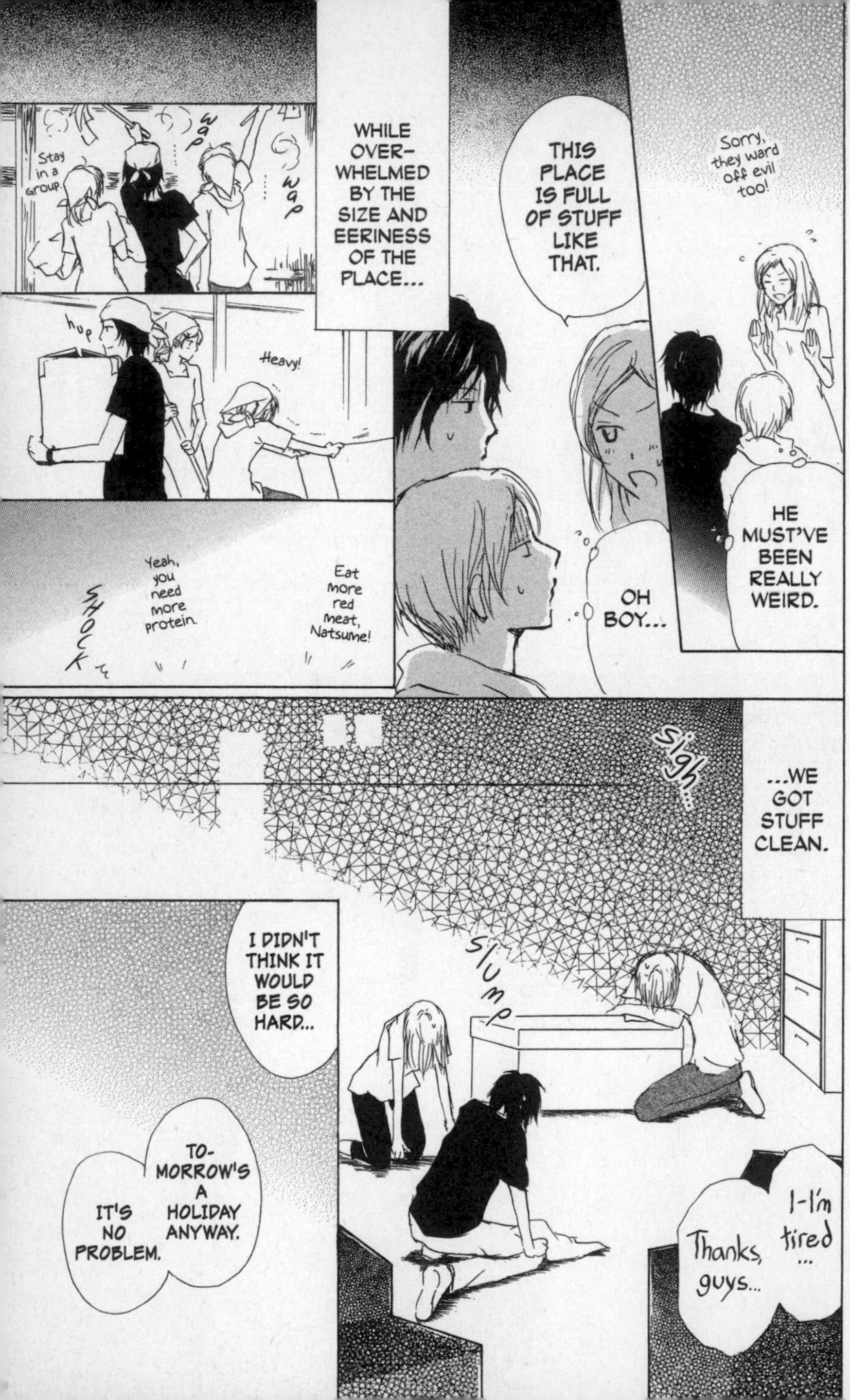
Sorry, they ward off evil too!
THIS PLACE IS FULL OF STUFF LIKE THAT.
HE MUST'VE BEEN REALLY WEIRD.
OH BOY...
WHILE OVER-WHELMED BY THE SIZE AND EERINESS OF THE PLACE...
wap
wap
Stay in a group.
hup
Heavy!
Eat more red meat, Natsume!
Yeah, you need more protein.
SHOCK
...WE GOT STUFF CLEAN.
sigh...
slump
I DIDN'T THINK IT WOULD BE SO HARD...
I-I'm tired...
Thanks, guys...
TO-MORROW'S A HOLIDAY ANYWAY.
IT'S NO PROBLEM.

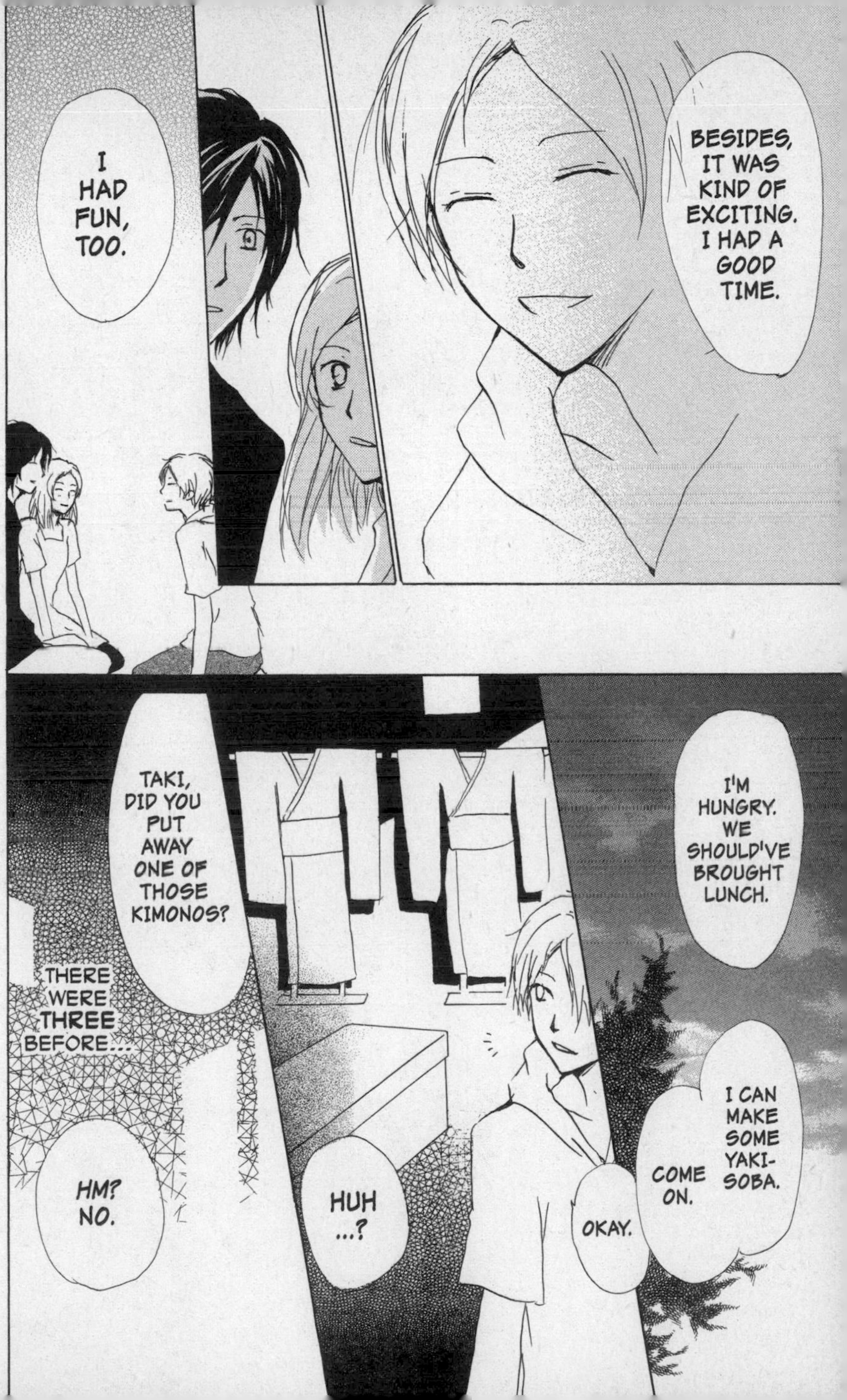
BESIDES, IT WAS KIND OF EXCITING. I HAD A GOOD TIME.
I HAD FUN, TOO.
I'M HUNGRY. WE SHOULD'VE BROUGHT LUNCH.
I CAN MAKE SOME YAKI-SOBA.
COME ON.
OKAY.
TAKI, DID YOU PUT AWAY ONE OF THOSE KIMONOS?
HM? NO.
THERE WERE THREE BEFORE...
HUH ...?

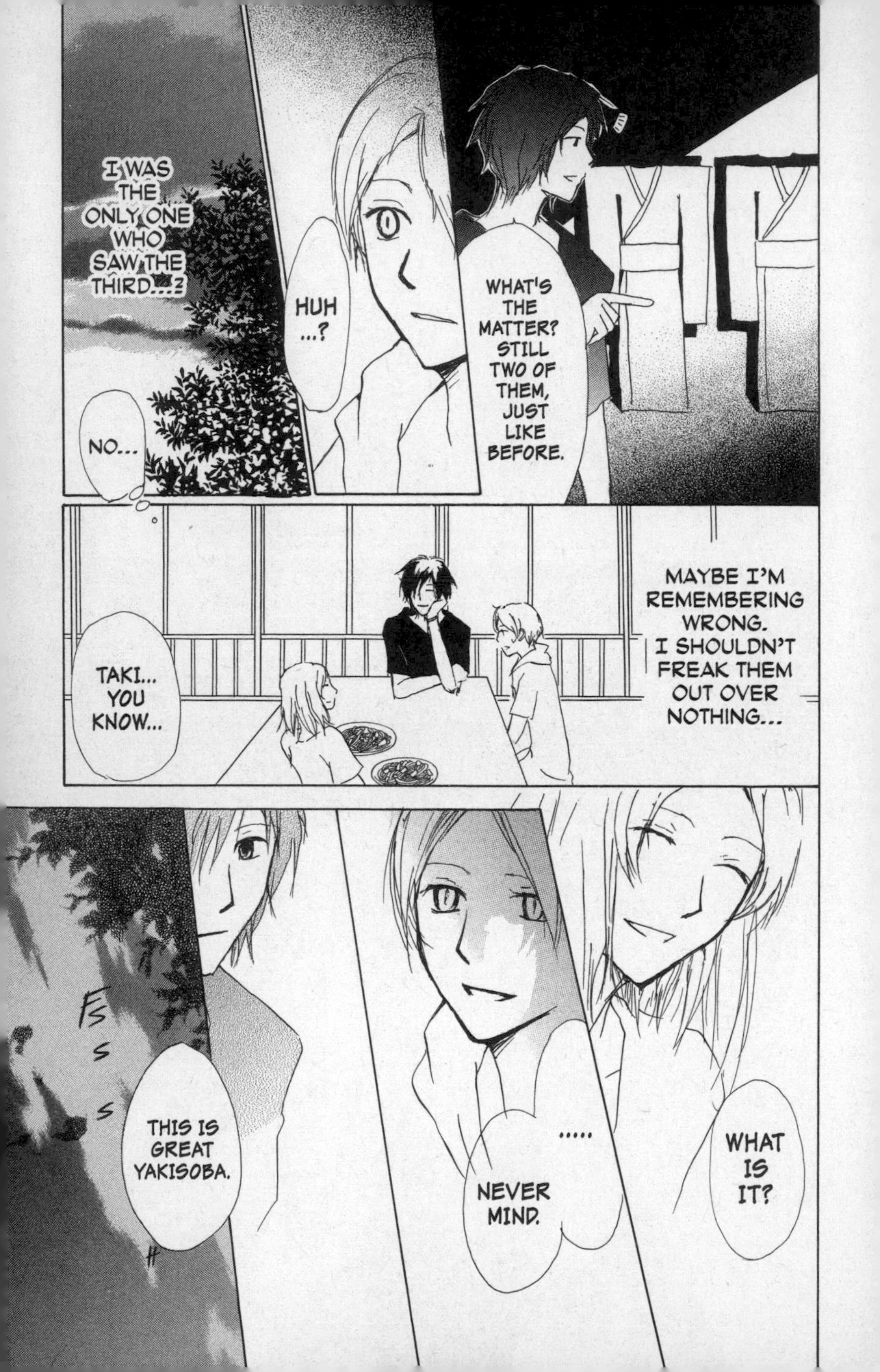
WHAT'S THE MATTER? STILL TWO OF THEM, JUST LIKE BEFORE.
HUH ...?
I WAS THE ONLY ONE WHO SAW THE THIRD...?
NO...
MAYBE I'M REMEMBERING WRONG. I SHOULDN'T FREAK THEM OUT OVER NOTHING...
TAKI... YOU KNOW...
WHAT IS IT?
.....
NEVER MIND.
THIS IS GREAT YAKISOBA.
FSSSH

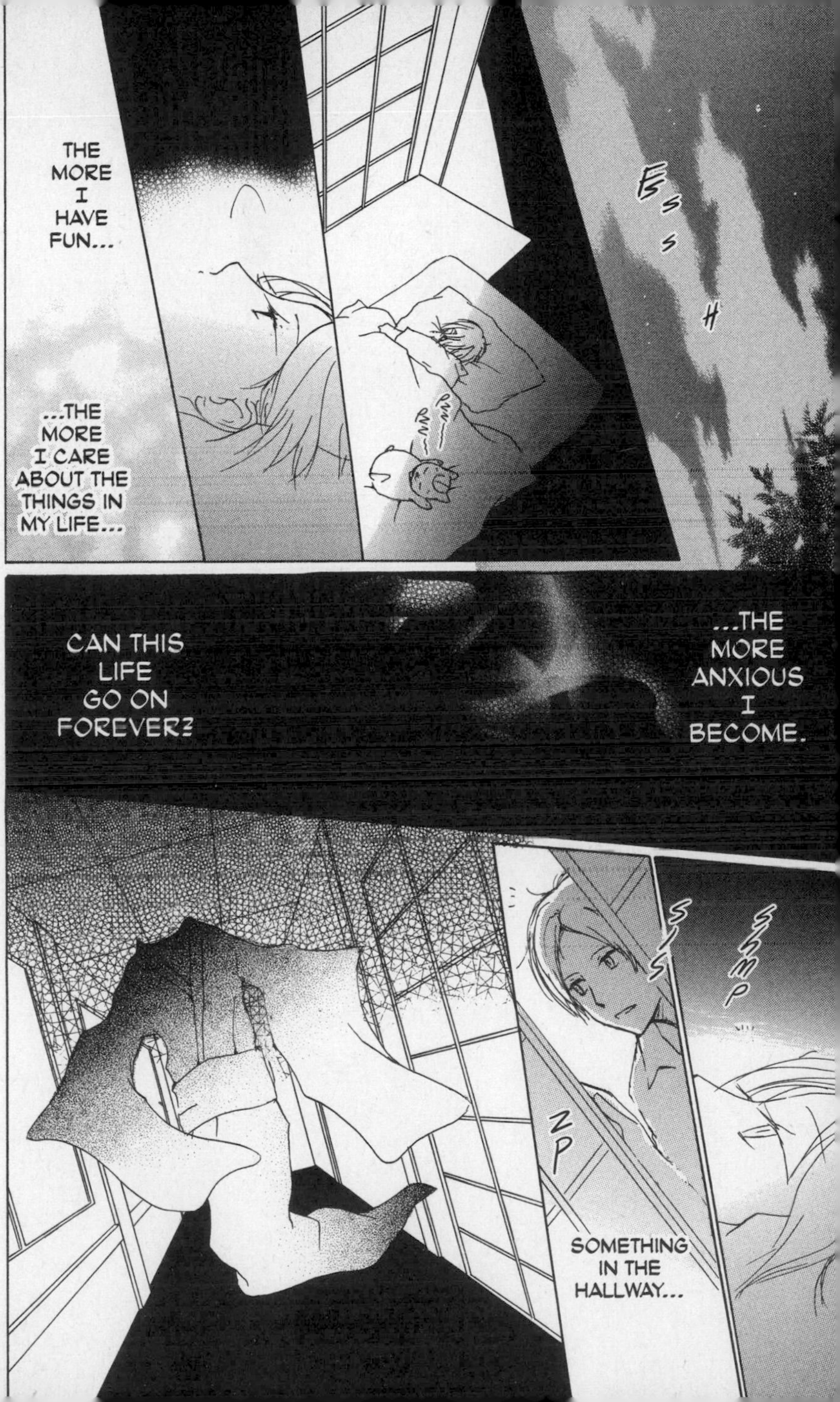
FSSH
THE MORE I HAVE FUN...
...THE MORE I CARE ABOUT THE THINGS IN MY LIFE...
...THE MORE ANXIOUS I BECOME.
CAN THIS LIFE GO ON FOREVER?
SHMP
SHS
ZP
SOMETHING IN THE HALLWAY...

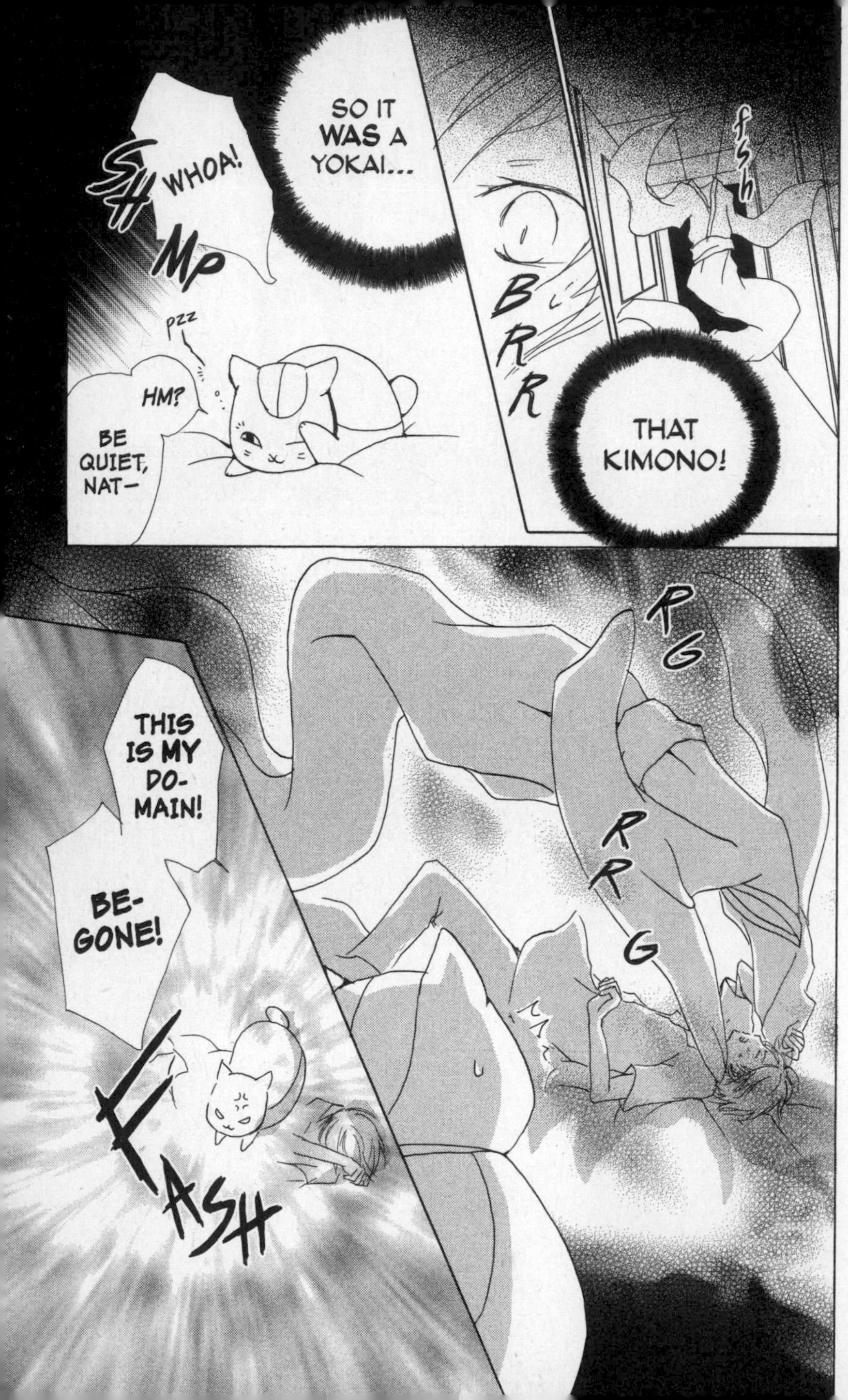
fsh
BRRR
THAT KIMONO!
SO IT WAS A YOKAI...
SHMP
WHOA!
pzz
HM?
BE QUIET, NAT—
RG
RRG
THIS IS MY DO-MAIN!
BE-GONE!
FASH

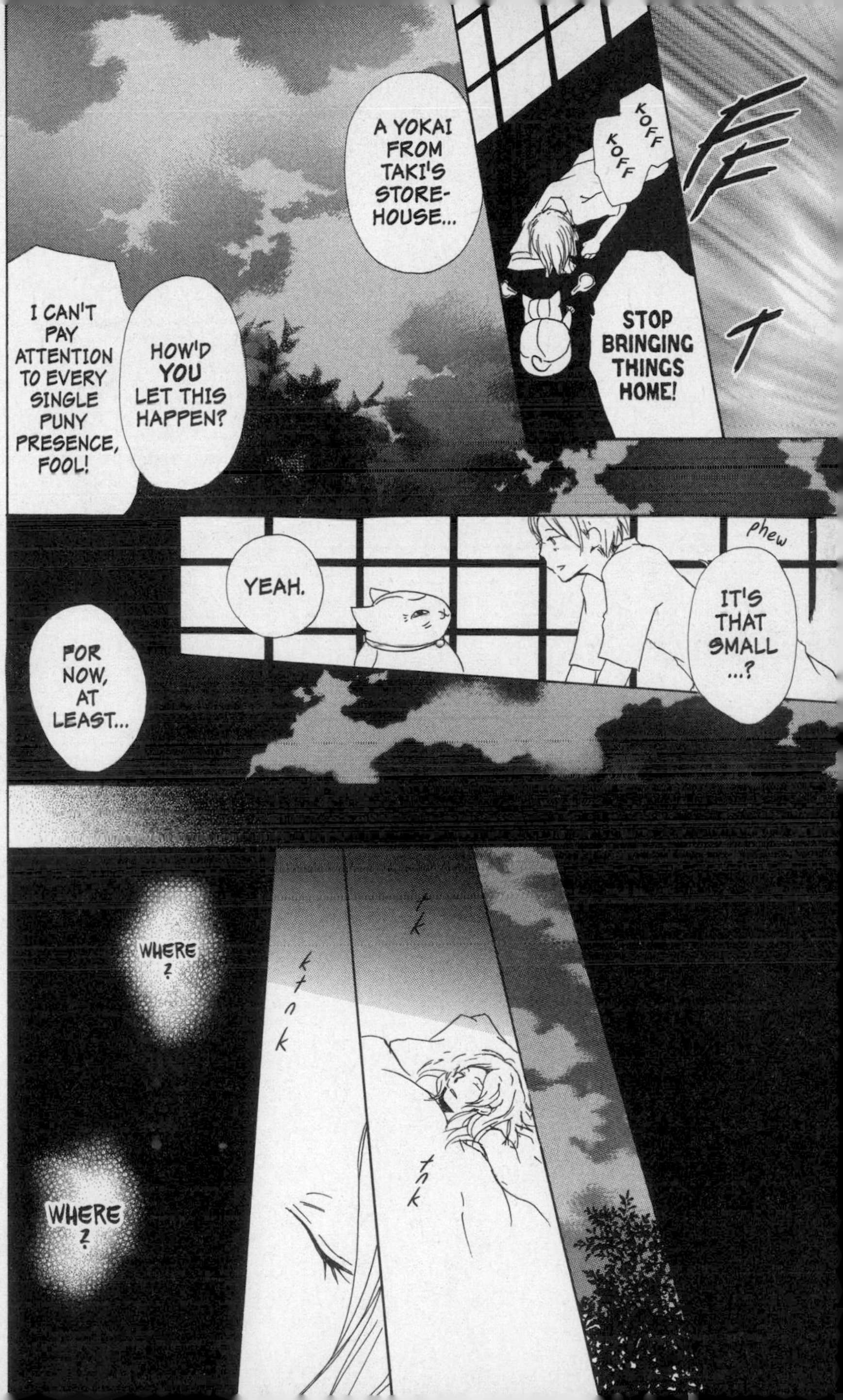
KOFF KOFF
STOP BRINGING THINGS HOME!
A YOKAI FROM TAKI'S STORE-HOUSE...
HOW'D YOU LET THIS HAPPEN?
I CAN'T PAY ATTENTION TO EVERY SINGLE PUNY PRESENCE, FOOL!
phew
IT'S THAT SMALL ...?
YEAH.
FOR NOW, AT LEAST...
WHERE?
WHERE?

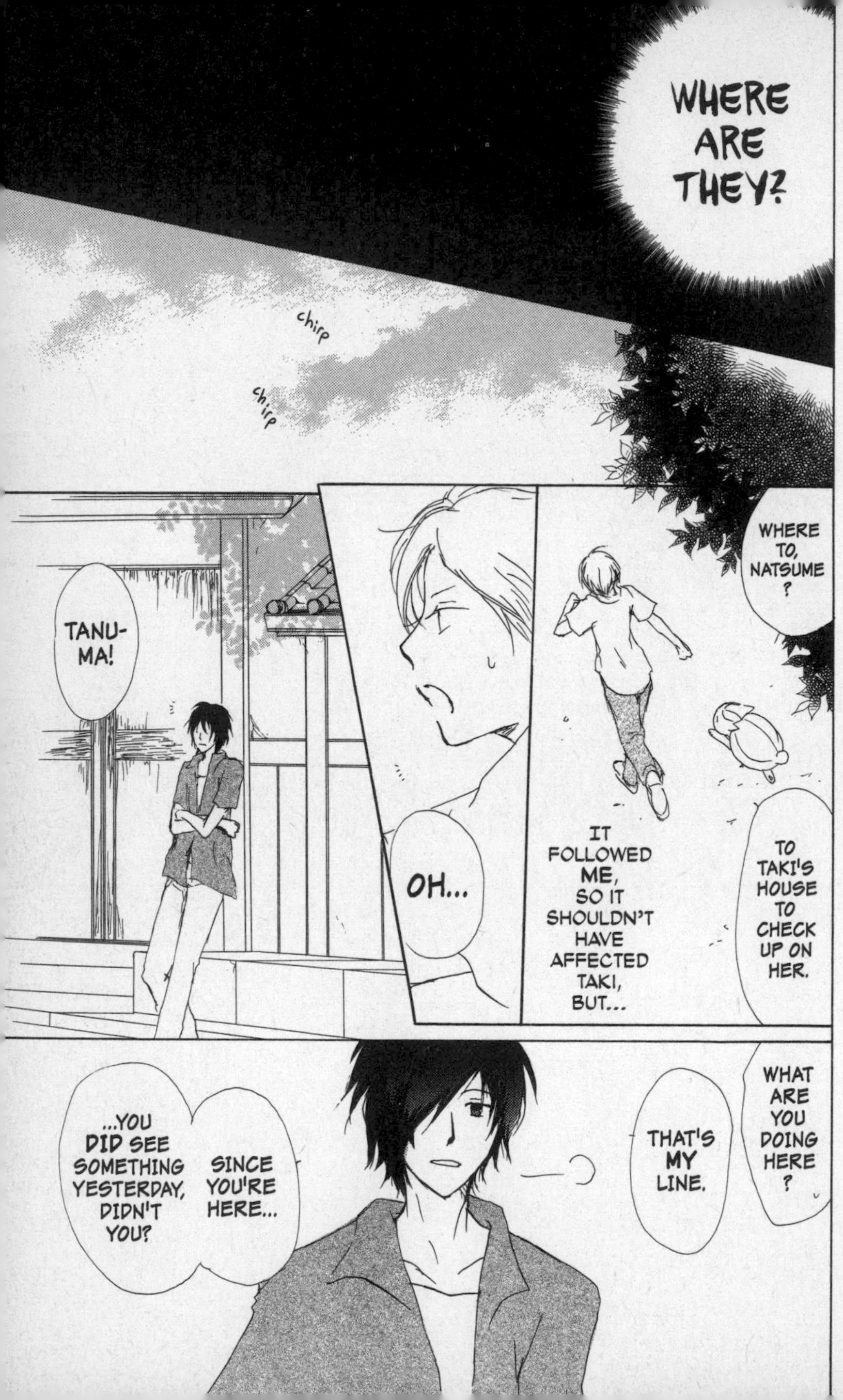
WHERE ARE THEY?
chirp
chirp
WHERE TO, NATSUME?
TO TAKI'S HOUSE TO CHECK UP ON HER.
IT FOLLOWED ME, SO IT SHOULDN'T HAVE AFFECTED TAKI, BUT...
OH...
TANU-MA!
WHAT ARE YOU DOING HERE?
THAT'S MY LINE.
SINCE YOU'RE HERE...
...YOU DID SEE SOMETHING YESTERDAY, DIDN'T YOU?

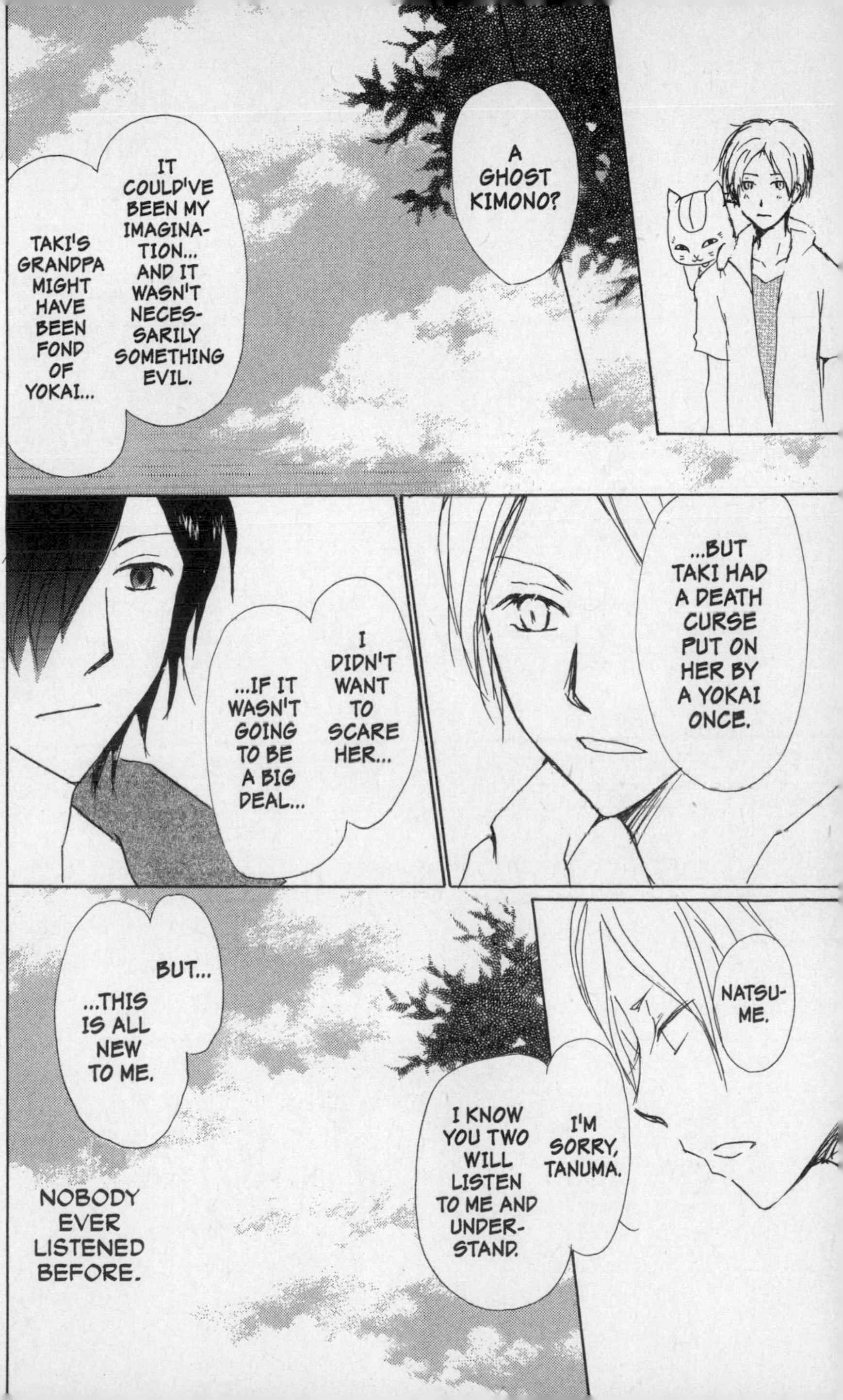
A GHOST KIMONO?
IT COULD'VE BEEN MY IMAGINATION... AND IT WASN'T NECES-SARILY SOMETHING EVIL.
TAKI'S GRANDPA MIGHT HAVE BEEN FOND OF YOKAI...
...BUT TAKI HAD A DEATH CURSE PUT ON HER BY A YOKAI ONCE.
I DIDN'T WANT TO SCARE HER...
...IF IT WASN'T GOING TO BE A BIG DEAL...
NATSU-ME.
I'M SORRY, TANUMA.
I KNOW YOU TWO WILL LISTEN TO ME AND UNDER-STAND.
BUT...
...THIS IS ALL NEW TO ME.
NOBODY EVER LISTENED BEFORE.

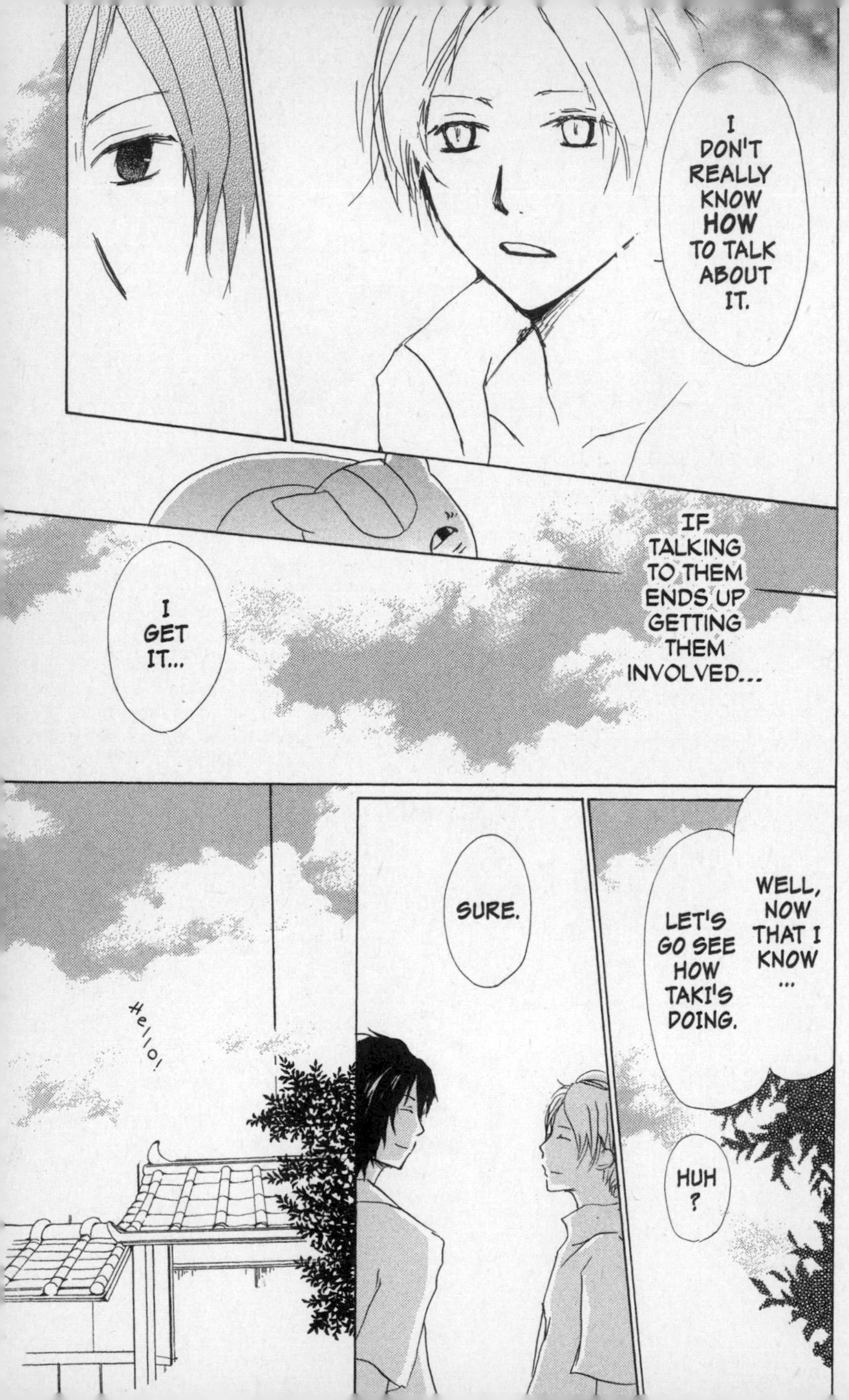
I DON'T REALLY KNOW HOW TO TALK ABOUT IT.
IF TALKING TO THEM ENDS UP GETTING THEM INVOLVED...
I GET IT...
WELL, NOW THAT I KNOW ...
LET'S GO SEE HOW TAKI'S DOING.
SURE.
HUH?
Hello!

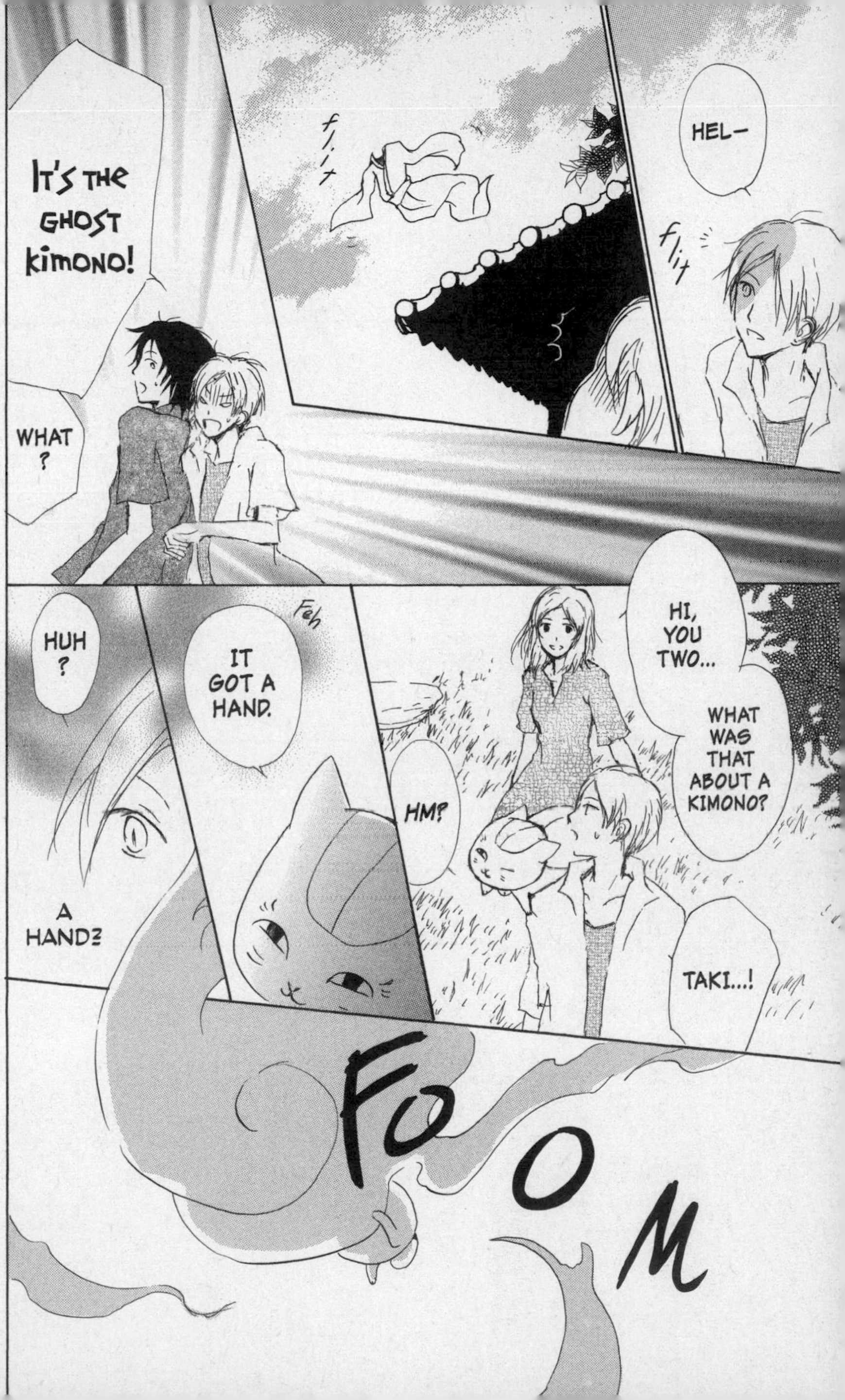
HEL–
flit
flit
IT'S THE GHOST KIMONO!
WHAT?
HI, YOU TWO...
WHAT WAS THAT ABOUT A KIMONO?
TAKI...!
HM?
Feh
IT GOT A HAND.
HUH?
A HAND?
FOOM

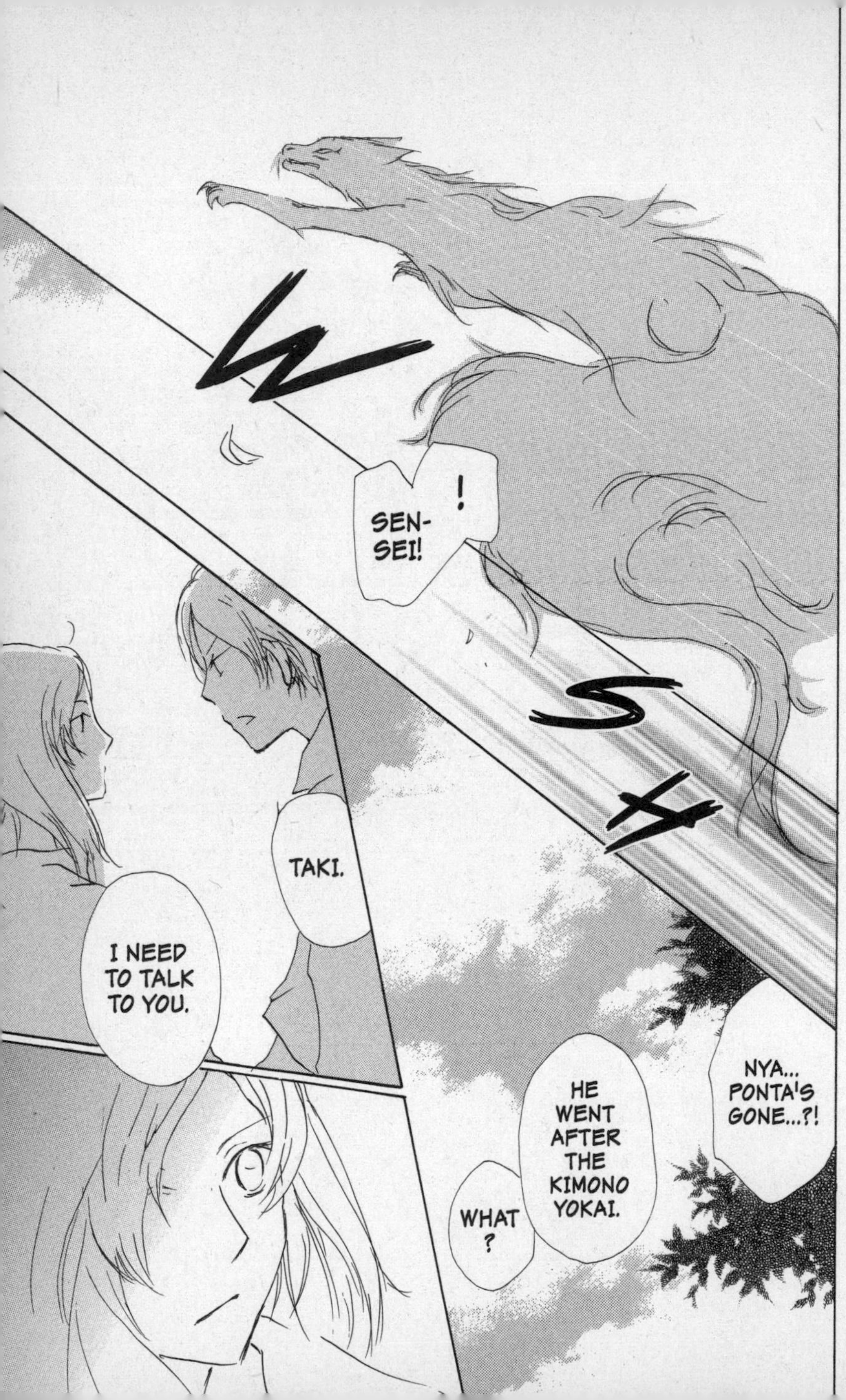
WSH
!
SEN-SEI!
NYA... PONTA'S GONE...?!
HE WENT AFTER THE KIMONO YOKAI.
WHAT?
TAKI.
I NEED TO TALK TO YOU.

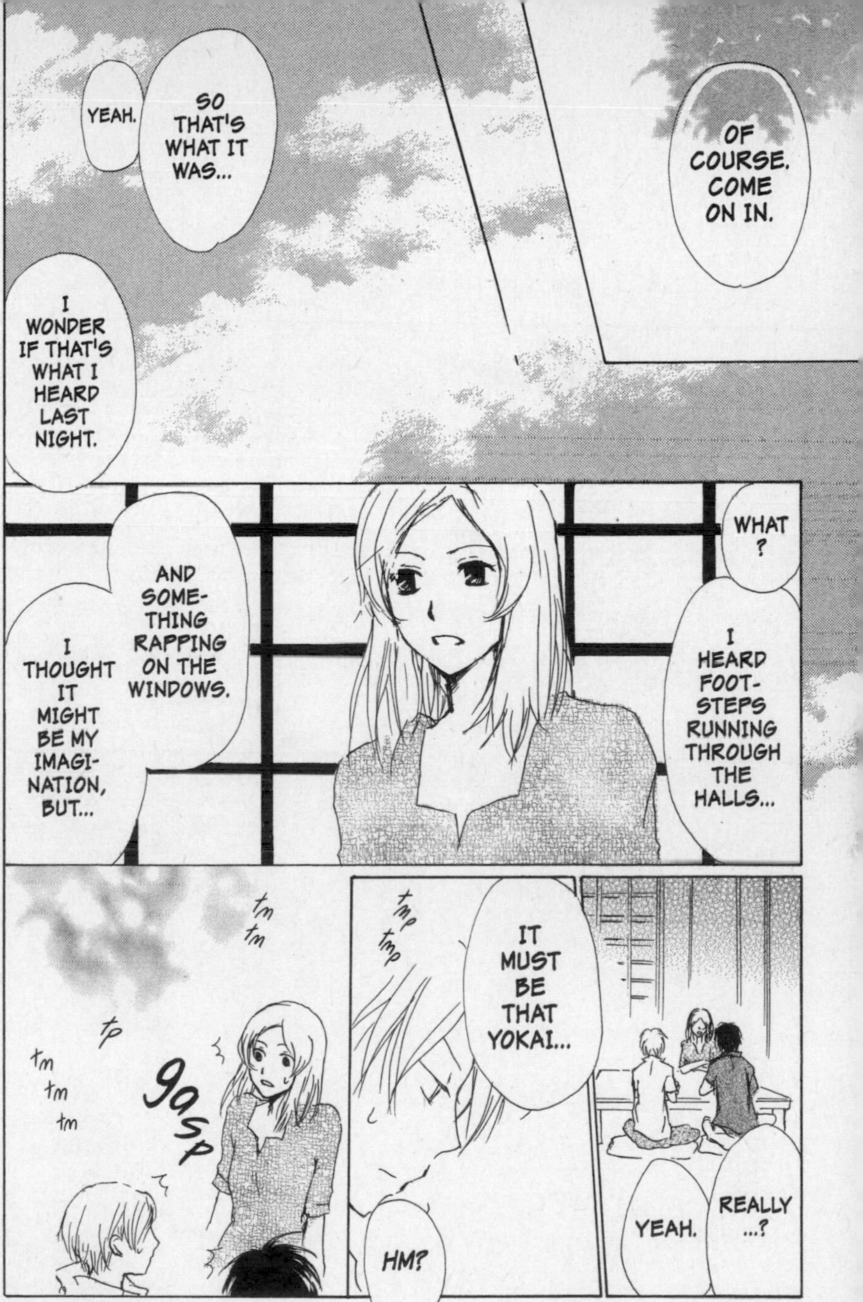
OF COURSE. COME ON IN.
SO THAT'S WHAT IT WAS...
YEAH.
I WONDER IF THAT'S WHAT I HEARD LAST NIGHT.
WHAT?
I HEARD FOOT-STEPS RUNNING THROUGH THE HALLS...
AND SOME-THING RAPPING ON THE WINDOWS.
I THOUGHT IT MIGHT BE MY IMAGI-NATION, BUT...
REALLY...?
YEAH.
IT MUST BE THAT YOKAI...
tmp tmp
HM?
tm tm
gasp
tp
tm tm tm

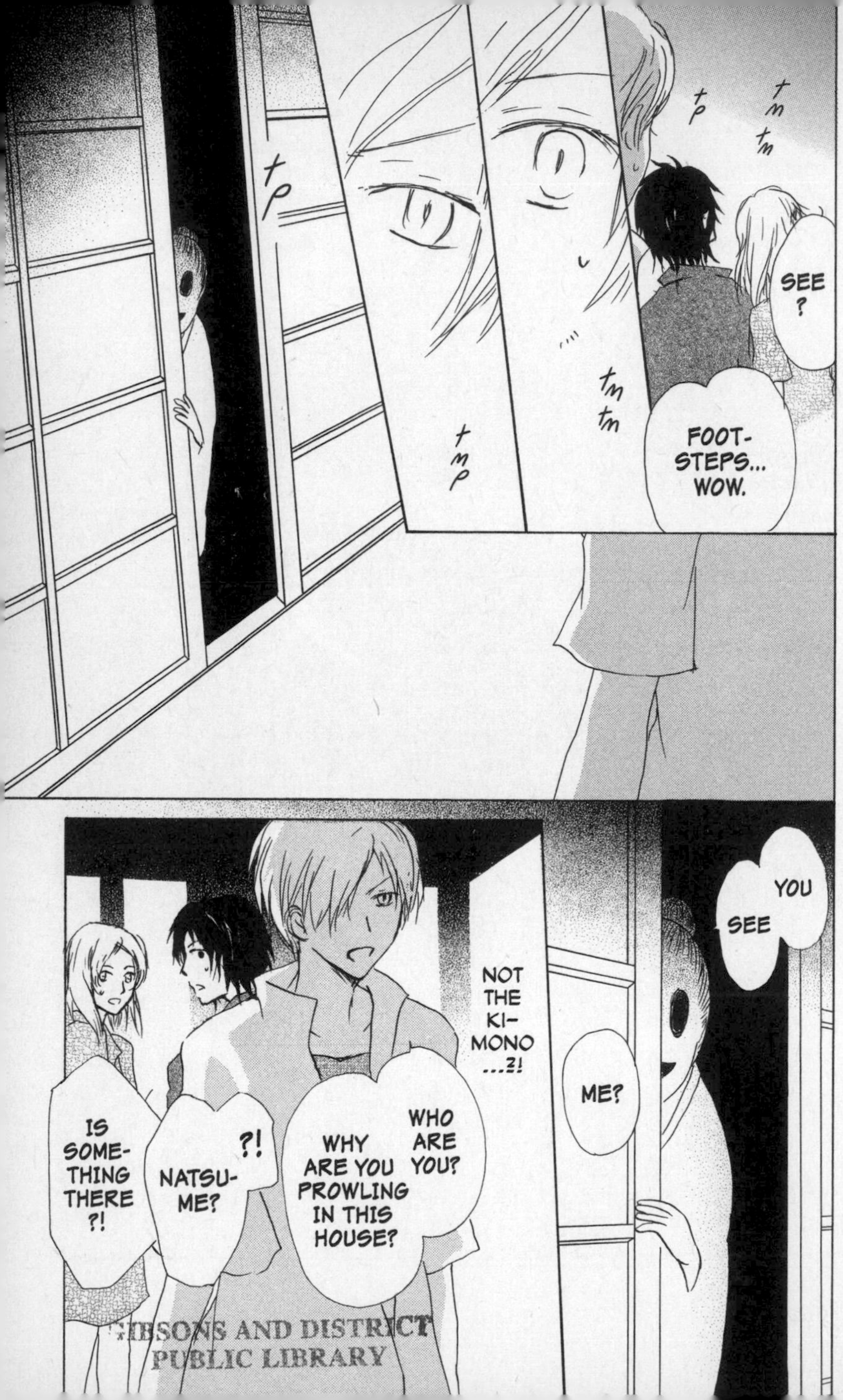

tm tm
tp
SEE?
FOOT-STEPS... WOW.
tm tm
tmp
tp
YOU SEE
ME?
NOT THE KI-MONO...?!
WHO ARE YOU?
WHY ARE YOU PROWLING IN THIS HOUSE?
?!
NATSU-ME?
IS SOME-THING THERE?!

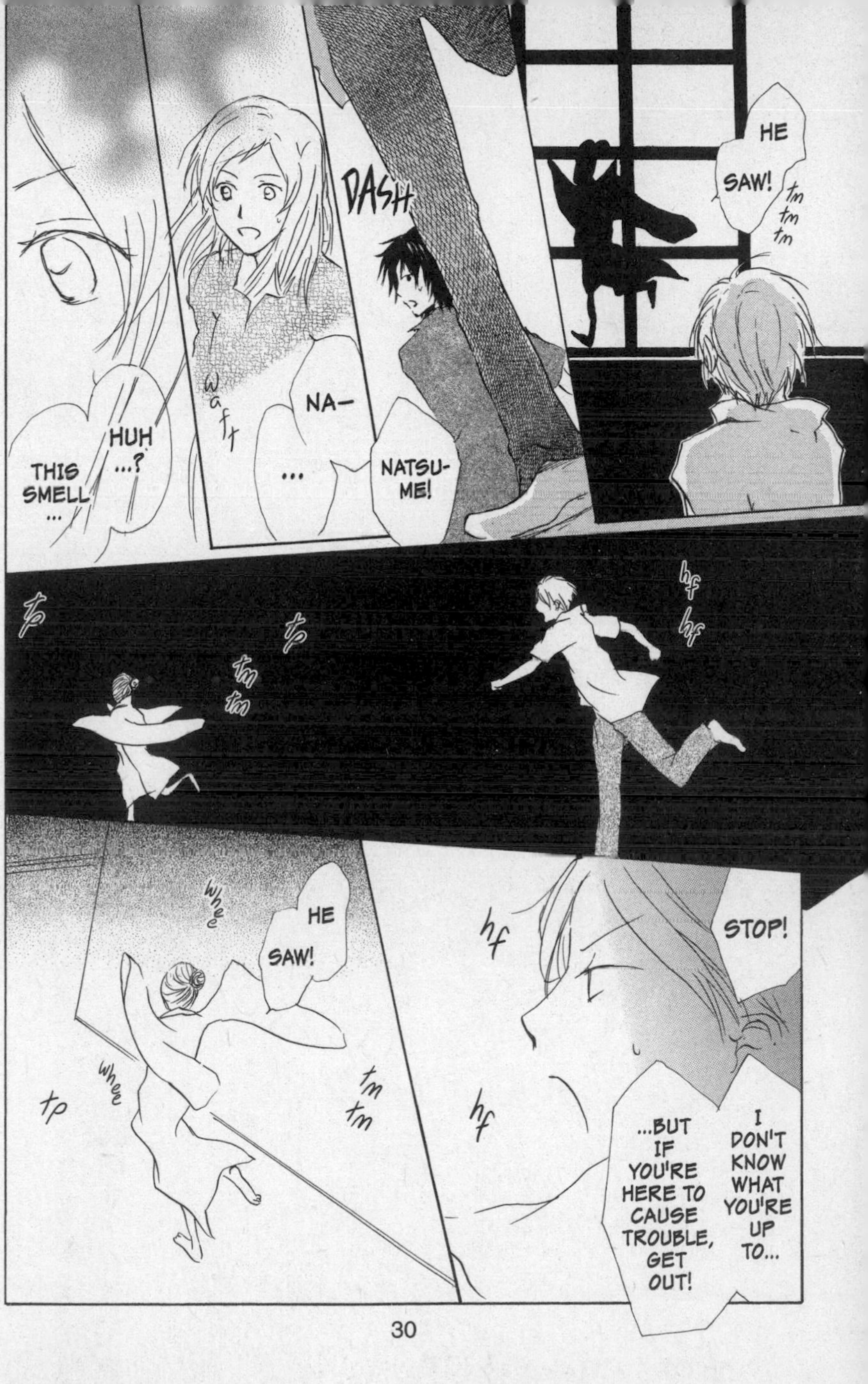
HE SAW!
tm tm tn
DASH
NATSU-ME!
NA- ...
waft
HUH ...?
THIS SMELL ...
hf hf
tm tm
tp
tp
STOP!
hf
I DON'T KNOW WHAT YOU'RE UP TO...
...BUT IF YOU'RE HERE TO CAUSE TROUBLE, GET OUT!
hf
HE SAW!
whee
tm tm
whee
tp

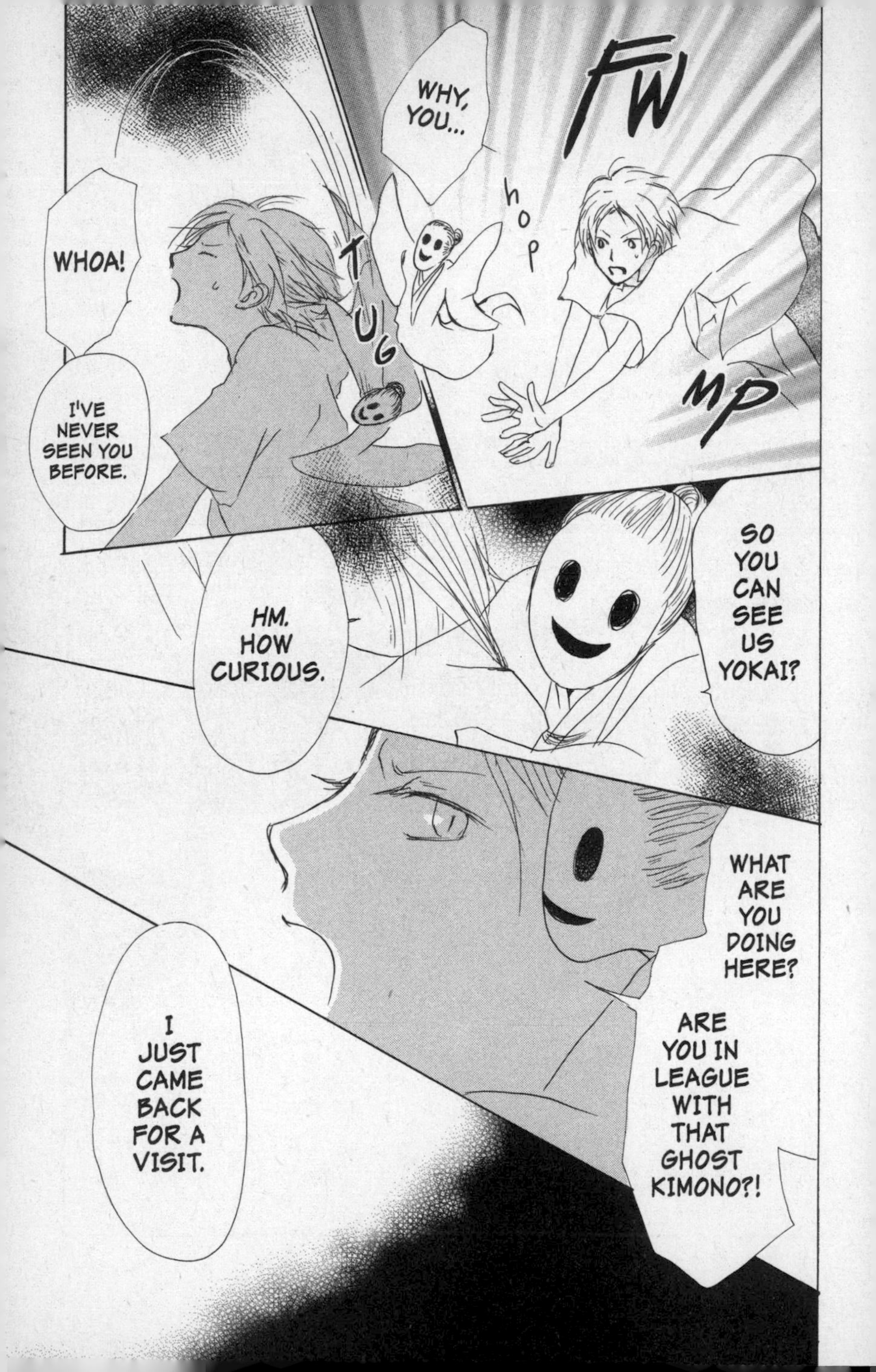
FW
MP
hop
WHY, YOU...
TUG
WHOA!
I'VE NEVER SEEN YOU BEFORE.
SO YOU CAN SEE US YOKAI?
HM. HOW CURIOUS.
WHAT ARE YOU DOING HERE?
ARE YOU IN LEAGUE WITH THAT GHOST KIMONO?!
I JUST CAME BACK FOR A VISIT.

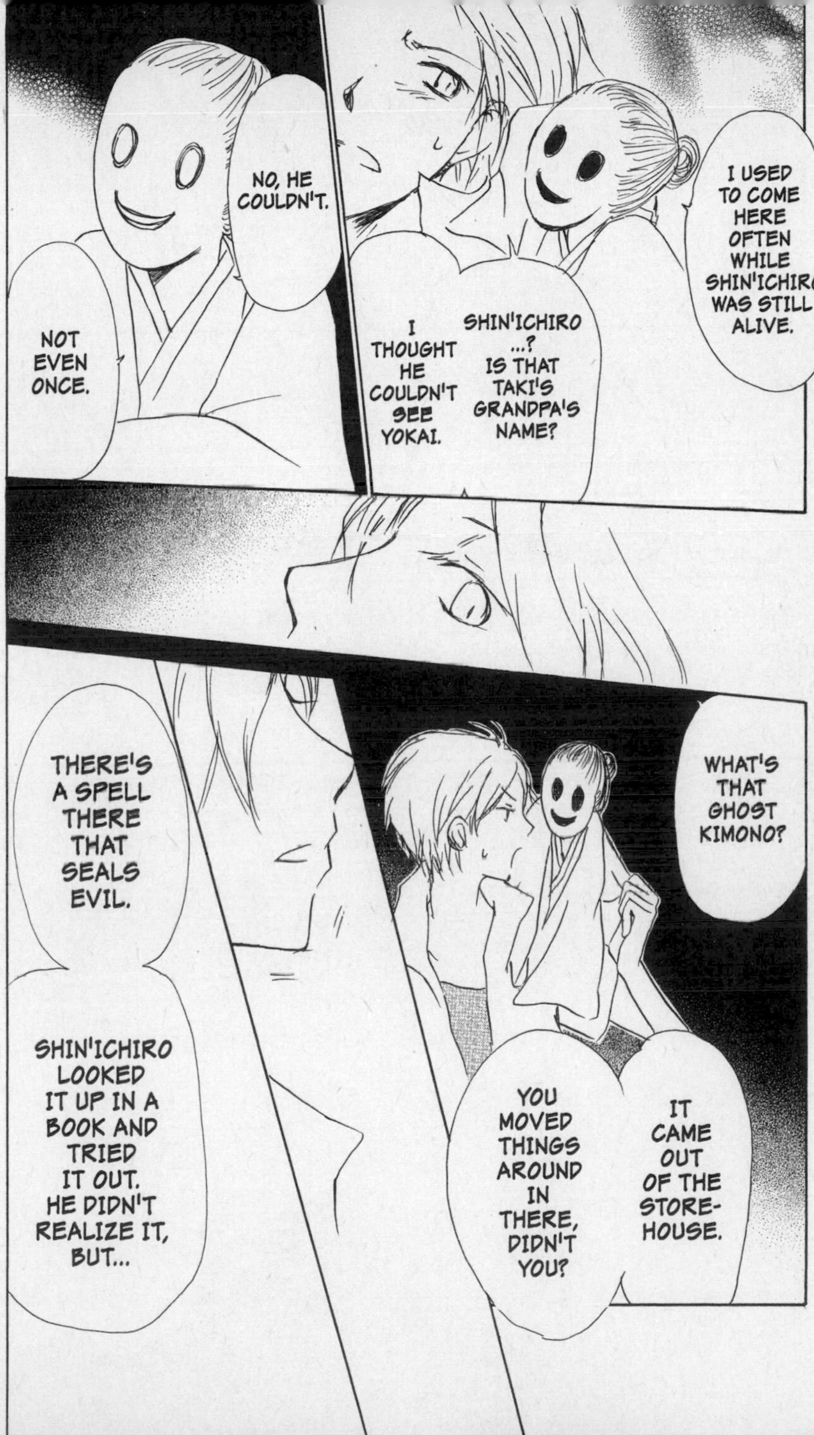
I USED TO COME HERE OFTEN WHILE SHIN'ICHIRO WAS STILL ALIVE.
SHIN'ICHIRO ...? IS THAT TAKI'S GRANDPA'S NAME?
I THOUGHT HE COULDN'T SEE YOKAI.
NO, HE COULDN'T.
NOT EVEN ONCE.
WHAT'S THAT GHOST KIMONO?
IT CAME OUT OF THE STORE-HOUSE.
YOU MOVED THINGS AROUND IN THERE, DIDN'T YOU?
THERE'S A SPELL THERE THAT SEALS EVIL.
SHIN'ICHIRO LOOKED IT UP IN A BOOK AND TRIED IT OUT. HE DIDN'T REALIZE IT, BUT...

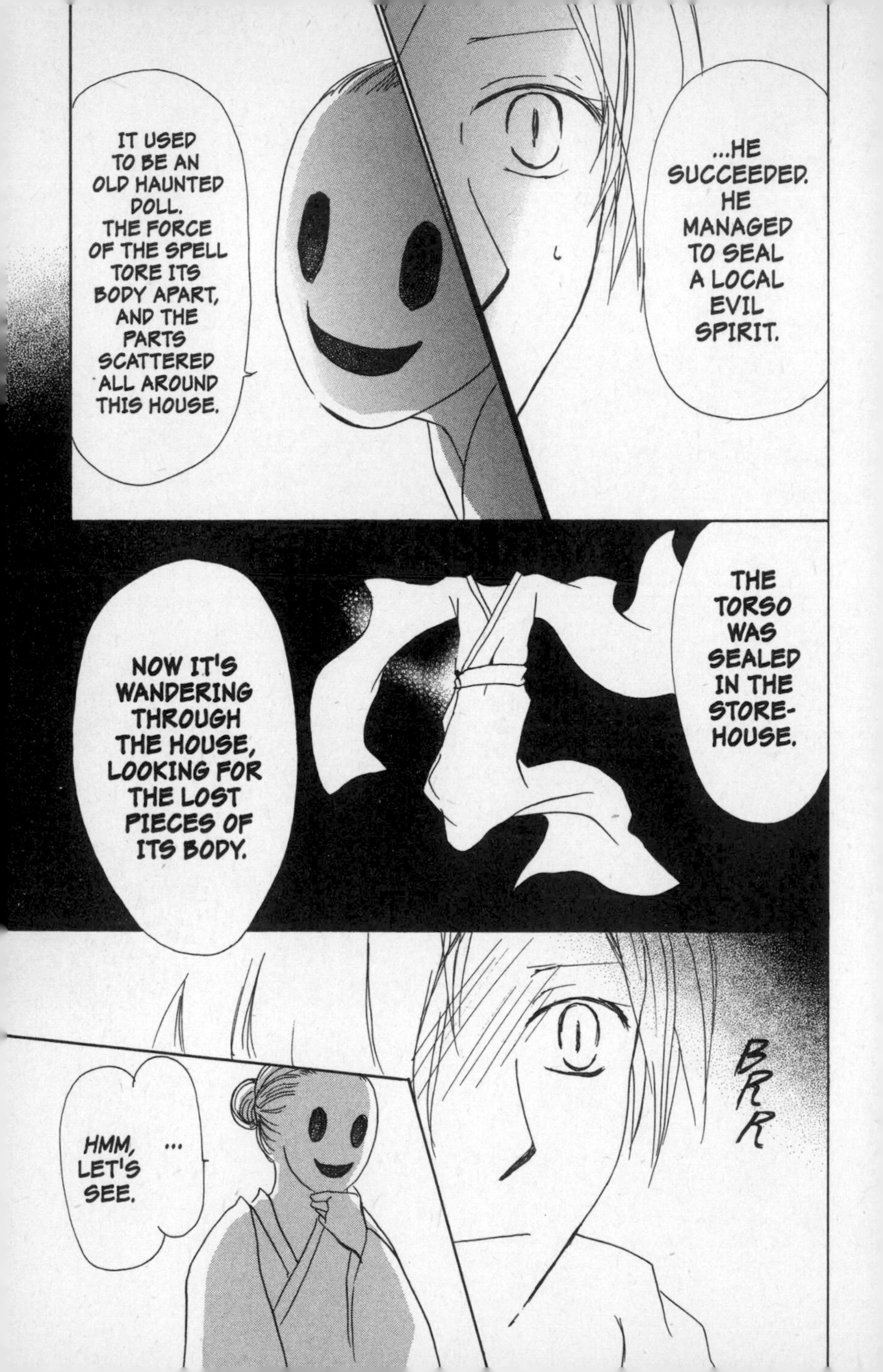
...HE SUCCEEDED. HE MANAGED TO SEAL A LOCAL EVIL SPIRIT.
IT USED TO BE AN OLD HAUNTED DOLL. THE FORCE OF THE SPELL TORE ITS BODY APART, AND THE PARTS SCATTERED ALL AROUND THIS HOUSE.
THE TORSO WAS SEALED IN THE STORE-HOUSE.
NOW IT'S WANDERING THROUGH THE HOUSE, LOOKING FOR THE LOST PIECES OF ITS BODY.
BRR
...
HMM, LET'S SEE.

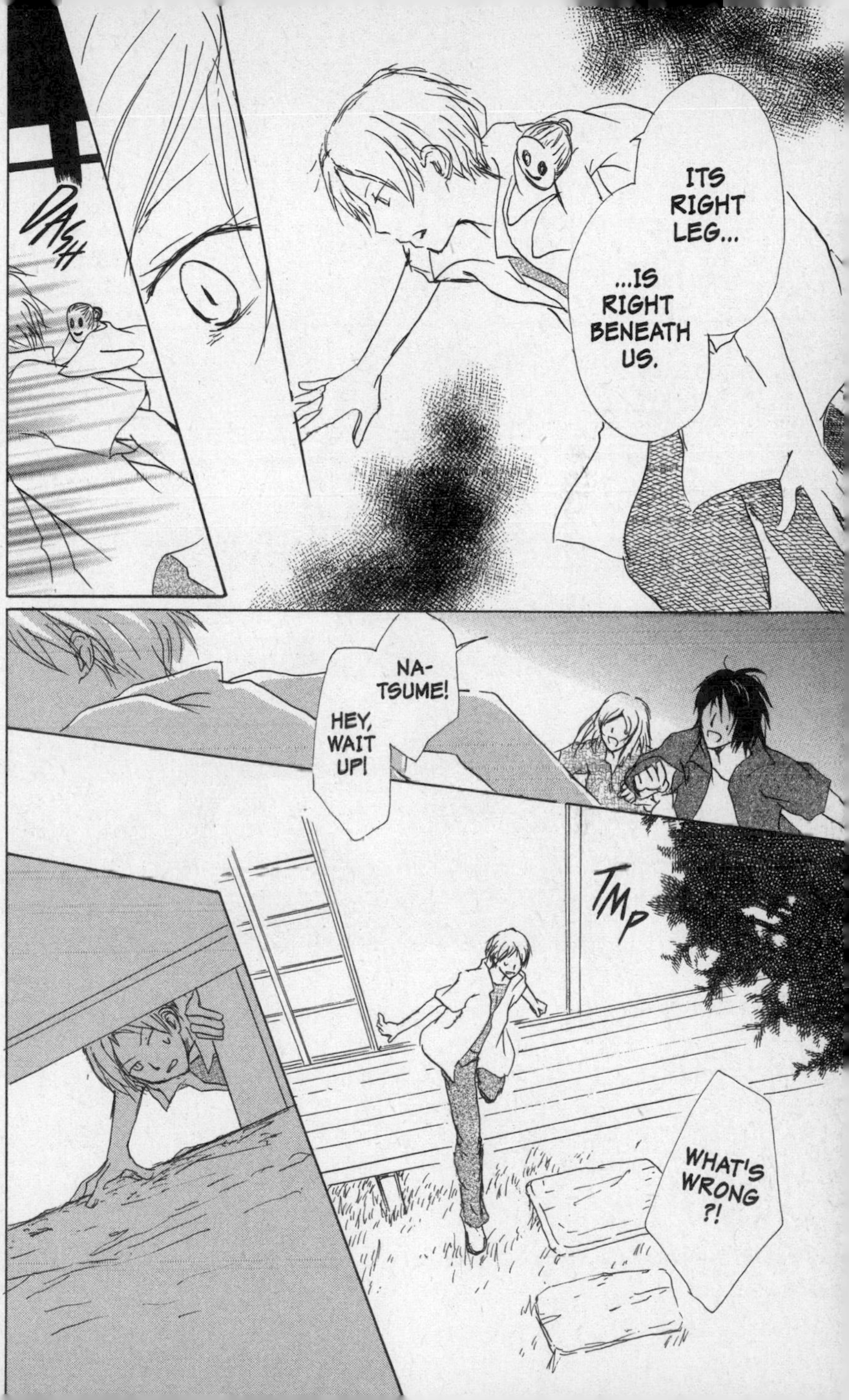
ITS RIGHT LEG...
...IS RIGHT BENEATH US.
DASH
NA-TSUME!
HEY, WAIT UP!
TMP
WHAT'S WRONG ?!

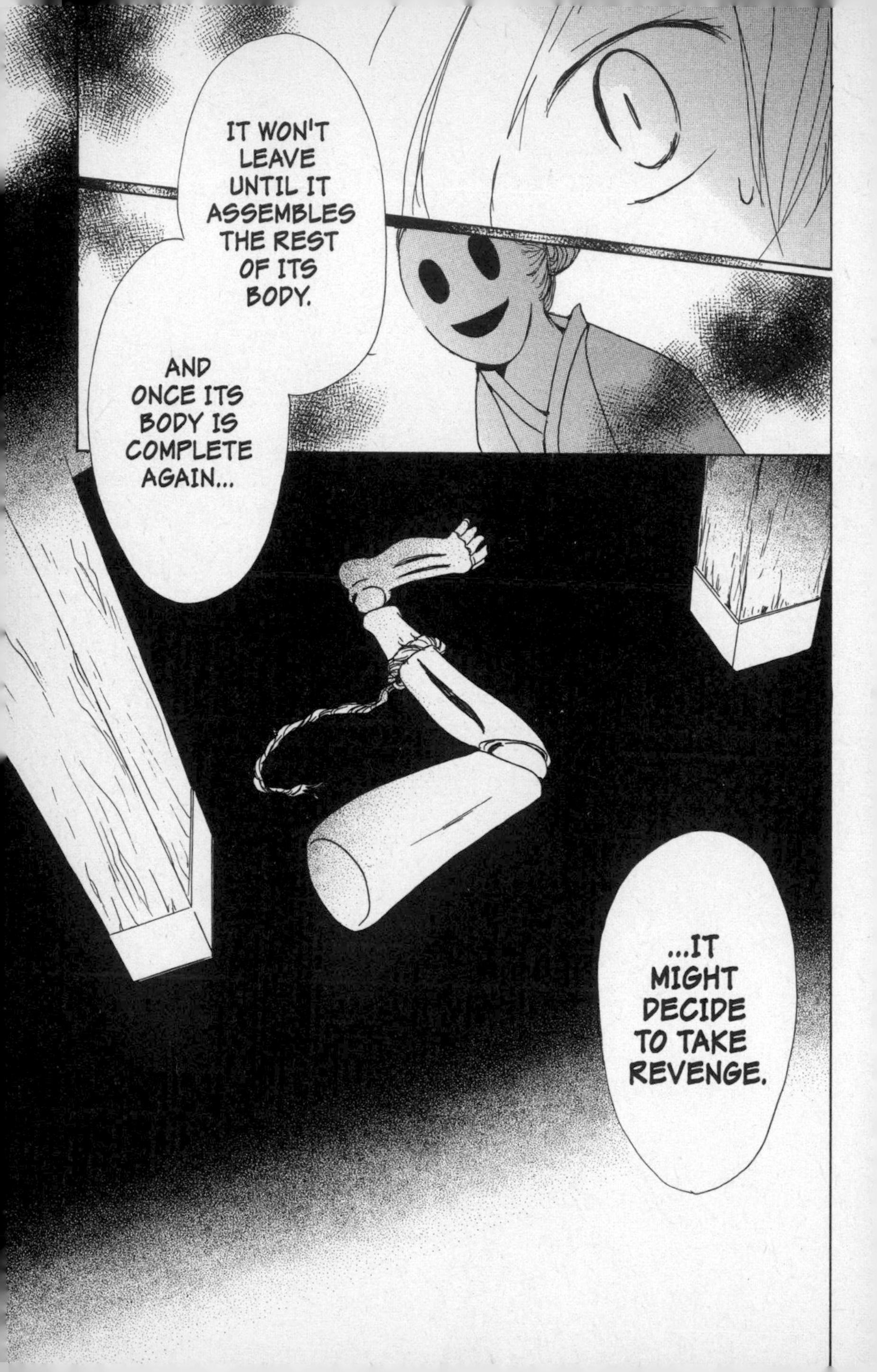
IT WON'T LEAVE UNTIL IT ASSEMBLES THE REST OF ITS BODY.
AND ONCE ITS BODY IS COMPLETE AGAIN...
...IT MIGHT DECIDE TO TAKE REVENGE.

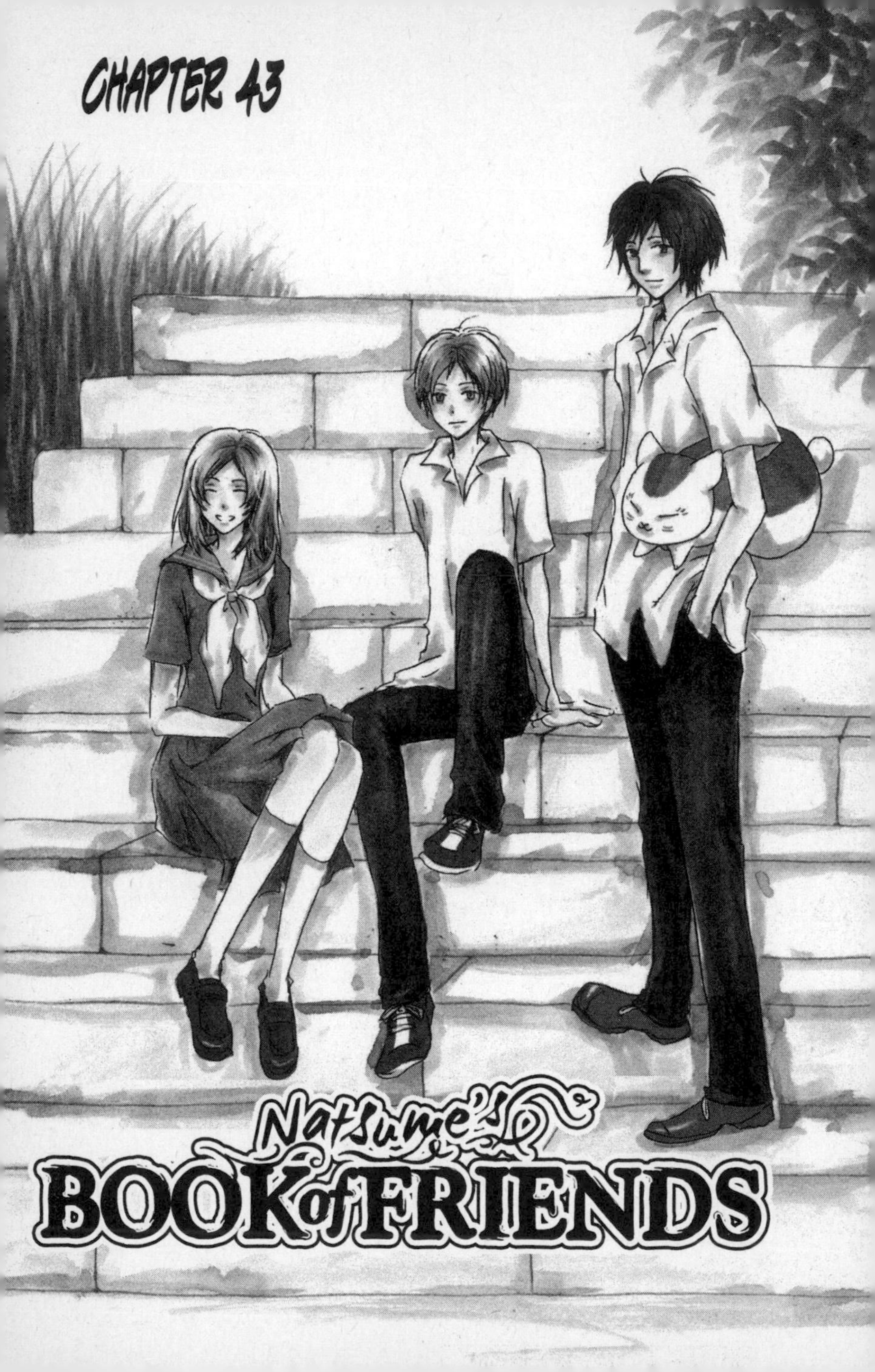
CHAPTER 43
Natsume's
BOOK of FRIENDS

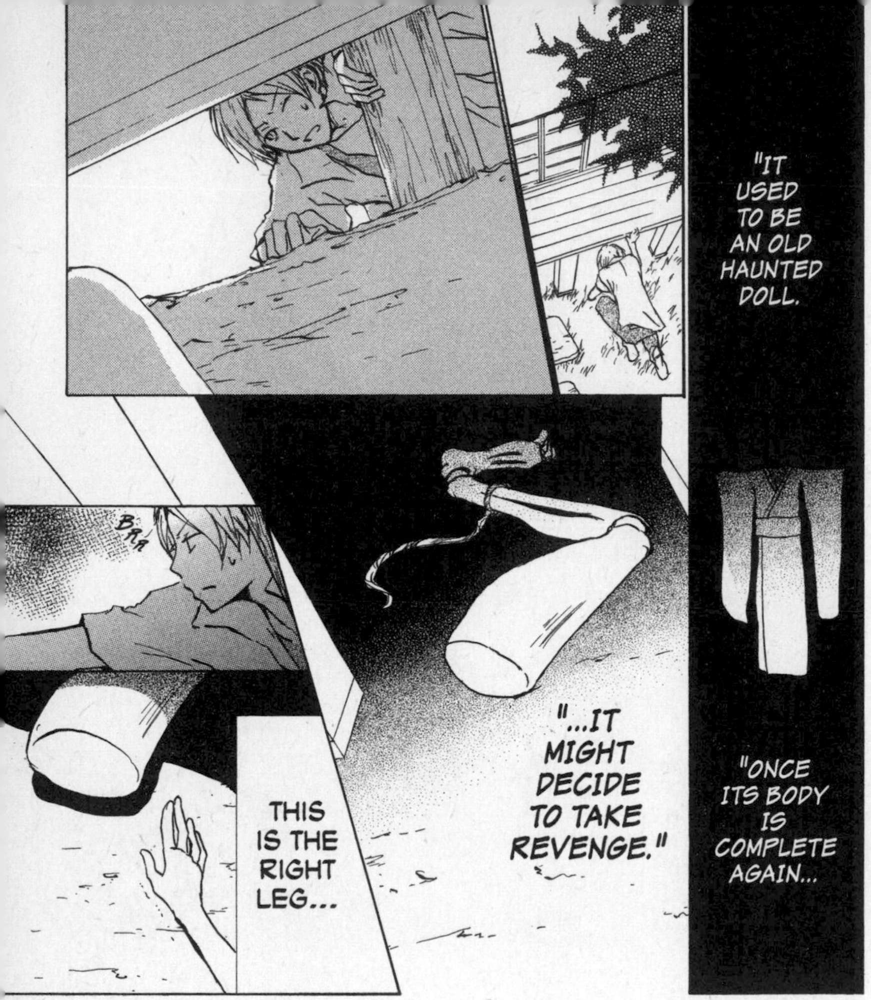
"IT USED TO BE AN OLD HAUNTED DOLL.
"ONCE ITS BODY IS COMPLETE AGAIN...
"...IT MIGHT DECIDE TO TAKE REVENGE."
BRR
THIS IS THE RIGHT LEG...

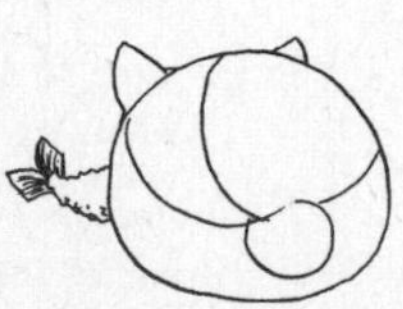

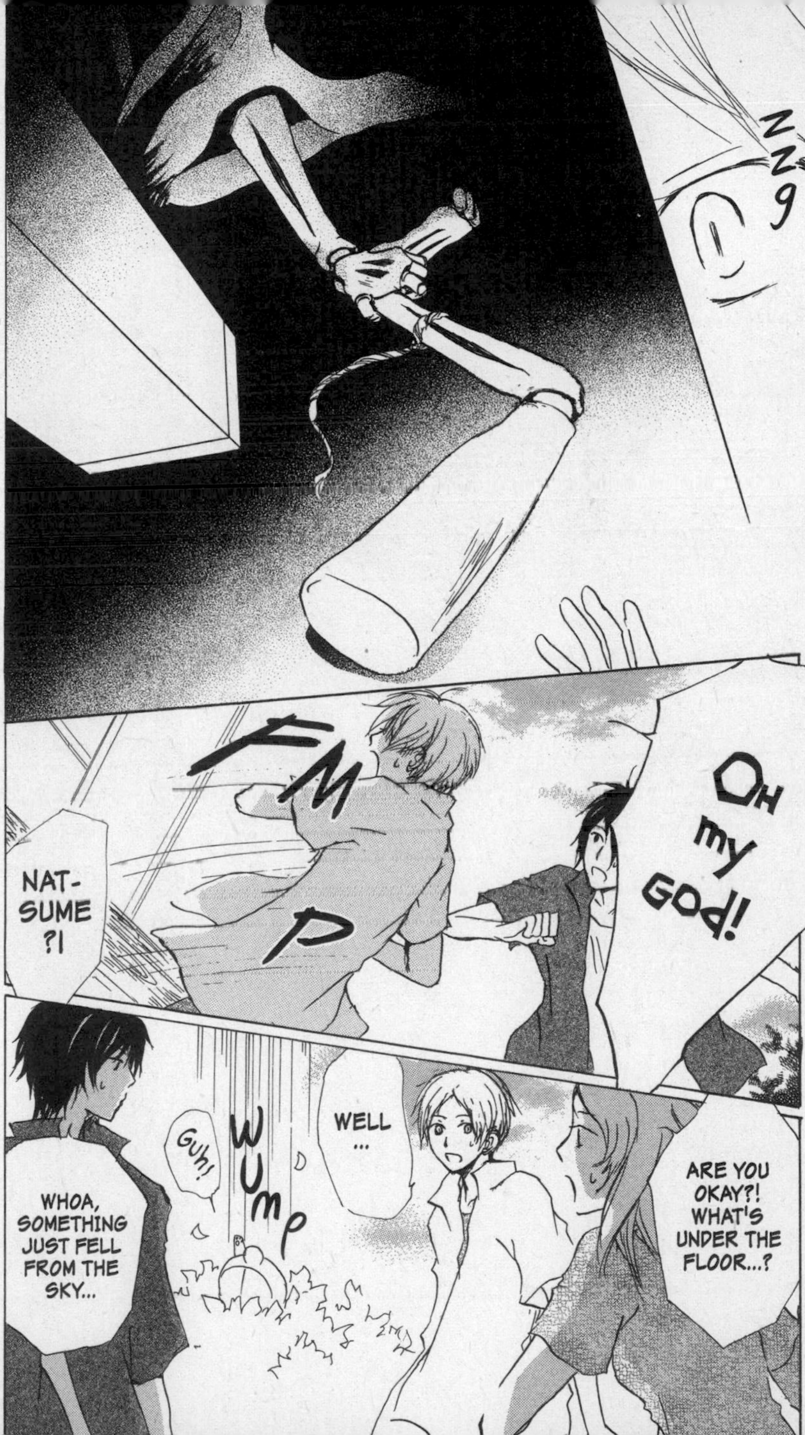
Oh my God!
FMP
NAT-SUME ?!
ARE YOU OKAY?! WHAT'S UNDER THE FLOOR...?
WELL ...
WUMP
Guh!
WHOA, SOMETHING JUST FELL FROM THE SKY...

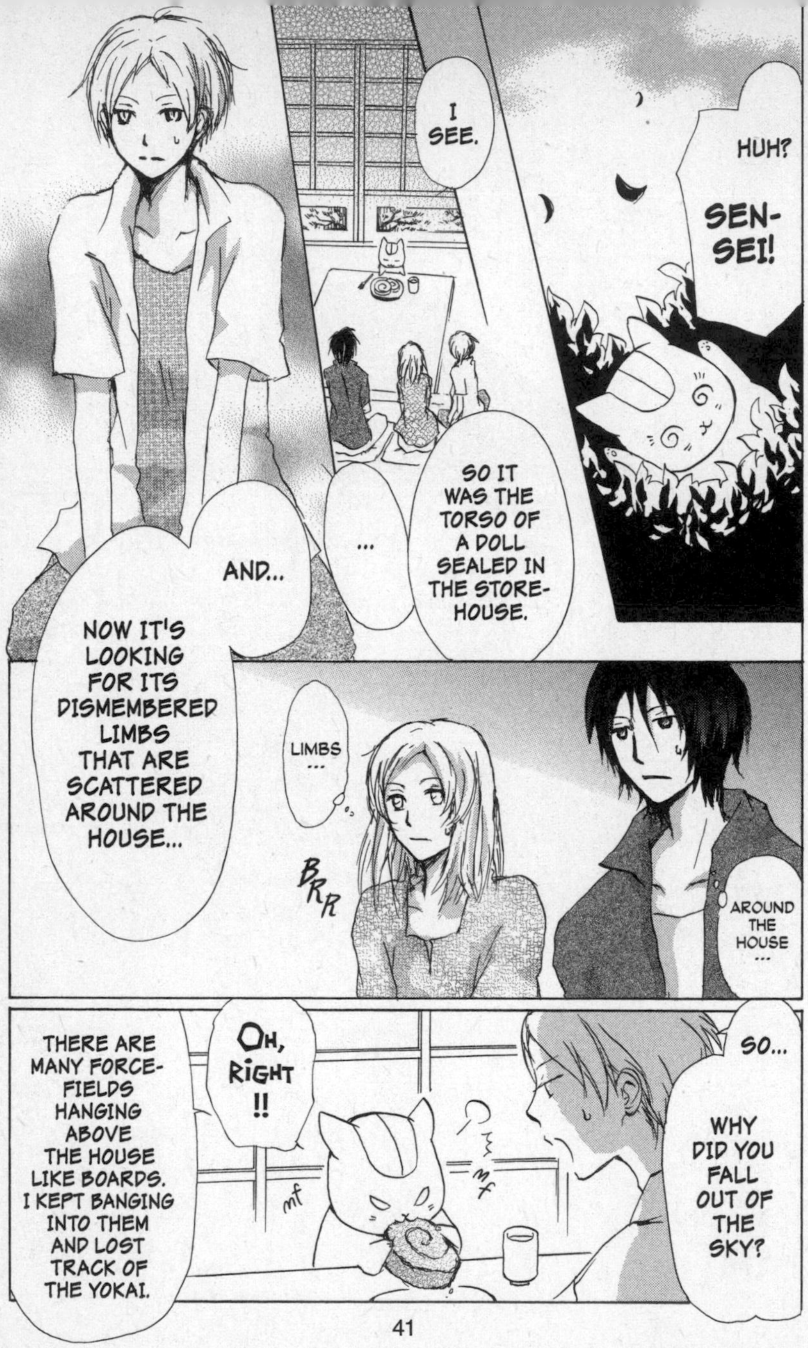
HUH?
SEN-SEI!
I SEE.
SO IT WAS THE TORSO OF A DOLL SEALED IN THE STORE-HOUSE.
...
AND...
NOW IT'S LOOKING FOR ITS DISMEMBERED LIMBS THAT ARE SCATTERED AROUND THE HOUSE...
AROUND THE HOUSE ...
LIMBS ...
BRR
SO...
WHY DID YOU FALL OUT OF THE SKY?
mf
mf
OH, RIGHT !!
mf
THERE ARE MANY FORCE-FIELDS HANGING ABOVE THE HOUSE LIKE BOARDS. I KEPT BANGING INTO THEM AND LOST TRACK OF THE YOKAI.

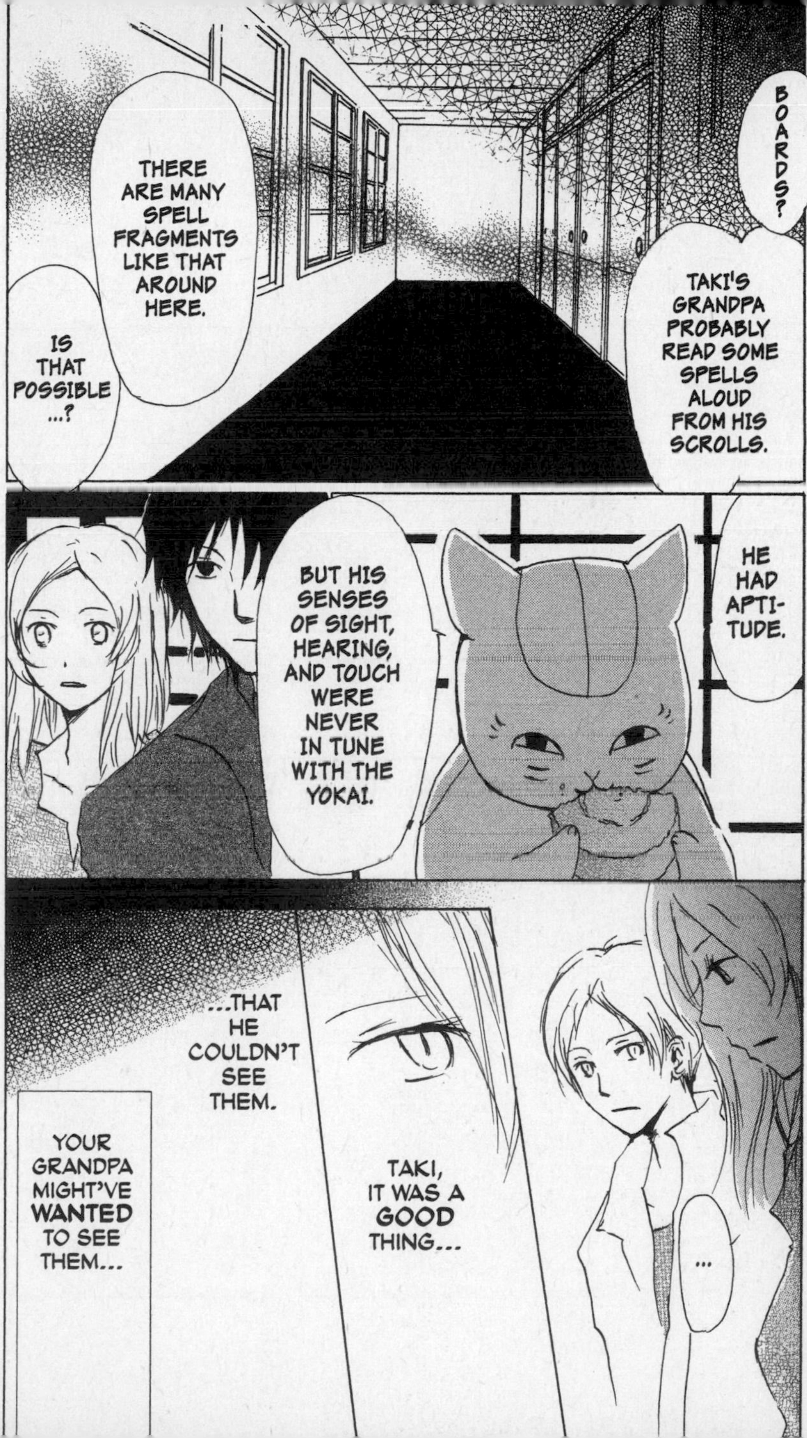
BOARDS?
TAKI'S GRANDPA PROBABLY READ SOME SPELLS ALOUD FROM HIS SCROLLS.
THERE ARE MANY SPELL FRAGMENTS LIKE THAT AROUND HERE.
IS THAT POSSIBLE ...?
HE HAD APTI-TUDE.
BUT HIS SENSES OF SIGHT, HEARING, AND TOUCH WERE NEVER IN TUNE WITH THE YOKAI.
...
TAKI, IT WAS A GOOD THING...
...THAT HE COULDN'T SEE THEM.
YOUR GRANDPA MIGHT'VE WANTED TO SEE THEM...

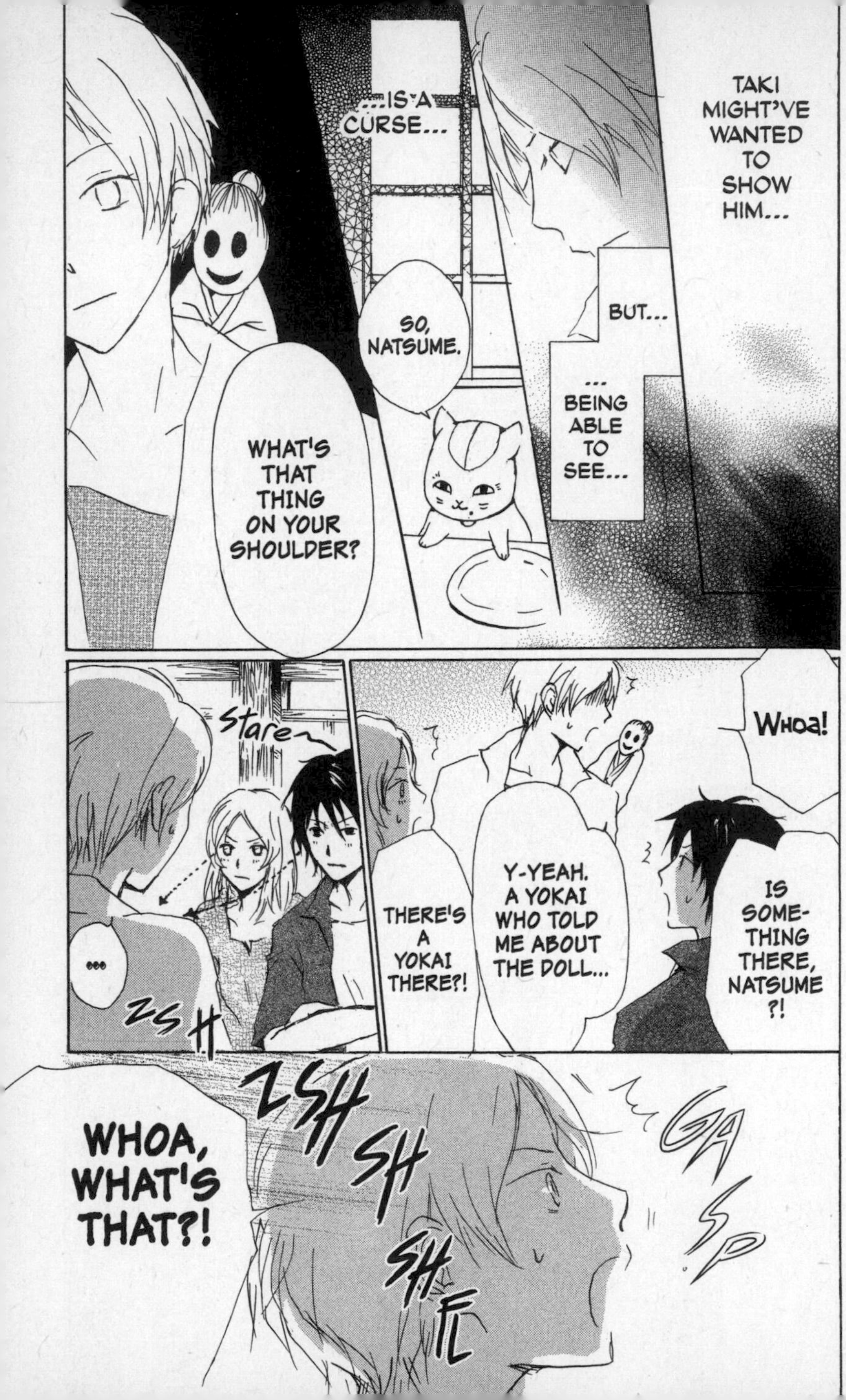
TAKI MIGHT'VE WANTED TO SHOW HIM...
BUT...
...BEING ABLE TO SEE...
...IS A CURSE...
SO, NATSUME.
WHAT'S THAT THING ON YOUR SHOULDER?
Whoa!
IS SOMETHING THERE, NATSUME?!
Y-YEAH. A YOKAI WHO TOLD ME ABOUT THE DOLL...
THERE'S A YOKAI THERE?!
Stare
...
ZSH
GASP
ZSH SH SH FL
WHOA, WHAT'S THAT?!

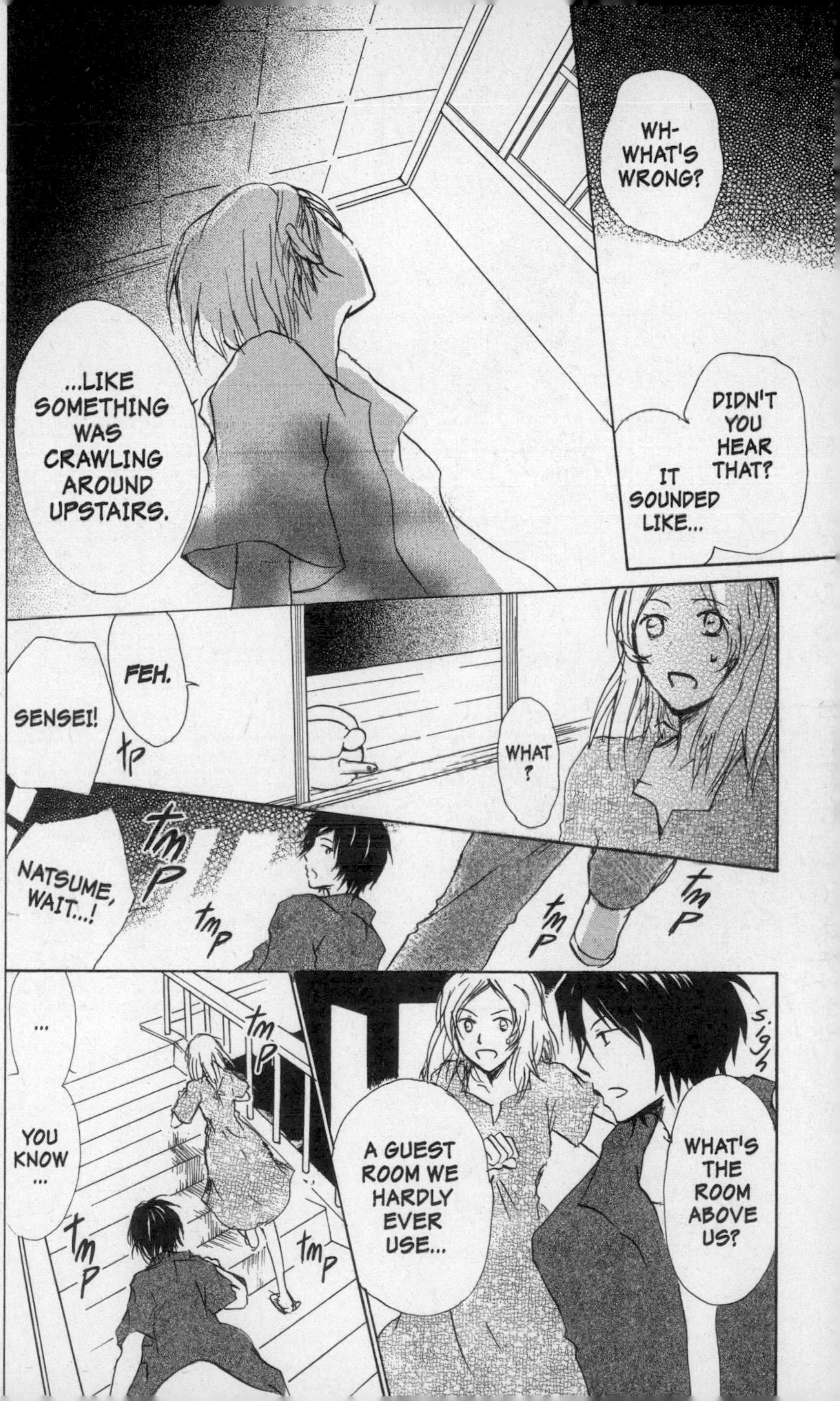
WH- WHAT'S WRONG?
DIDN'T YOU HEAR THAT?
IT SOUNDED LIKE...
...LIKE SOMETHING WAS CRAWLING AROUND UPSTAIRS.
WHAT?
FEH.
SENSEI!
tp
tmp
tmp
NATSUME, WAIT...!
tmp
tmp
sigh
WHAT'S THE ROOM ABOVE US?
A GUEST ROOM WE HARDLY EVER USE...
...
YOU KNOW ...
tmp
tmp
tmp

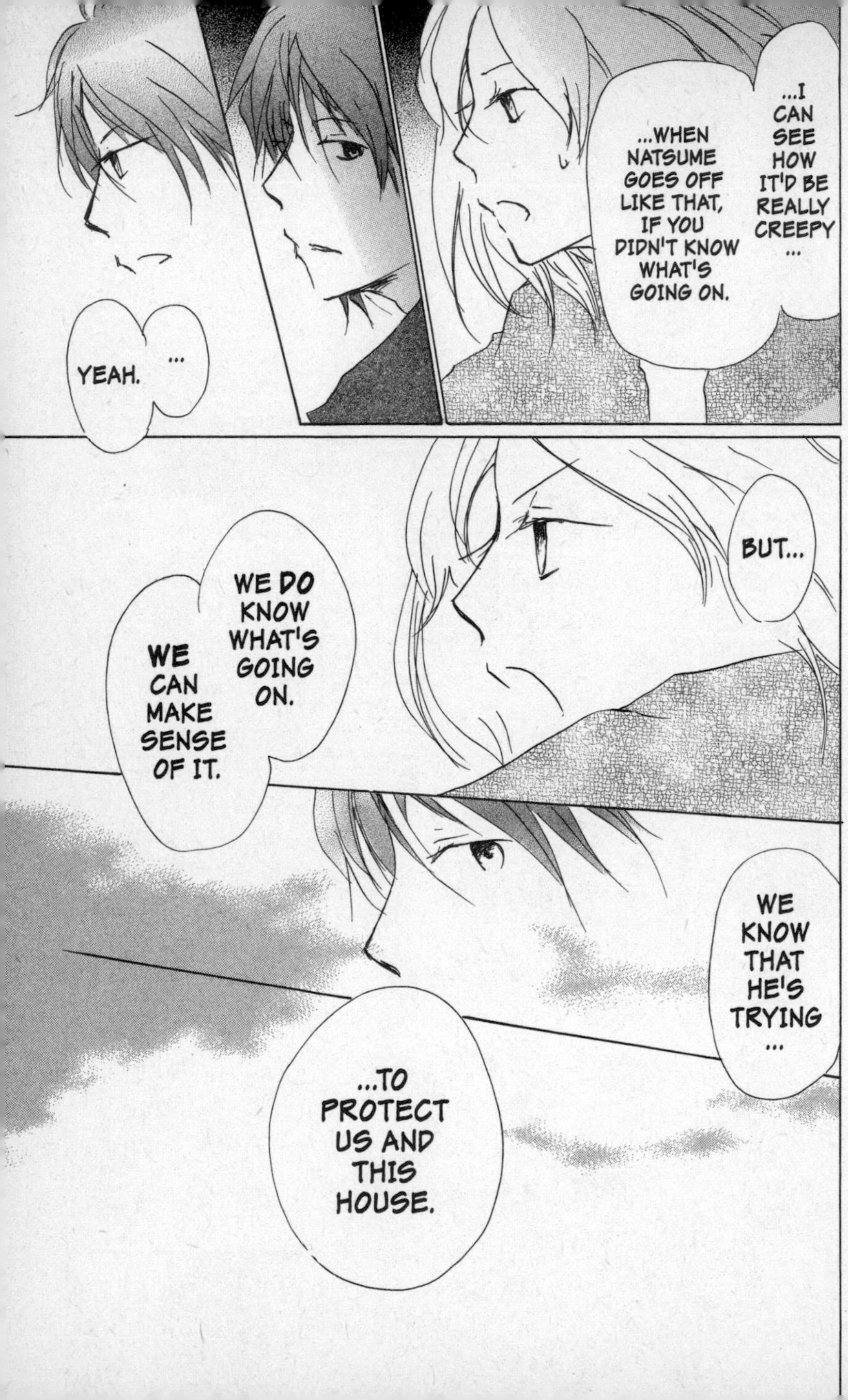
...I CAN SEE HOW IT'D BE REALLY CREEPY...
...WHEN NATSUME GOES OFF LIKE THAT, IF YOU DIDN'T KNOW WHAT'S GOING ON.
...
YEAH.
BUT...
WE DO KNOW WHAT'S GOING ON.
WE CAN MAKE SENSE OF IT.
WE KNOW THAT HE'S TRYING...
...TO PROTECT US AND THIS HOUSE.

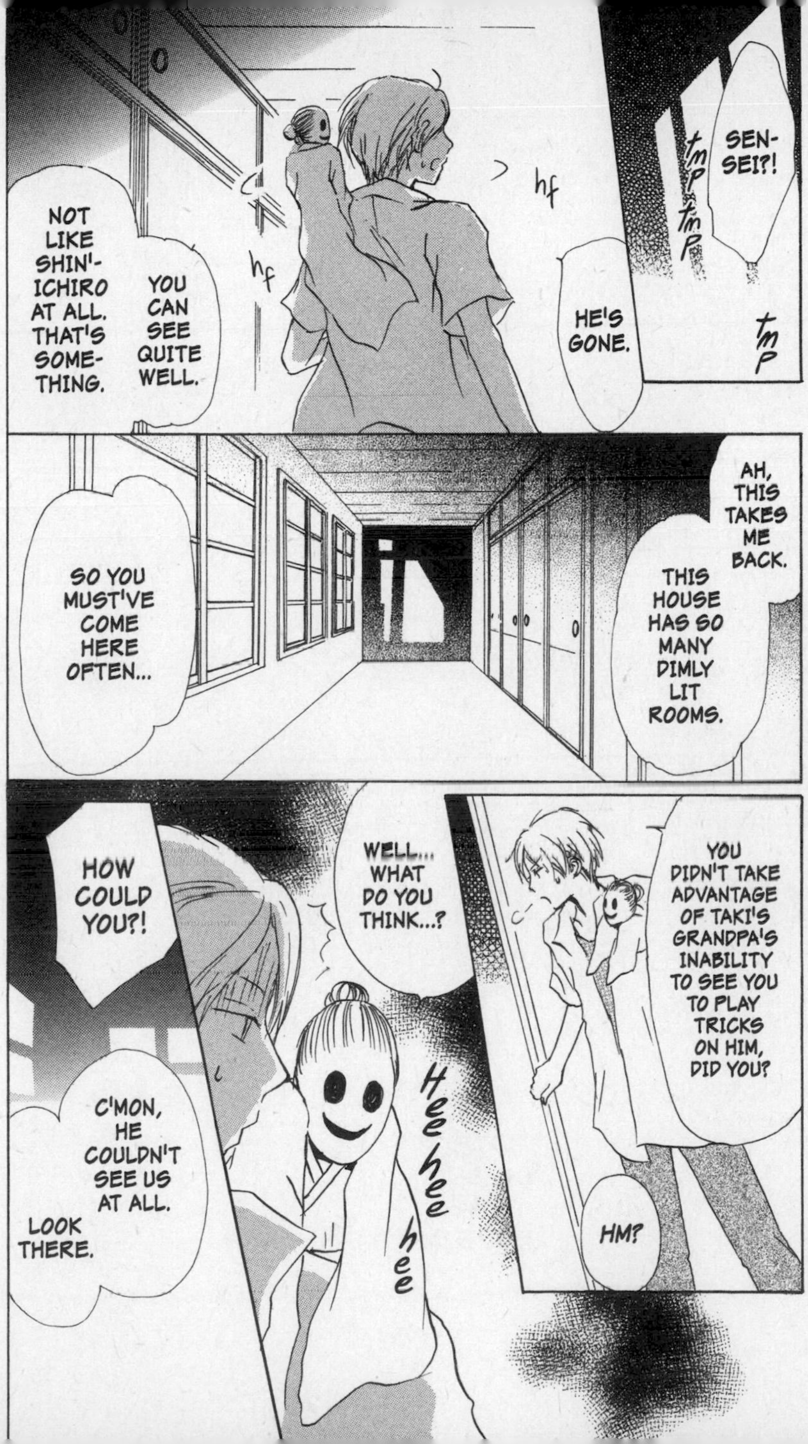
SEN-SEI?!
tmp tmp tmp
tmp
HE'S GONE.
hf
hf
YOU CAN SEE QUITE WELL.
NOT LIKE SHIN'ICHIRO AT ALL. THAT'S SOMETHING.
AH, THIS TAKES ME BACK.
THIS HOUSE HAS SO MANY DIMLY LIT ROOMS.
SO YOU MUST'VE COME HERE OFTEN...
YOU DIDN'T TAKE ADVANTAGE OF TAKI'S GRANDPA'S INABILITY TO SEE YOU TO PLAY TRICKS ON HIM, DID YOU?
HM?
WELL... WHAT DO YOU THINK...?
HOW COULD YOU?!
Hee hee hee
C'MON, HE COULDN'T SEE US AT ALL.
LOOK THERE.

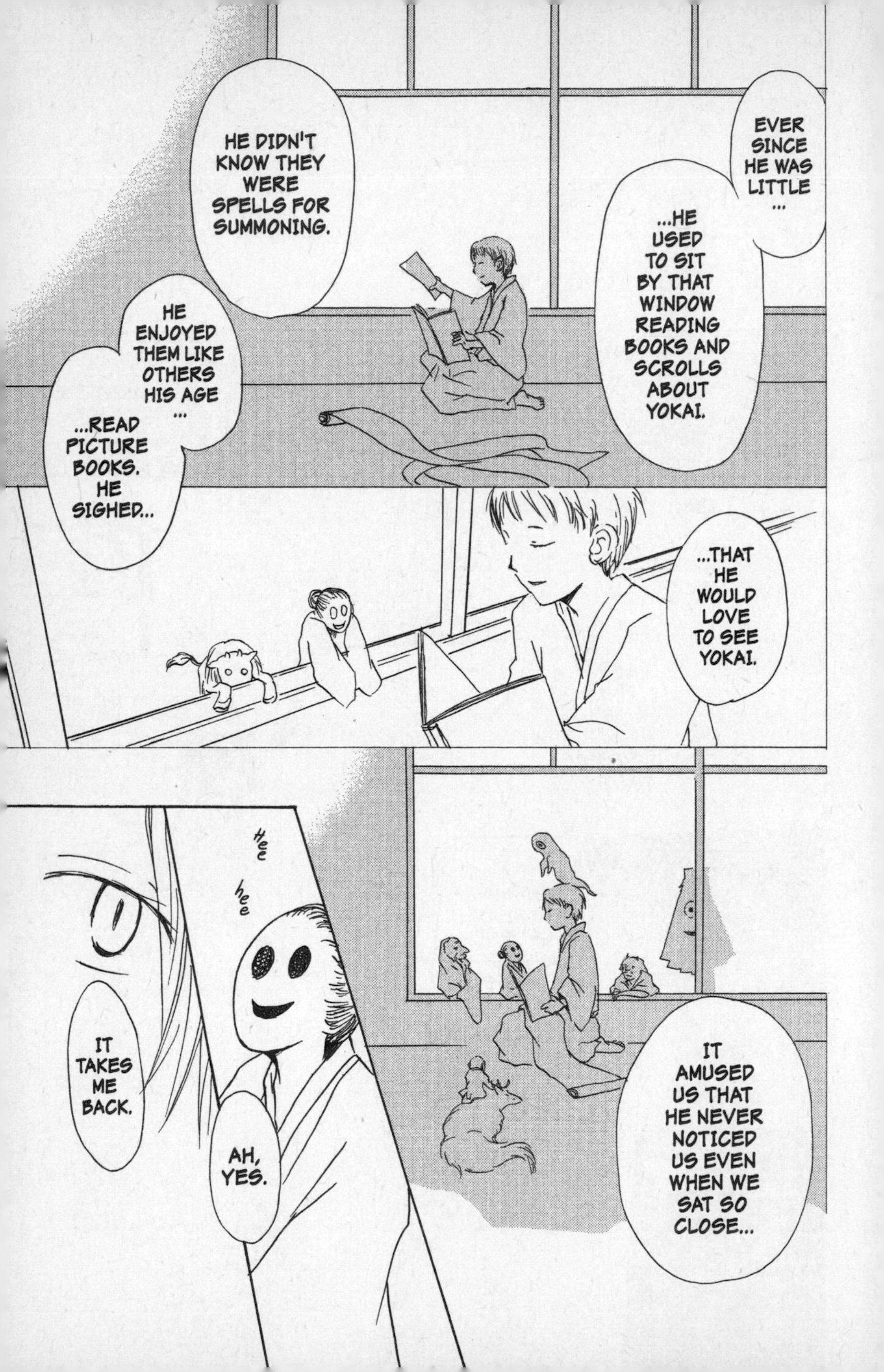
EVER SINCE HE WAS LITTLE...
...HE USED TO SIT BY THAT WINDOW READING BOOKS AND SCROLLS ABOUT YOKAI.
HE DIDN'T KNOW THEY WERE SPELLS FOR SUMMONING.
HE ENJOYED THEM LIKE OTHERS HIS AGE...
...READ PICTURE BOOKS. HE SIGHED...
...THAT HE WOULD LOVE TO SEE YOKAI.
IT AMUSED US THAT HE NEVER NOTICED US EVEN WHEN WE SAT SO CLOSE...
Hee
hee
AH, YES.
IT TAKES ME BACK.

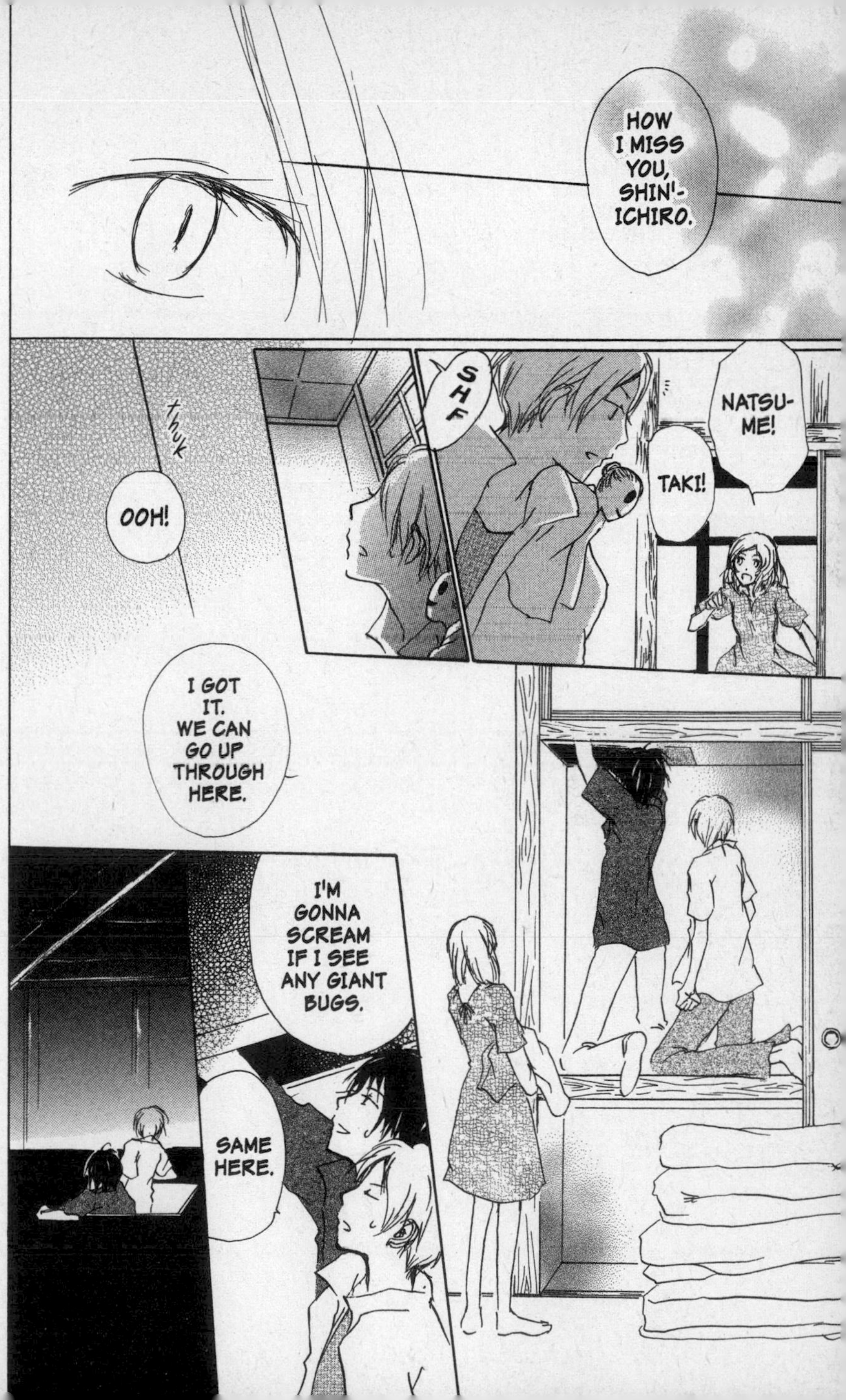
HOW I MISS YOU, SHIN'-ICHIRO.
NATSU-ME!
TAKI!
SHF
thuk
OOH!
I GOT IT. WE CAN GO UP THROUGH HERE.
I'M GONNA SCREAM IF I SEE ANY GIANT BUGS.
SAME HERE.

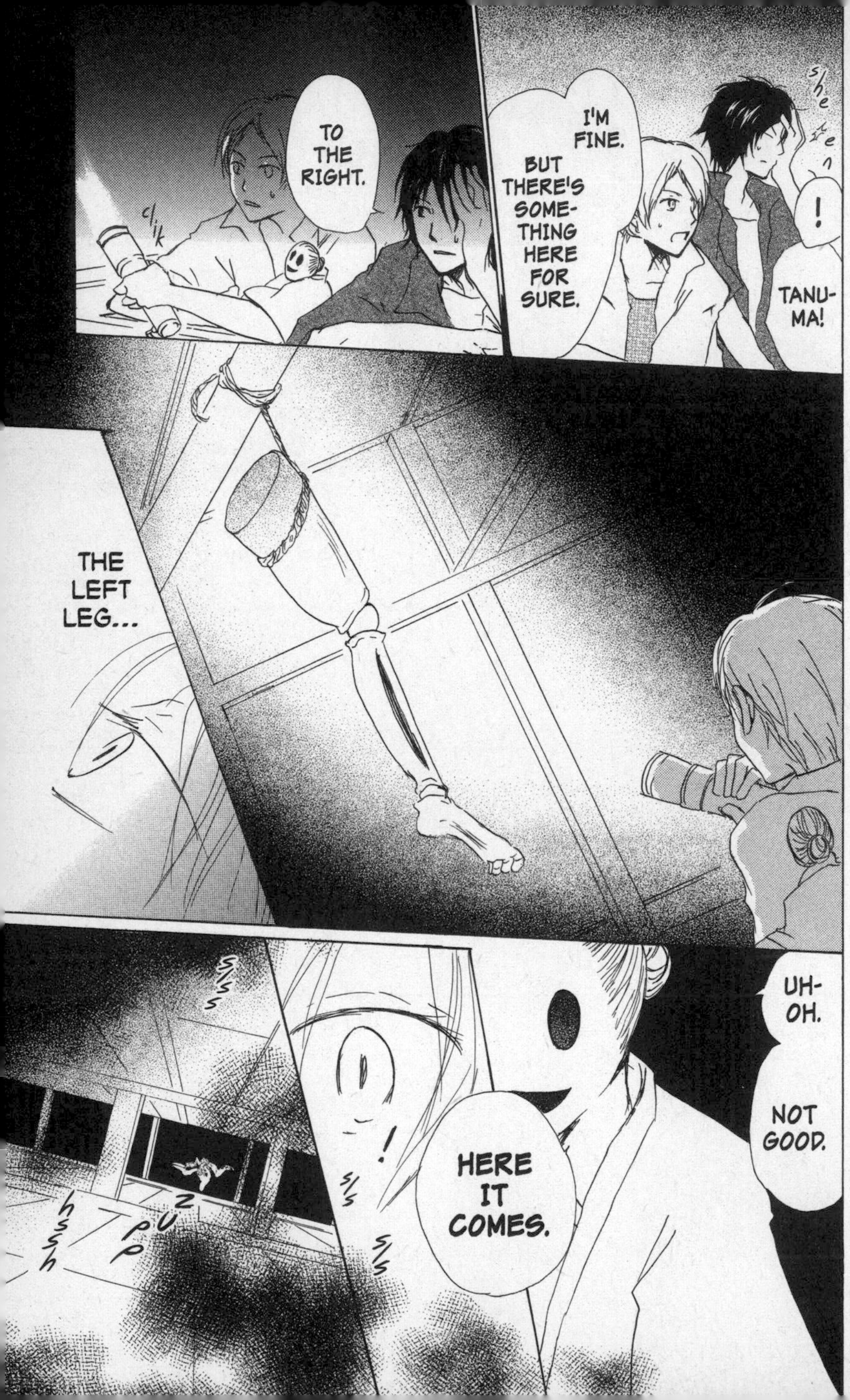
!
TANU-MA!
I'M FINE.
BUT THERE'S SOME-THING HERE FOR SURE.
TO THE RIGHT.
THE LEFT LEG...
UH-OH.
NOT GOOD.
HERE IT COMES.
!

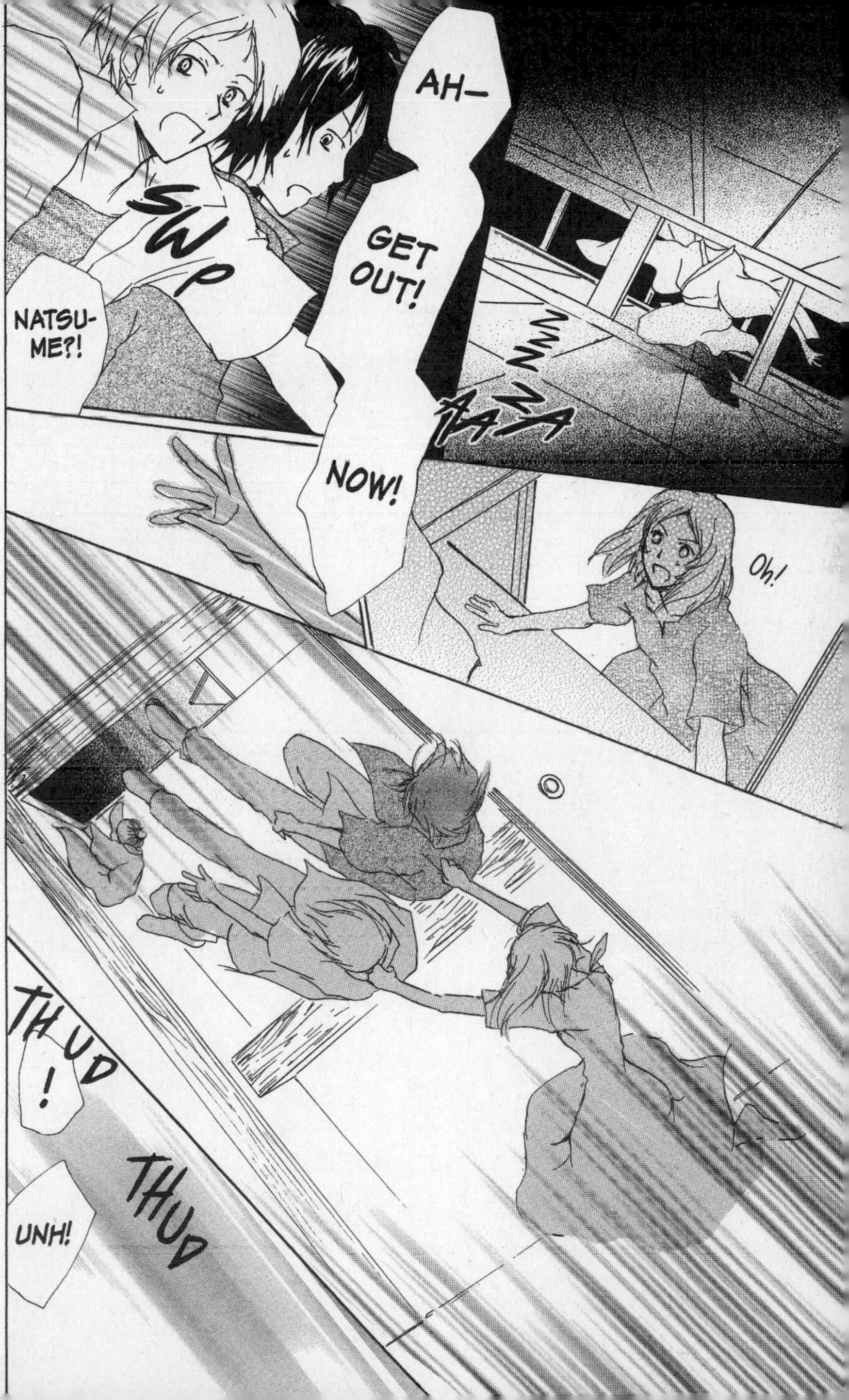
ZZZZAAA
AH— GET OUT! NOW!
SWP
NATSUME?!
Oh!
THUD!
THUD
UNH!

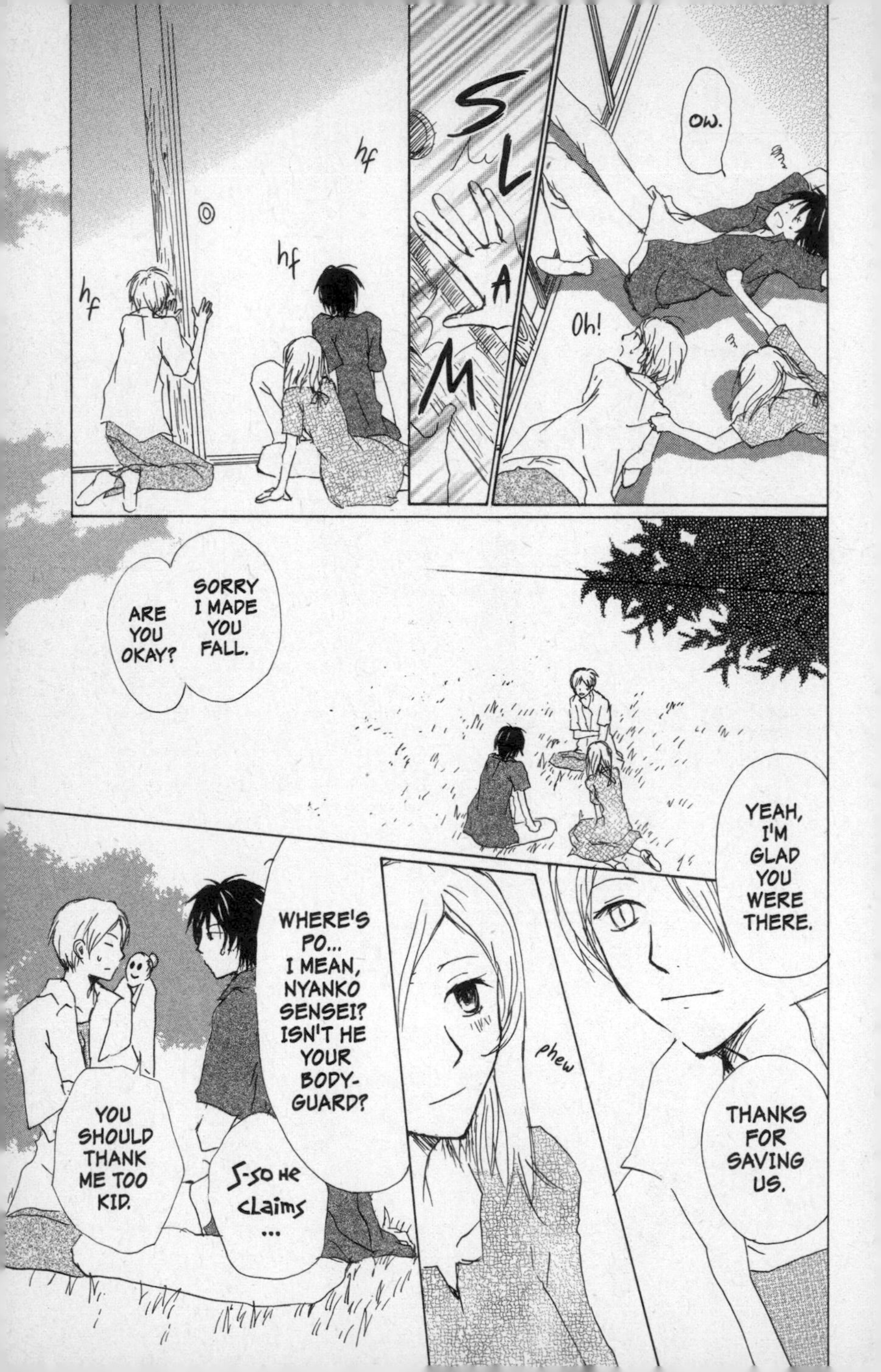
OW.
Oh!
SLAM
hf
hf
hf
SORRY I MADE YOU FALL.
ARE YOU OKAY?
YEAH, I'M GLAD YOU WERE THERE.
phew
THANKS FOR SAVING US.
WHERE'S PO... I MEAN, NYANKO SENSEI? ISN'T HE YOUR BODY-GUARD?
S-SO HE CLAIMS...
YOU SHOULD THANK ME TOO KID.

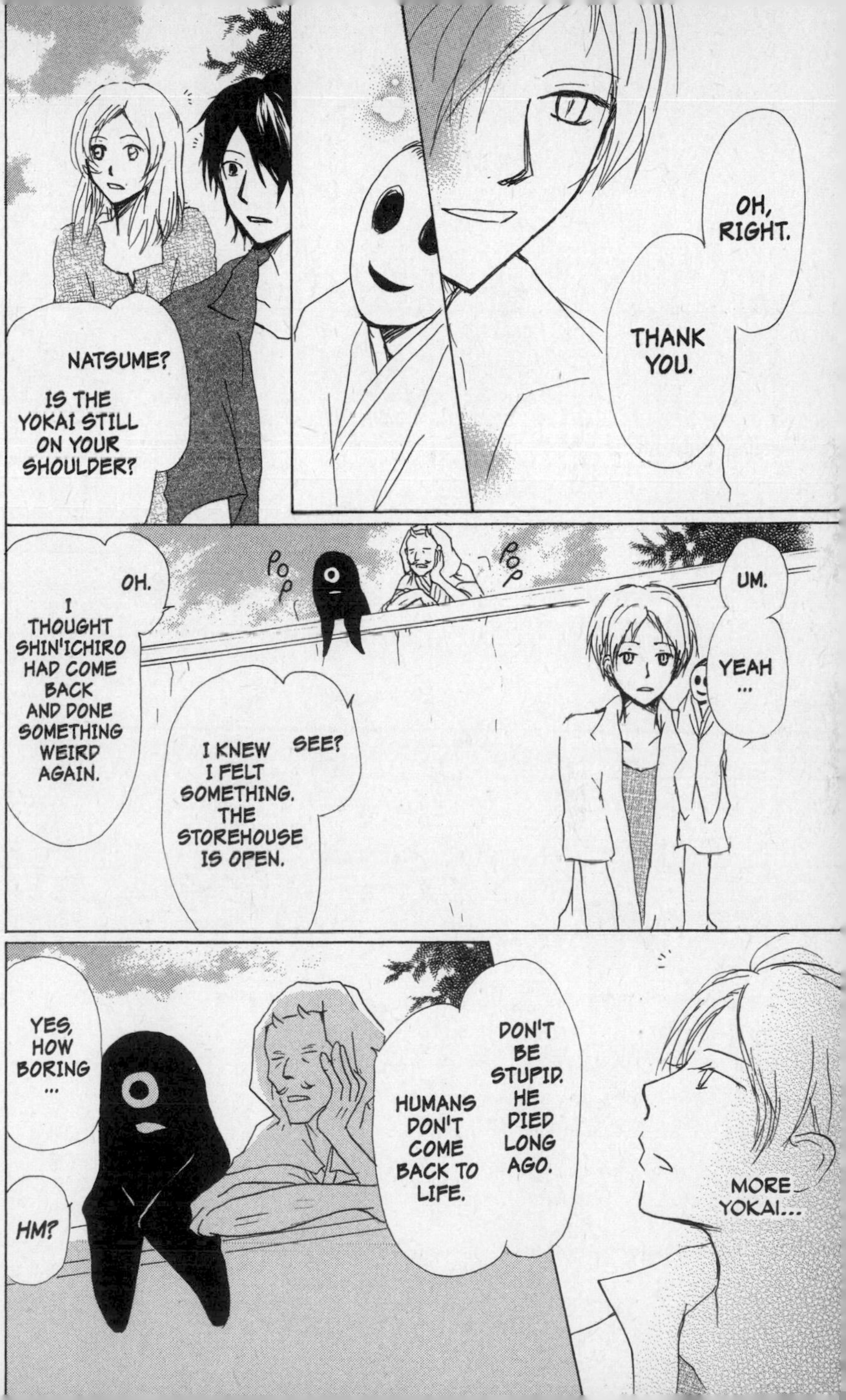
OH, RIGHT.
THANK YOU.
NATSUME?
IS THE YOKAI STILL ON YOUR SHOULDER?
UM.
YEAH ...
POP
POP
SEE?
I KNEW I FELT SOMETHING. THE STOREHOUSE IS OPEN.
OH.
I THOUGHT SHIN'ICHIRO HAD COME BACK AND DONE SOMETHING WEIRD AGAIN.
MORE YOKAI...
DON'T BE STUPID. HE DIED LONG AGO.
HUMANS DON'T COME BACK TO LIFE.
YES, HOW BORING ...
HM?

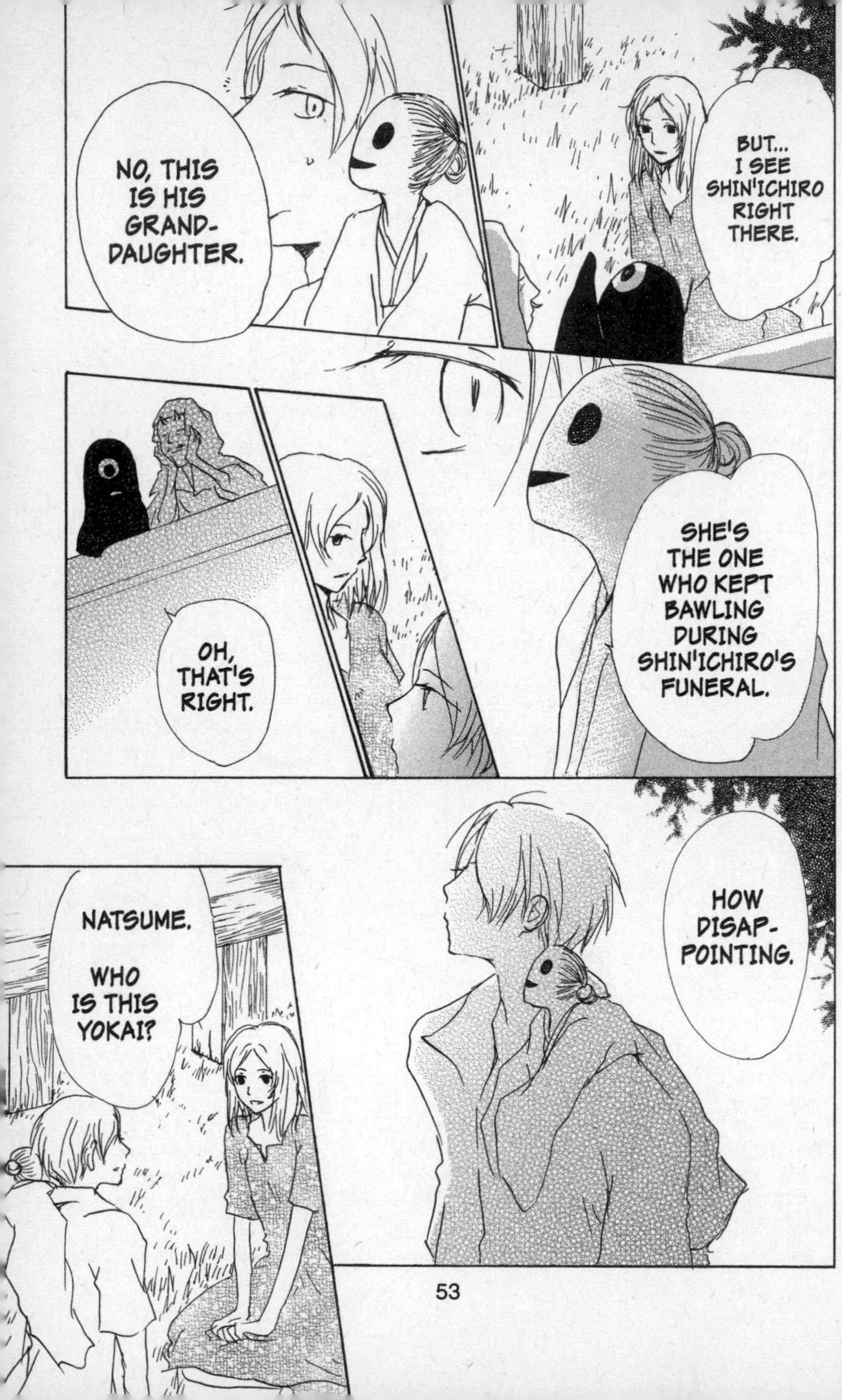
BUT... I SEE SHIN'ICHIRO RIGHT THERE.
NO, THIS IS HIS GRAND-DAUGHTER.
SHE'S THE ONE WHO KEPT BAWLING DURING SHIN'ICHIRO'S FUNERAL.
OH, THAT'S RIGHT.
HOW DISAP-POINTING.
NATSUME.
WHO IS THIS YOKAI?

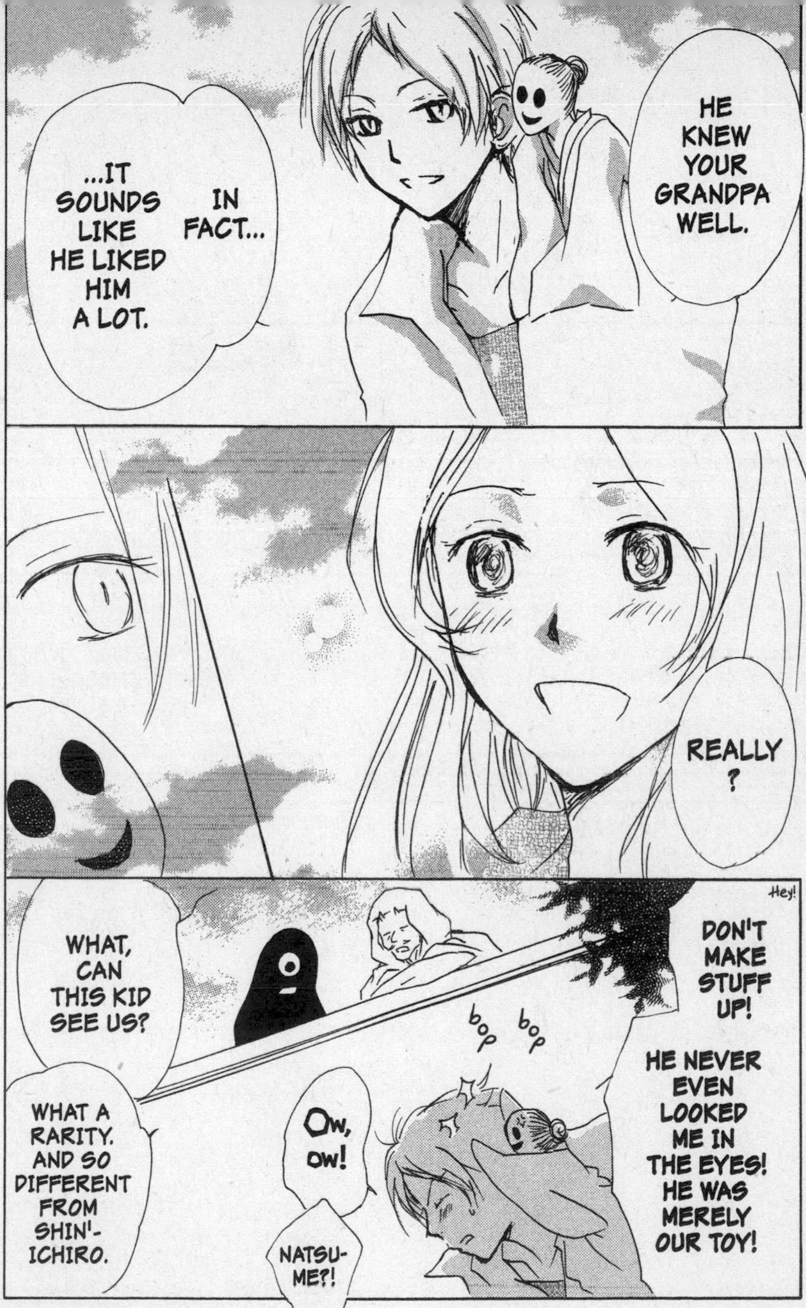
HE KNEW YOUR GRANDPA WELL.
IN FACT...
...IT SOUNDS LIKE HE LIKED HIM A LOT.
REALLY?
Hey!
DON'T MAKE STUFF UP!
HE NEVER EVEN LOOKED ME IN THE EYES! HE WAS MERELY OUR TOY!
bop bop
WHAT, CAN THIS KID SEE US?
WHAT A RARITY. AND SO DIFFERENT FROM SHIN'-ICHIRO.
OW, OW!
NATSU-ME?!

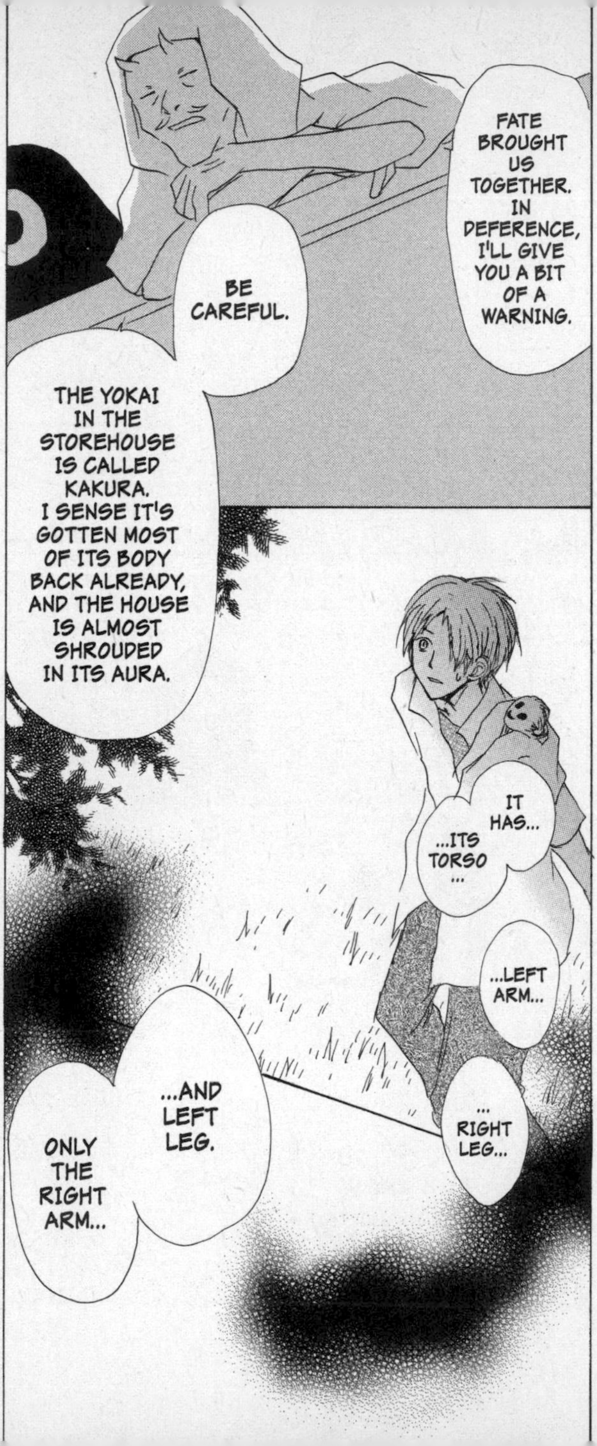
FATE BROUGHT US TOGETHER. IN DEFERENCE, I'LL GIVE YOU A BIT OF A WARNING.
BE CAREFUL.
THE YOKAI IN THE STOREHOUSE IS CALLED KAKURA. I SENSE IT'S GOTTEN MOST OF ITS BODY BACK ALREADY, AND THE HOUSE IS ALMOST SHROUDED IN ITS AURA.
IT HAS...
...ITS TORSO...
...LEFT ARM...
...RIGHT LEG...
...AND LEFT LEG.
ONLY THE RIGHT ARM...

02

❋The third season of the anime

Believe it or not, thanks to the wonderful staff who created the first and second seasons of the anime and all the supporting fans, they're going to be making a third season.

It's another view of the world of Natsume that is vivid, gentle, mischievous, and heartwarming. There is nothing that could make me happier. I love the anime so much.

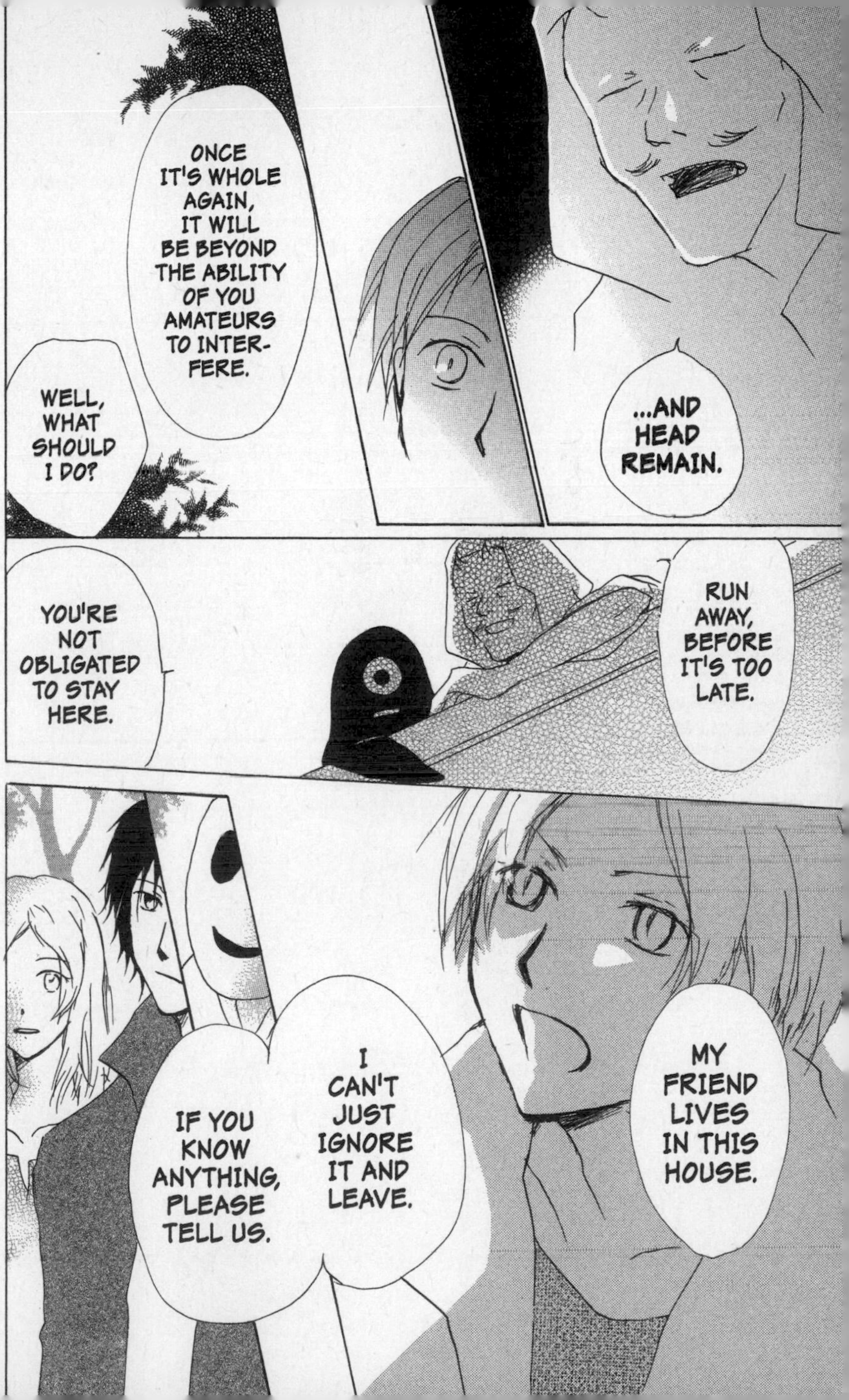
...AND HEAD REMAIN.
ONCE IT'S WHOLE AGAIN, IT WILL BE BEYOND THE ABILITY OF YOU AMATEURS TO INTER-FERE.
WELL, WHAT SHOULD I DO?
RUN AWAY, BEFORE IT'S TOO LATE.
YOU'RE NOT OBLIGATED TO STAY HERE.
MY FRIEND LIVES IN THIS HOUSE.
I CAN'T JUST IGNORE IT AND LEAVE.
IF YOU KNOW ANYTHING, PLEASE TELL US.

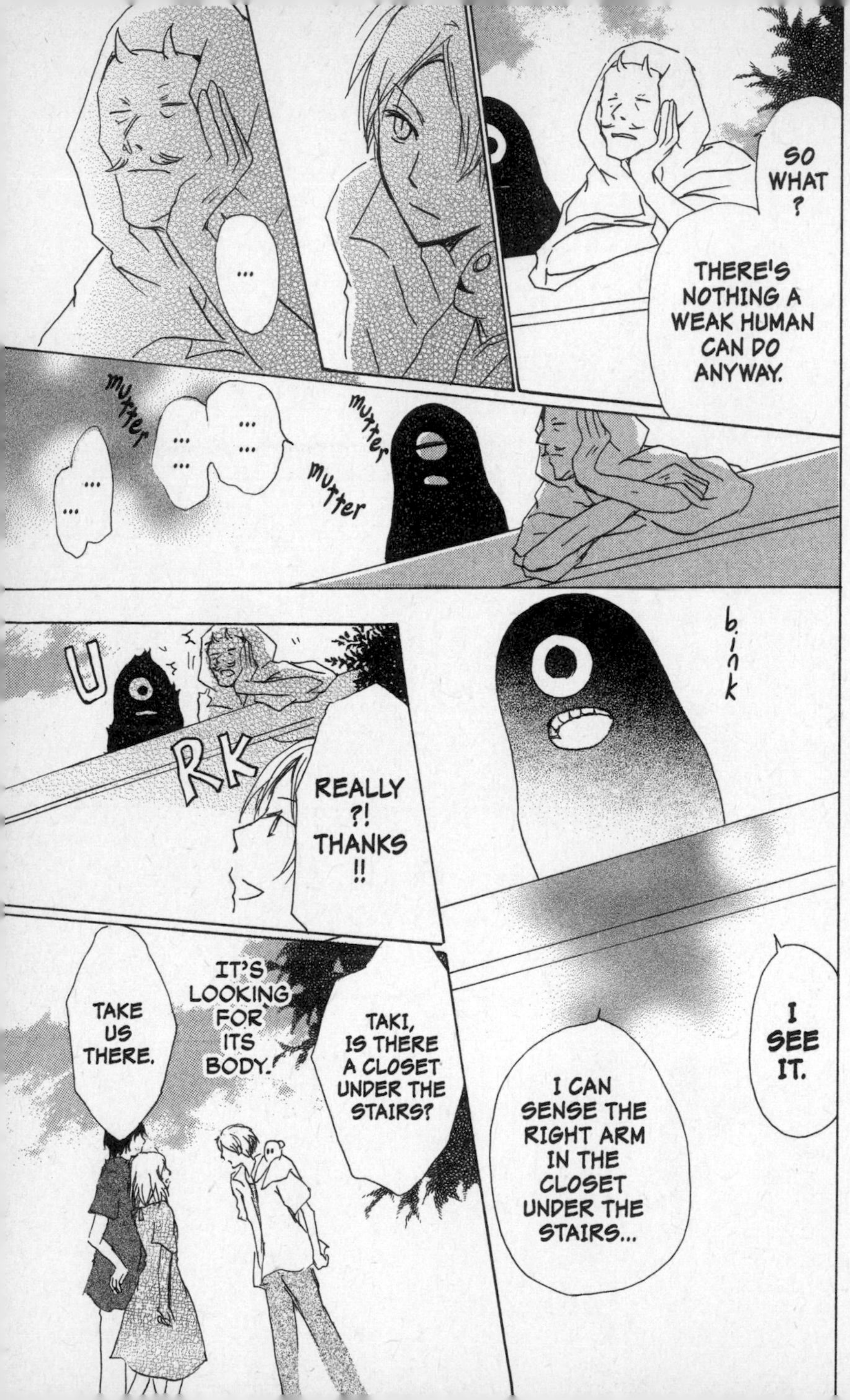
SO WHAT?
THERE'S NOTHING A WEAK HUMAN CAN DO ANYWAY.
...
mutter mutter
... ...
... ...
mutter
blink
REALLY?! THANKS!!
URK
I SEE IT.
I CAN SENSE THE RIGHT ARM IN THE CLOSET UNDER THE STAIRS...
TAKI, IS THERE A CLOSET UNDER THE STAIRS?
IT'S LOOKING FOR ITS BODY.
TAKE US THERE.

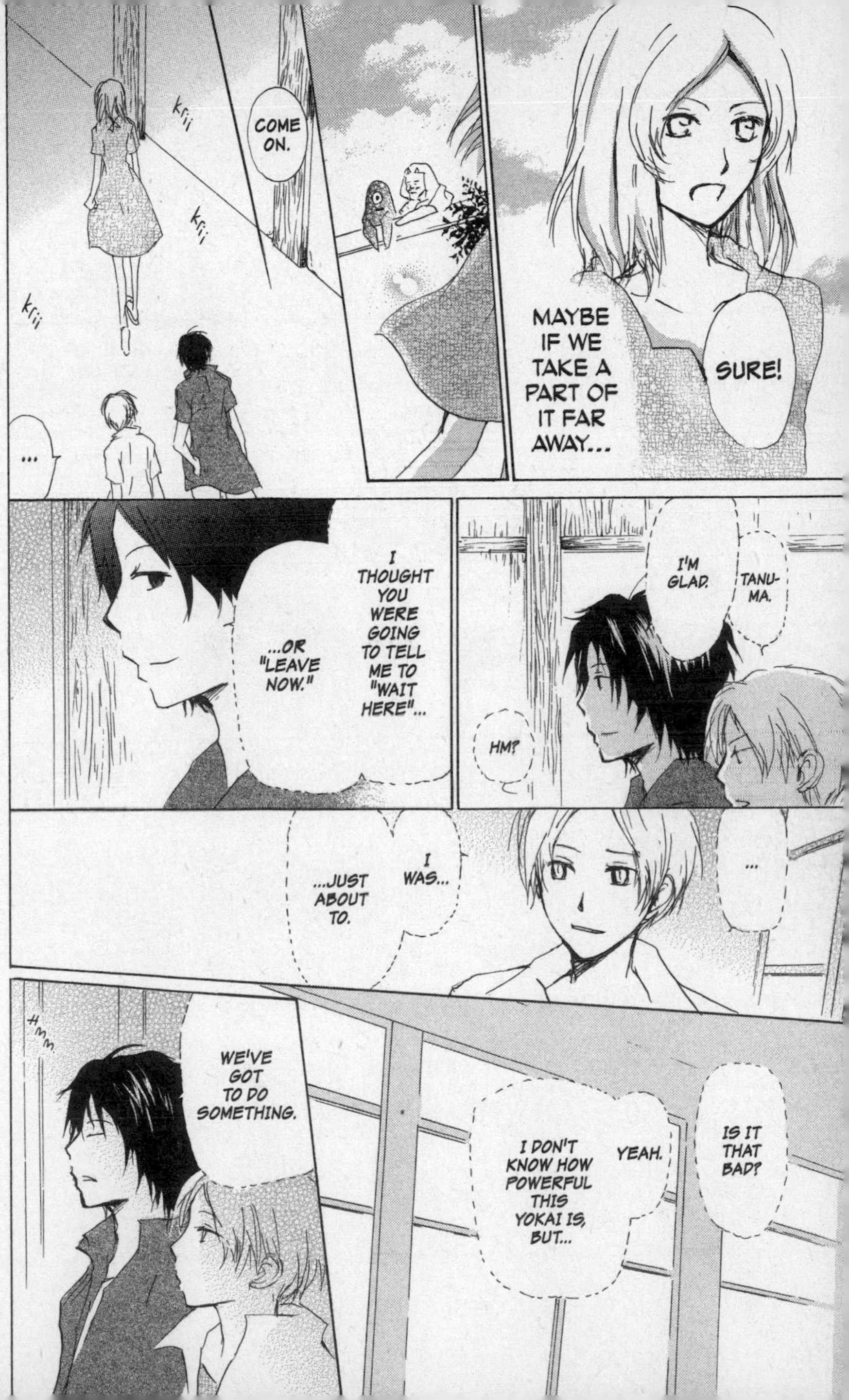
SURE!
MAYBE IF WE TAKE A PART OF IT FAR AWAY...
COME ON.
krii
krii
krii
...
TANU-MA.
I'M GLAD.
HM?
I THOUGHT YOU WERE GOING TO TELL ME TO "WAIT HERE"...
...OR "LEAVE NOW."
...
I WAS...
...JUST ABOUT TO.
IS IT THAT BAD?
YEAH.
I DON'T KNOW HOW POWERFUL THIS YOKAI IS, BUT...
WE'VE GOT TO DO SOMETHING.
HMM.

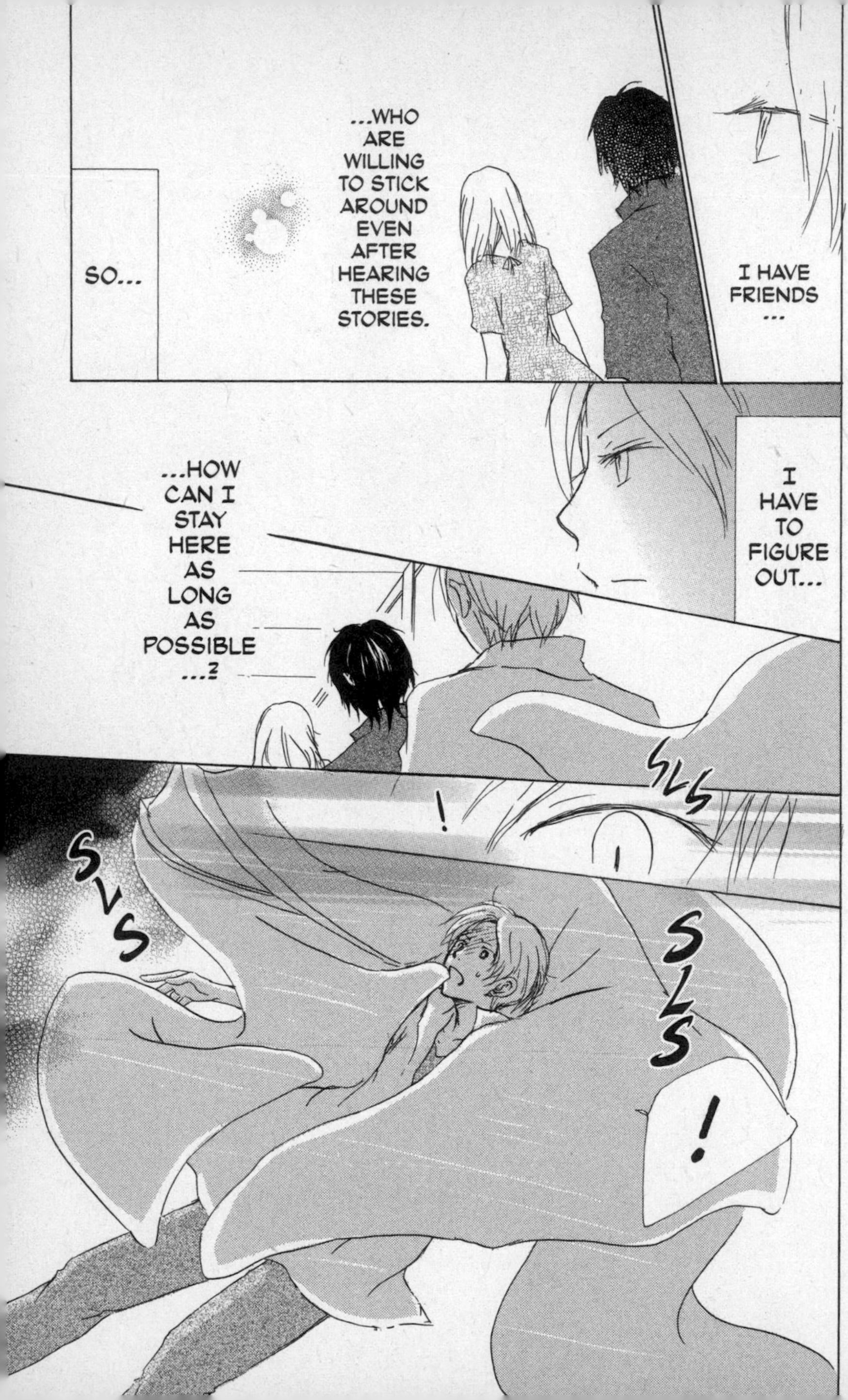
I HAVE FRIENDS...
...WHO ARE WILLING TO STICK AROUND EVEN AFTER HEARING THESE STORIES.
SO...
I HAVE TO FIGURE OUT...
...HOW CAN I STAY HERE AS LONG AS POSSIBLE...?
SLS
!
SLS
SVS
!

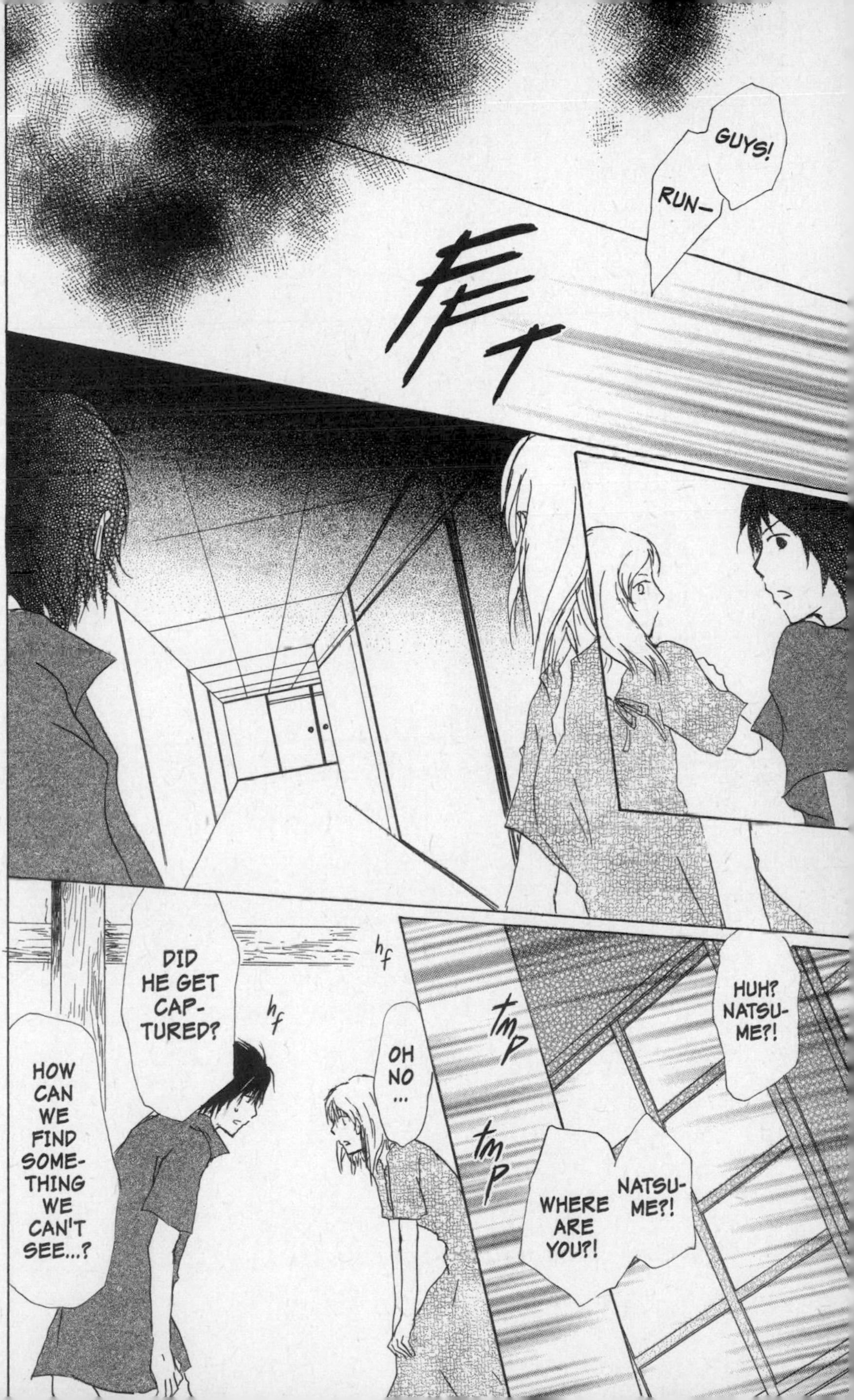
GUYS!
RUN—
FFT
HUH? NATSU-ME?!
tmp
tmp
NATSU-ME?!
WHERE ARE YOU?!
hf
hf
DID HE GET CAP-TURED?
OH NO ...
HOW CAN WE FIND SOME-THING WE CAN'T SEE...?

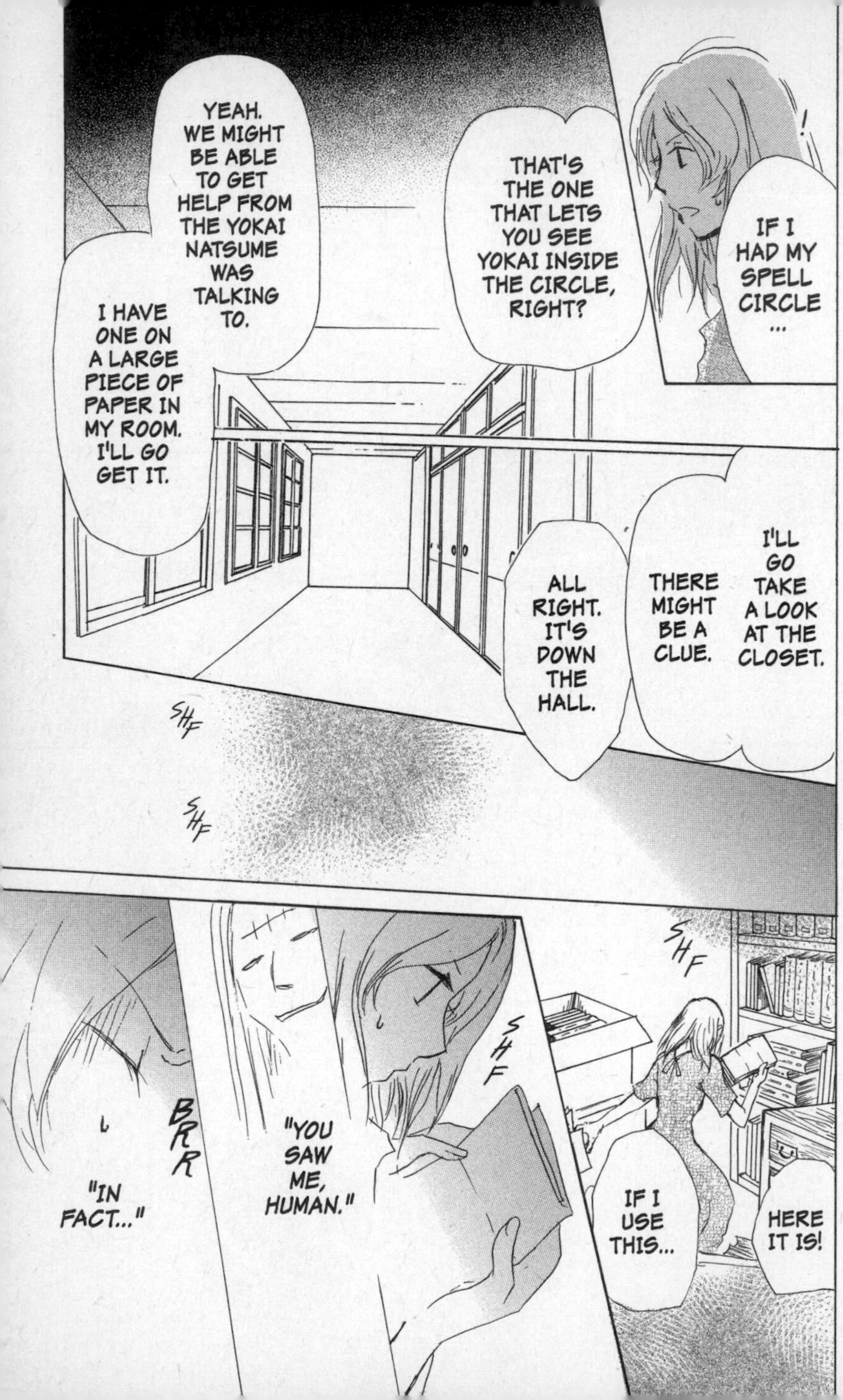
!
IF I HAD MY SPELL CIRCLE ...
THAT'S THE ONE THAT LETS YOU SEE YOKAI INSIDE THE CIRCLE, RIGHT?
YEAH. WE MIGHT BE ABLE TO GET HELP FROM THE YOKAI NATSUME WAS TALKING TO.
I HAVE ONE ON A LARGE PIECE OF PAPER IN MY ROOM. I'LL GO GET IT.
I'LL GO TAKE A LOOK AT THE CLOSET.
THERE MIGHT BE A CLUE.
ALL RIGHT. IT'S DOWN THE HALL.
SHF
SHF
SHF
HERE IT IS!
IF I USE THIS...
SHF
"YOU SAW ME, HUMAN."
BRR
"IN FACT..."

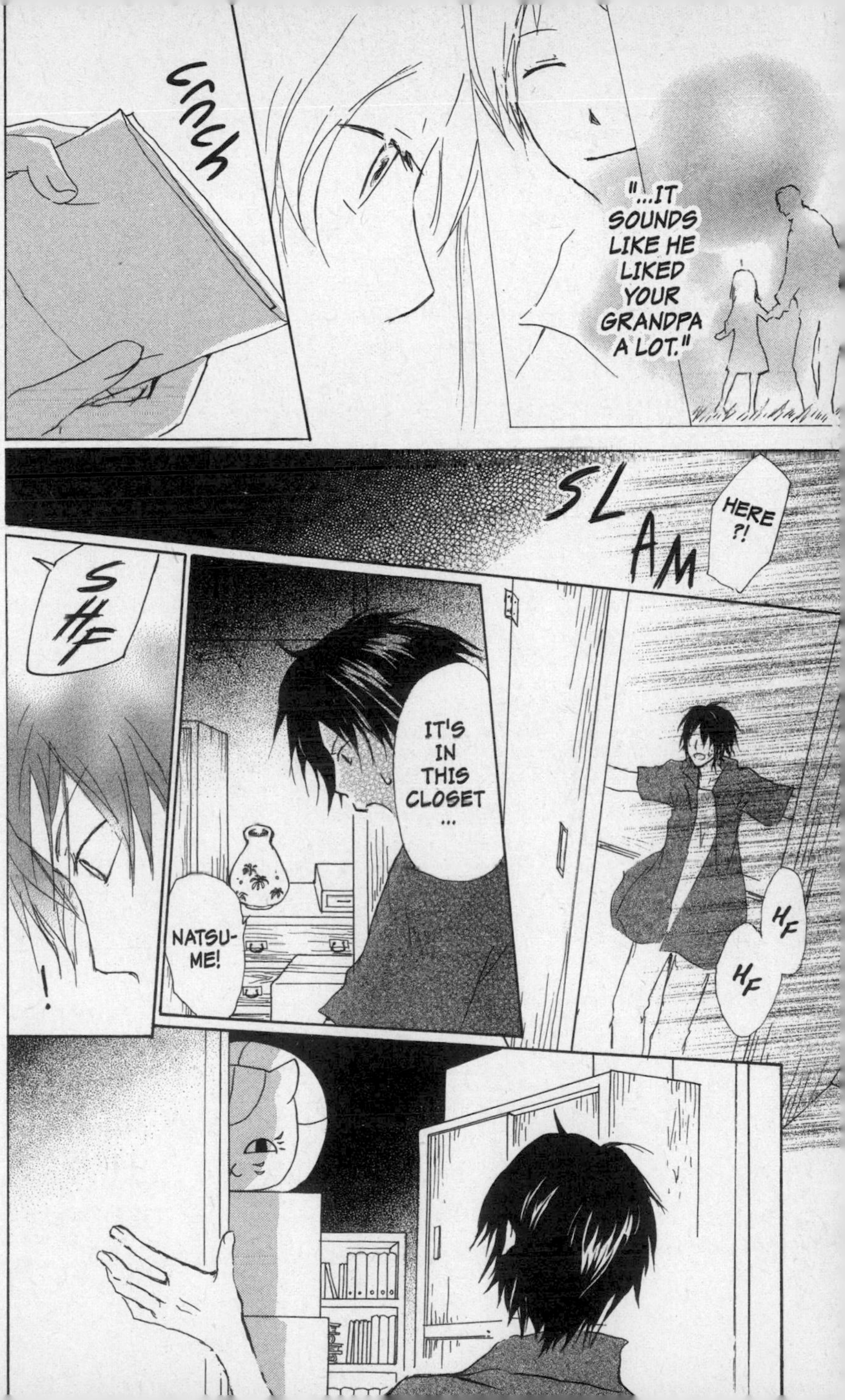
"...IT SOUNDS LIKE HE LIKED YOUR GRANDPA A LOT."
crnch
HERE?!
SLAM
HF
HF
IT'S IN THIS CLOSET ...
NATSU-ME!
SHF
!

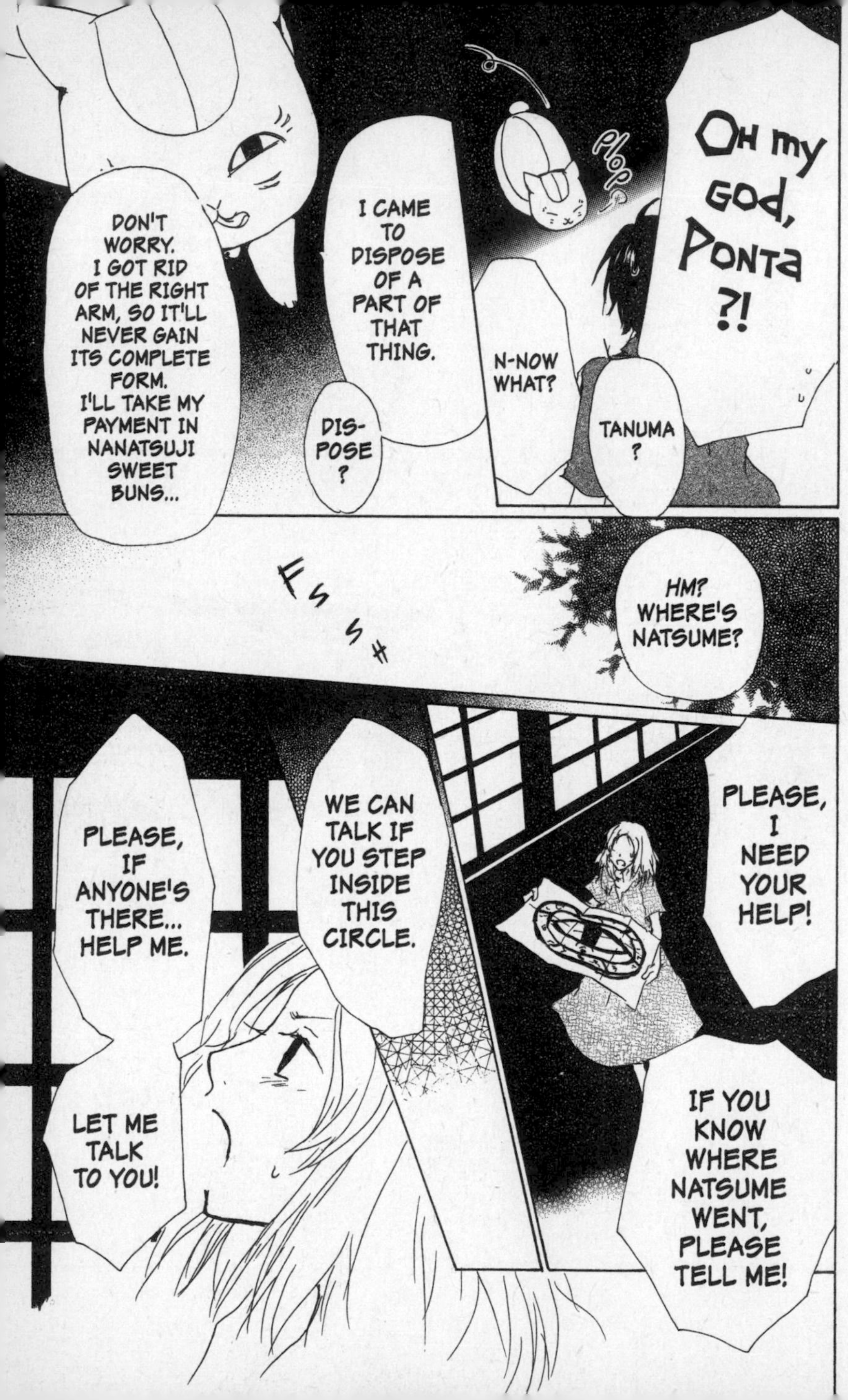
OH my GOD, PONTA ?!
TANUMA ?
N-NOW WHAT?
I CAME TO DISPOSE OF A PART OF THAT THING.
DIS-POSE ?
DON'T WORRY. I GOT RID OF THE RIGHT ARM, SO IT'LL NEVER GAIN ITS COMPLETE FORM. I'LL TAKE MY PAYMENT IN NANATSUJI SWEET BUNS...
HM? WHERE'S NATSUME?
FSSH
PLEASE, I NEED YOUR HELP!
IF YOU KNOW WHERE NATSUME WENT, PLEASE TELL ME!
WE CAN TALK IF YOU STEP INSIDE THIS CIRCLE.
PLEASE, IF ANYONE'S THERE... HELP ME.
LET ME TALK TO YOU!

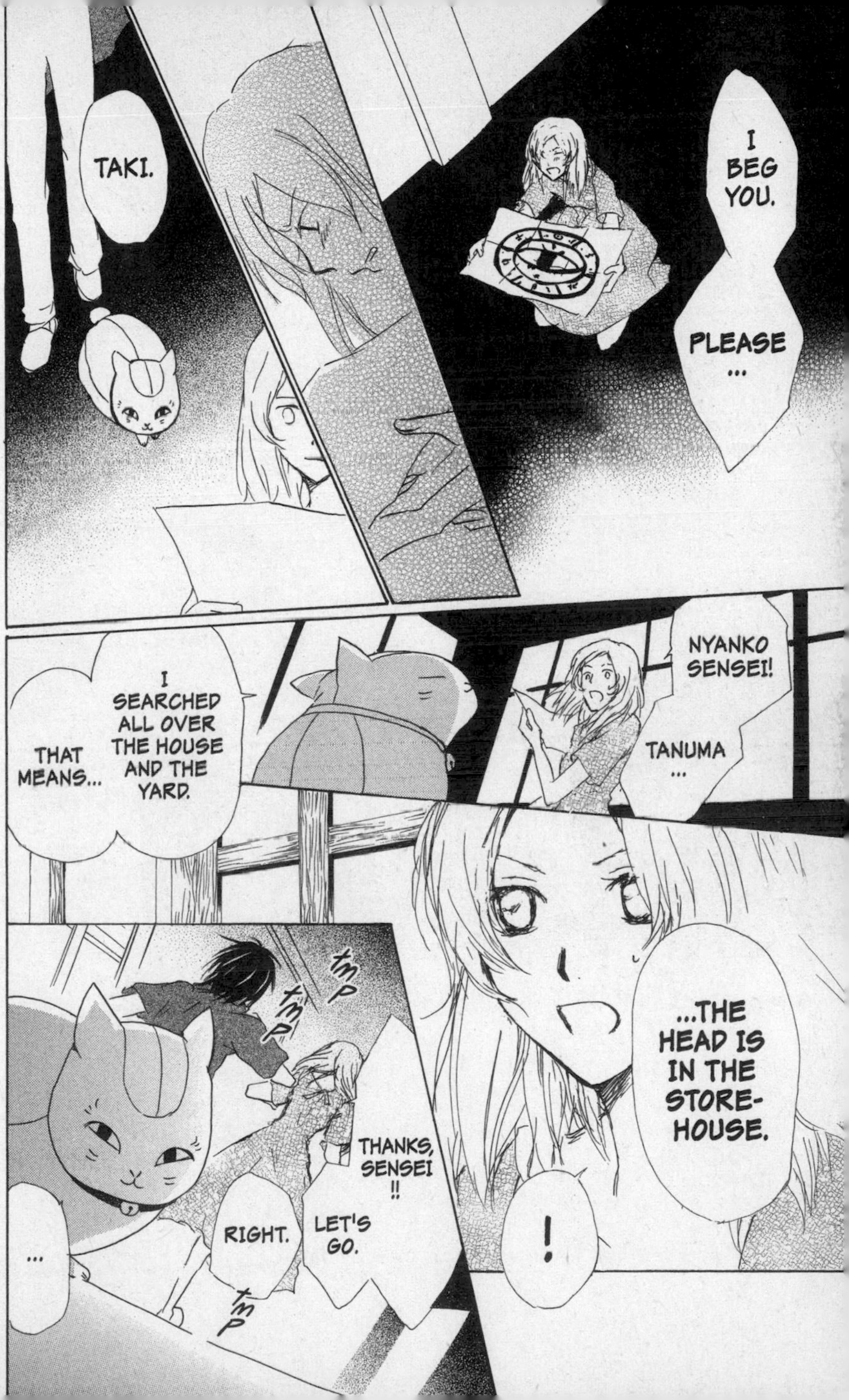
I BEG YOU.
PLEASE ...
TAKI.
NYANKO SENSEI!
TANUMA ...
I SEARCHED ALL OVER THE HOUSE AND THE YARD.
THAT MEANS...
...THE HEAD IS IN THE STORE-HOUSE.
!
tmp tmp
THANKS, SENSEI !!
LET'S GO.
RIGHT.
...
tmp

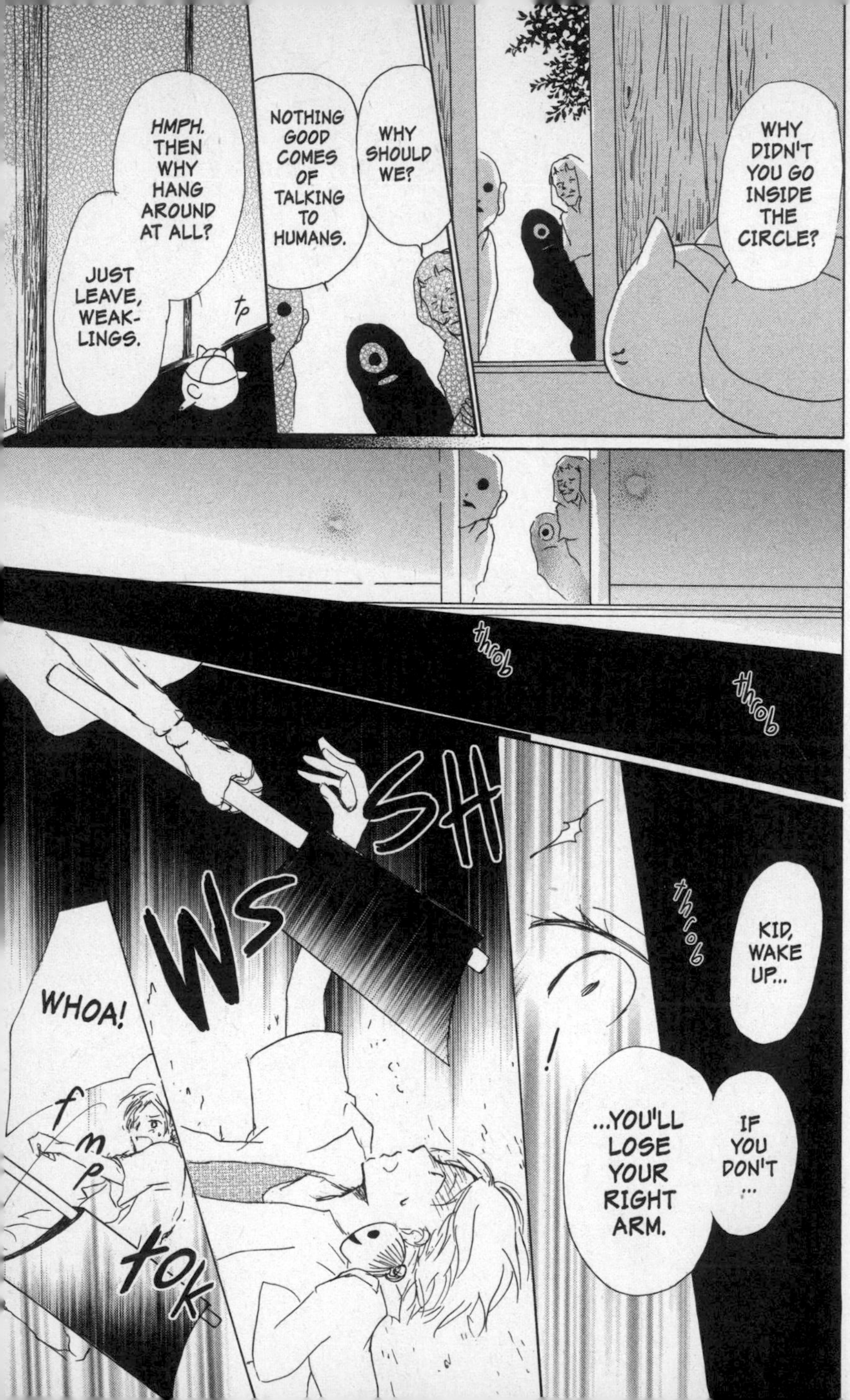
WHY DIDN'T YOU GO INSIDE THE CIRCLE?
WHY SHOULD WE?
NOTHING GOOD COMES OF TALKING TO HUMANS.
HMPH. THEN WHY HANG AROUND AT ALL?
JUST LEAVE, WEAK-LINGS.
tp
throb
throb
throb
KID, WAKE UP...
IF YOU DON'T...
...YOU'LL LOSE YOUR RIGHT ARM.
!
WSSH
WHOA!
fmp
tok

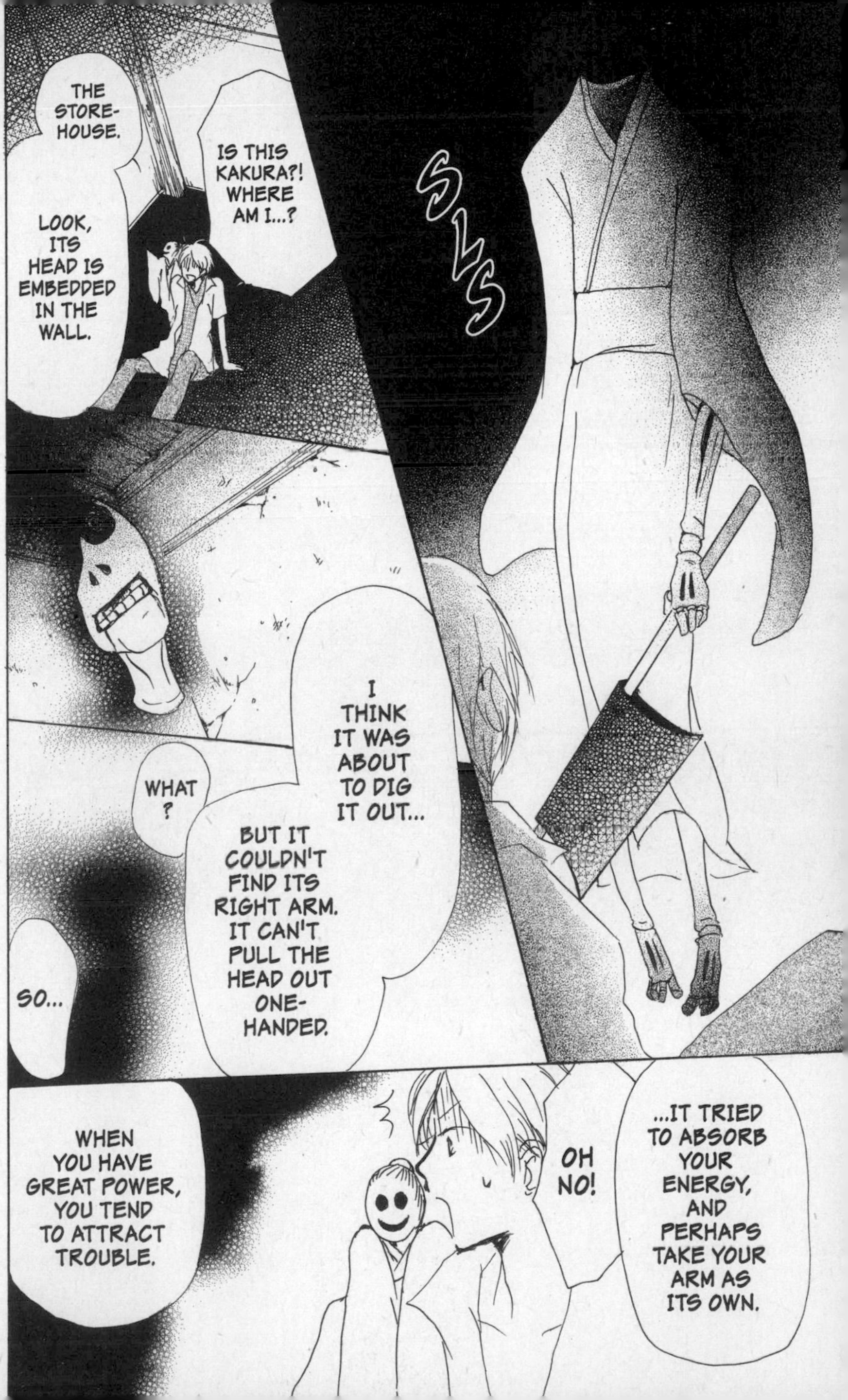
SLS
IS THIS KAKURA?! WHERE AM I...?
THE STOREHOUSE.
LOOK, ITS HEAD IS EMBEDDED IN THE WALL.
I THINK IT WAS ABOUT TO DIG IT OUT...
WHAT?
BUT IT COULDN'T FIND ITS RIGHT ARM. IT CAN'T PULL THE HEAD OUT ONE-HANDED.
SO...
...IT TRIED TO ABSORB YOUR ENERGY, AND PERHAPS TAKE YOUR ARM AS ITS OWN.
OH NO!
WHEN YOU HAVE GREAT POWER, YOU TEND TO ATTRACT TROUBLE.

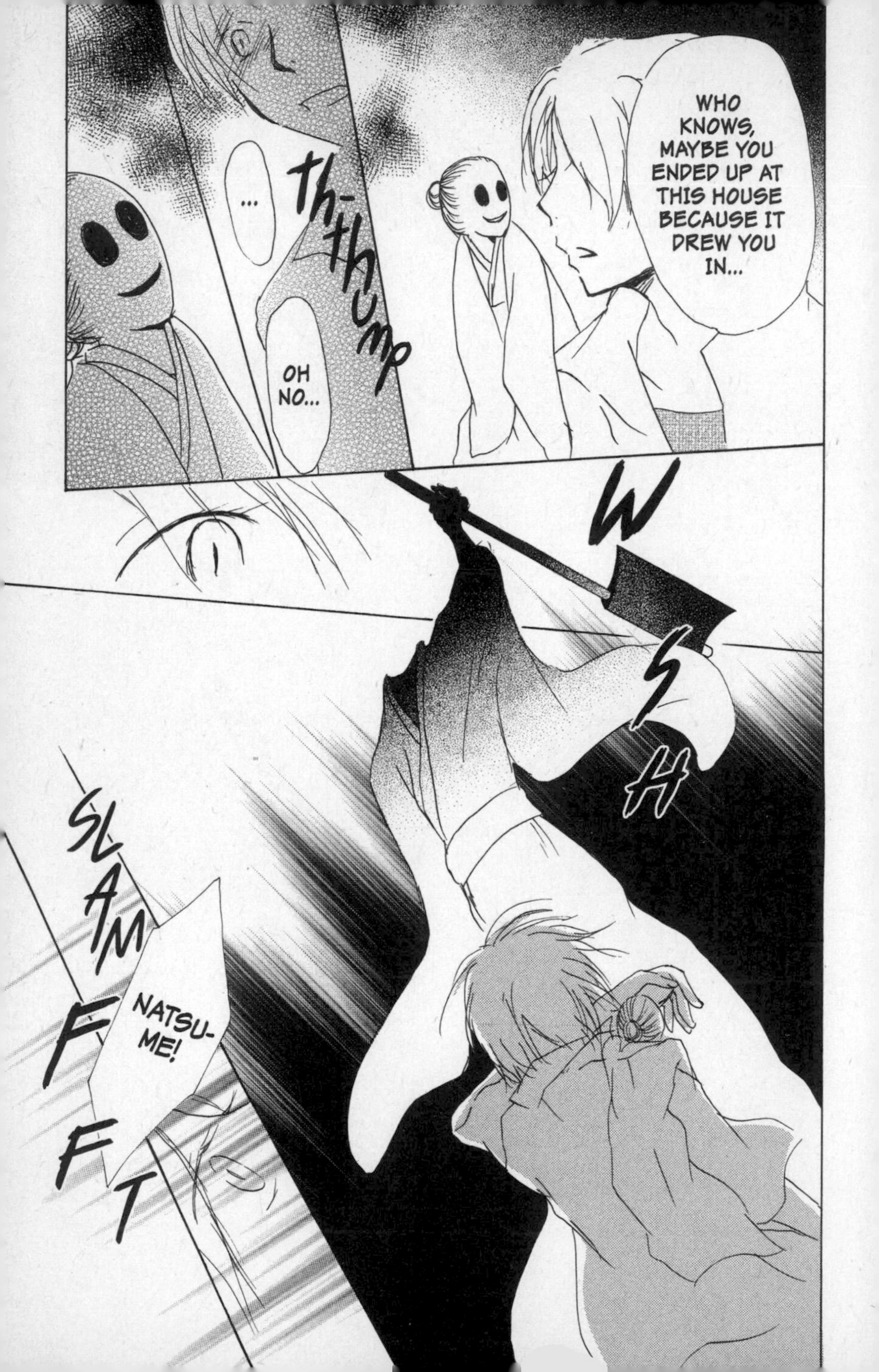
WHO KNOWS, MAYBE YOU ENDED UP AT THIS HOUSE BECAUSE IT DREW YOU IN...
th-thump
...
OH NO...
WSH
SLAM
FFFT
NATSU-ME!

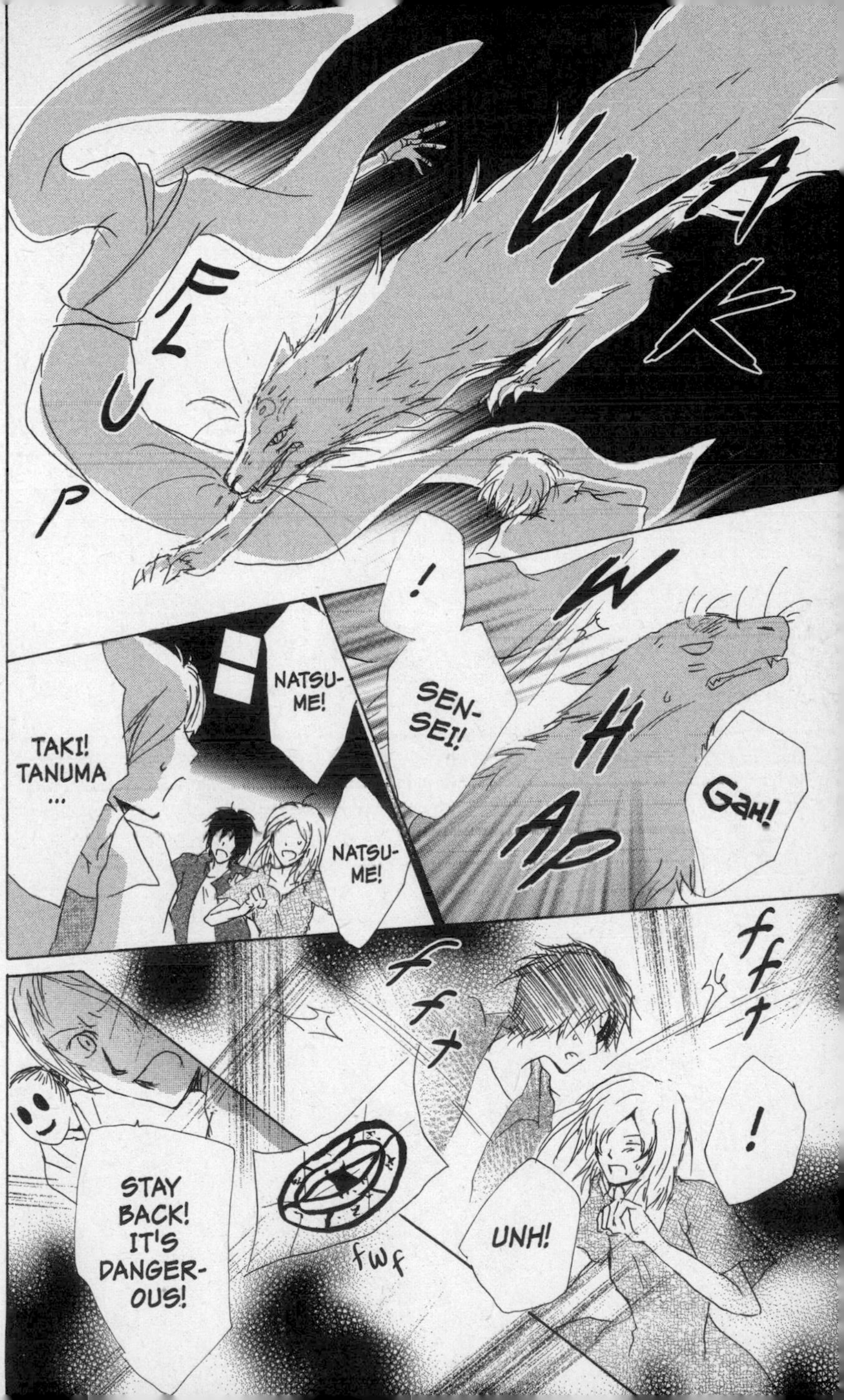
WAK
FLUP
!
SEN-SEI!
WHAP
Gah!
NATSU-ME!
NATSU-ME!
TAKI! TANUMA ...
fft
!
fft
UNH!
fwf
STAY BACK! IT'S DANGER-OUS!

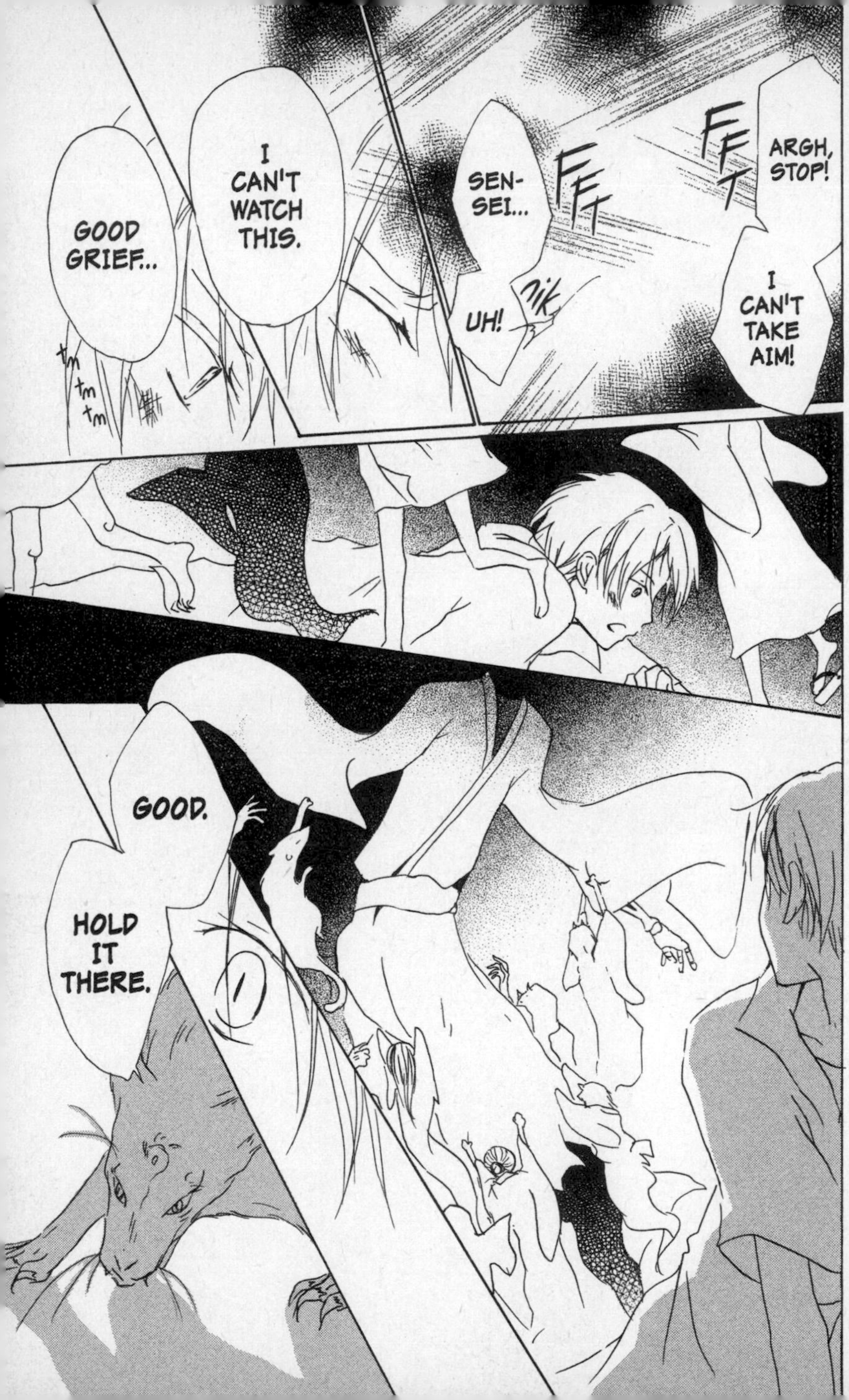
FFT
ARGH, STOP!
I CAN'T TAKE AIM!
SEN-SEI...
FFT
nik
UH!
I CAN'T WATCH THIS.
GOOD GRIEF...
tm tm tm
GOOD.
HOLD IT THERE.

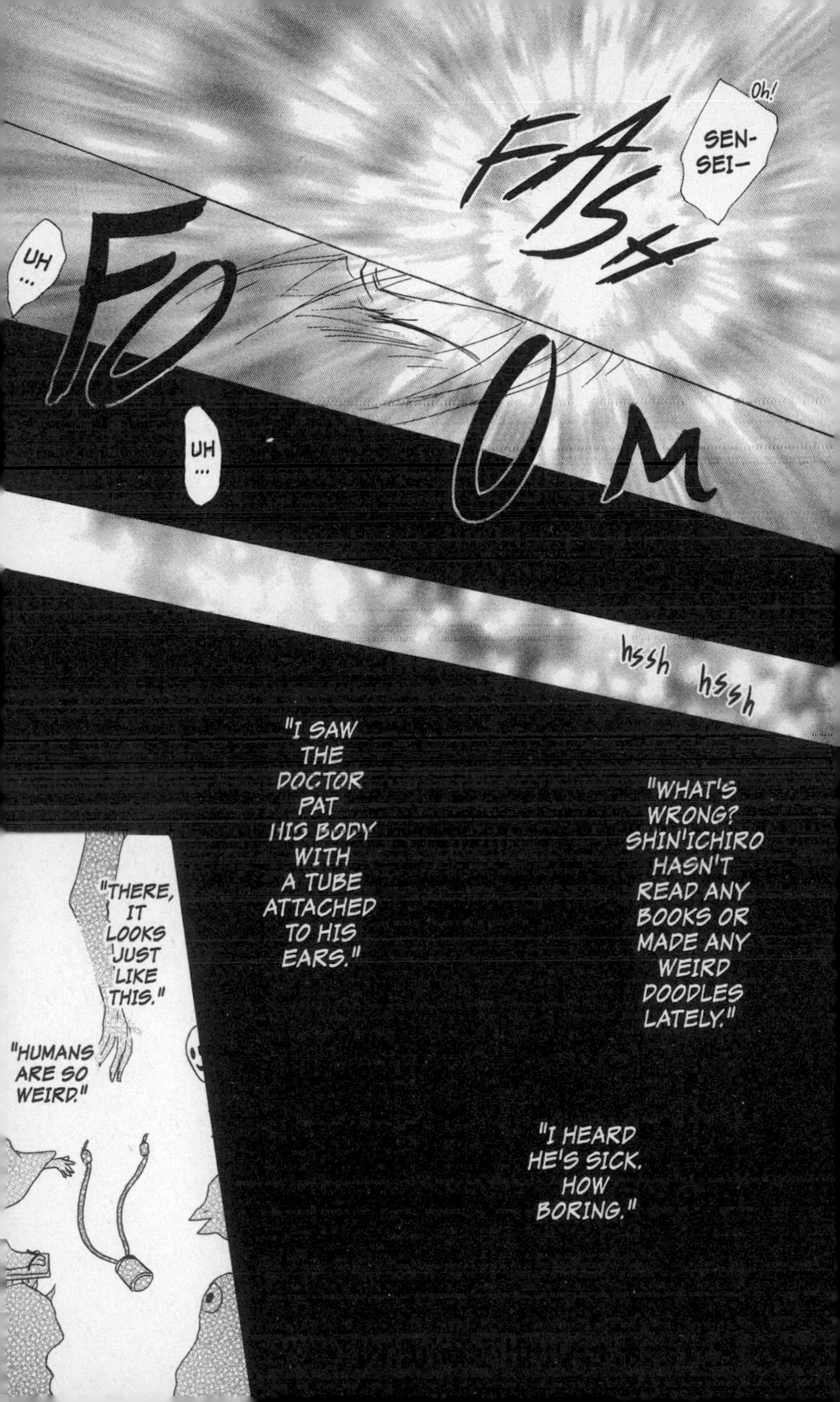
Oh!
SEN-SEI—
FASH
FOOM
UH...
UH...
hssh hssh
"WHAT'S WRONG? SHIN'ICHIRO HASN'T READ ANY BOOKS OR MADE ANY WEIRD DOODLES LATELY."
"I HEARD HE'S SICK. HOW BORING."
"I SAW THE DOCTOR PAT HIS BODY WITH A TUBE ATTACHED TO HIS EARS."
"THERE, IT LOOKS JUST LIKE THIS."
"HUMANS ARE SO WEIRD."

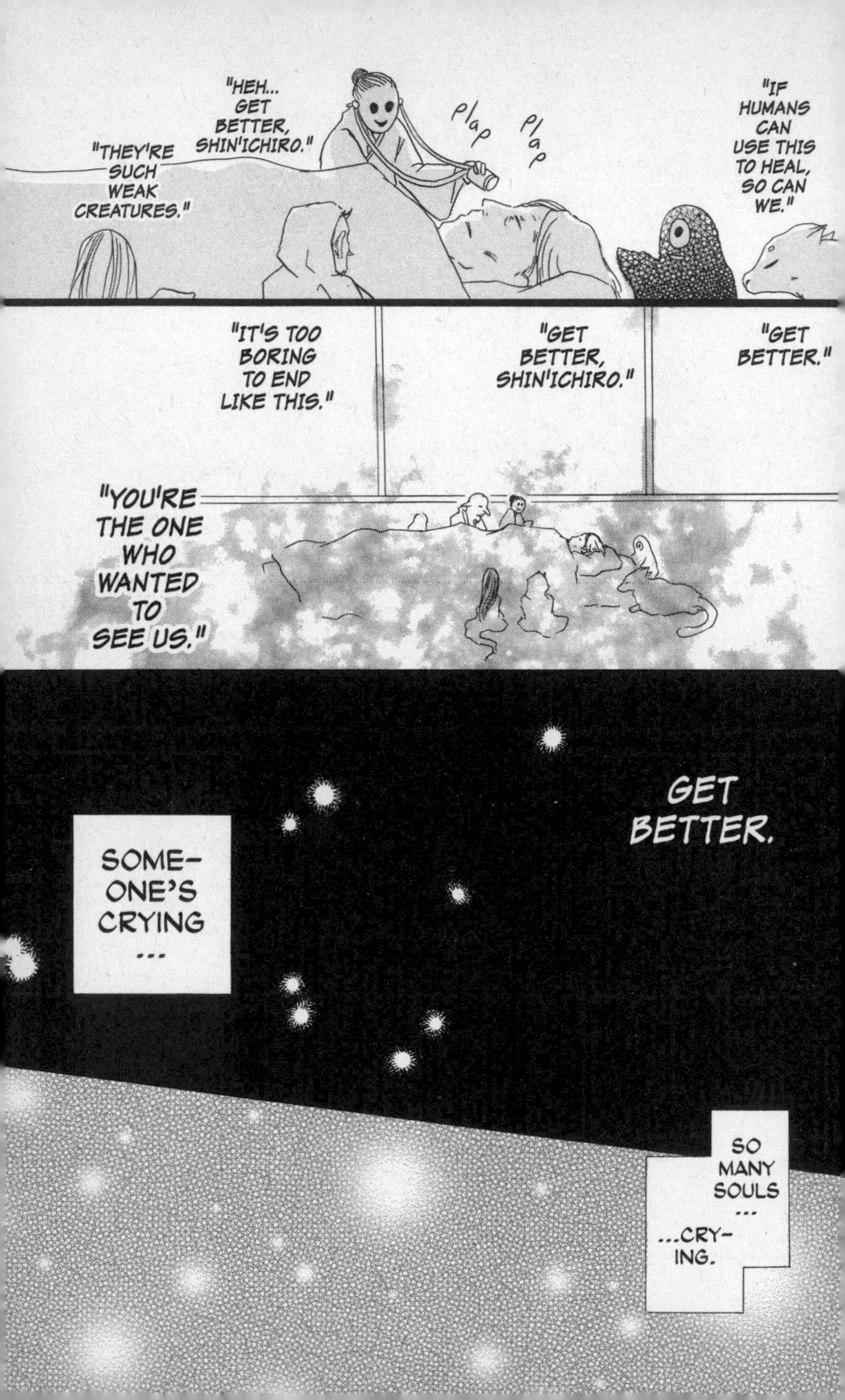
"IF HUMANS CAN USE THIS TO HEAL, SO CAN WE."
plap
plap
"HEH... GET BETTER, SHIN'ICHIRO."
"THEY'RE SUCH WEAK CREATURES."
"GET BETTER."
"GET BETTER, SHIN'ICHIRO."
"IT'S TOO BORING TO END LIKE THIS."
"YOU'RE THE ONE WHO WANTED TO SEE US."
GET BETTER.
SOME-ONE'S CRYING...
SO MANY SOULS...
...CRY-ING.

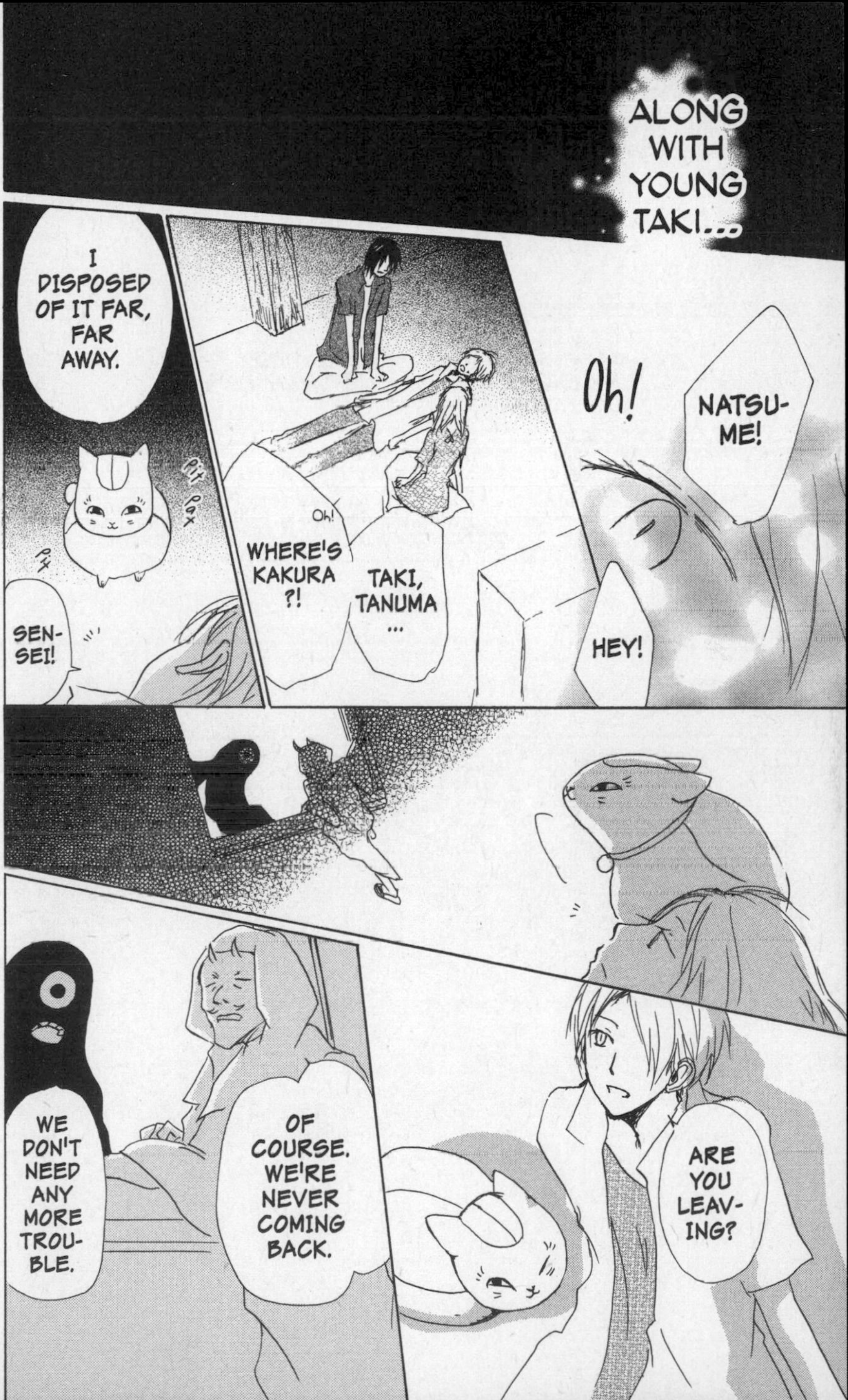
ALONG WITH YOUNG TAKI...
NATSU-ME!
Oh!
HEY!
Oh!
TAKI, TANUMA ...
WHERE'S KAKURA ?!
I DISPOSED OF IT FAR, FAR AWAY.
Pit Pat
Pit
SEN-SEI!
ARE YOU LEAVING?
OF COURSE. WE'RE NEVER COMING BACK.
WE DON'T NEED ANY MORE TROUBLE.

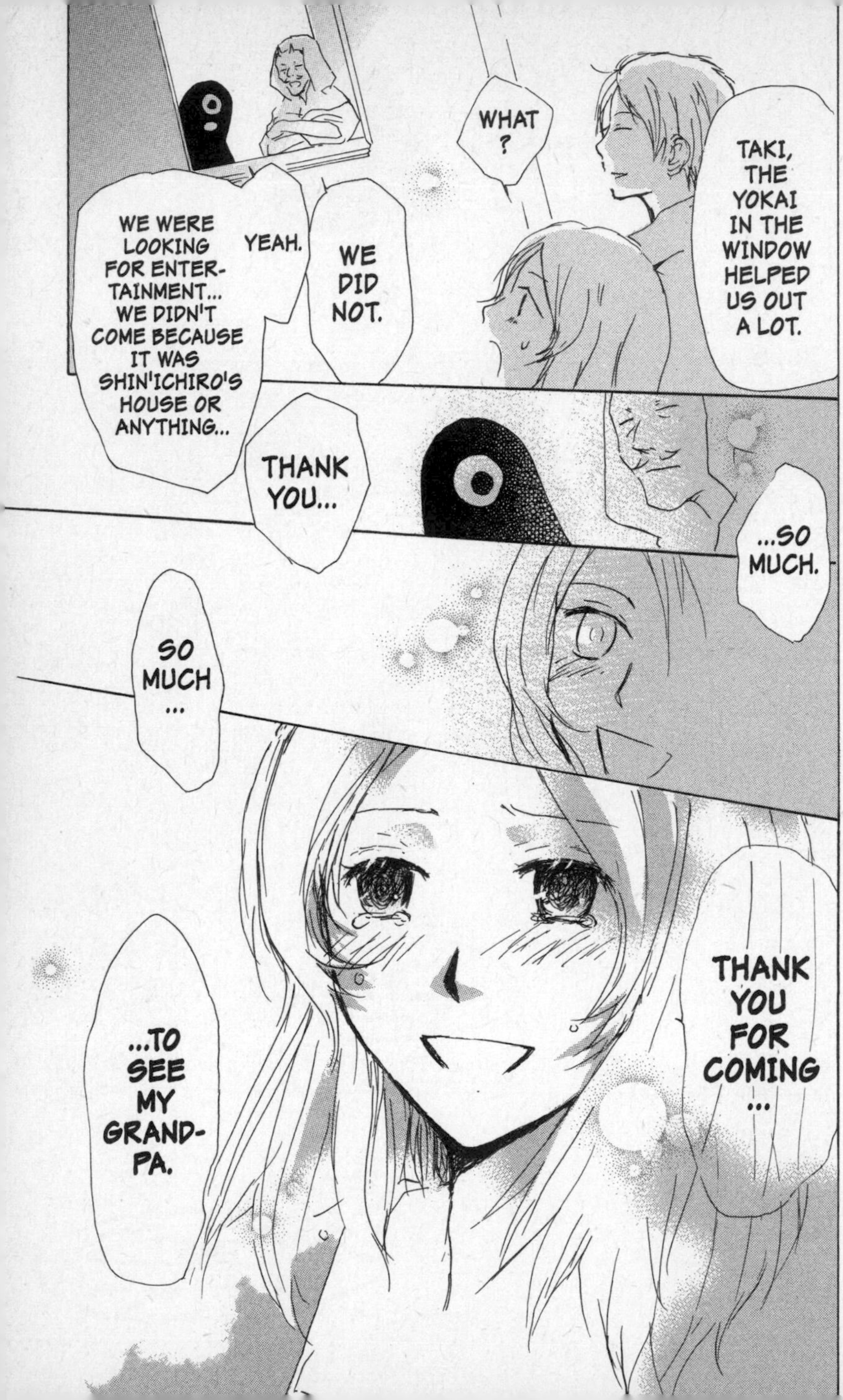
TAKI, THE YOKAI IN THE WINDOW HELPED US OUT A LOT.
WHAT?
WE DID NOT.
YEAH.
WE WERE LOOKING FOR ENTER-TAINMENT... WE DIDN'T COME BECAUSE IT WAS SHIN'ICHIRO'S HOUSE OR ANYTHING...
THANK YOU...
...SO MUCH.
SO MUCH ...
THANK YOU FOR COMING ...
...TO SEE MY GRAND-PA.

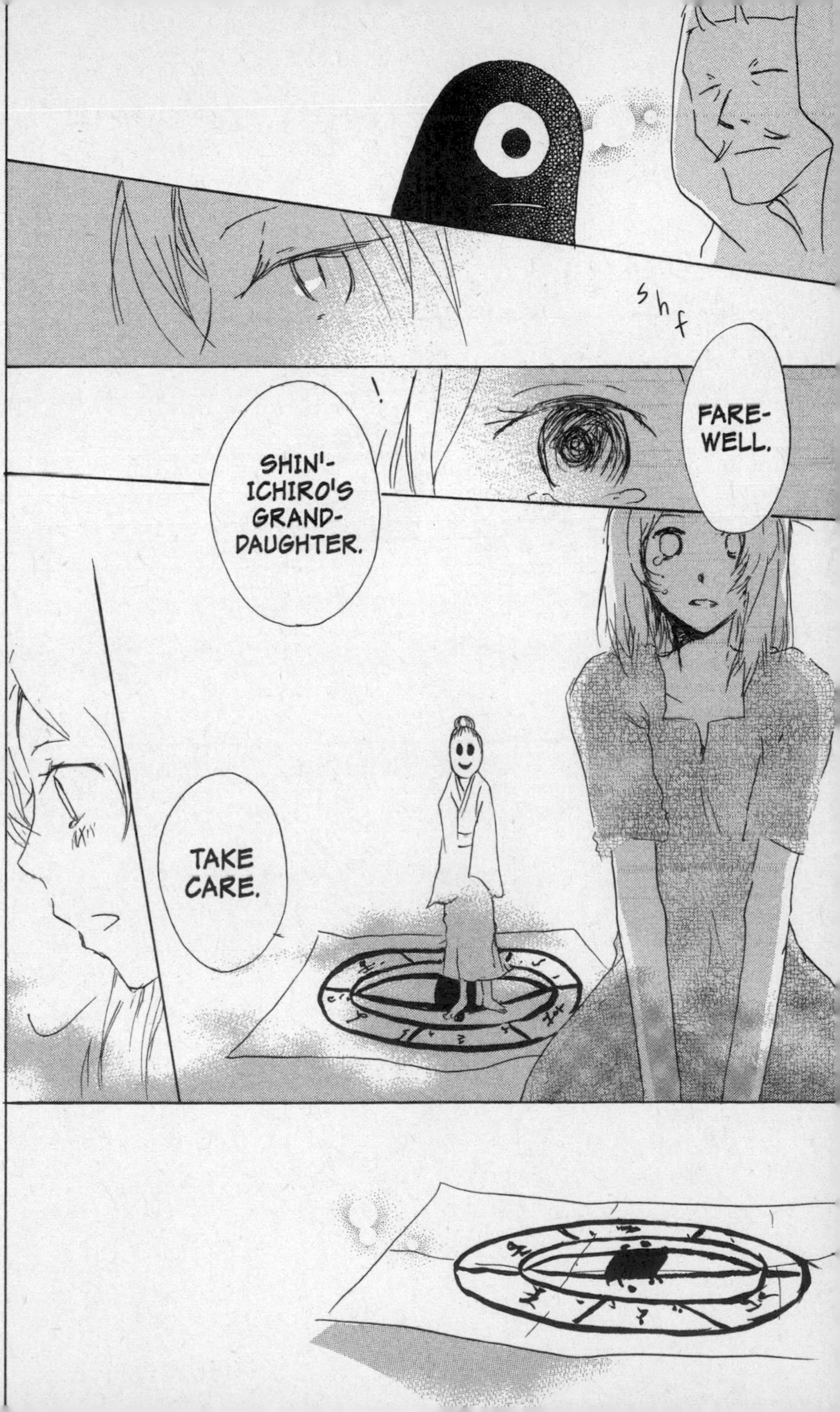
shf
FARE-WELL.
!
SHIN'-ICHIRO'S GRAND-DAUGHTER.
TAKE CARE.

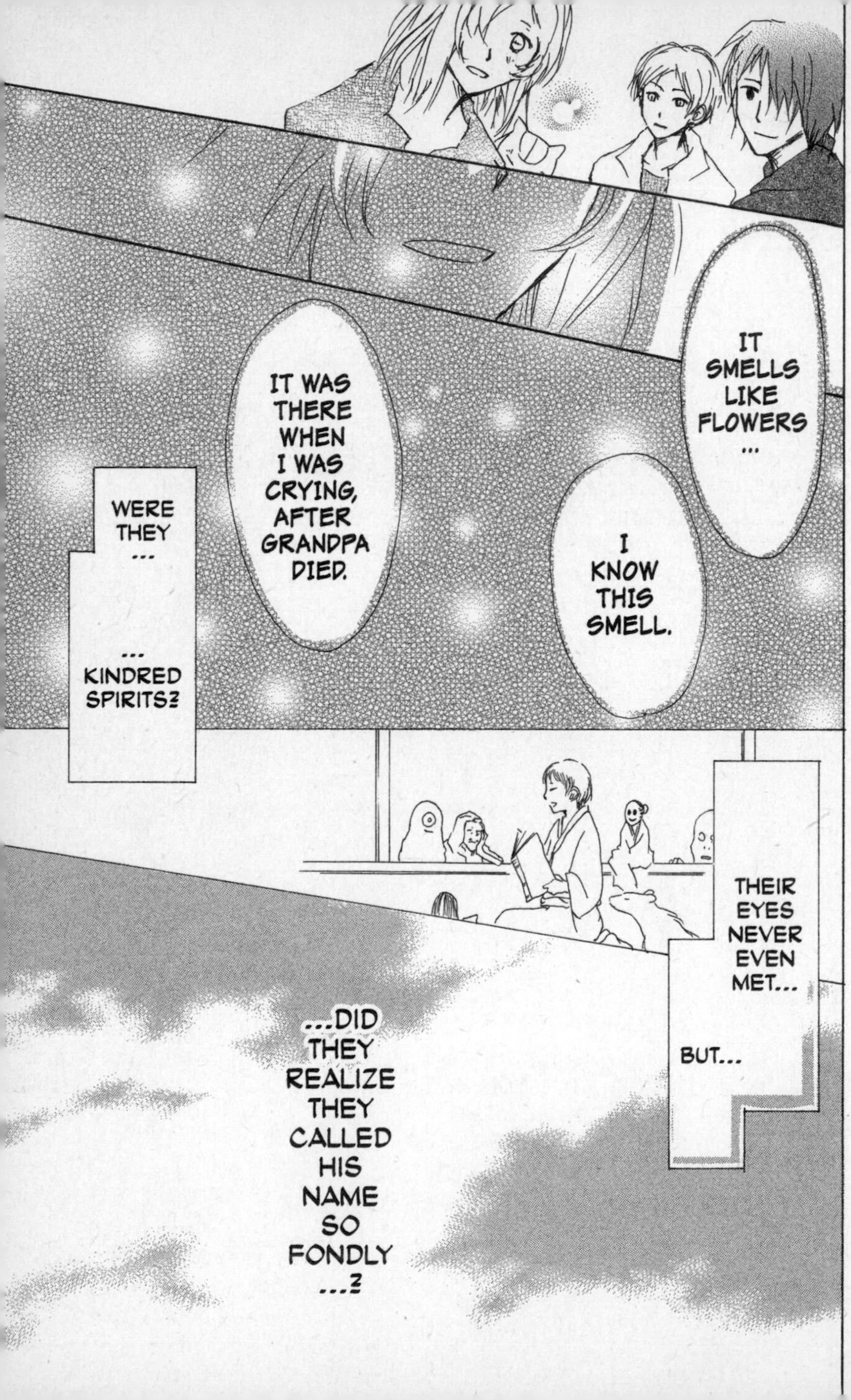
IT SMELLS LIKE FLOWERS...
I KNOW THIS SMELL.
IT WAS THERE WHEN I WAS CRYING, AFTER GRANDPA DIED.
WERE THEY...
...KINDRED SPIRITS?
THEIR EYES NEVER EVEN MET...
BUT...
...DID THEY REALIZE THEY CALLED HIS NAME SO FONDLY...?

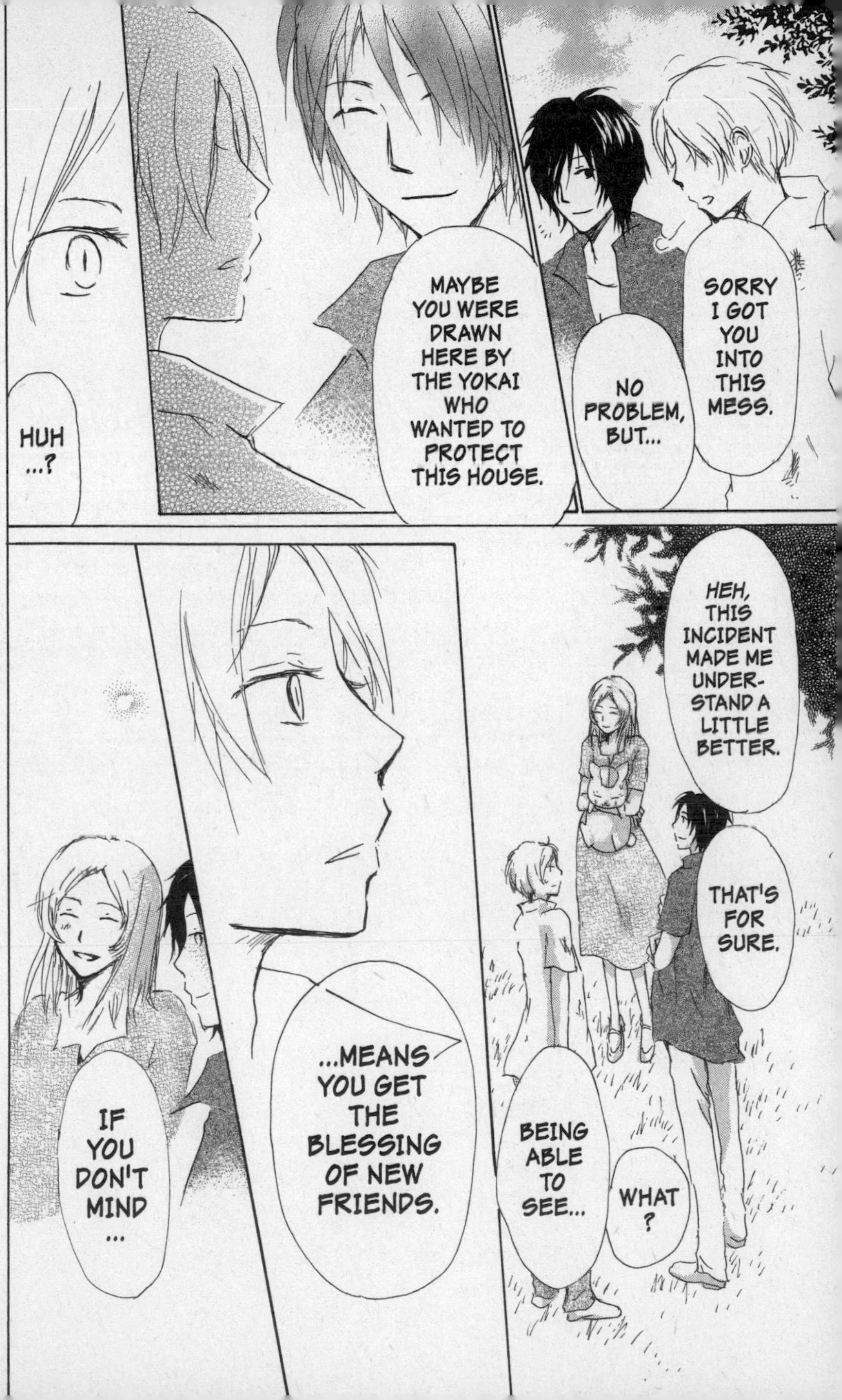
SORRY I GOT YOU INTO THIS MESS.
NO PROBLEM, BUT...
MAYBE YOU WERE DRAWN HERE BY THE YOKAI WHO WANTED TO PROTECT THIS HOUSE.
HUH ...?
HEH, THIS INCIDENT MADE ME UNDER-STAND A LITTLE BETTER.
THAT'S FOR SURE.
WHAT?
BEING ABLE TO SEE...
...MEANS YOU GET THE BLESSING OF NEW FRIENDS.
IF YOU DON'T MIND ...

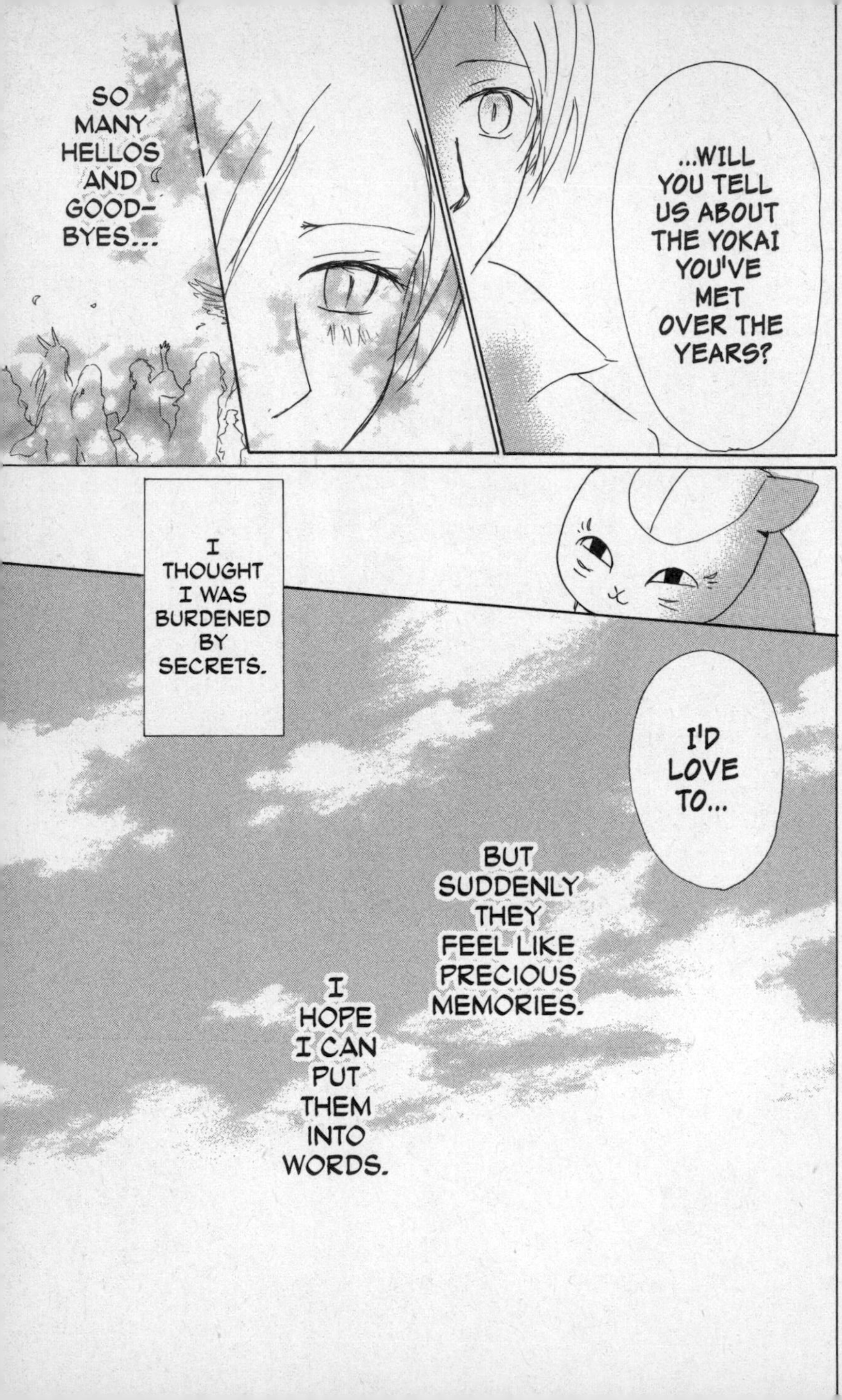
...WILL YOU TELL US ABOUT THE YOKAI YOU'VE MET OVER THE YEARS?
SO MANY HELLOS AND GOOD-BYES...
I THOUGHT I WAS BURDENED BY SECRETS.
I'D LOVE TO...
BUT SUDDENLY THEY FEEL LIKE PRECIOUS MEMORIES.
I HOPE I CAN PUT THEM INTO WORDS.

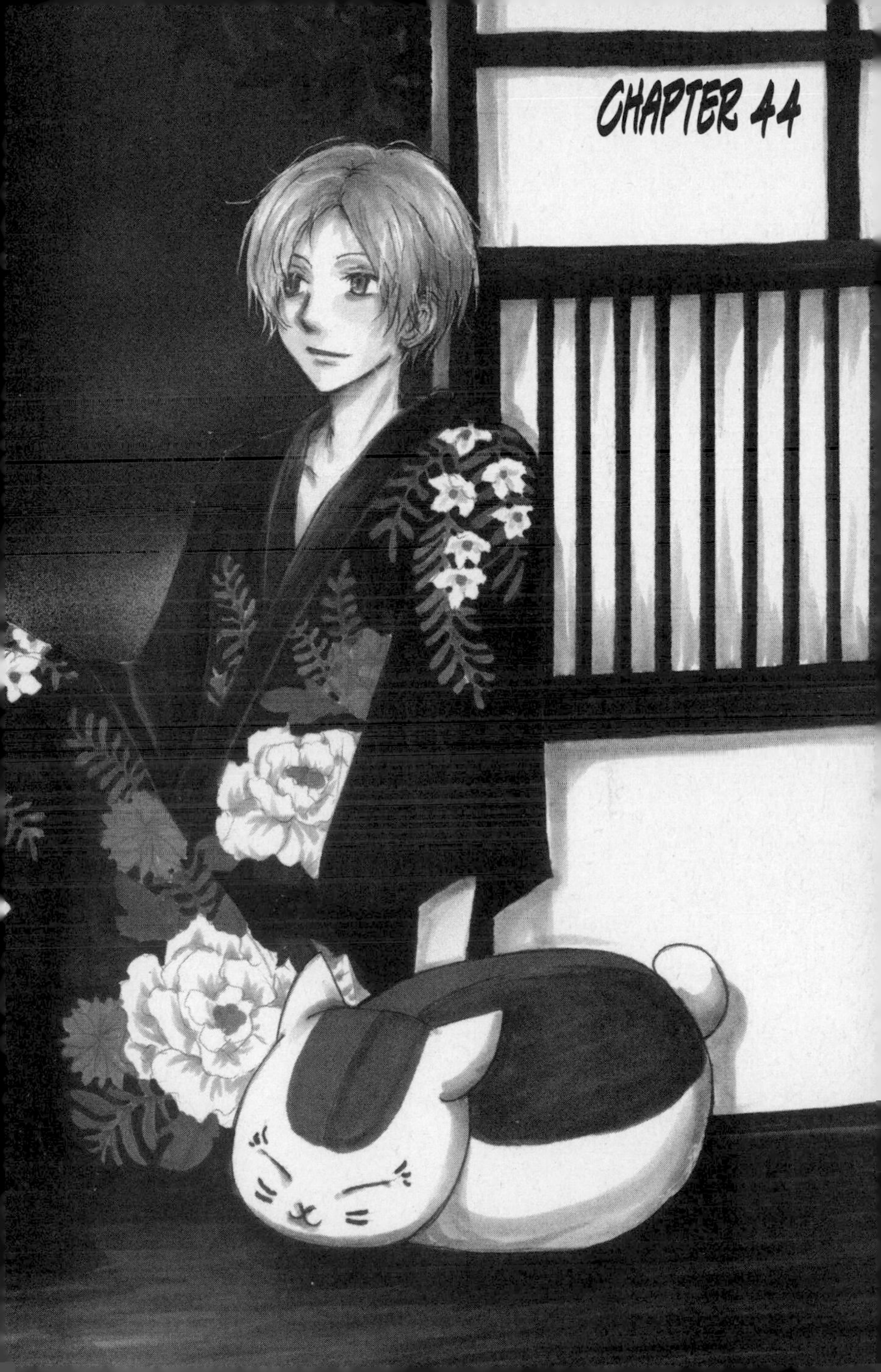
CHAPTER 44

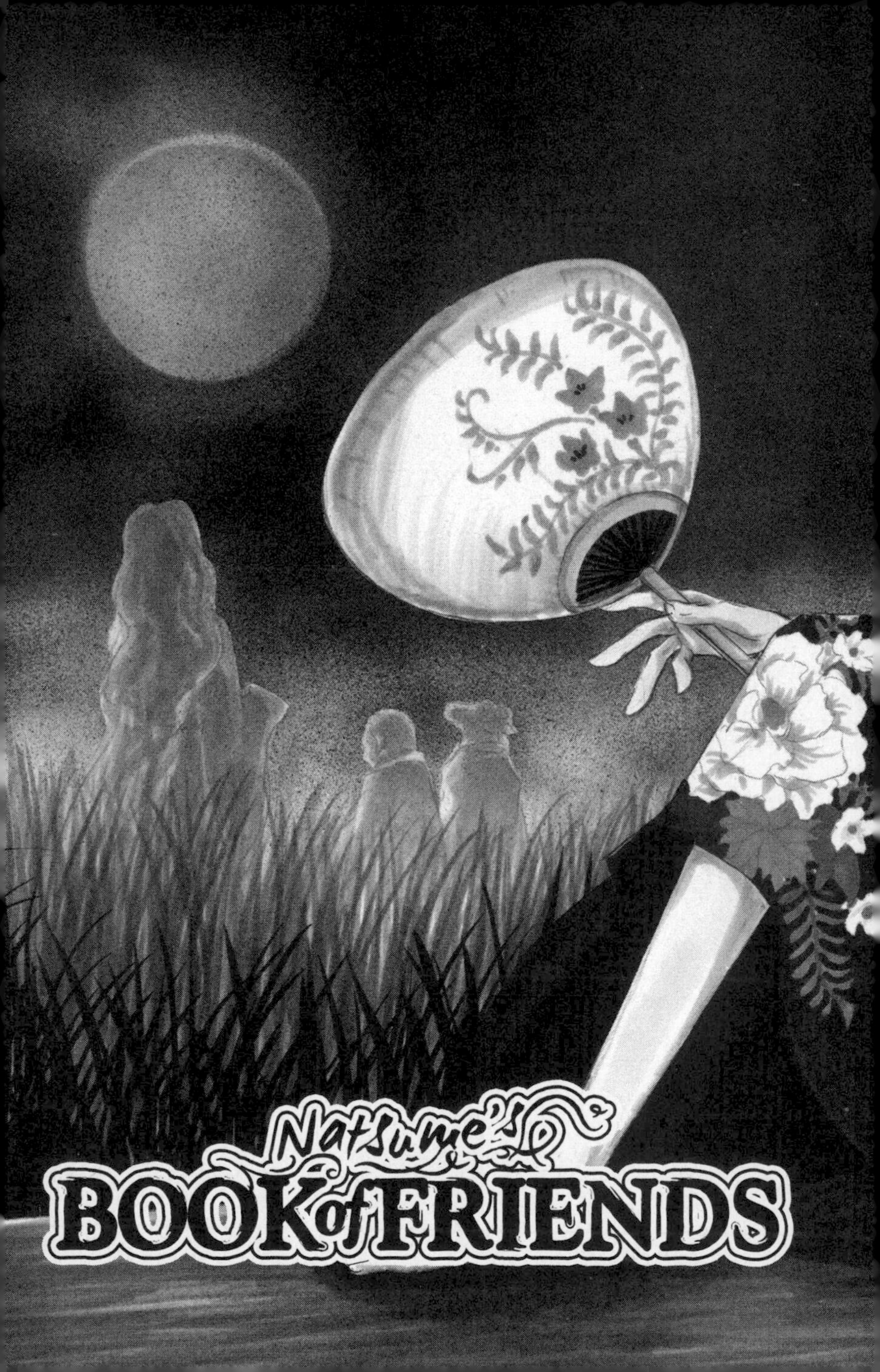
Natsume's
BOOK of FRIENDS

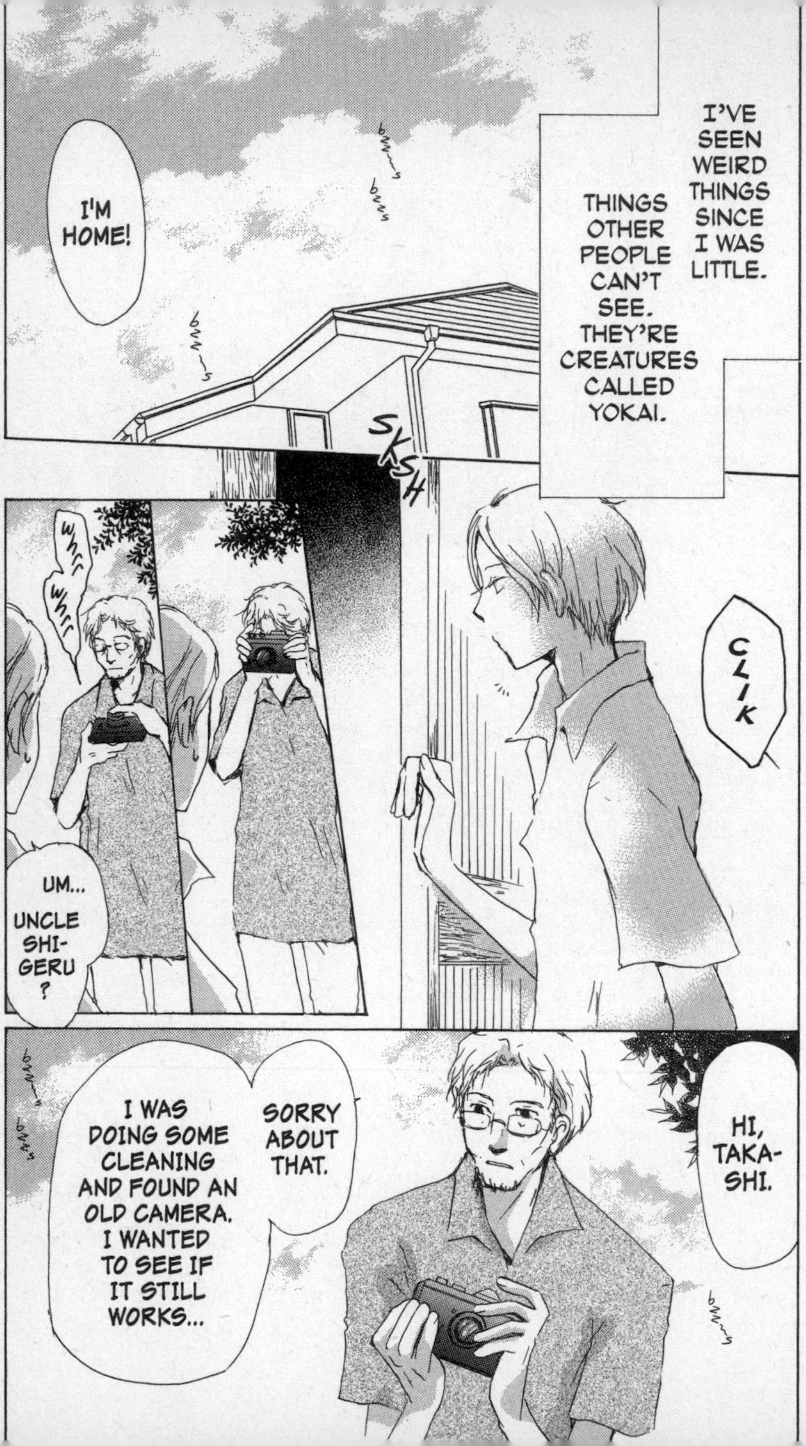
I'VE SEEN WEIRD THINGS SINCE I WAS LITTLE.
THINGS OTHER PEOPLE CAN'T SEE. THEY'RE CREATURES CALLED YOKAI.
I'M HOME!
SKSH
CLIK
WHRR WHRR
UM... UNCLE SHIGERU?
HI, TAKASHI.
SORRY ABOUT THAT.
I WAS DOING SOME CLEANING AND FOUND AN OLD CAMERA. I WANTED TO SEE IF IT STILL WORKS...

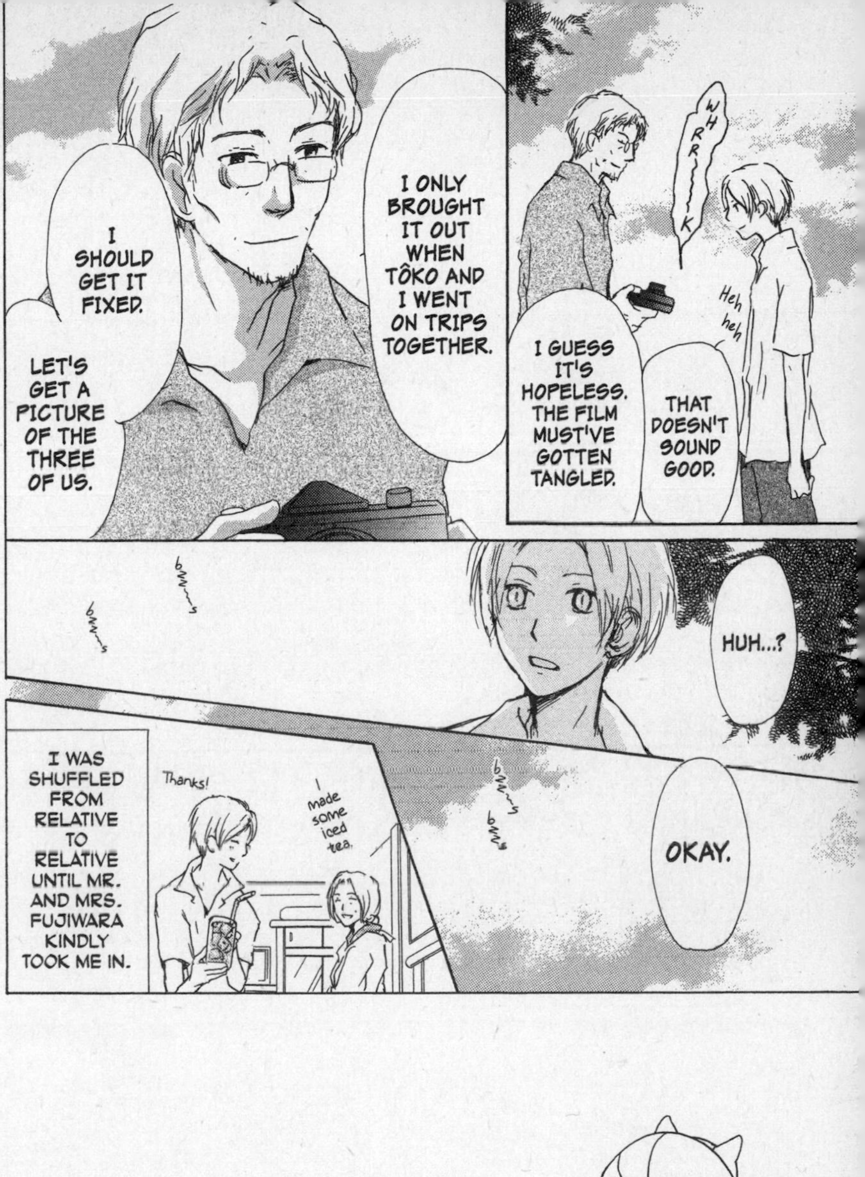
WHRRIK
Heh heh
THAT DOESN'T SOUND GOOD.
I GUESS IT'S HOPELESS. THE FILM MUST'VE GOTTEN TANGLED.
I ONLY BROUGHT IT OUT WHEN TÔKO AND I WENT ON TRIPS TOGETHER.
I SHOULD GET IT FIXED.
LET'S GET A PICTURE OF THE THREE OF US.
HUH...?
bzzz
bzzz
OKAY.
bzzz
bzzz
I made some iced tea.
Thanks!
I WAS SHUFFLED FROM RELATIVE TO RELATIVE UNTIL MR. AND MRS. FUJIWARA KINDLY TOOK ME IN.

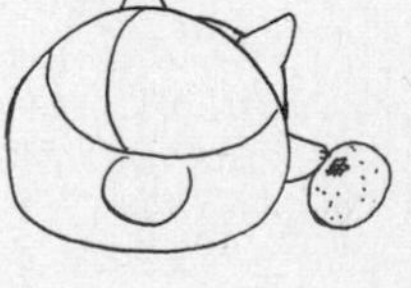

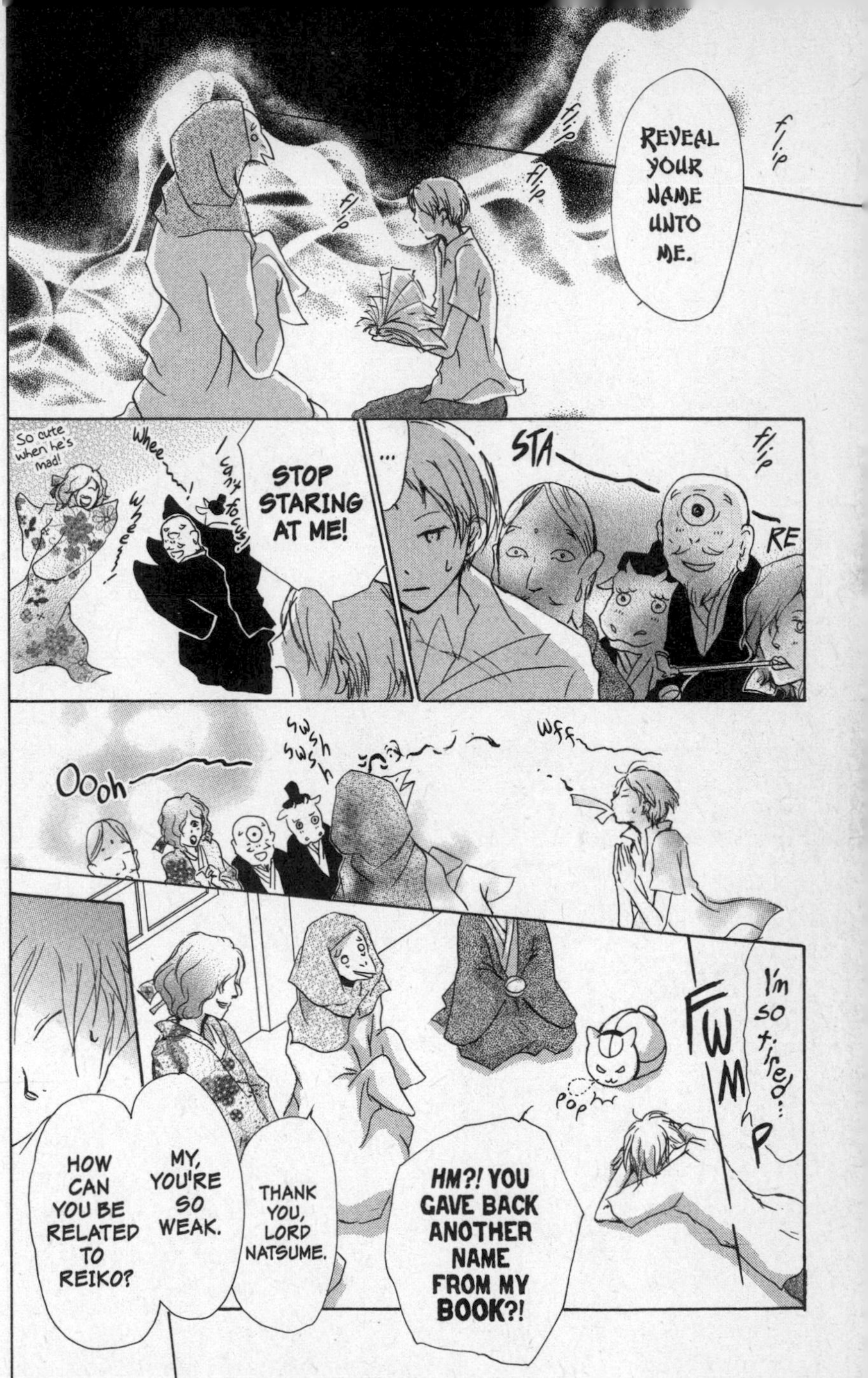
flip
REVEAL YOUR NAME UNTO ME.
flip
flip
flip
flip
STA—RE
...
STOP STARING AT ME!
I can't focus!
Whee—!
whee—!
So cute when he's mad!
wff
swsh swsh
Oooh
I'm so tired...
FWMP
pop
HM?! YOU GAVE BACK ANOTHER NAME FROM MY BOOK?!
THANK YOU, LORD NATSUME.
MY, YOU'RE SO WEAK.
HOW CAN YOU BE RELATED TO REIKO?

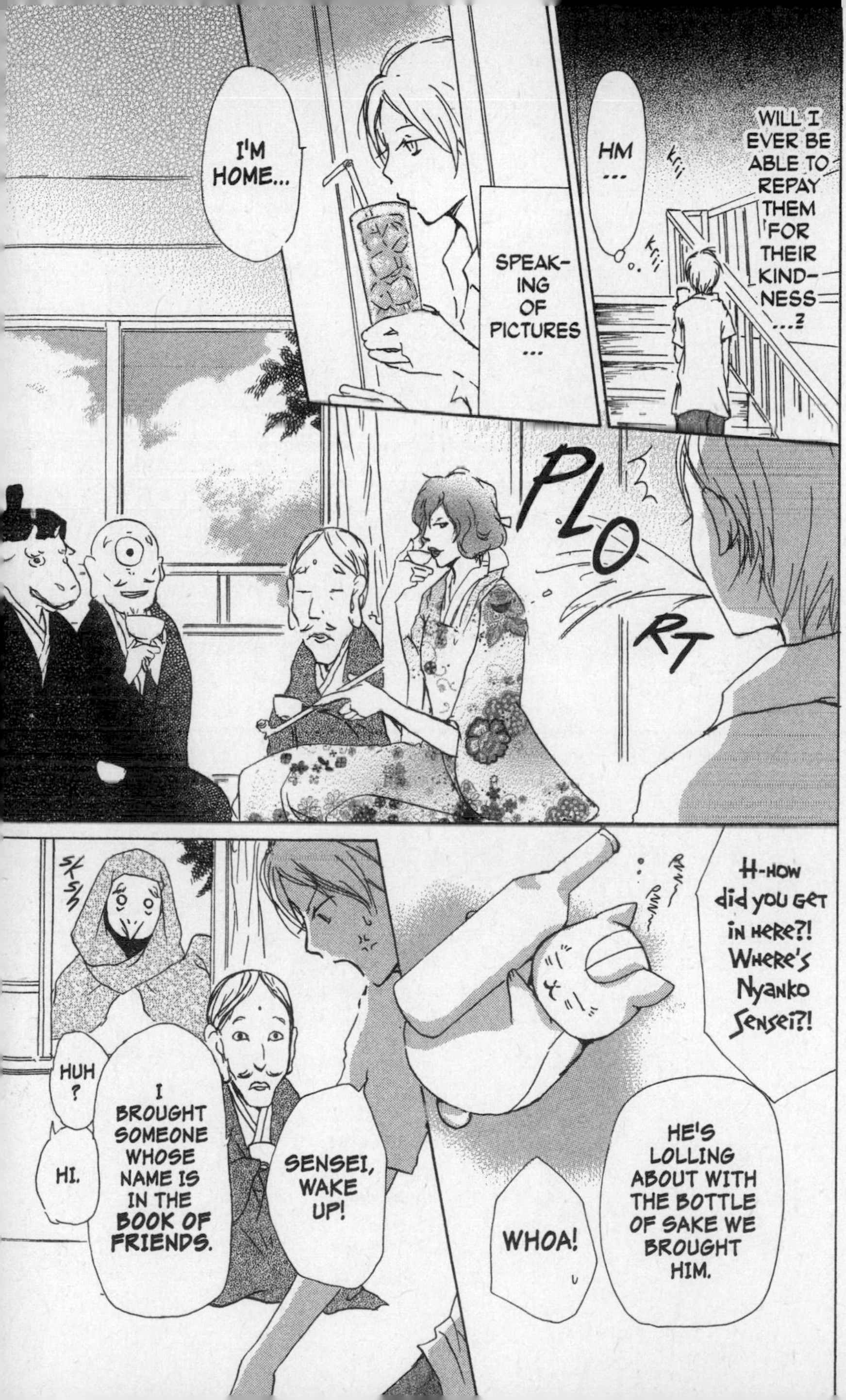WILL I EVER BE ABLE TO REPAY THEM FOR THEIR KINDNESS...?
HM...
kriii
kriii
SPEAKING OF PICTURES...
I'M HOME...
PLORT
H-how did you get in here?! Where's Nyanko Sensei?!
HE'S LOLLING ABOUT WITH THE BOTTLE OF SAKE WE BROUGHT HIM.
WHOA!
SENSEI, WAKE UP!
I BROUGHT SOMEONE WHOSE NAME IS IN THE BOOK OF FRIENDS.
HUH?
HI.
SKSH

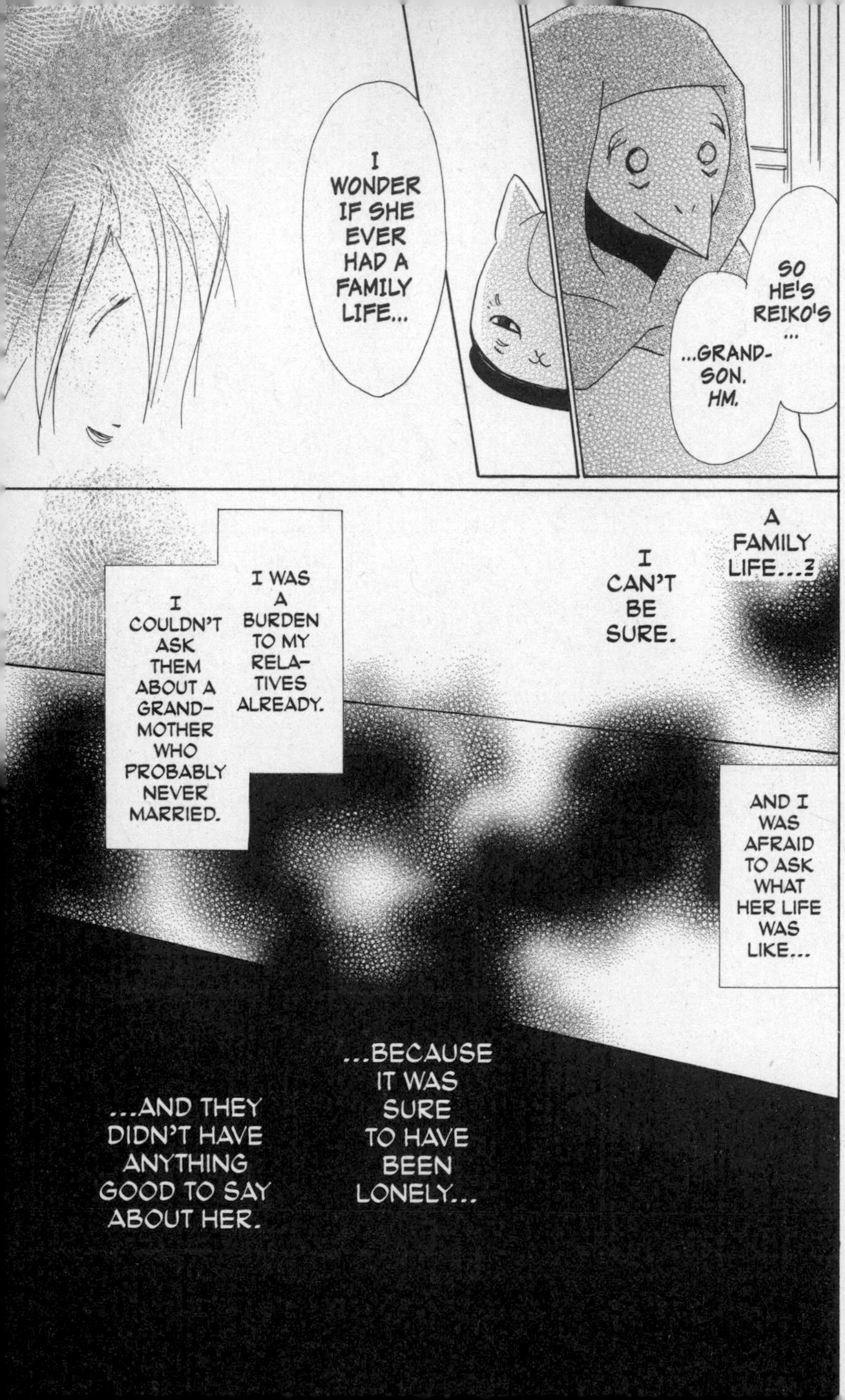

SO HE'S REIKO'S ...
...GRAND-SON. HM.
I WONDER IF SHE EVER HAD A FAMILY LIFE...
A FAMILY LIFE...?
I CAN'T BE SURE.
I WAS A BURDEN TO MY RELA-TIVES ALREADY.
I COULDN'T ASK THEM ABOUT A GRAND-MOTHER WHO PROBABLY NEVER MARRIED.
AND I WAS AFRAID TO ASK WHAT HER LIFE WAS LIKE...
...BECAUSE IT WAS SURE TO HAVE BEEN LONELY...
...AND THEY DIDN'T HAVE ANYTHING GOOD TO SAY ABOUT HER.

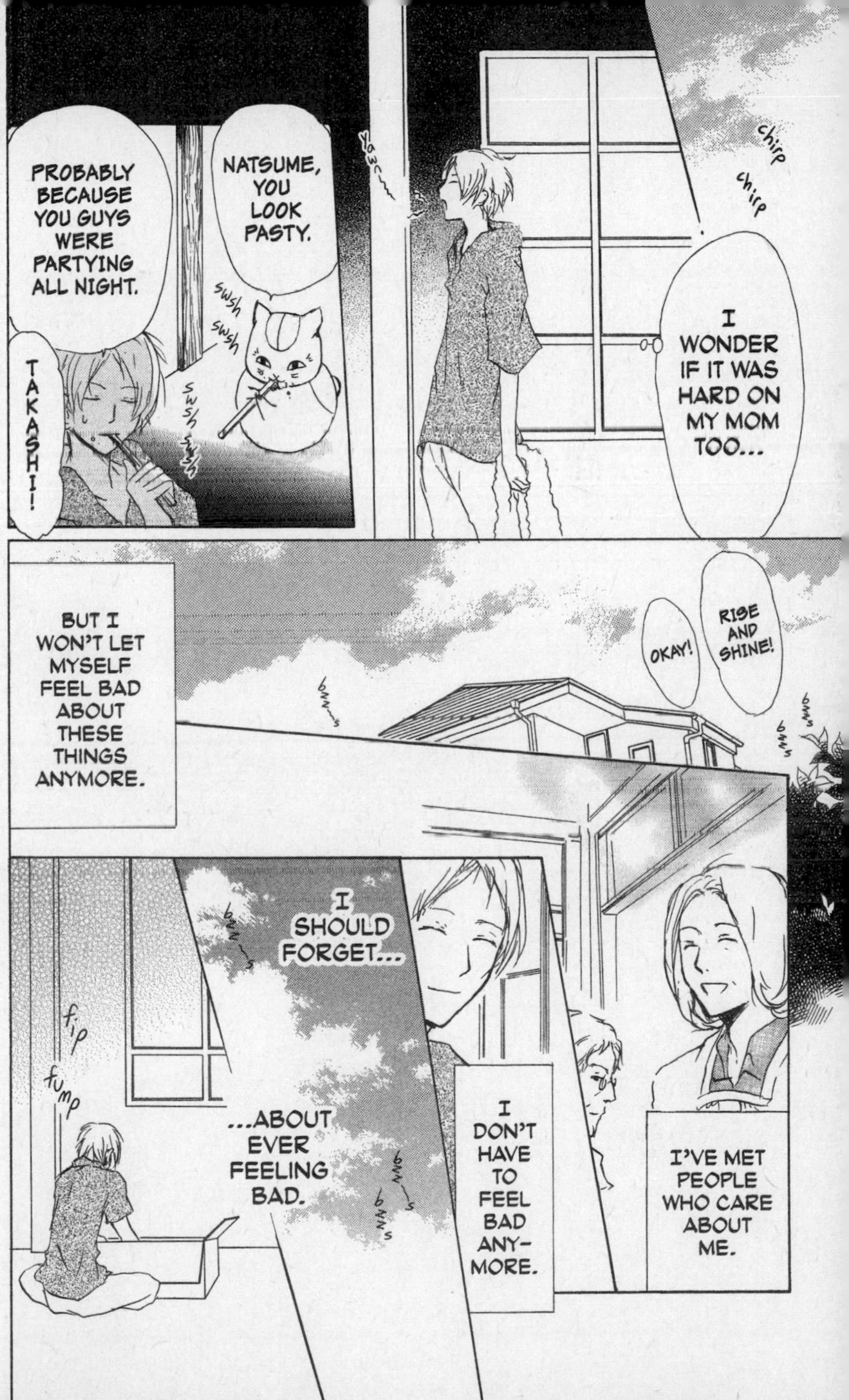
chirp
chirp
Yawn~
I WONDER IF IT WAS HARD ON MY MOM TOO...
NATSUME, YOU LOOK PASTY.
PROBABLY BECAUSE YOU GUYS WERE PARTYING ALL NIGHT.
swsh
swsh
swsh
swsh
TAKASHI!
RISE AND SHINE!
OKAY!
bzzs
bzzs
bzzs
BUT I WON'T LET MYSELF FEEL BAD ABOUT THESE THINGS ANYMORE.
I'VE MET PEOPLE WHO CARE ABOUT ME.
I DON'T HAVE TO FEEL BAD ANYMORE.
I SHOULD FORGET...
bzzs
...ABOUT EVER FEELING BAD.
bzzs
bzzs
flip
fump

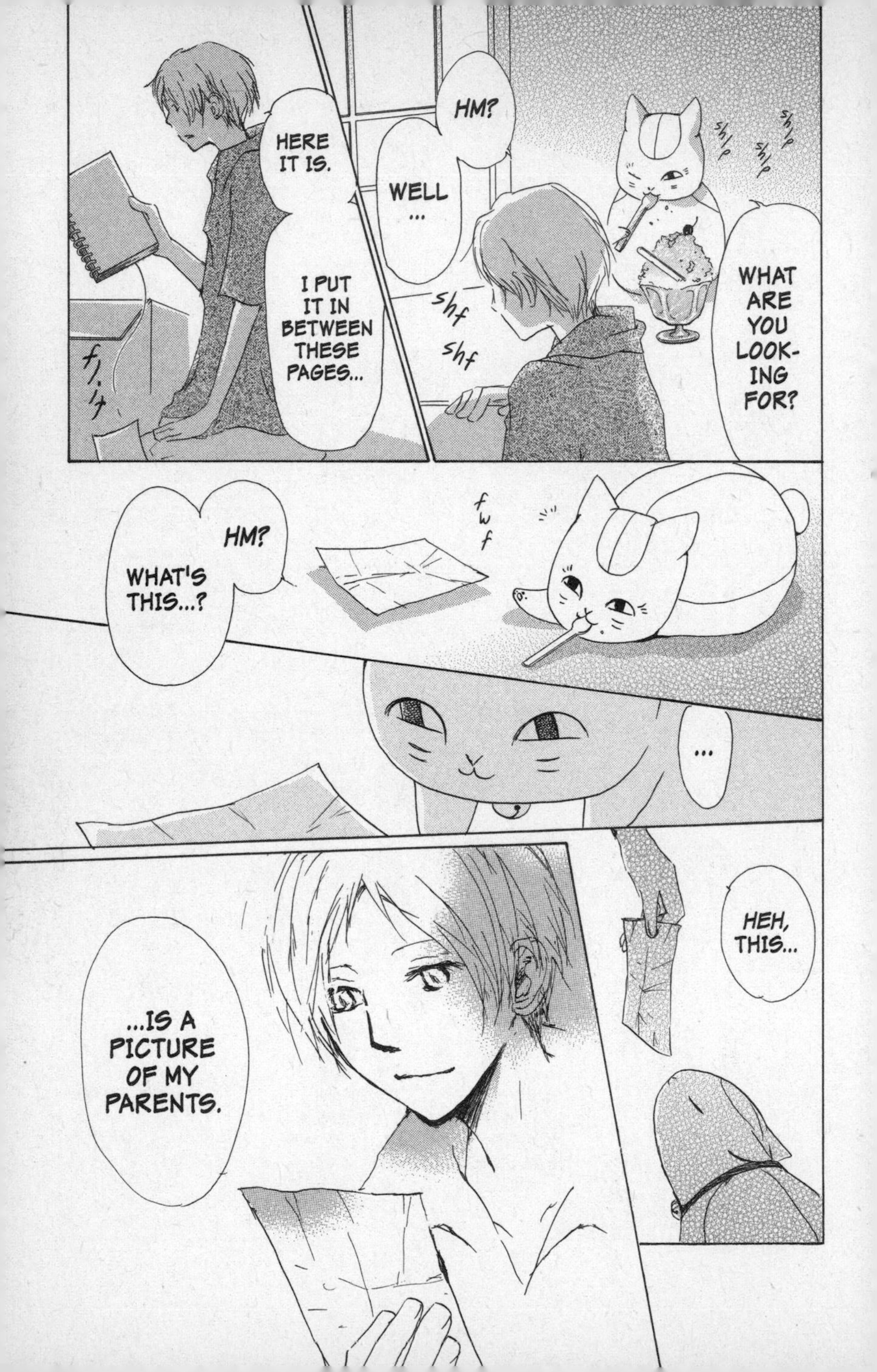
shlp
shlp
shlp
WHAT ARE YOU LOOKING FOR?
HM?
shf
shf
WELL ...
I PUT IT IN BETWEEN THESE PAGES...
HERE IT IS.
fwf
HM?
WHAT'S THIS...?
...
HEH, THIS...
...IS A PICTURE OF MY PARENTS.

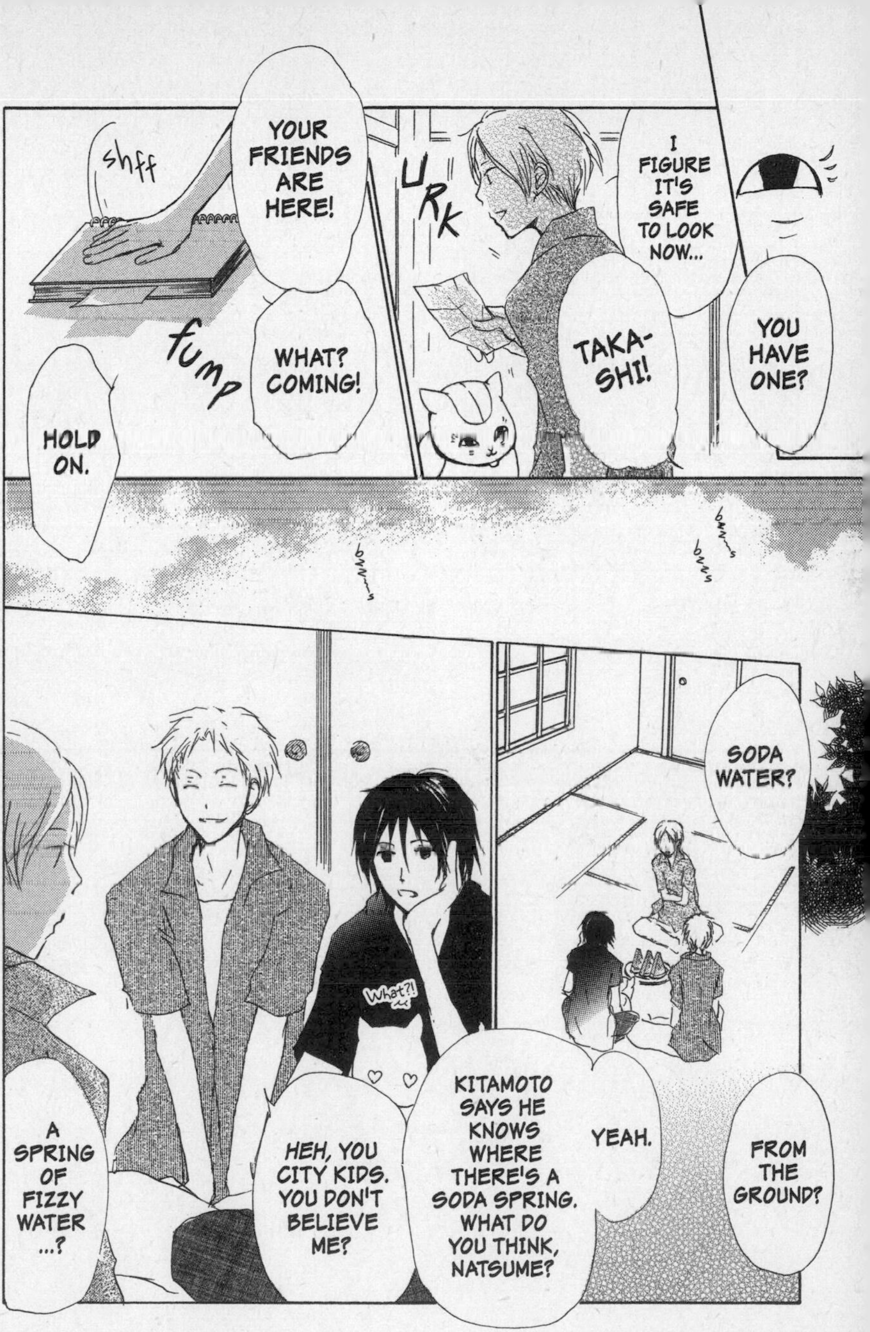
YOU HAVE ONE?
I FIGURE IT'S SAFE TO LOOK NOW...
TAKA-SHI!
URK
YOUR FRIENDS ARE HERE!
shff
WHAT? COMING!
fump
HOLD ON.
bzzz
bzzz
bzzz
SODA WATER?
FROM THE GROUND?
YEAH.
KITAMOTO SAYS HE KNOWS WHERE THERE'S A SODA SPRING. WHAT DO YOU THINK, NATSUME?
HEH, YOU CITY KIDS. YOU DON'T BELIEVE ME?
A SPRING OF FIZZY WATER ...?
What?!

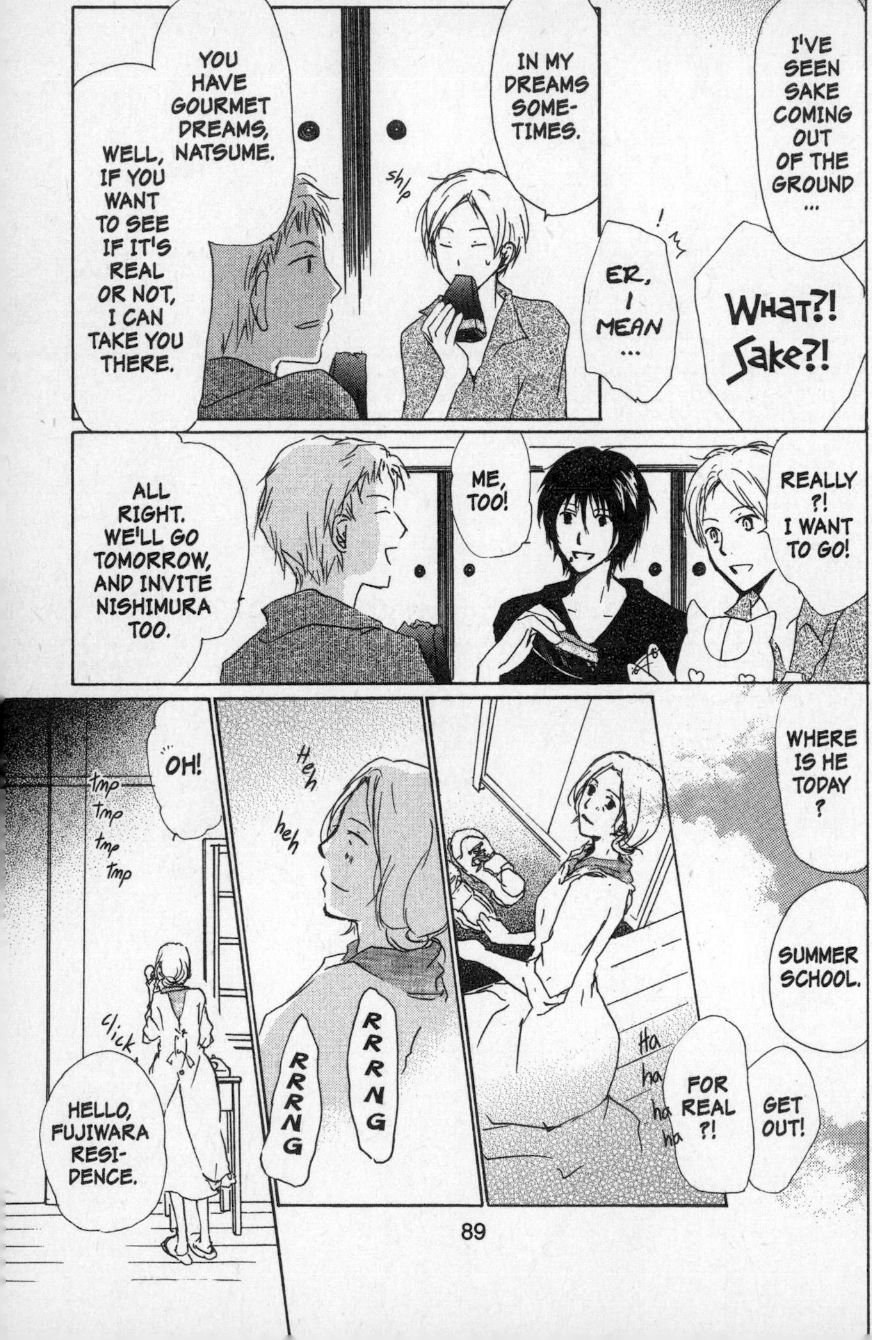
I'VE SEEN SAKE COMING OUT OF THE GROUND ...
WHAT?! Sake?!
!
ER, I MEAN ...
IN MY DREAMS SOMETIMES.
shlp
YOU HAVE GOURMET DREAMS, NATSUME.
WELL, IF YOU WANT TO SEE IF IT'S REAL OR NOT, I CAN TAKE YOU THERE.
REALLY?! I WANT TO GO!
ME, TOO!
ALL RIGHT. WE'LL GO TOMORROW, AND INVITE NISHIMURA TOO.
WHERE IS HE TODAY?
SUMMER SCHOOL.
GET OUT!
FOR REAL?!
Ha ha ha ha
RRRNG
RRRNG
Heh heh
OH!
tmp tmp tmp tmp
click
HELLO, FUJIWARA RESIDENCE.

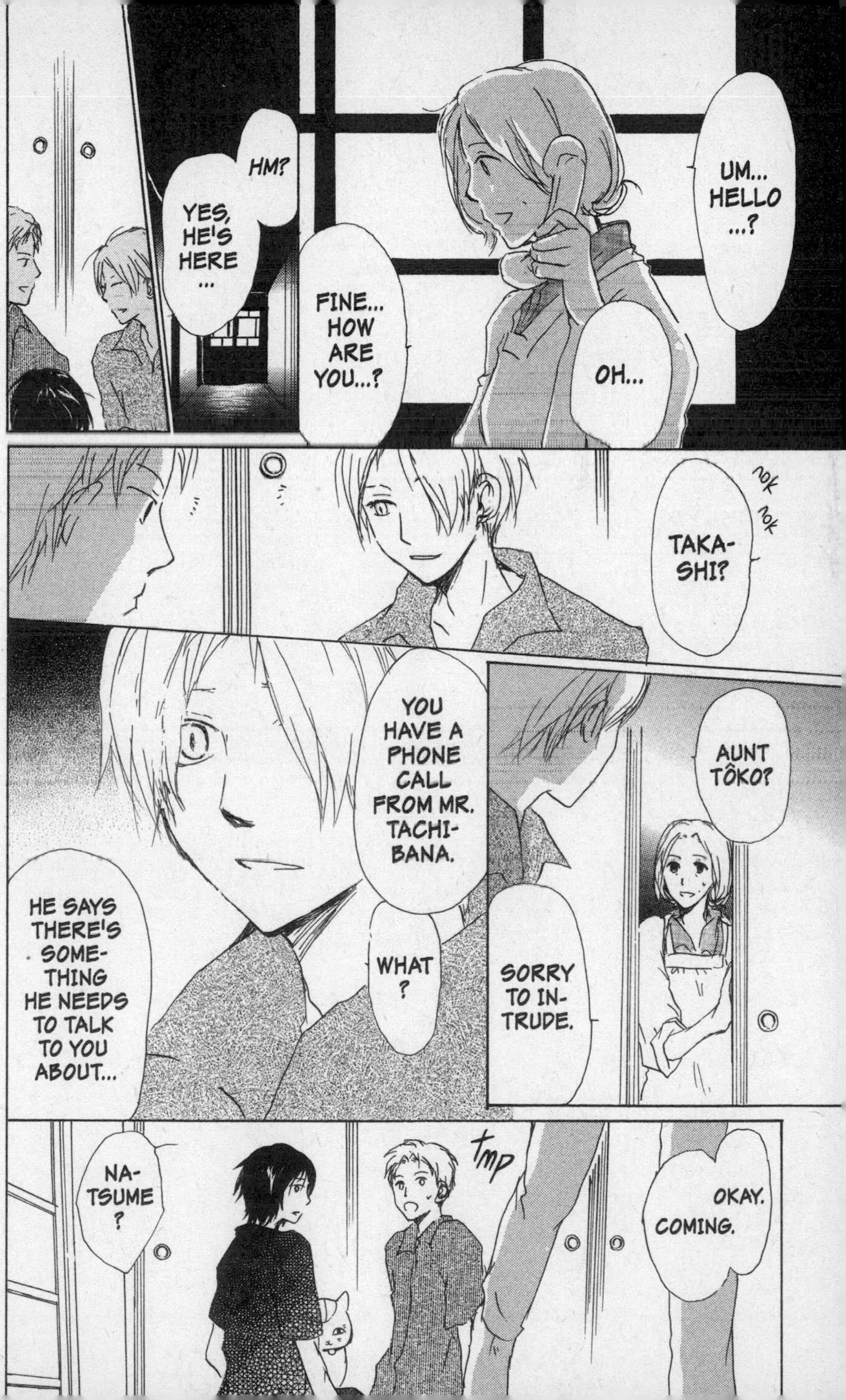
UM... HELLO ...?
OH...
FINE... HOW ARE YOU...?
HM?
YES, HE'S HERE ...
nok nok
TAKA-SHI?
AUNT TÔKO?
SORRY TO IN-TRUDE.
YOU HAVE A PHONE CALL FROM MR. TACHI-BANA.
WHAT ?
HE SAYS THERE'S SOME-THING HE NEEDS TO TALK TO YOU ABOUT...
OKAY. COMING.
tmp
NA-TSUME ?

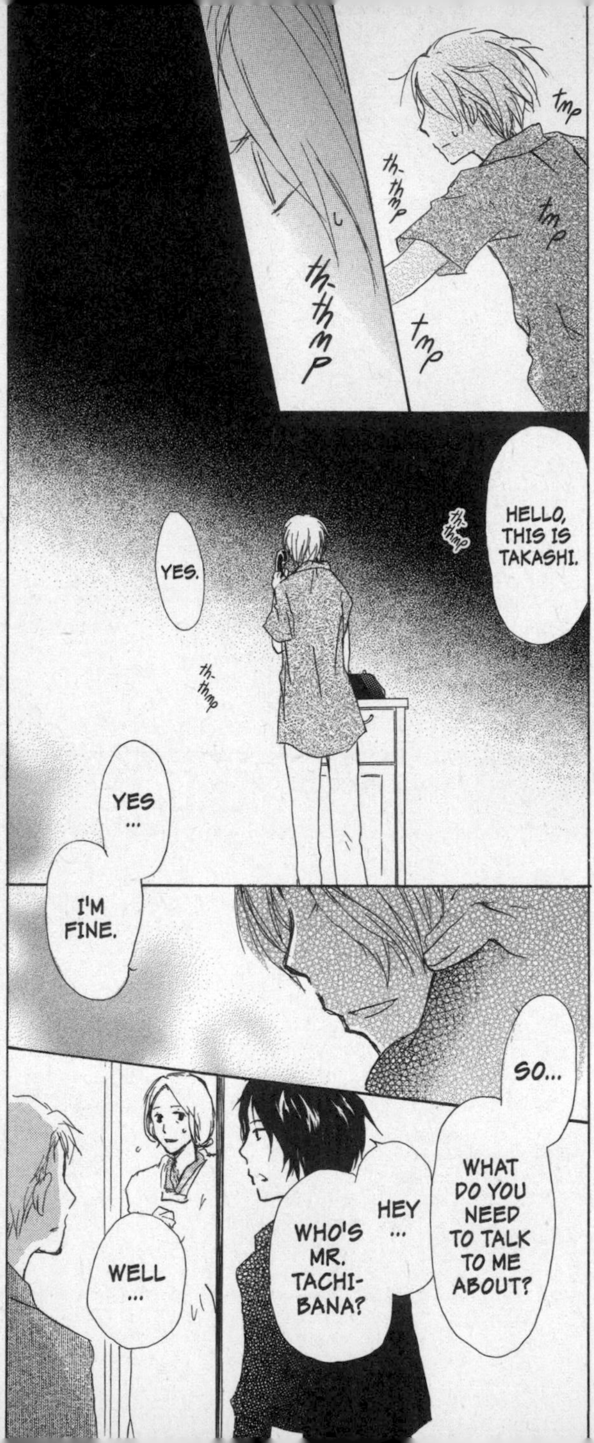
tmp
th-thmp
tmp
th-thmp
tmp
HELLO, THIS IS TAKASHI.
th-thmp
YES.
th-thmp
YES ...
I'M FINE.
SO...
WHAT DO YOU NEED TO TALK TO ME ABOUT?
HEY ...
WHO'S MR. TACHIBANA?
WELL ...

03

❋Location scouting: Part 1

The director and the anime production staff came all the way to Kumamoto again for location scouting. I'm so excited that I get to see all those nostalgic and spiritual scenes again.

They asked me to recommend some locations, and I ended up making them walk up some rather steep hills. There were some times during our meetings when I couldn't verbalize my sentiments as effectively as I wanted. But as they talked, asked questions, and carefully considered every single detail, I had to keep myself from shouting out loud, "This makes me so happy!"

← Continued in part 04

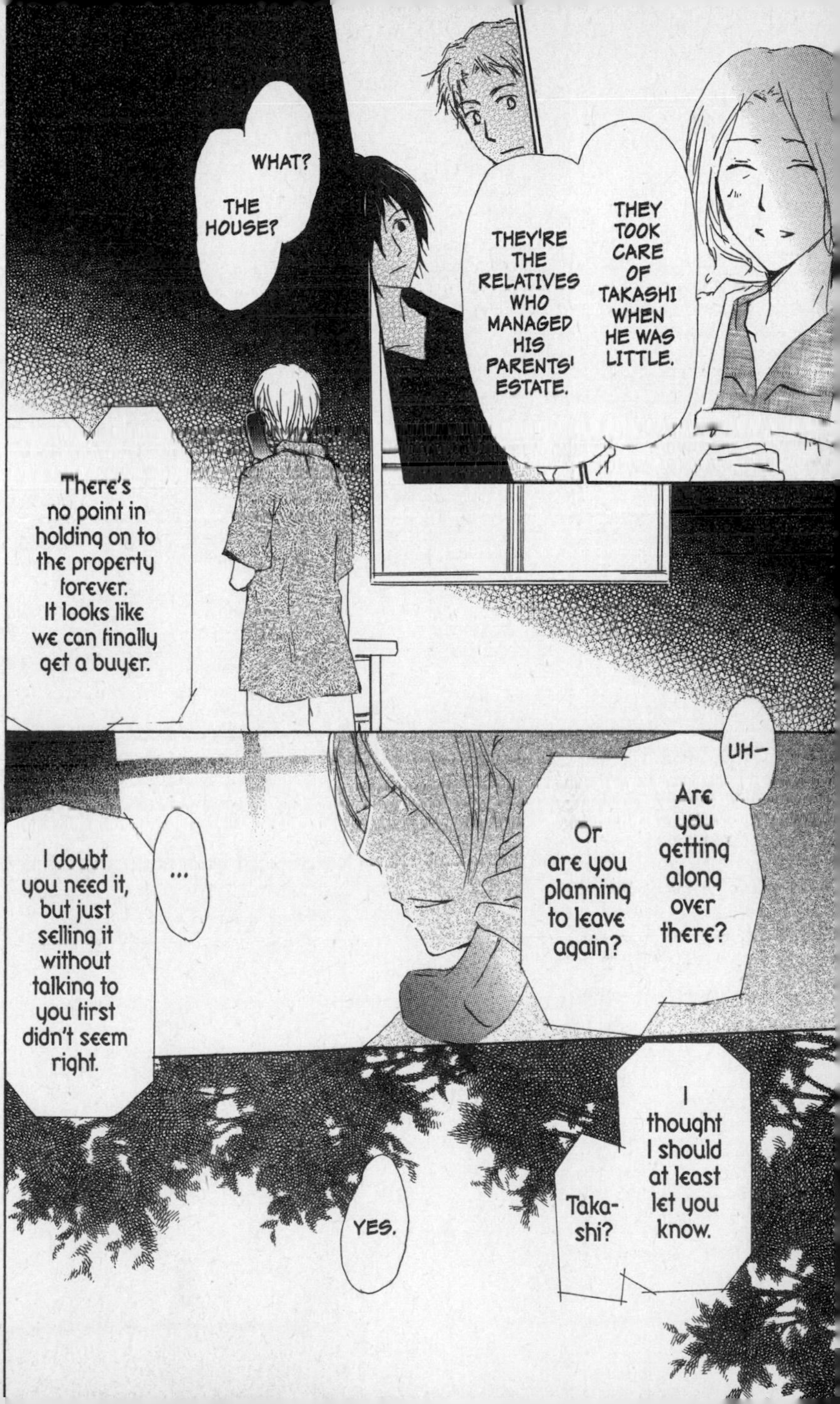
THEY TOOK CARE OF TAKASHI WHEN HE WAS LITTLE.
THEY'RE THE RELATIVES WHO MANAGED HIS PARENTS' ESTATE.
WHAT?
THE HOUSE?
There's no point in holding on to the property forever. It looks like we can finally get a buyer.
UH—
Are you getting along over there?
Or are you planning to leave again?
...
I doubt you need it, but just selling it without talking to you first didn't seem right.
I thought I should at least let you know.
Taka-shi?
YES.

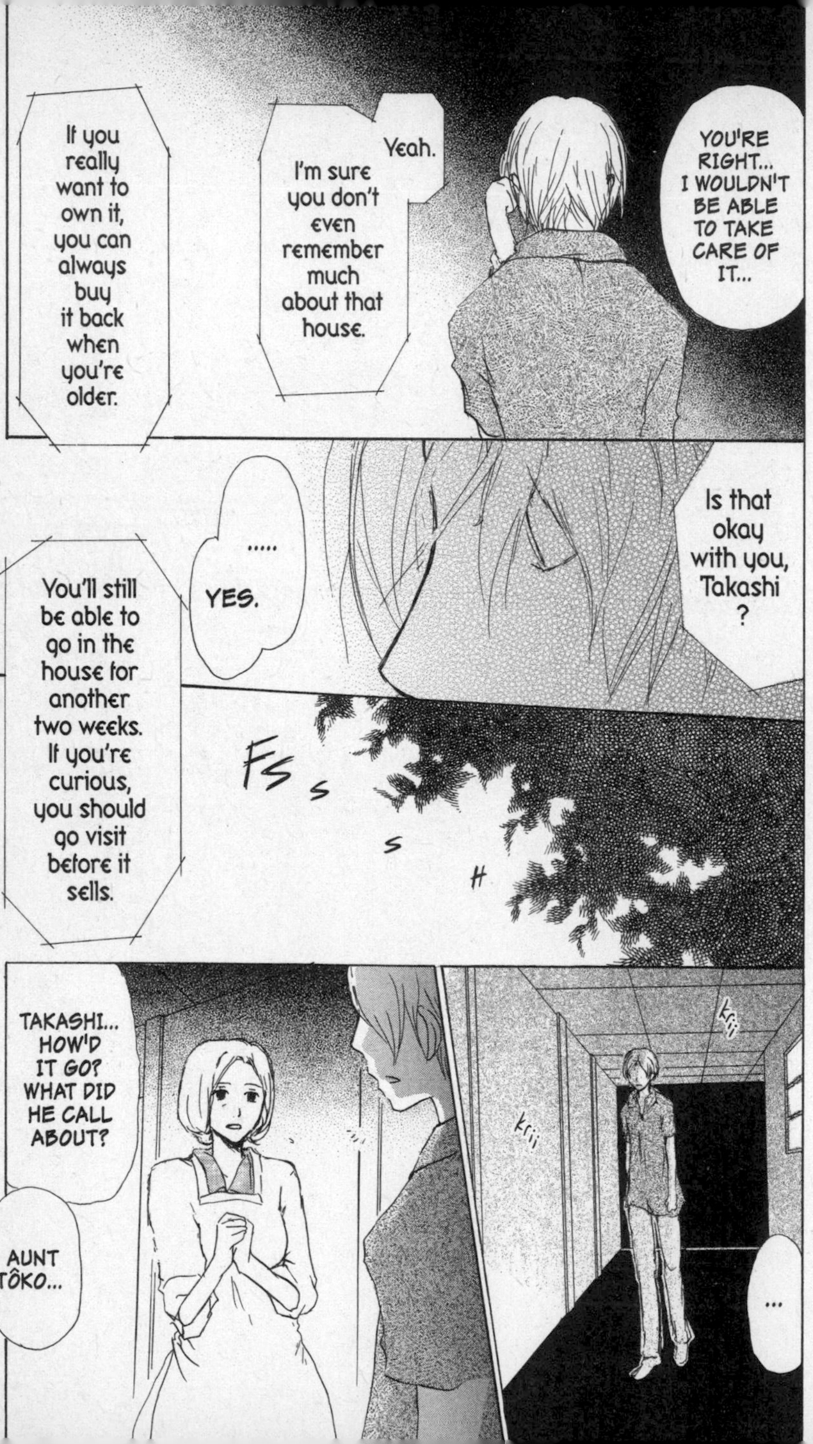
YOU'RE RIGHT... I WOULDN'T BE ABLE TO TAKE CARE OF IT...
Yeah. I'm sure you don't even remember much about that house.
If you really want to own it, you can always buy it back when you're older.
Is that okay with you, Takashi?
..... YES.
You'll still be able to go in the house for another two weeks. If you're curious, you should go visit before it sells.
FSSSH
...
krii
krii
TAKASHI... HOW'D IT GO? WHAT DID HE CALL ABOUT?
AUNT TÔKO...

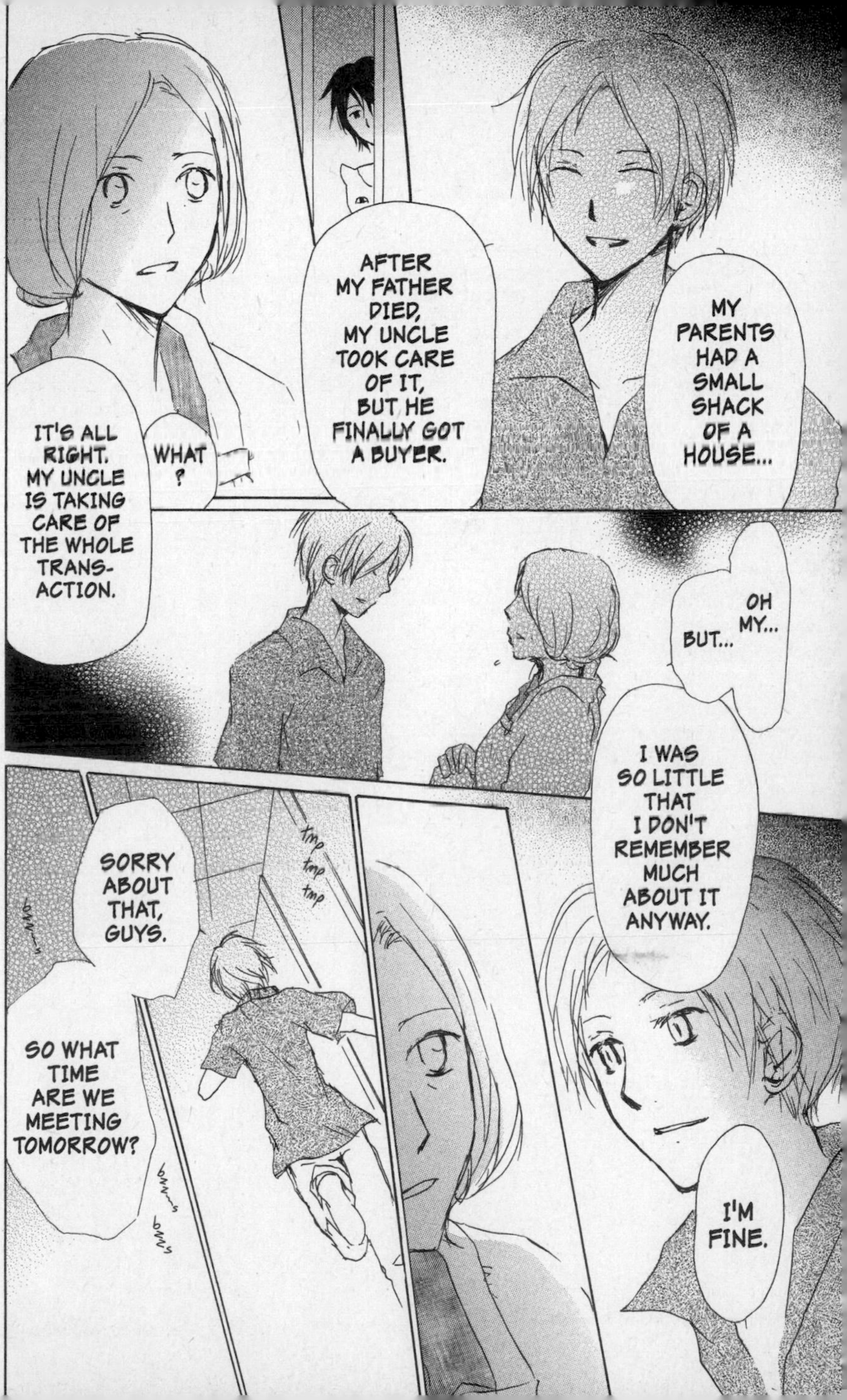
MY PARENTS HAD A SMALL SHACK OF A HOUSE...
AFTER MY FATHER DIED, MY UNCLE TOOK CARE OF IT, BUT HE FINALLY GOT A BUYER.
WHAT?
IT'S ALL RIGHT. MY UNCLE IS TAKING CARE OF THE WHOLE TRANS-ACTION.
OH MY...
BUT...
I WAS SO LITTLE THAT I DON'T REMEMBER MUCH ABOUT IT ANYWAY.
I'M FINE.
tmp tmp tmp
SORRY ABOUT THAT, GUYS.
SO WHAT TIME ARE WE MEETING TOMORROW?
bzzs bzzs

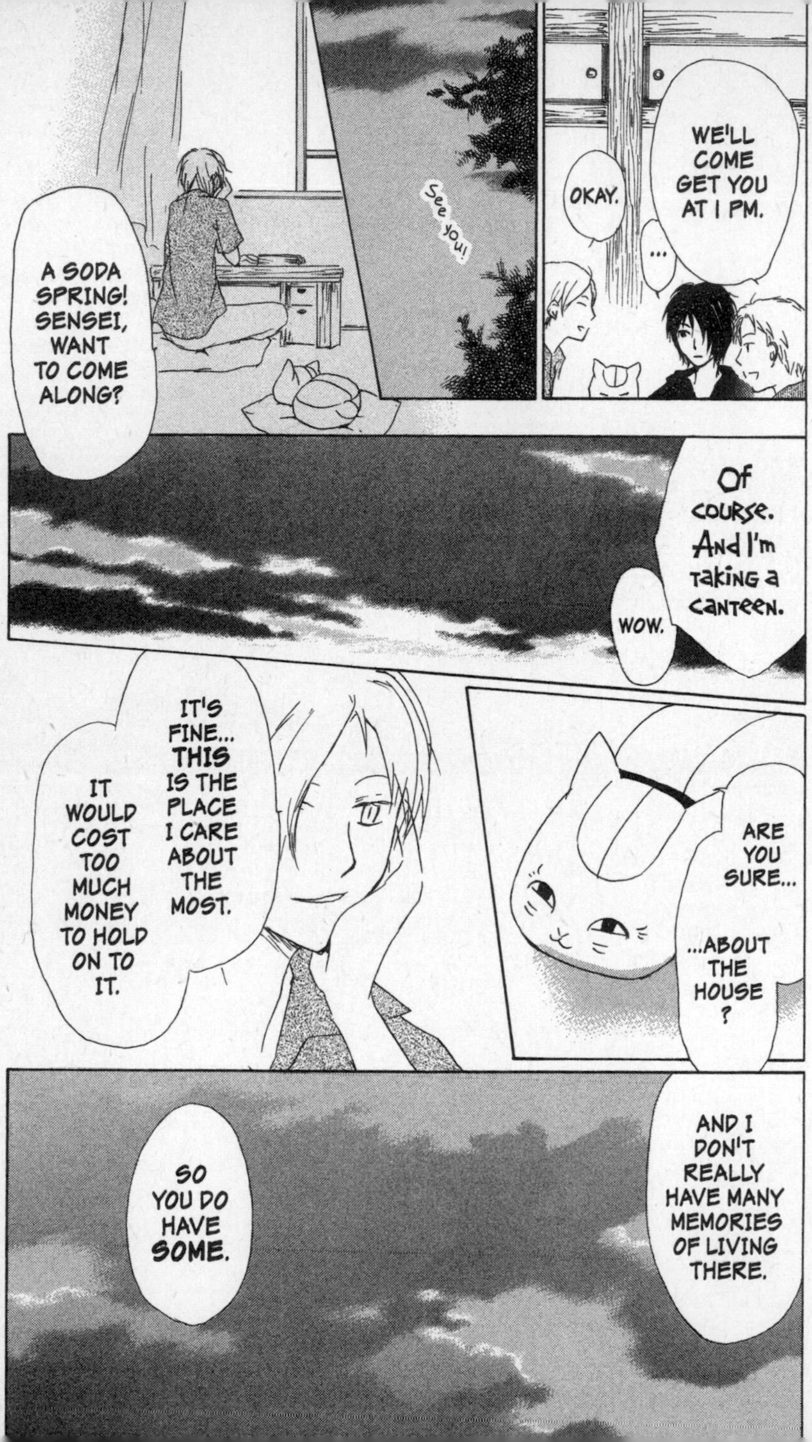
WE'LL COME GET YOU AT 1 PM.
...
OKAY.
See you!
A SODA SPRING! SENSEI, WANT TO COME ALONG?
Of course. And I'm taking a canteen.
WOW.
ARE YOU SURE...
...ABOUT THE HOUSE?
IT'S FINE... THIS IS THE PLACE I CARE ABOUT THE MOST.
IT WOULD COST TOO MUCH MONEY TO HOLD ON TO IT.
AND I DON'T REALLY HAVE MANY MEMORIES OF LIVING THERE.
SO YOU DO HAVE SOME.

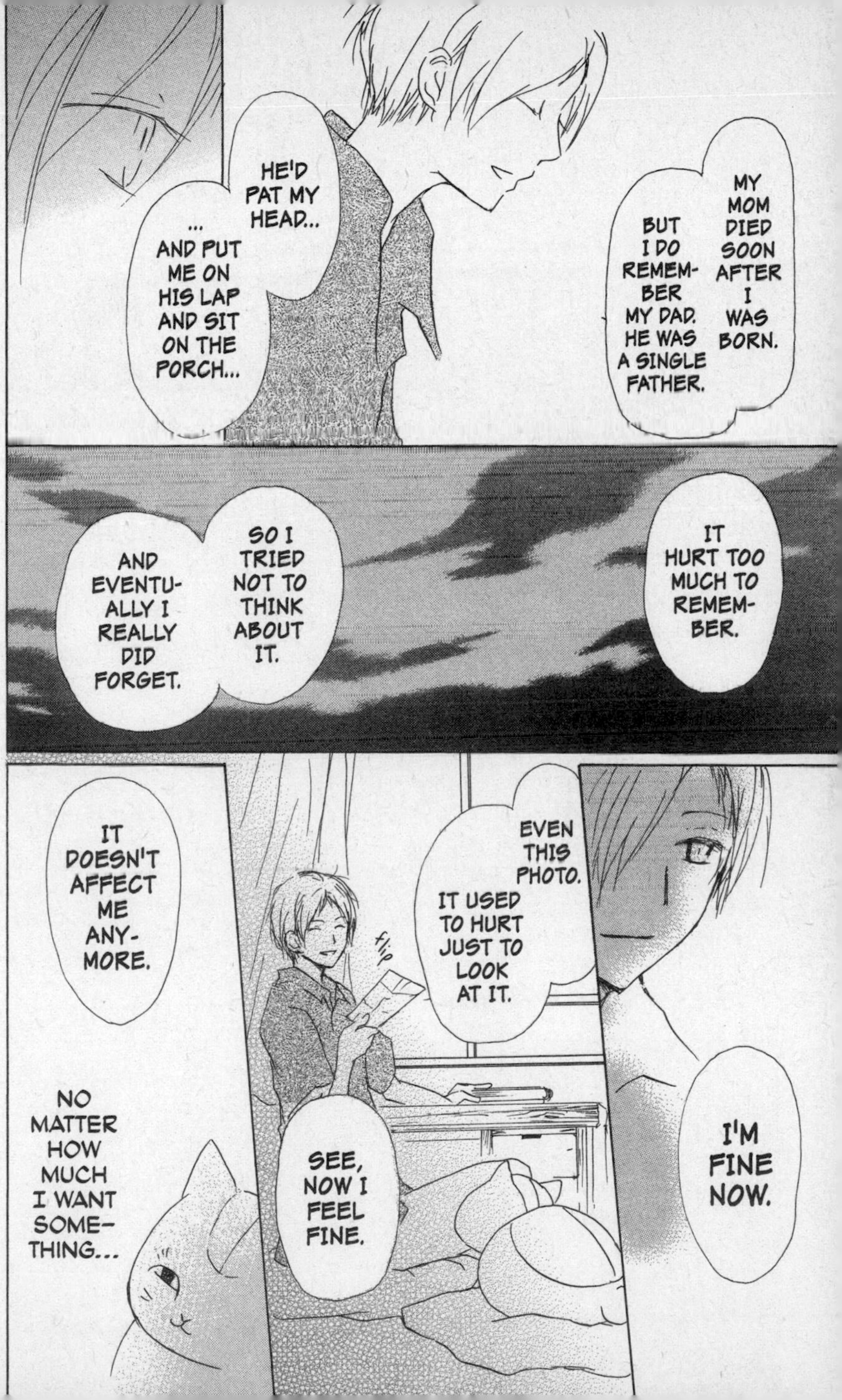
MY MOM DIED SOON AFTER I WAS BORN.
BUT I DO REMEMBER MY DAD. HE WAS A SINGLE FATHER.
HE'D PAT MY HEAD...
... AND PUT ME ON HIS LAP AND SIT ON THE PORCH...
IT HURT TOO MUCH TO REMEMBER.
SO I TRIED NOT TO THINK ABOUT IT.
AND EVENTUALLY I REALLY DID FORGET.
EVEN THIS PHOTO.
IT USED TO HURT JUST TO LOOK AT IT.
flip
SEE, NOW I FEEL FINE.
I'M FINE NOW.
IT DOESN'T AFFECT ME ANYMORE.
NO MATTER HOW MUCH I WANT SOMETHING...

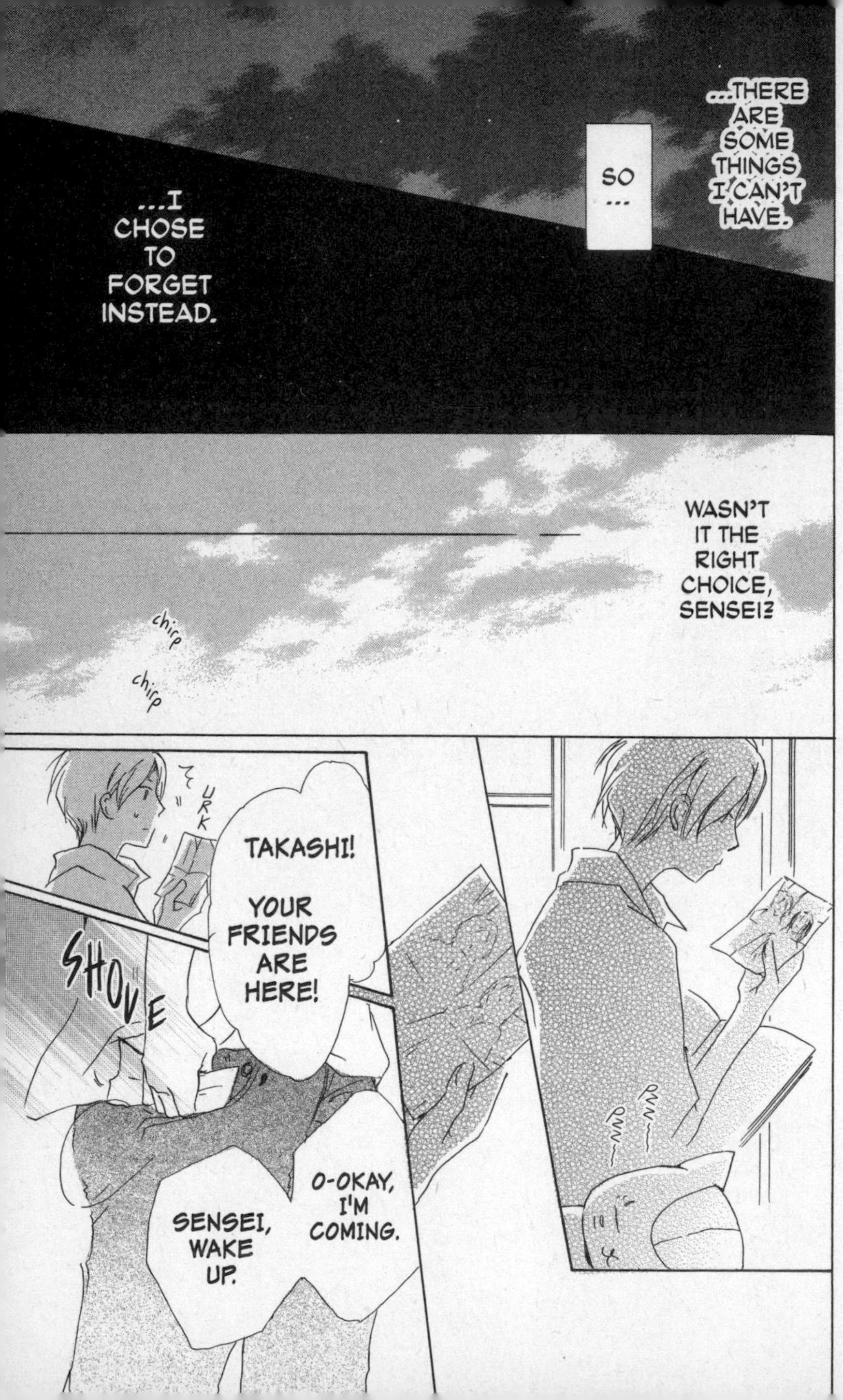
...THERE ARE SOME THINGS I CAN'T HAVE.
SO...
...I CHOSE TO FORGET INSTEAD.
WASN'T IT THE RIGHT CHOICE, SENSEI?
chirp
chirp
TAKASHI!
YOUR FRIENDS ARE HERE!
URK
SHOVE
O-OKAY, I'M COMING.
SENSEI, WAKE UP.

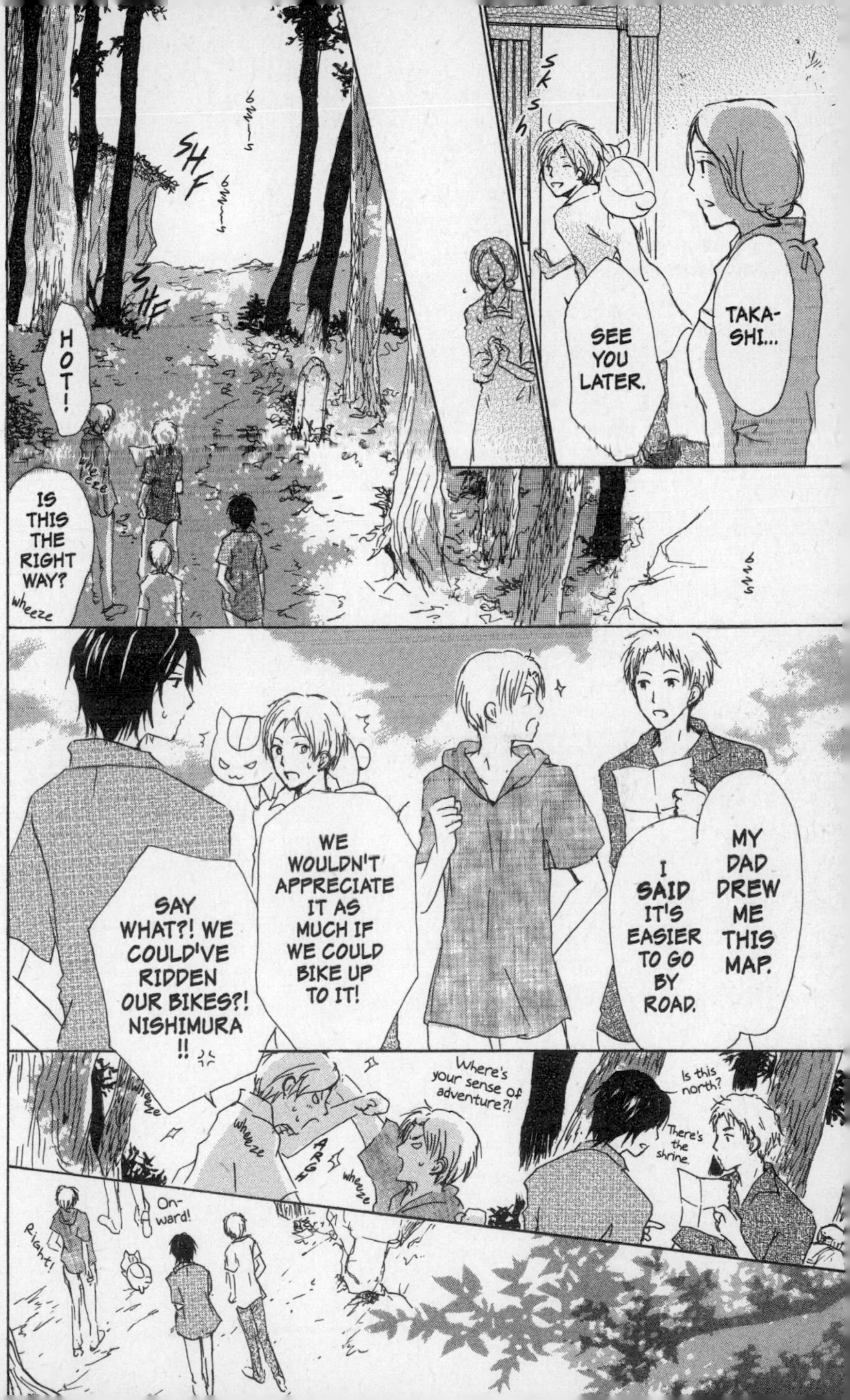
sksh
TAKA-SHI...
SEE YOU LATER.
SHF
SHF
HOT!
IS THIS THE RIGHT WAY?
wheeze
wheeze
MY DAD DREW ME THIS MAP.
I SAID IT'S EASIER TO GO BY ROAD.
WE WOULDN'T APPRECIATE IT AS MUCH IF WE COULD BIKE UP TO IT!
SAY WHAT?! WE COULD'VE RIDDEN OUR BIKES?! NISHIMURA !!
Is this north?
There's the shrine.
Where's your sense of adventure?!
wheeze
wheeze
ARGH
wheeze
On-ward!
Right!

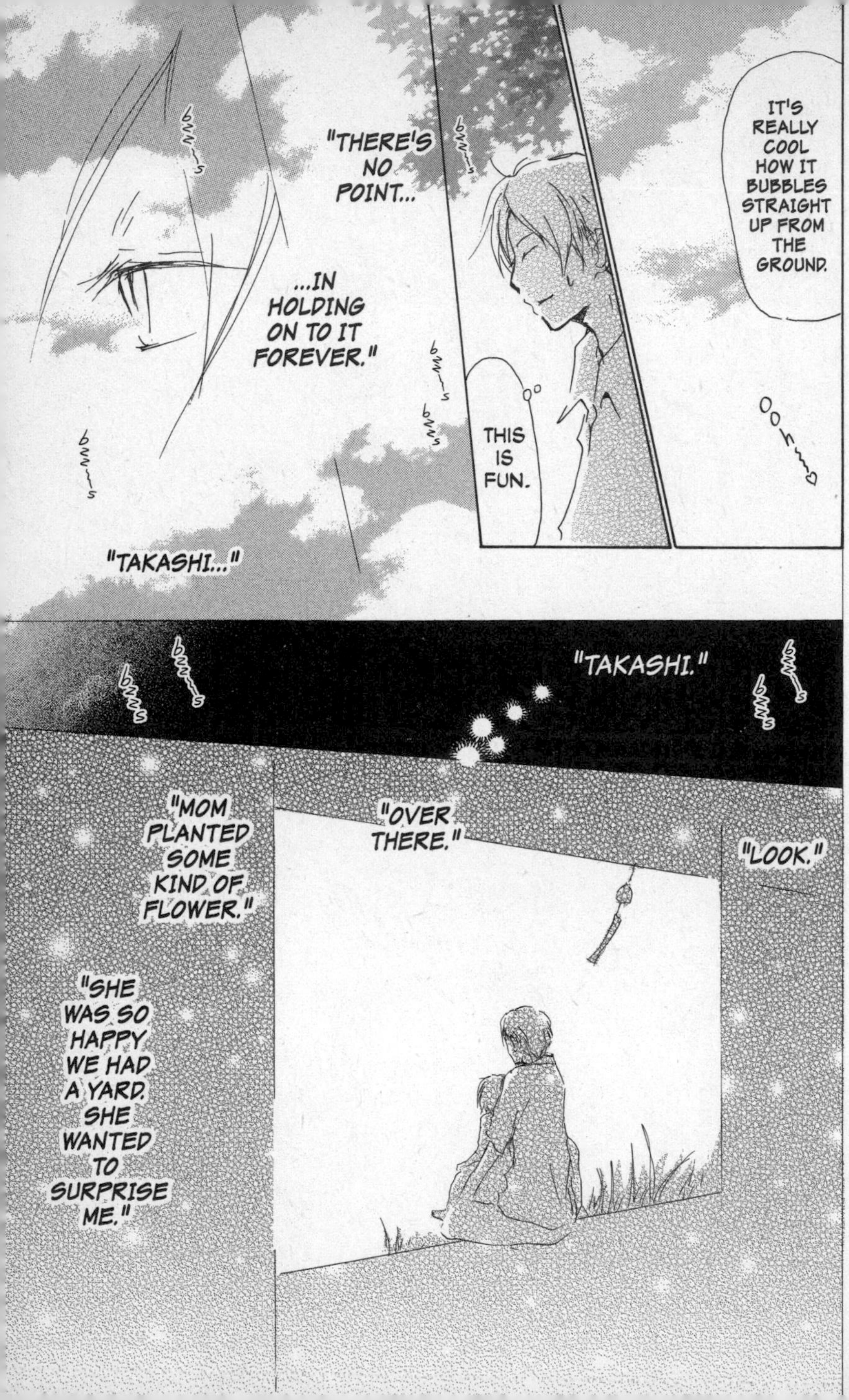
IT'S REALLY COOL HOW IT BUBBLES STRAIGHT UP FROM THE GROUND.
THIS IS FUN.
"THERE'S NO POINT...
...IN HOLDING ON TO IT FOREVER."
"TAKASHI..."
"TAKASHI."
"LOOK."
"OVER THERE."
"MOM PLANTED SOME KIND OF FLOWER."
"SHE WAS SO HAPPY WE HAD A YARD. SHE WANTED TO SURPRISE ME."

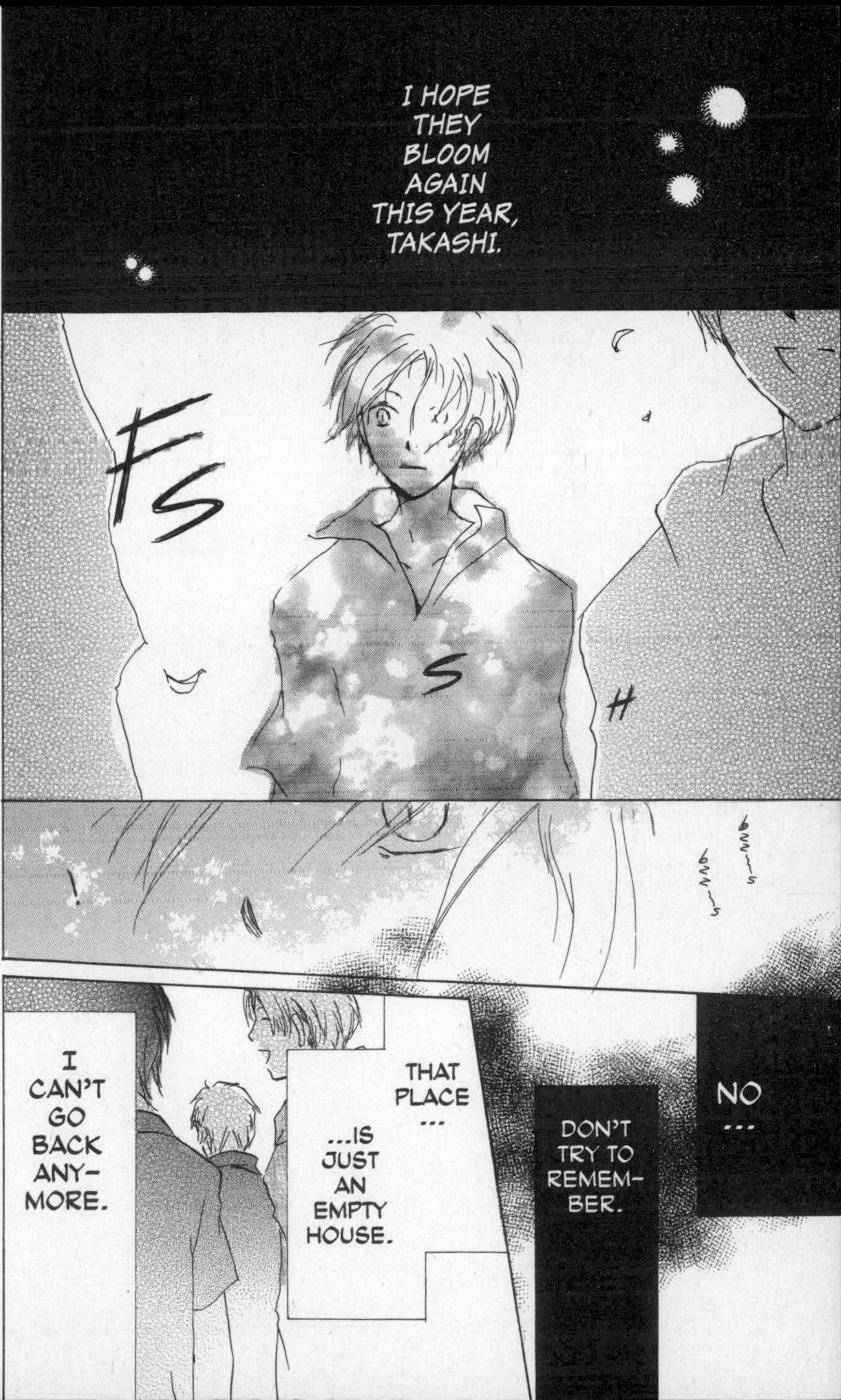
I HOPE THEY BLOOM AGAIN THIS YEAR, TAKASHI.
FS
S
H
NO ---
DON'T TRY TO REMEMBER.
THAT PLACE ---
...IS JUST AN EMPTY HOUSE.
I CAN'T GO BACK ANYMORE.

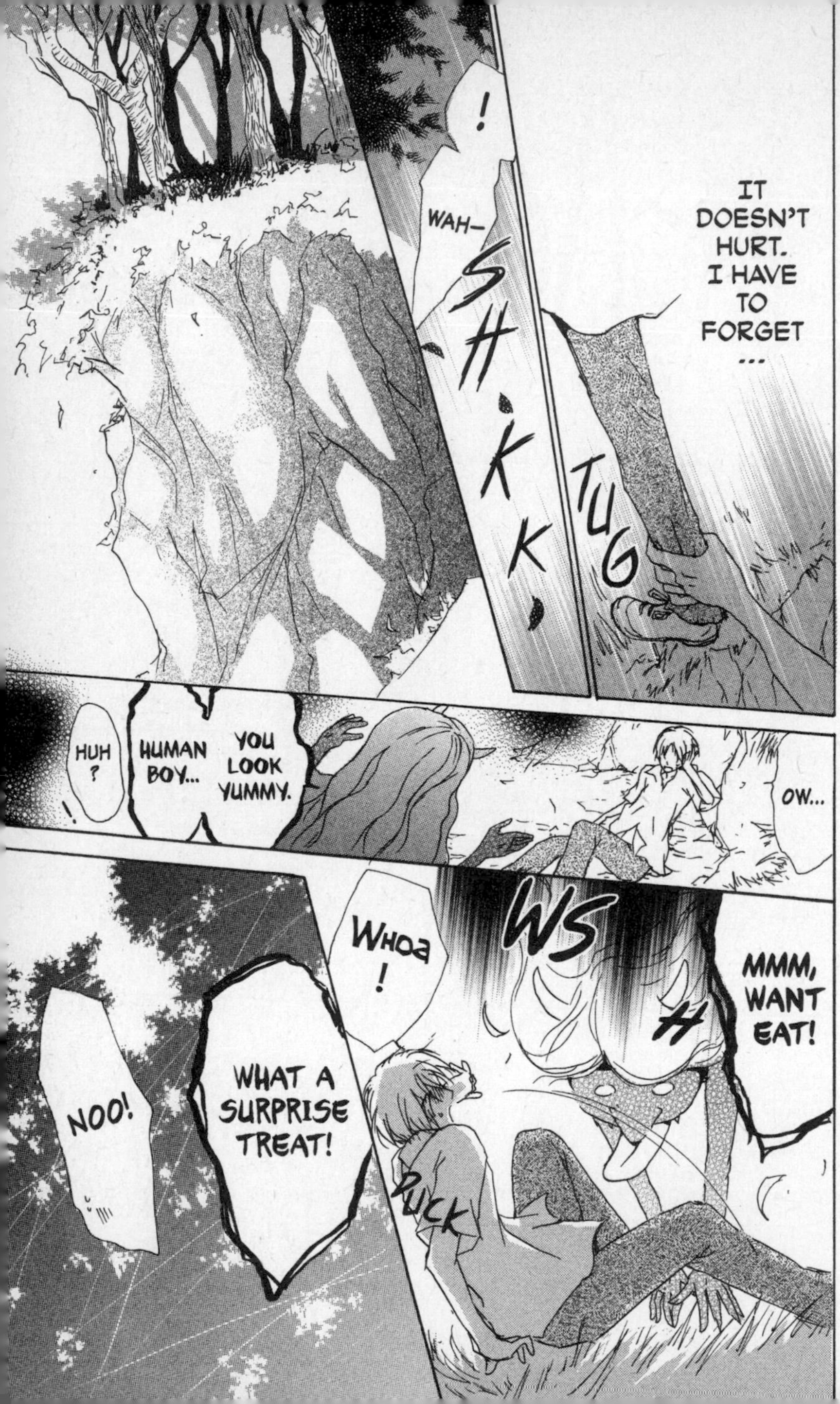
IT DOESN'T HURT. I HAVE TO FORGET...
TUG
!
WAH—
SHKK
OW...
HUMAN BOY... YOU LOOK YUMMY.
HUH?
!
MMM, WANT EAT!
WSH
Whoa!
DUCK
WHAT A SURPRISE TREAT!
NOO!

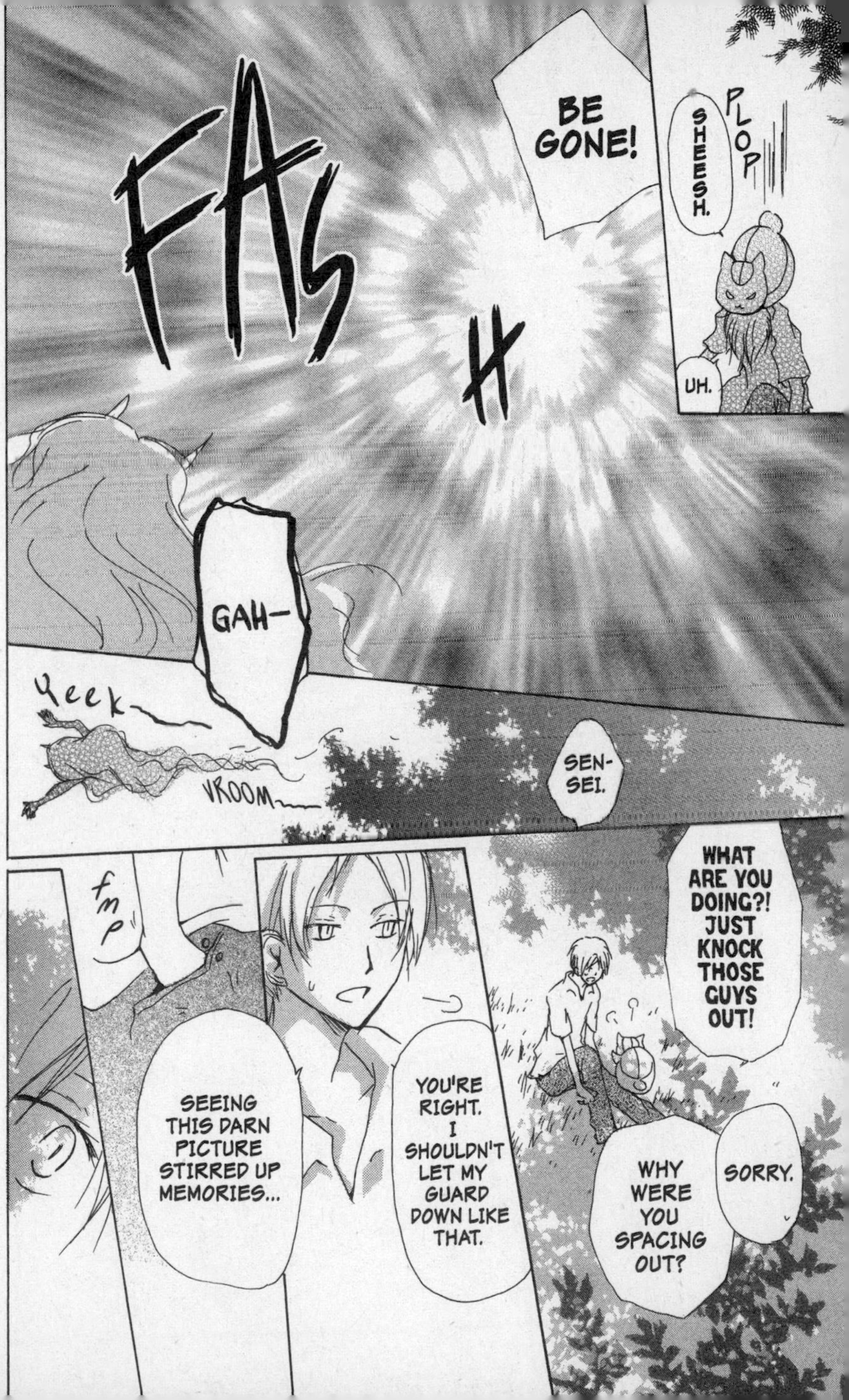
PLOP
SHEESH.
UH.
BE GONE!
FASH
GAH-
SEN-SEI.
VROOM
yeek
WHAT ARE YOU DOING?! JUST KNOCK THOSE GUYS OUT!
SORRY.
WHY WERE YOU SPACING OUT?
YOU'RE RIGHT. I SHOULDN'T LET MY GUARD DOWN LIKE THAT.
SEEING THIS DARN PICTURE STIRRED UP MEMORIES...
fmp

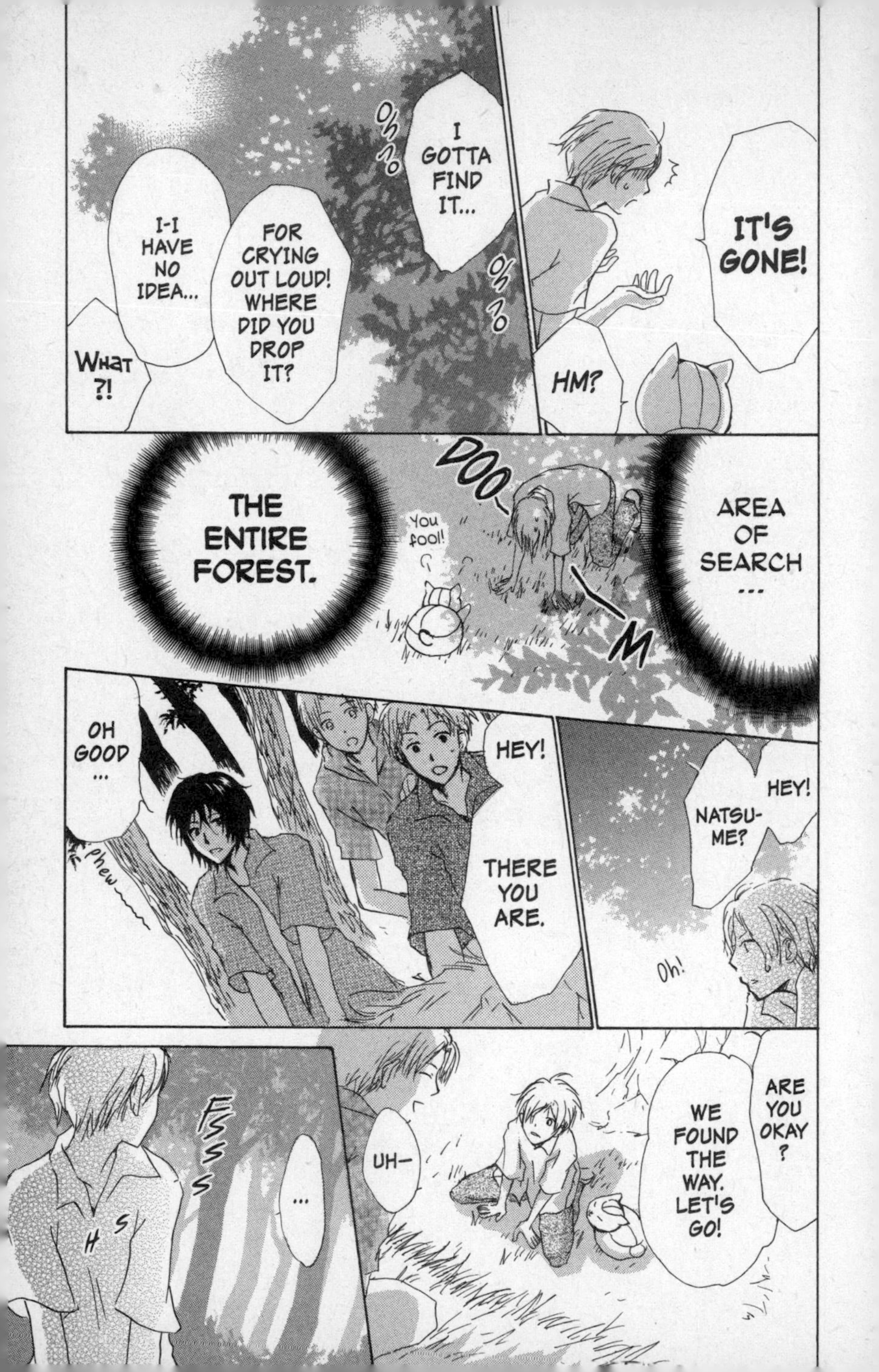
IT'S GONE!
HM?
Oh no
I GOTTA FIND IT...
Oh no
FOR CRYING OUT LOUD! WHERE DID YOU DROP IT?
I-I HAVE NO IDEA...
WHAT?!
AREA OF SEARCH ...
DOOM
You fool!
THE ENTIRE FOREST.
HEY!
NATSUME?
Oh!
HEY!
THERE YOU ARE.
OH GOOD ...
phew
ARE YOU OKAY?
WE FOUND THE WAY. LET'S GO!
UH—
...
FSSS
HS

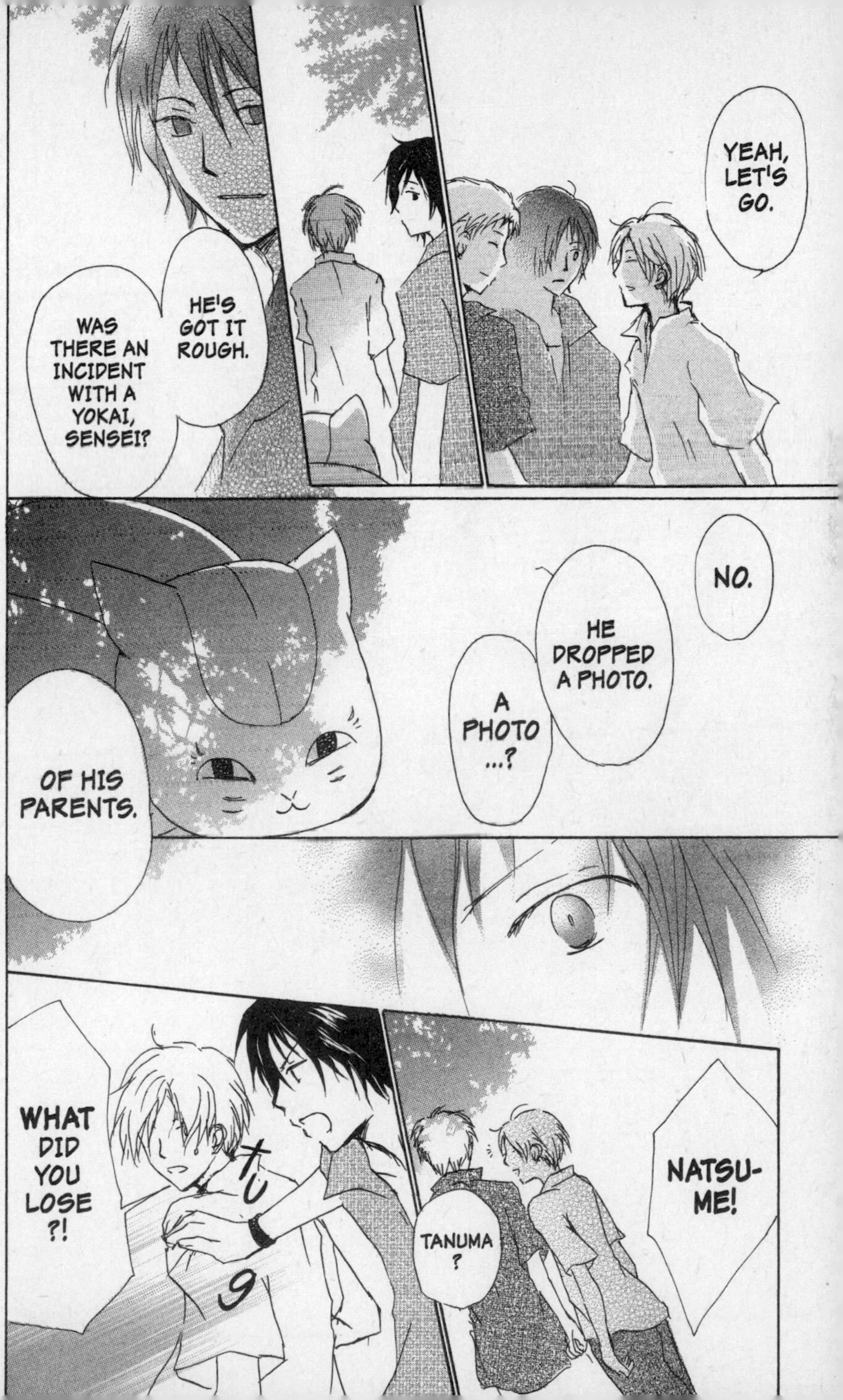
YEAH, LET'S GO.
HE'S GOT IT ROUGH.
WAS THERE AN INCIDENT WITH A YOKAI, SENSEI?
NO.
HE DROPPED A PHOTO.
A PHOTO ...?
OF HIS PARENTS.
NATSU-ME!
TANUMA ?
WHAT DID YOU LOSE ?!
TUG

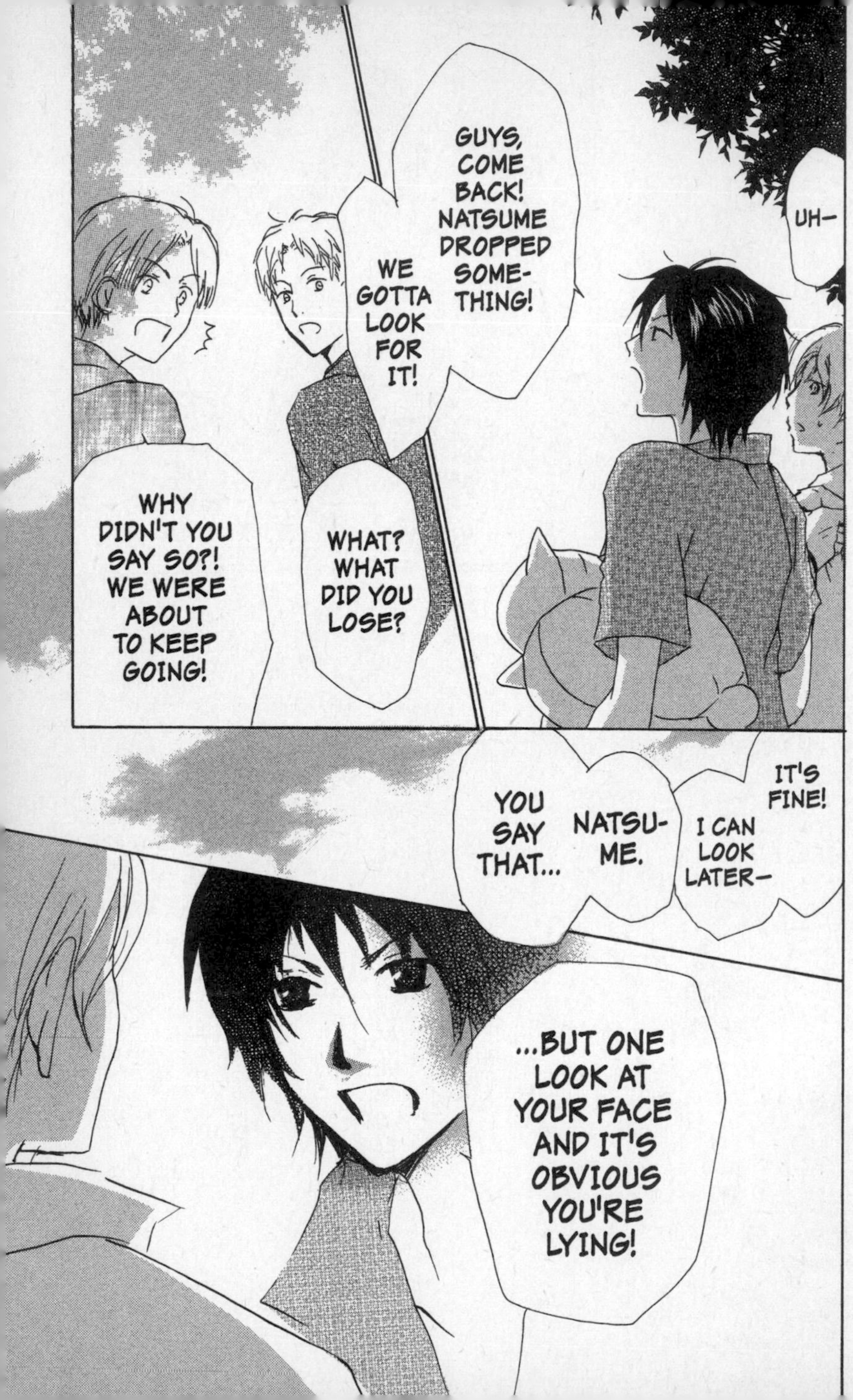
UH-
GUYS, COME BACK! NATSUME DROPPED SOME-THING!
WE GOTTA LOOK FOR IT!
WHAT? WHAT DID YOU LOSE?
WHY DIDN'T YOU SAY SO?! WE WERE ABOUT TO KEEP GOING!
IT'S FINE!
I CAN LOOK LATER—
NATSU-ME.
YOU SAY THAT...
...BUT ONE LOOK AT YOUR FACE AND IT'S OBVIOUS YOU'RE LYING!

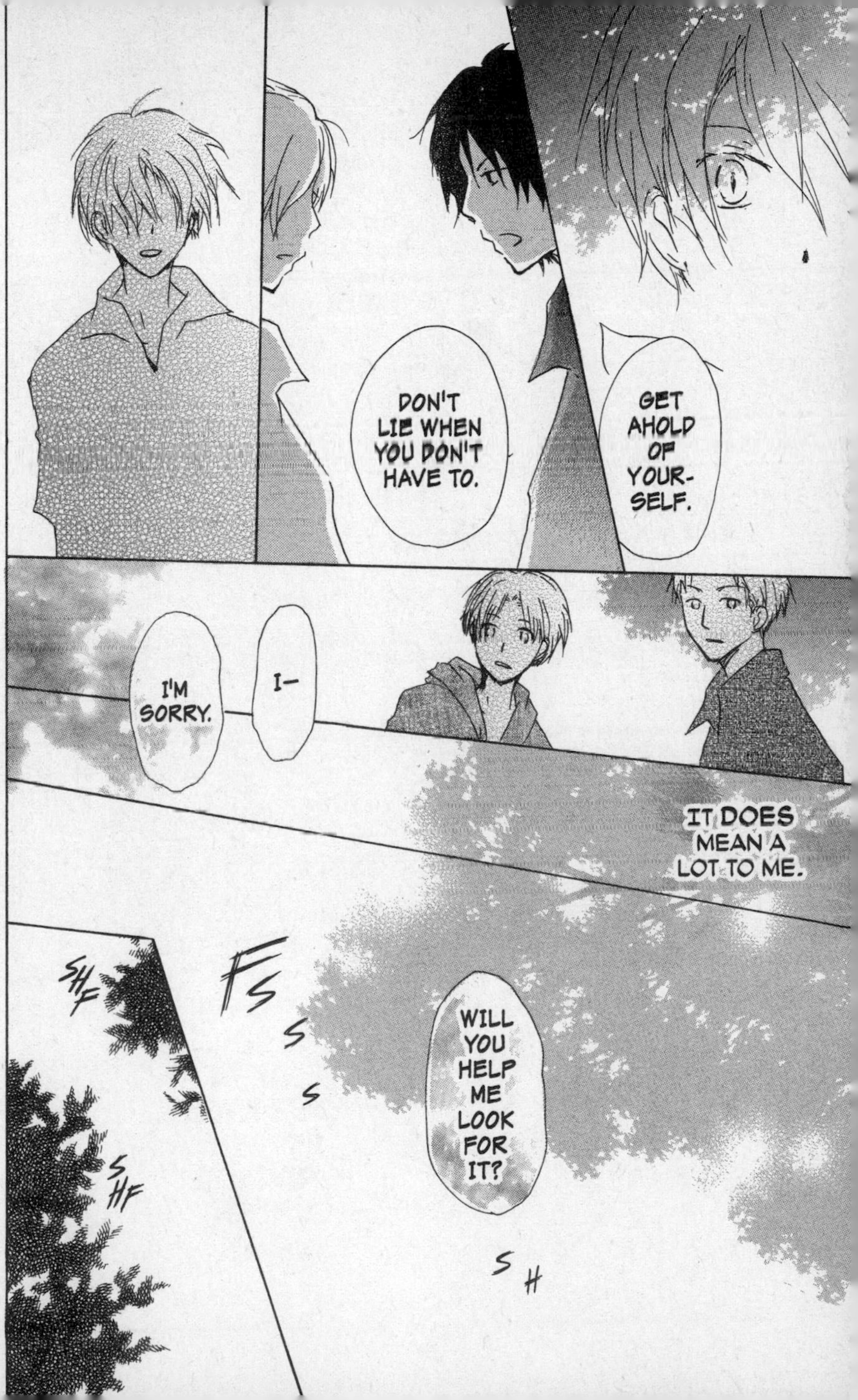
GET AHOLD OF YOURSELF.
DON'T LIE WHEN YOU DON'T HAVE TO.
I—
I'M SORRY.
IT DOES MEAN A LOT TO ME.
WILL YOU HELP ME LOOK FOR IT?
FSSS
SHF
SH
SHF

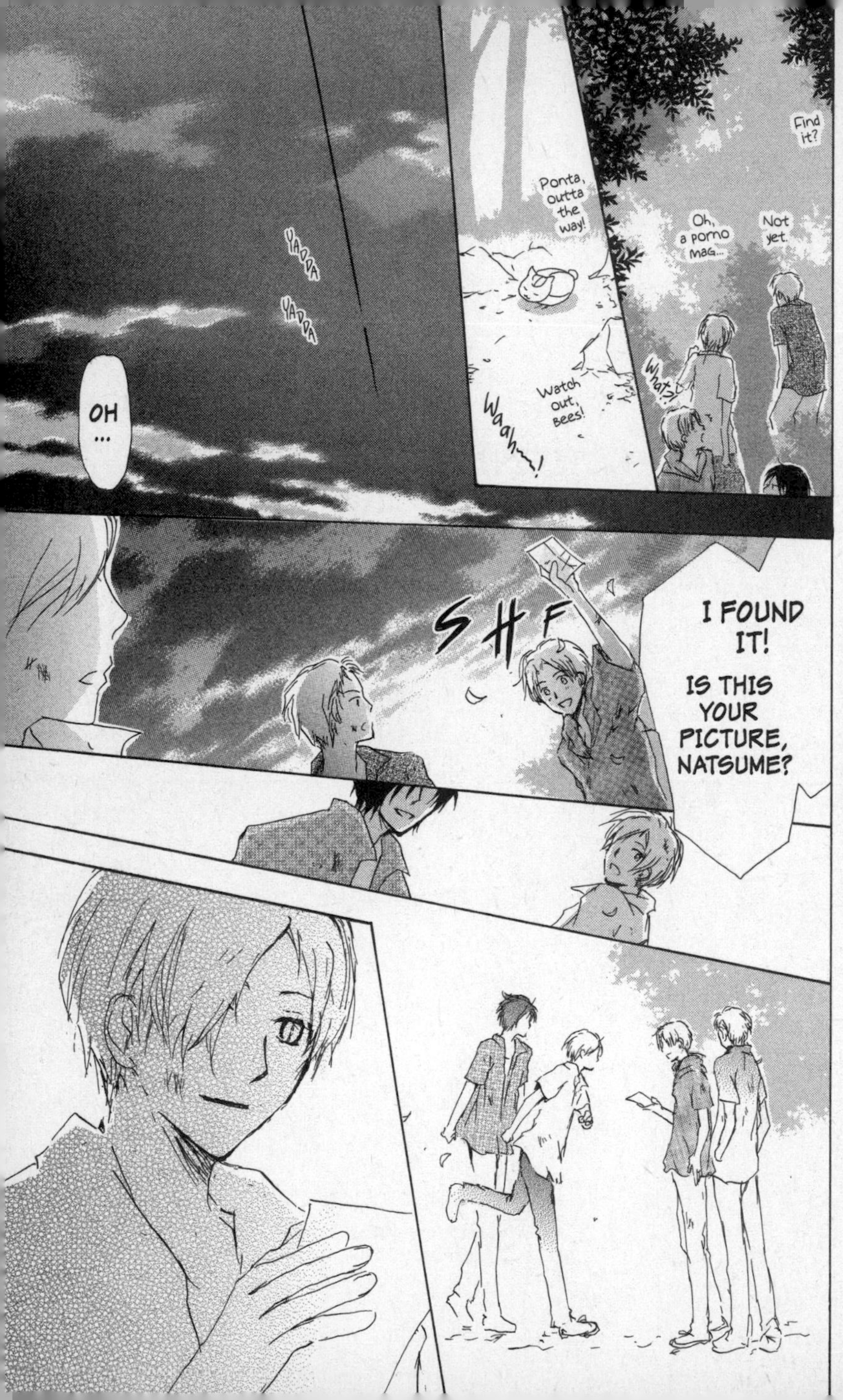

Find it?
Not yet.
Oh, a porno mag...
Ponta, outta the way!
What?!
Watch out, bees!
Waah~!
YADDA YADDA
OH...
I FOUND IT!
IS THIS YOUR PICTURE, NATSUME?
SHF

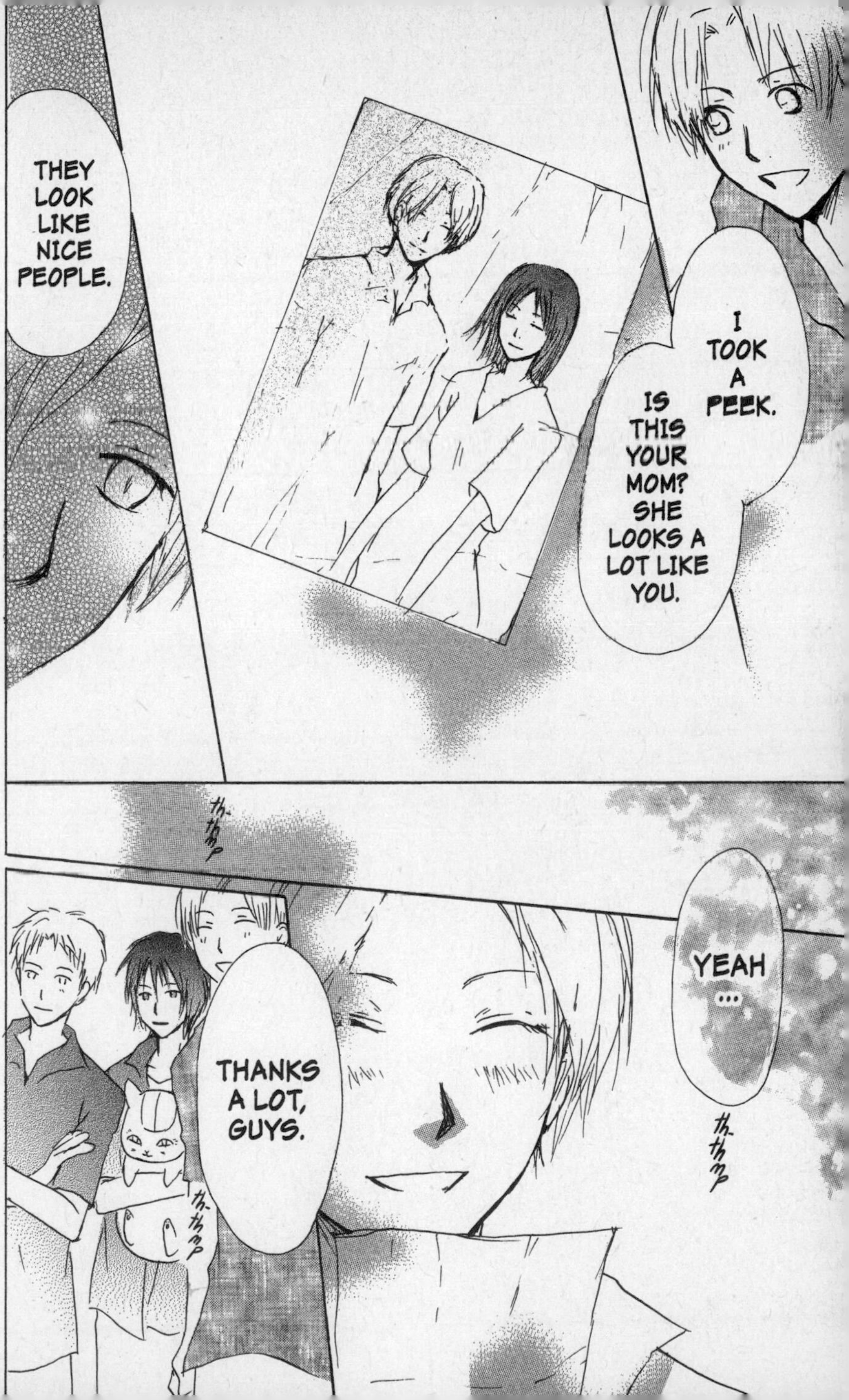
I TOOK A PEEK.
IS THIS YOUR MOM? SHE LOOKS A LOT LIKE YOU.
THEY LOOK LIKE NICE PEOPLE.
YEAH ...
THANKS A LOT, GUYS.

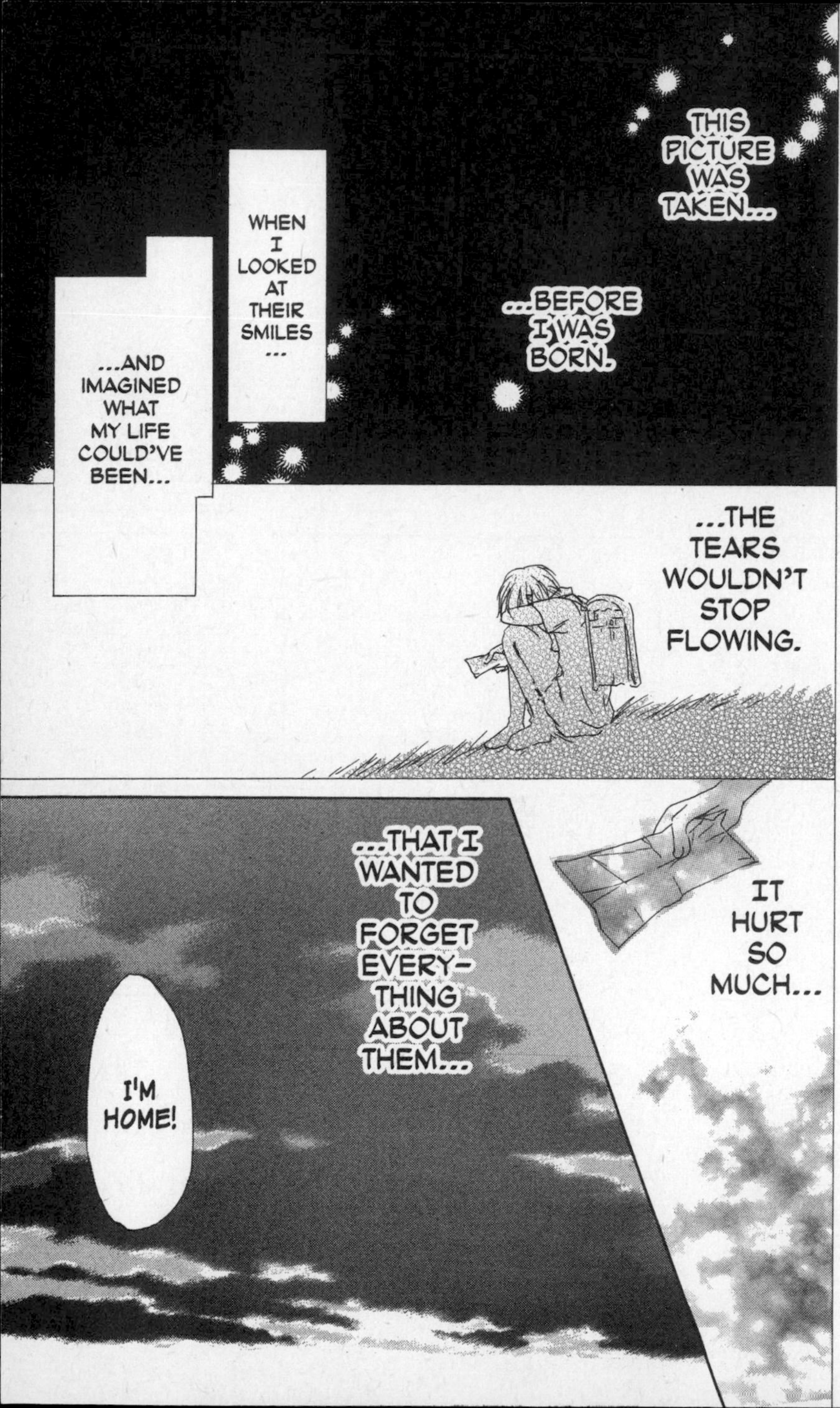
THIS PICTURE WAS TAKEN...
...BEFORE I WAS BORN.
WHEN I LOOKED AT THEIR SMILES...
...AND IMAGINED WHAT MY LIFE COULD'VE BEEN...
...THE TEARS WOULDN'T STOP FLOWING.
IT HURT SO MUCH...
...THAT I WANTED TO FORGET EVERYTHING ABOUT THEM...
I'M HOME!

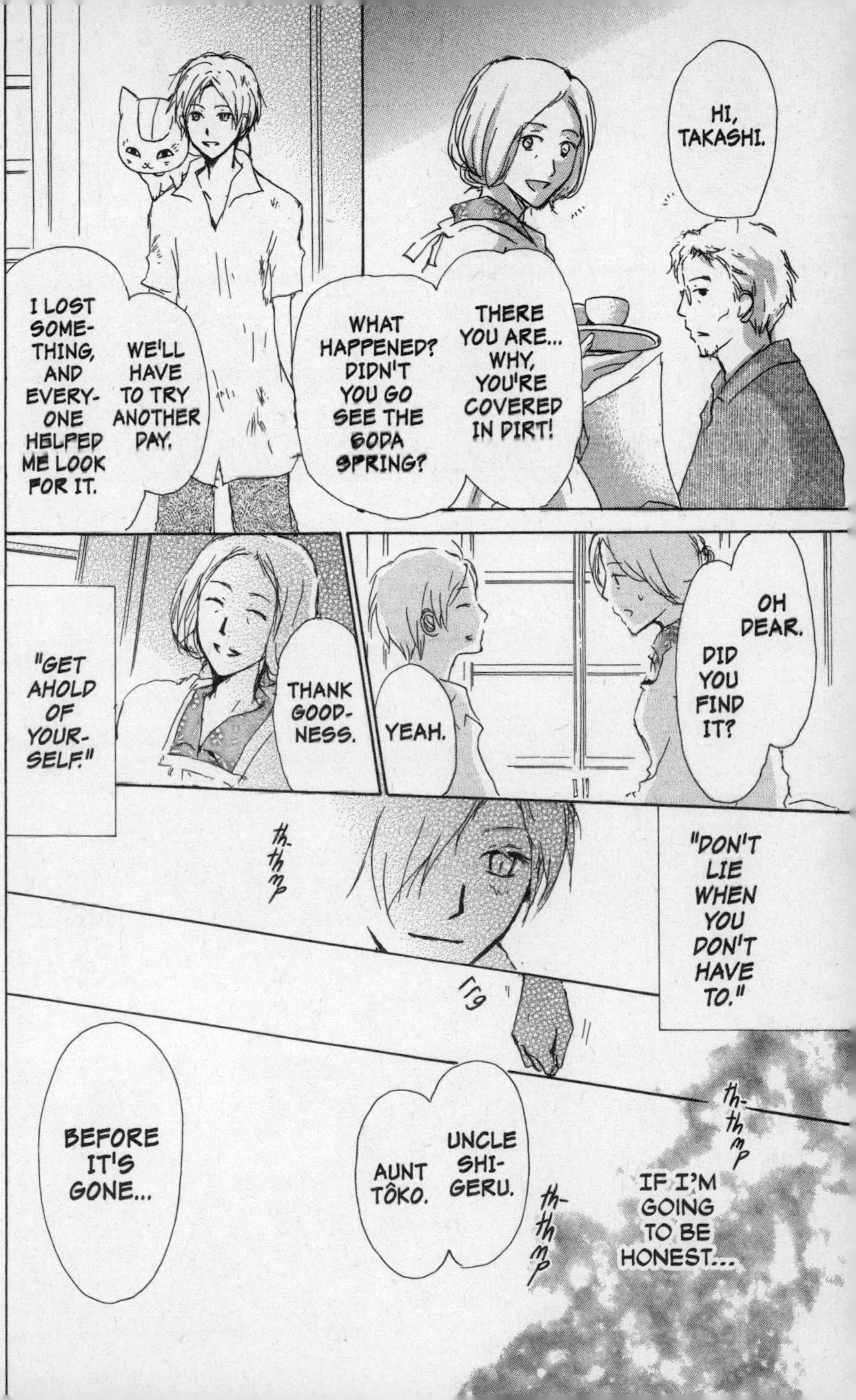
HI, TAKASHI.
THERE YOU ARE... WHY, YOU'RE COVERED IN DIRT!
WHAT HAPPENED? DIDN'T YOU GO SEE THE GODA SPRING?
WE'LL HAVE TO TRY ANOTHER DAY.
I LOST SOMETHING, AND EVERYONE HELPED ME LOOK FOR IT.
OH DEAR.
DID YOU FIND IT?
YEAH.
THANK GOODNESS.
"GET AHOLD OF YOURSELF."
"DON'T LIE WHEN YOU DON'T HAVE TO."
th-thmp
grip
th-thmp
IF I'M GOING TO BE HONEST...
th-thmp
UNCLE SHIGERU.
AUNT TÔKO.
BEFORE IT'S GONE...

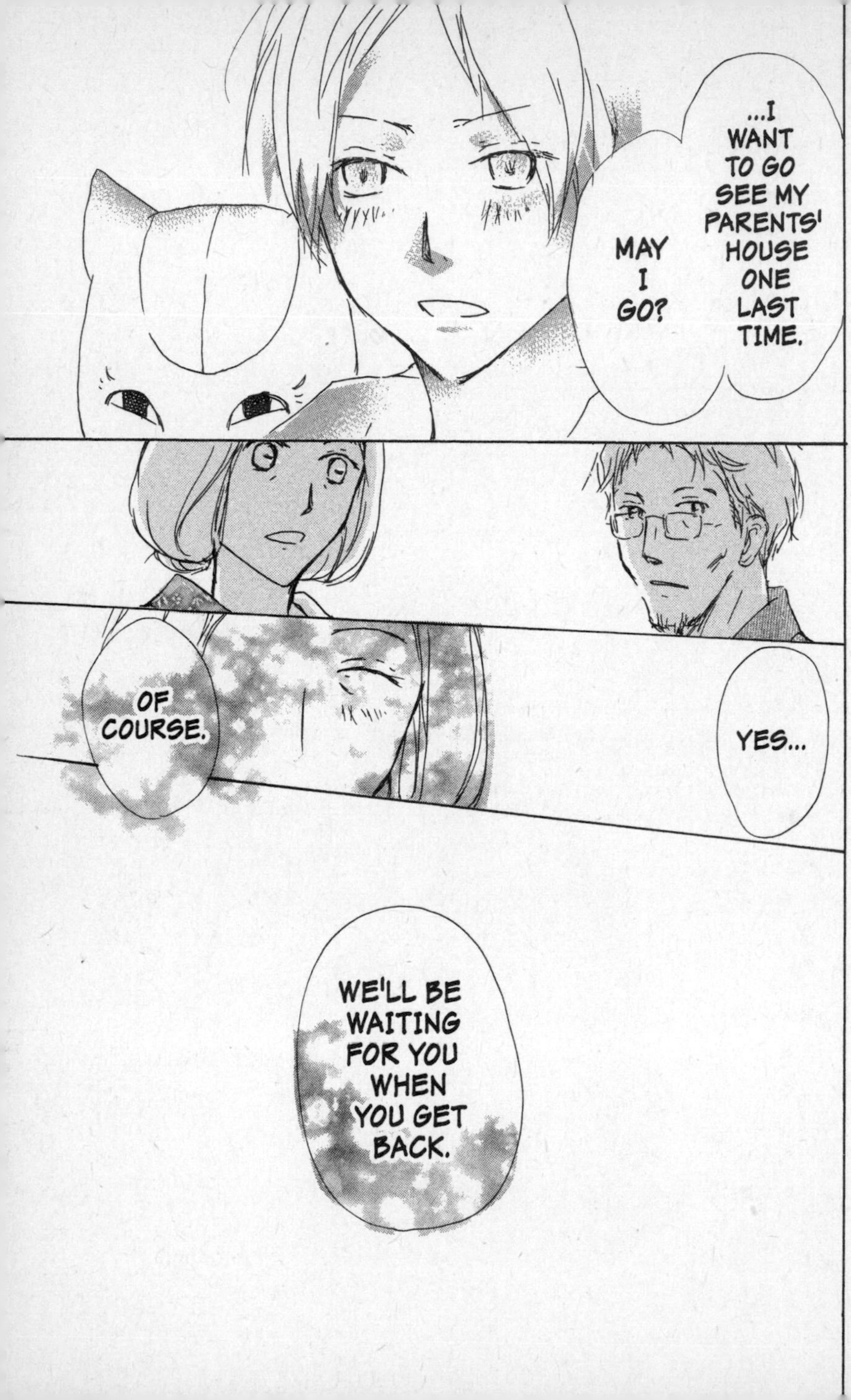
...I WANT TO GO SEE MY PARENTS' HOUSE ONE LAST TIME.
MAY I GO?
YES...
OF COURSE.
WE'LL BE WAITING FOR YOU WHEN YOU GET BACK.

Tohru Taki as a child

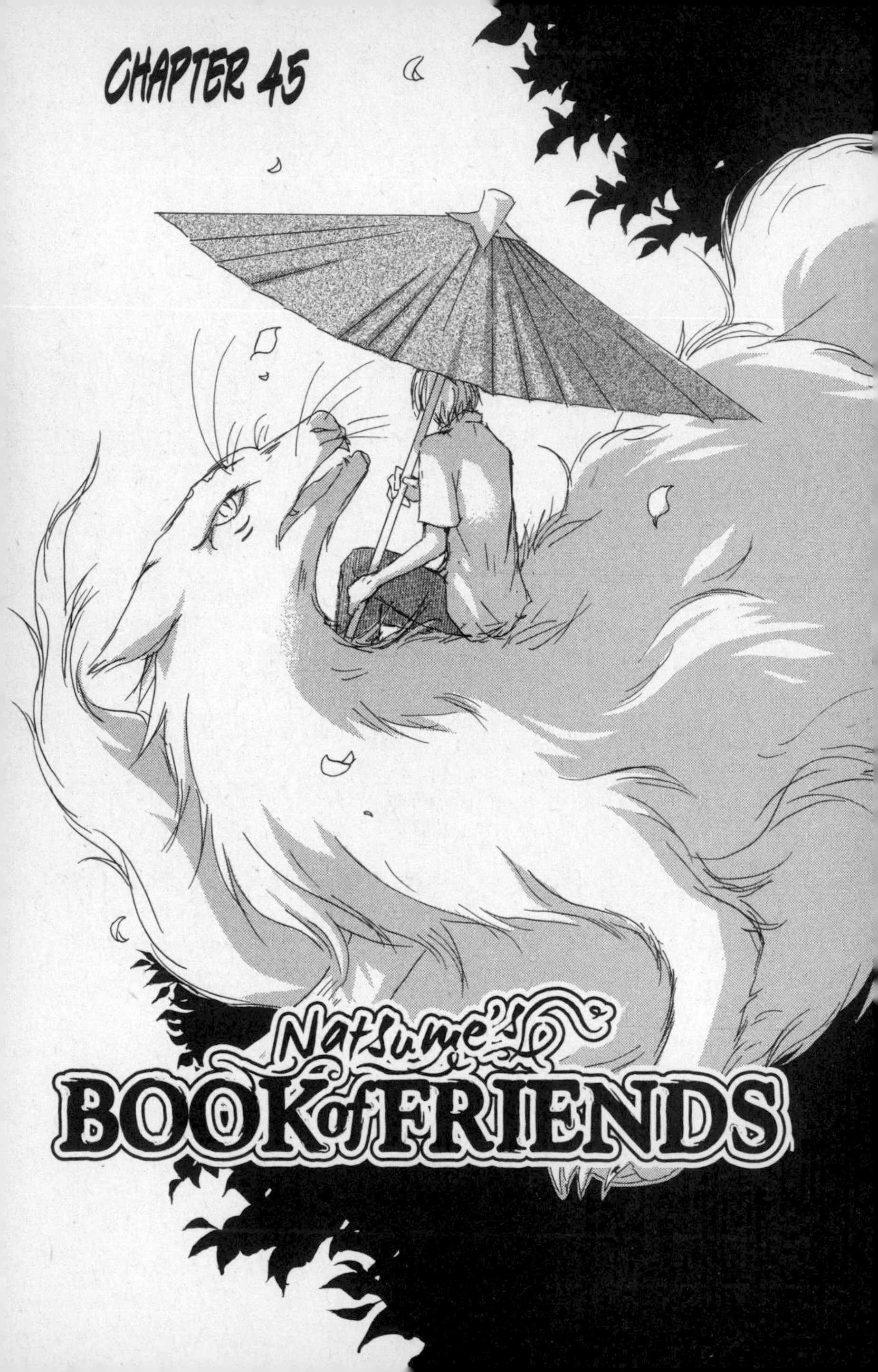
CHAPTER 45
Natsume's
BOOK of FRIENDS

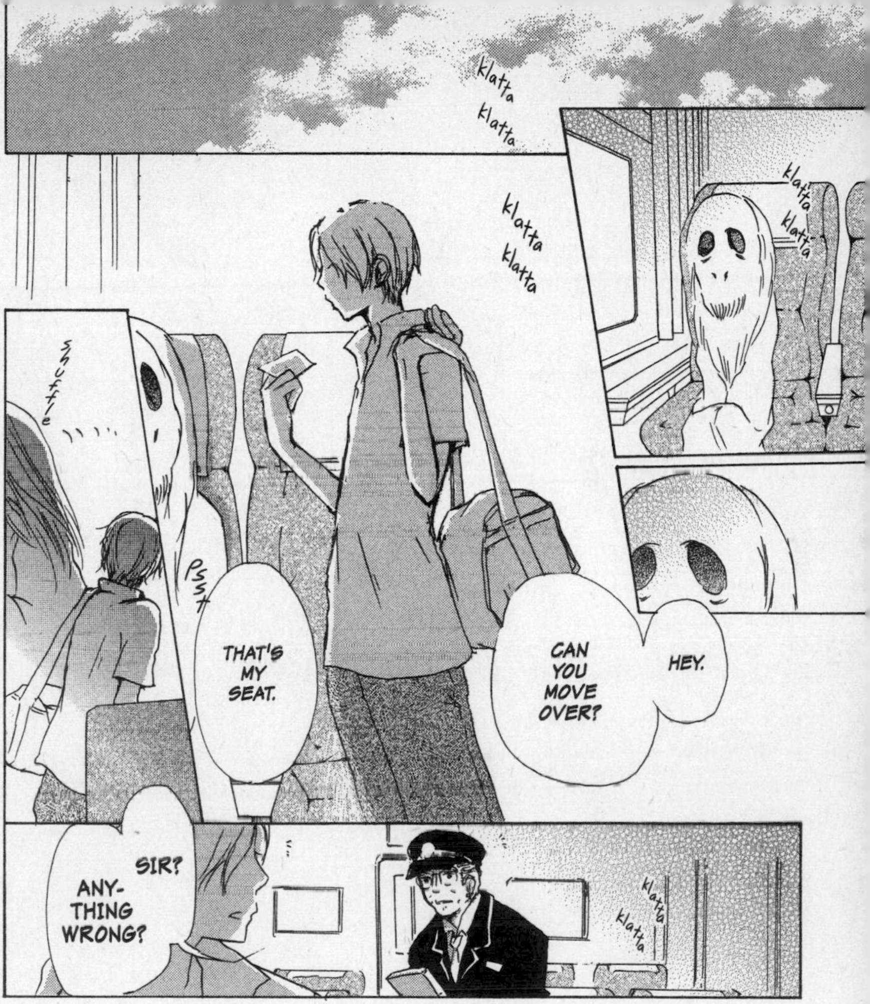
klatta klatta
klatta klatta
klatta klatta
HEY.
CAN YOU MOVE OVER?
Psst
THAT'S MY SEAT.
snuffle
klatta klatta
SIR? ANYTHING WRONG?

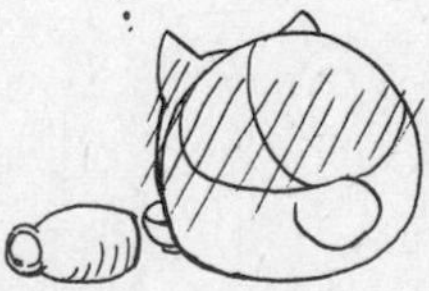

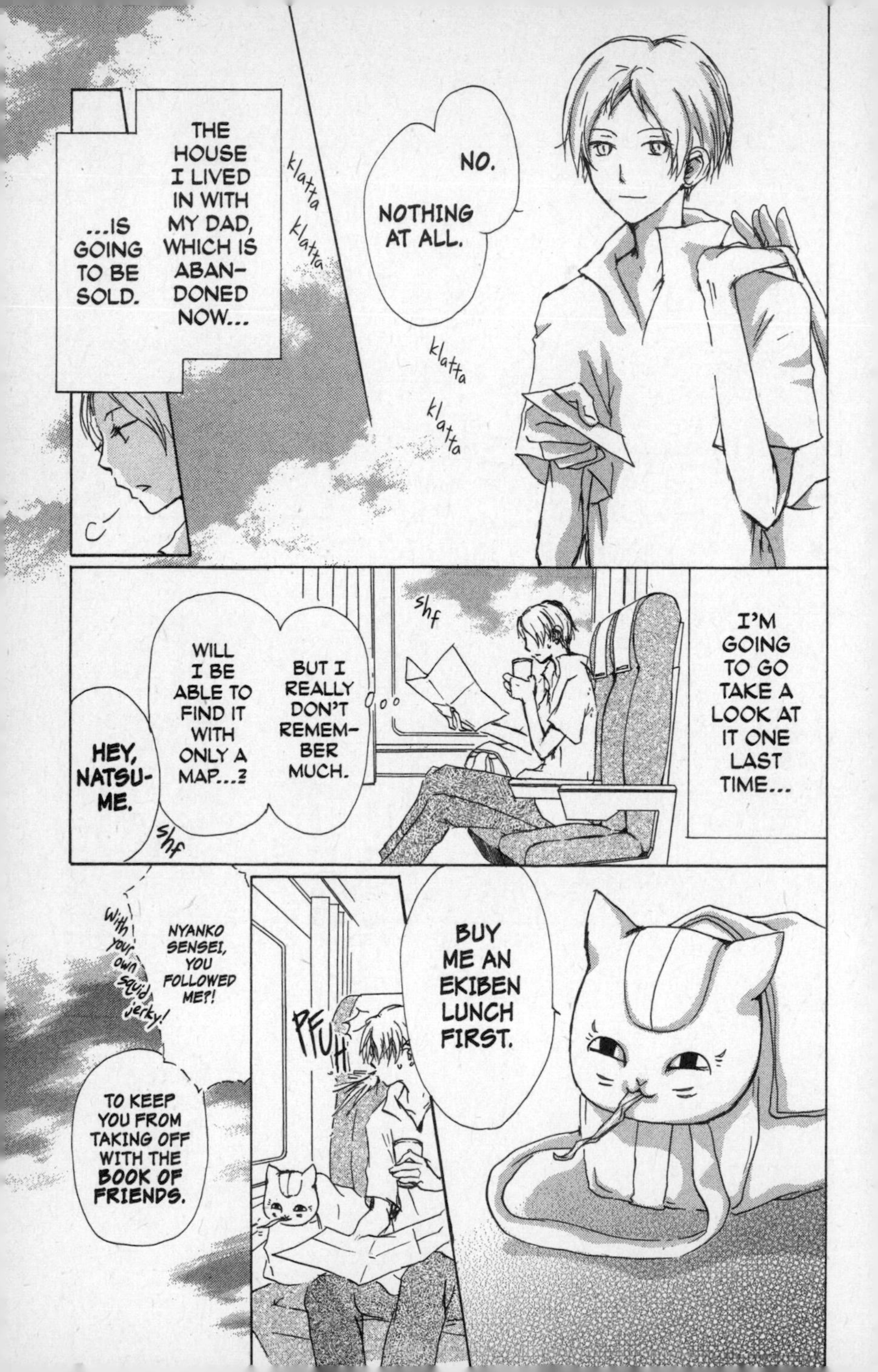
NO.
NOTHING AT ALL.
klatta klatta
klatta klatta
THE HOUSE I LIVED IN WITH MY DAD, WHICH IS ABANDONED NOW...
...IS GOING TO BE SOLD.
I'M GOING TO GO TAKE A LOOK AT IT ONE LAST TIME...
shf
BUT I REALLY DON'T REMEMBER MUCH.
WILL I BE ABLE TO FIND IT WITH ONLY A MAP...?
HEY, NATSUME.
shf
BUY ME AN EKIBEN LUNCH FIRST.
PFUH
NYANKO SENSEI, YOU FOLLOWED ME?!
With your own squid jerky!
TO KEEP YOU FROM TAKING OFF WITH THE BOOK OF FRIENDS.

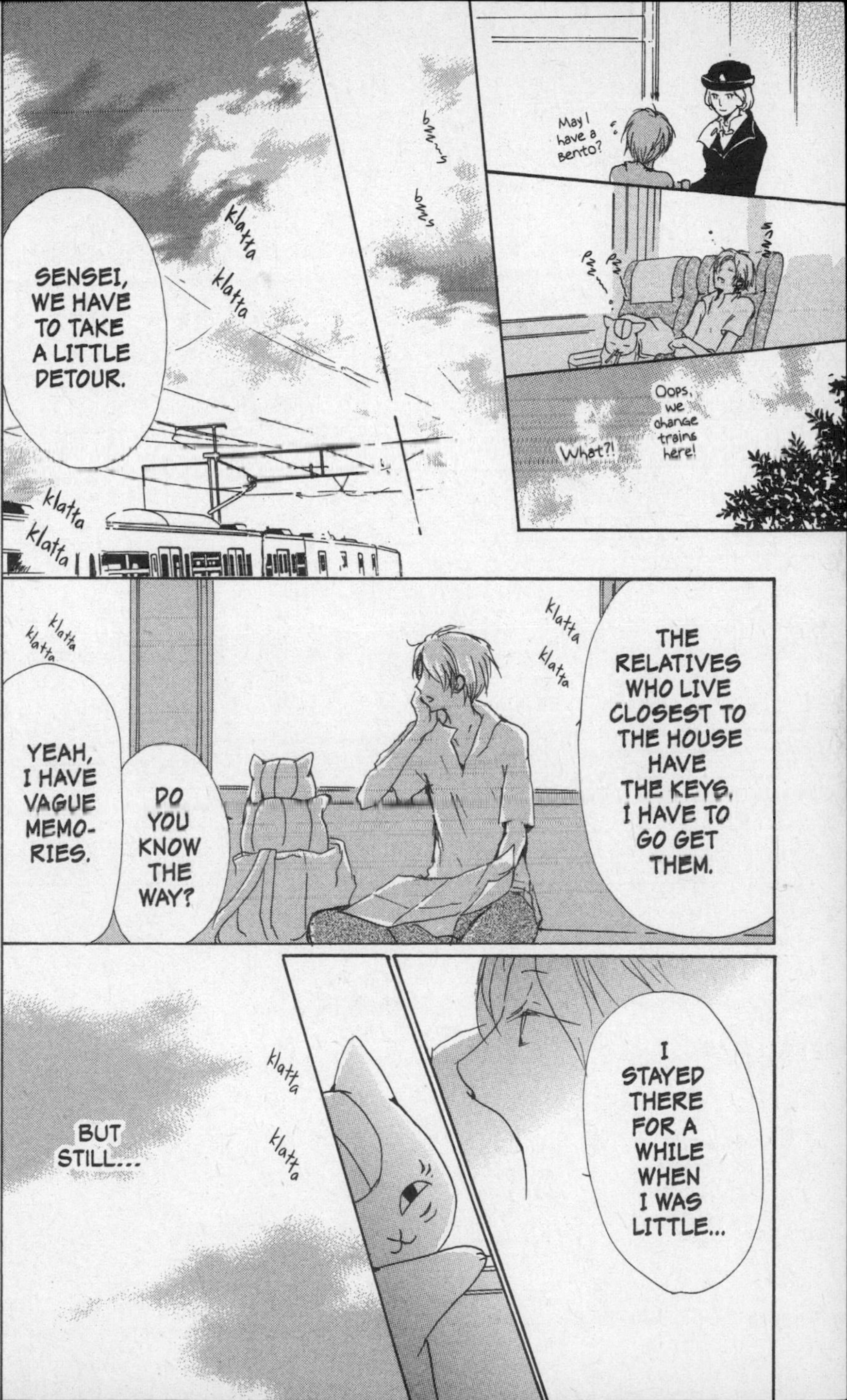
May I have a Bento?
Oops, we change trains here!
What?!
klatta
klatta
SENSEI, WE HAVE TO TAKE A LITTLE DETOUR.
klatta
klatta
klatta
klatta
THE RELATIVES WHO LIVE CLOSEST TO THE HOUSE HAVE THE KEYS. I HAVE TO GO GET THEM.
klatta
klatta
DO YOU KNOW THE WAY?
YEAH, I HAVE VAGUE MEMO-RIES.
I STAYED THERE FOR A WHILE WHEN I WAS LITTLE...
klatta
klatta
BUT STILL...

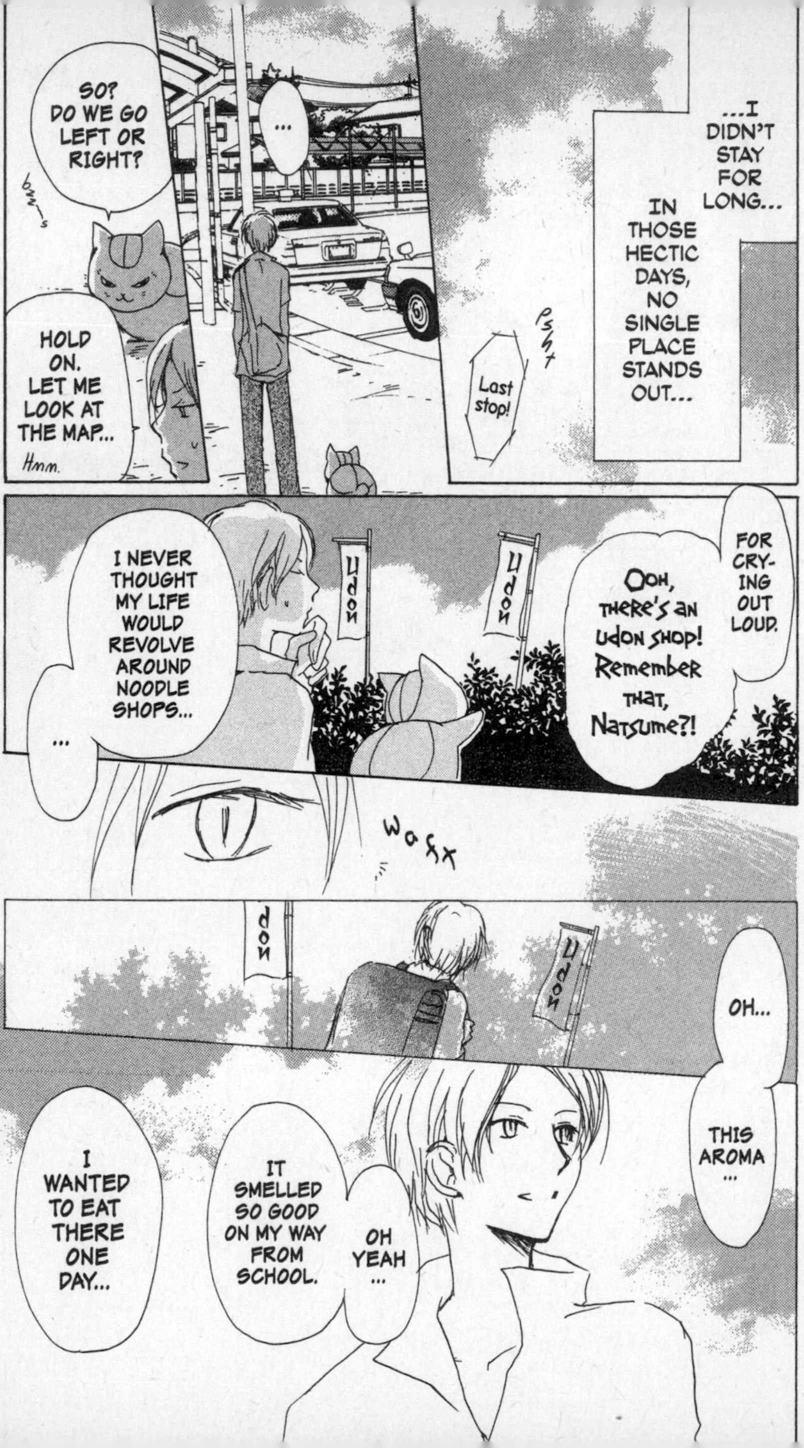
...I DIDN'T STAY FOR LONG...
IN THOSE HECTIC DAYS, NO SINGLE PLACE STANDS OUT...
Psht
Last stop!
...
SO? DO WE GO LEFT OR RIGHT?
HOLD ON. LET ME LOOK AT THE MAP...
Hmm.
FOR CRYING OUT LOUD.
OOH, THERE'S AN UDON SHOP! REMEMBER THAT, NATSUME?!
Udon
I NEVER THOUGHT MY LIFE WOULD REVOLVE AROUND NOODLE SHOPS...
...
Waft
OH...
THIS AROMA...
OH YEAH...
IT SMELLED SO GOOD ON MY WAY FROM SCHOOL.
I WANTED TO EAT THERE ONE DAY...

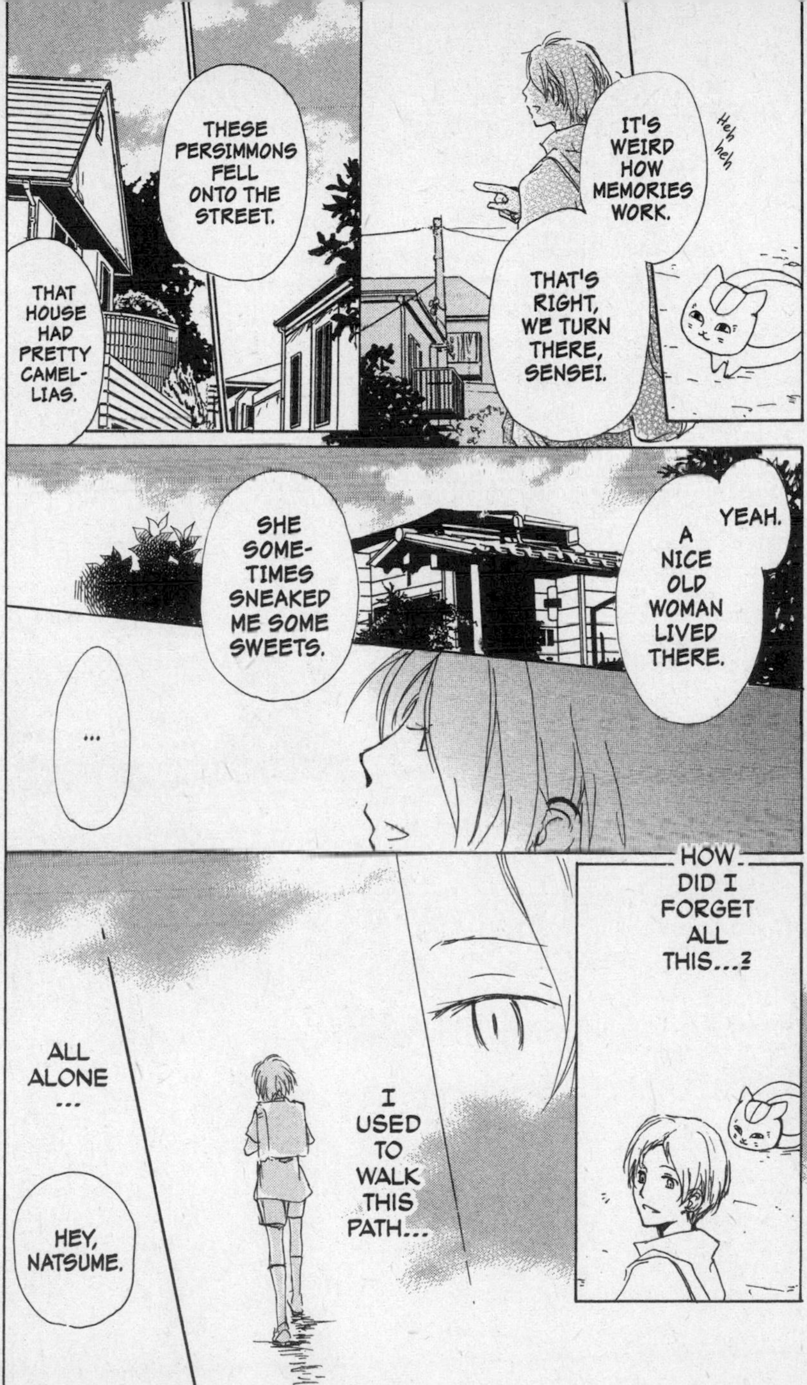
IT'S WEIRD HOW MEMORIES WORK.
Heh heh
THAT'S RIGHT, WE TURN THERE, SENSEI.
THESE PERSIMMONS FELL ONTO THE STREET.
THAT HOUSE HAD PRETTY CAMEL-LIAS.
YEAH.
A NICE OLD WOMAN LIVED THERE.
SHE SOME-TIMES SNEAKED ME SOME SWEETS.
...
HOW DID I FORGET ALL THIS...?
I USED TO WALK THIS PATH...
ALL ALONE...
HEY, NATSUME.

04

❋Location scouting: part 2

(continued)

The designers kept scribbling things in their notebooks while they talked during the meeting. I was dying to take a peek, but I couldn't summon the courage to ask. I'm determined to ask the next time I get such an opportunity.

Actually, this location scouting was intended to serve a dual purpose. They're going to animate "Hotarubi no Mori e," my short story about Hotaru, a young girl who wanders into the mountain god's forest and meets Gin, a boy who lives there. The director and most of the staff are the same as those working on Natsume. I hope everyone will check it out, both people who liked the story and people who haven't read it yet.

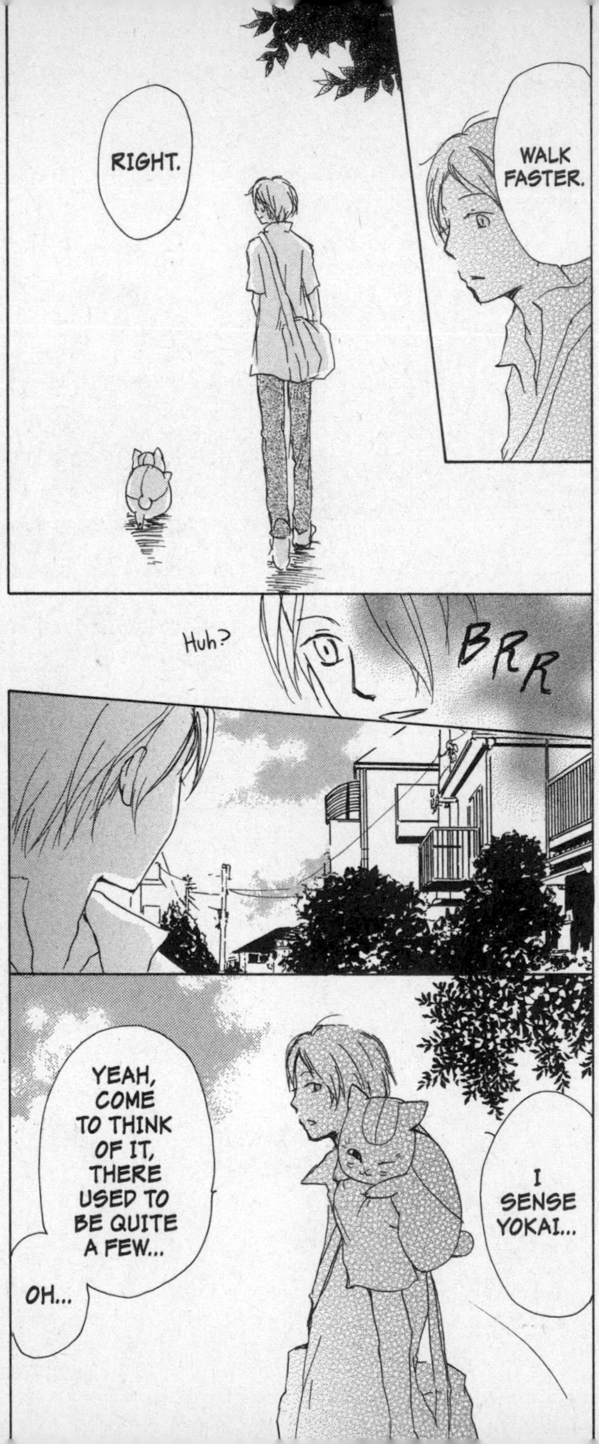
WALK FASTER.
RIGHT.
Huh?
BRRR
I SENSE YOKAI...
YEAH, COME TO THINK OF IT, THERE USED TO BE QUITE A FEW...
OH...

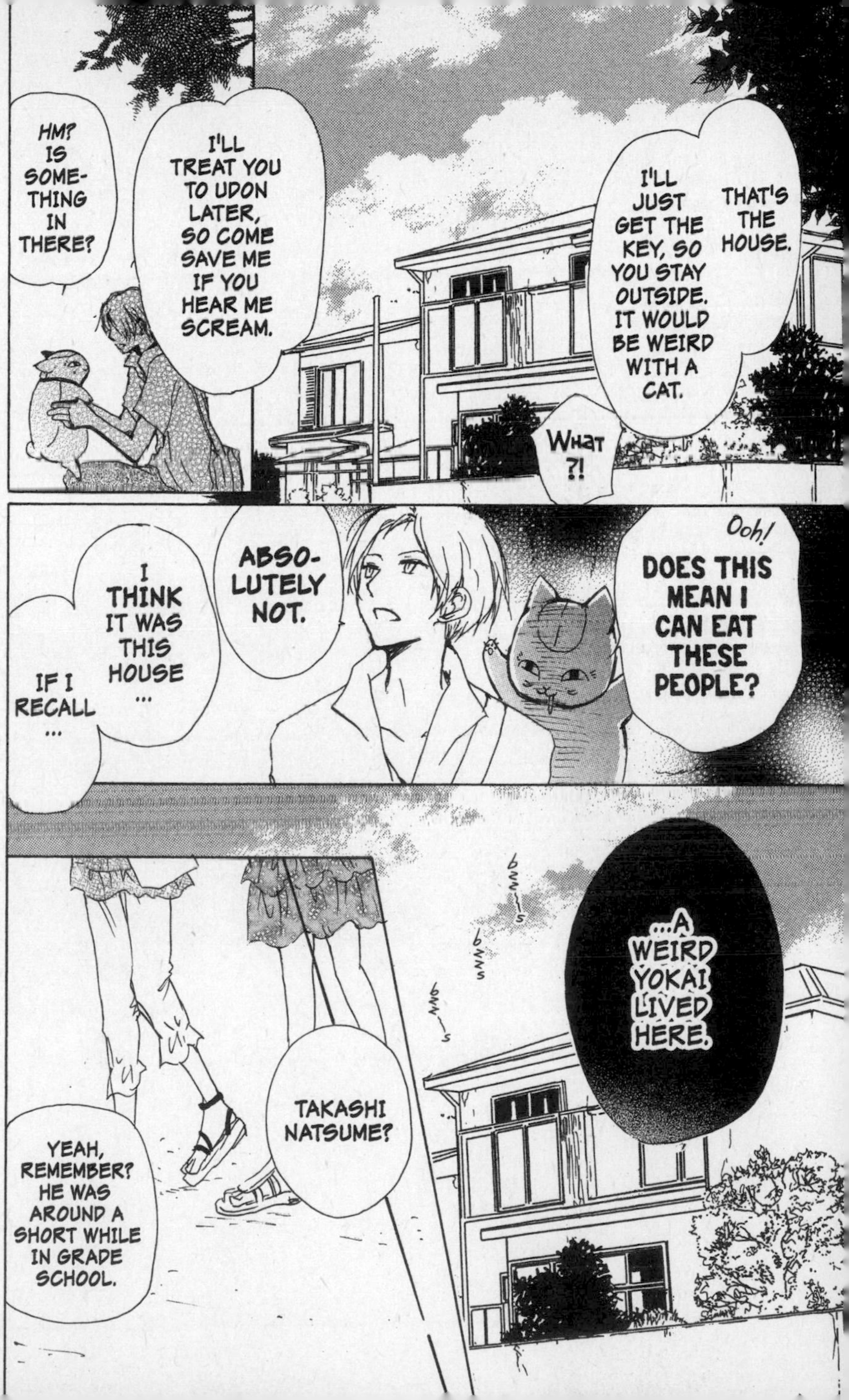
THAT'S THE HOUSE.
I'LL JUST GET THE KEY, SO YOU STAY OUTSIDE. IT WOULD BE WEIRD WITH A CAT.
WHAT?!
I'LL TREAT YOU TO UDON LATER, SO COME SAVE ME IF YOU HEAR ME SCREAM.
HM? IS SOME-THING IN THERE?
Ooh!
DOES THIS MEAN I CAN EAT THESE PEOPLE?
ABSO-LUTELY NOT.
I THINK IT WAS THIS HOUSE ...
IF I RECALL ...
...A WEIRD YOKAI LIVED HERE.
bzzzs
bzzs
bzzs
TAKASHI NATSUME?
YEAH, REMEMBER? HE WAS AROUND A SHORT WHILE IN GRADE SCHOOL.

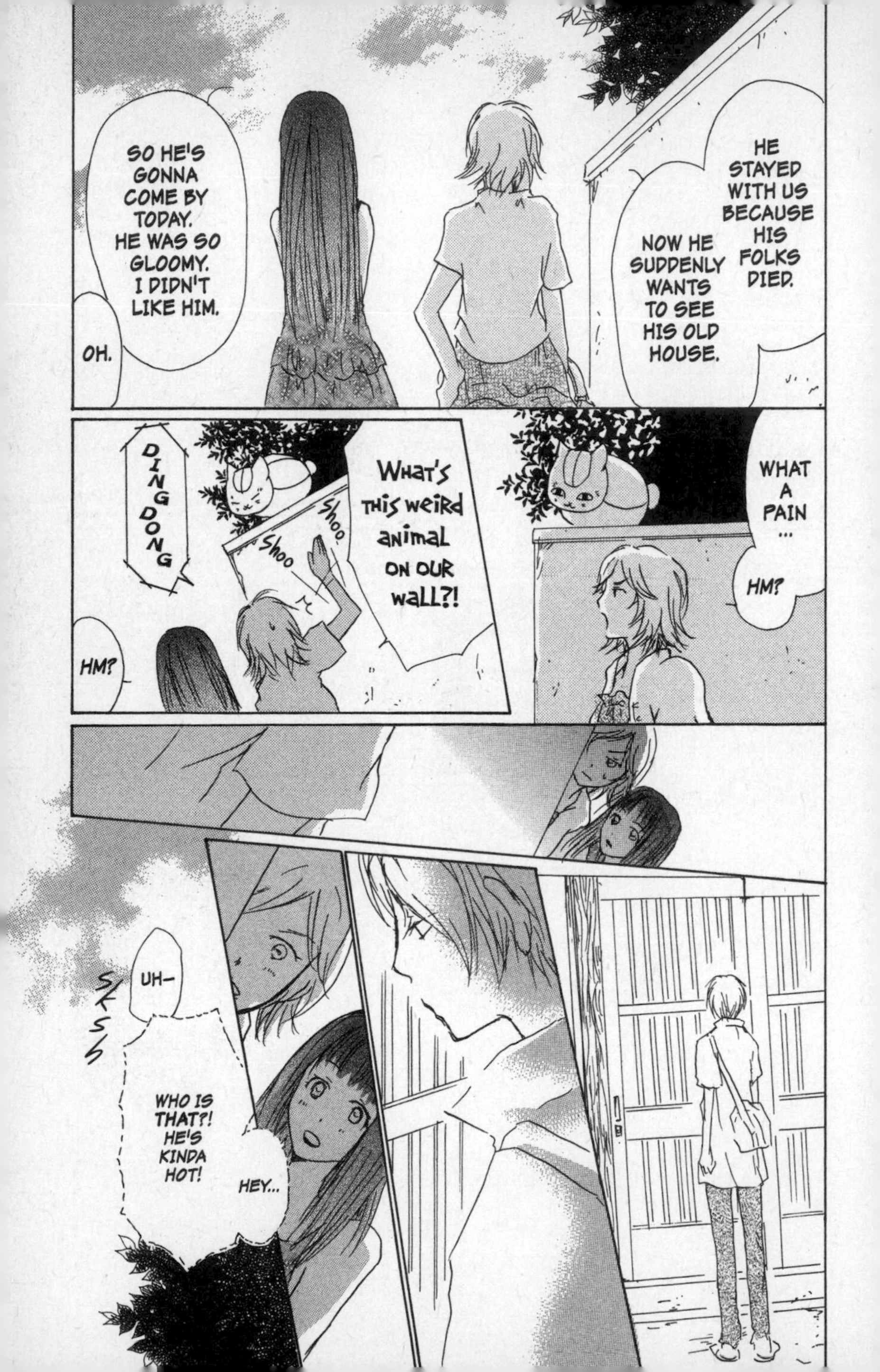
HE STAYED WITH US BECAUSE HIS FOLKS DIED.
NOW HE SUDDENLY WANTS TO SEE HIS OLD HOUSE.
SO HE'S GONNA COME BY TODAY. HE WAS SO GLOOMY. I DIDN'T LIKE HIM.
OH.
WHAT A PAIN ...
HM?
What's this weird animal on our wall?!
Shoo
Shoo
DING DONG
HM?
UH-
SKSS
WHO IS THAT?! HE'S KINDA HOT!
HEY...

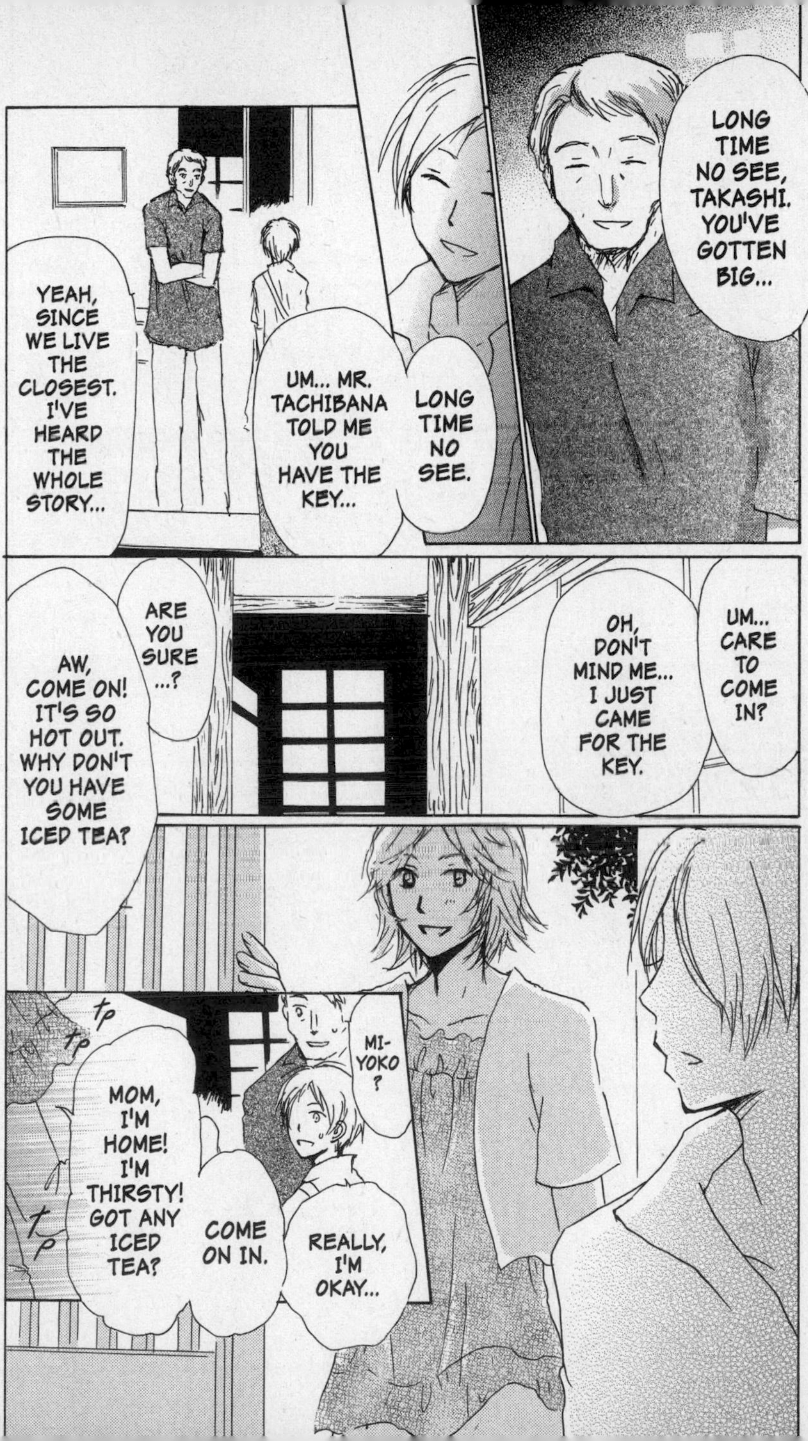
LONG TIME NO SEE, TAKASHI. YOU'VE GOTTEN BIG...
LONG TIME NO SEE.
UM... MR. TACHIBANA TOLD ME YOU HAVE THE KEY...
YEAH, SINCE WE LIVE THE CLOSEST. I'VE HEARD THE WHOLE STORY...
UM... CARE TO COME IN?
OH, DON'T MIND ME... I JUST CAME FOR THE KEY.
ARE YOU SURE ...?
AW, COME ON! IT'S SO HOT OUT. WHY DON'T YOU HAVE SOME ICED TEA?
REALLY, I'M OKAY...
COME ON IN.
tp tp tp
MOM, I'M HOME! I'M THIRSTY! GOT ANY ICED TEA?
MI-YOKO?

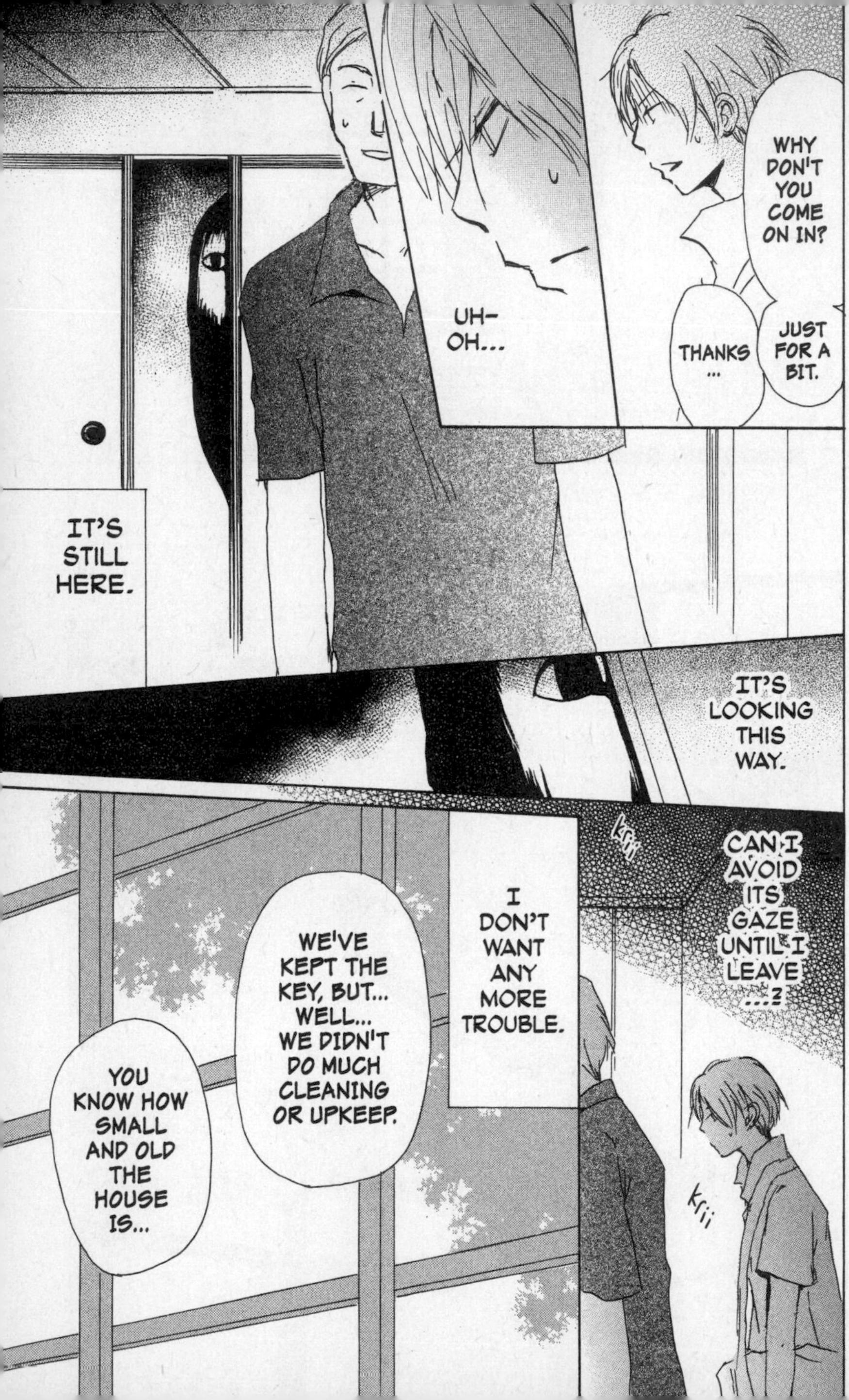
WHY DON'T YOU COME ON IN?
JUST FOR A BIT.
THANKS...
UH-OH...
IT'S STILL HERE.
IT'S LOOKING THIS WAY.
CAN I AVOID ITS GAZE UNTIL I LEAVE...?
krii
krii
I DON'T WANT ANY MORE TROUBLE.
WE'VE KEPT THE KEY, BUT... WELL... WE DIDN'T DO MUCH CLEANING OR UPKEEP.
YOU KNOW HOW SMALL AND OLD THE HOUSE IS...

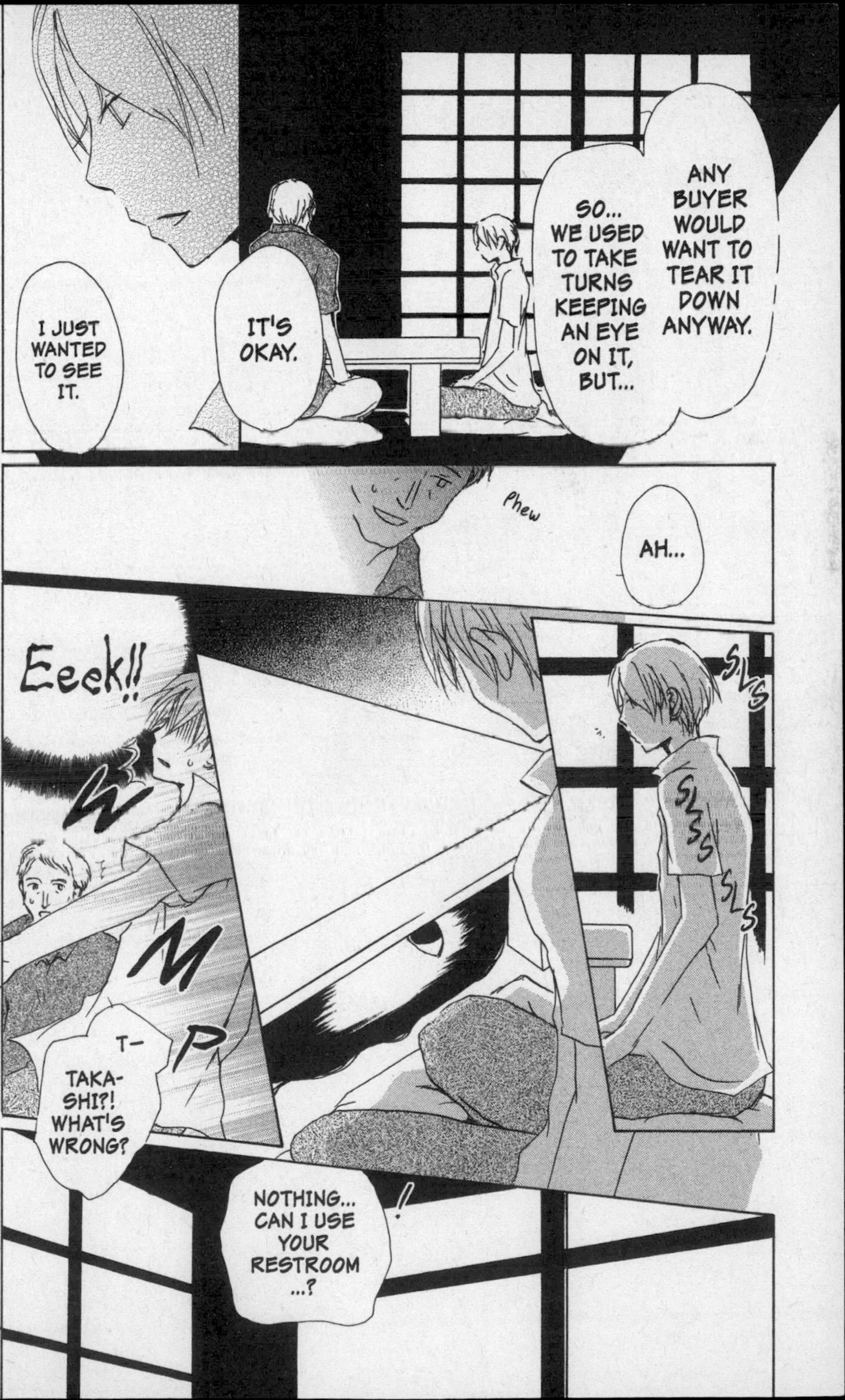
ANY BUYER WOULD WANT TO TEAR IT DOWN ANYWAY.
SO... WE USED TO TAKE TURNS KEEPING AN EYE ON IT, BUT...
IT'S OKAY.
I JUST WANTED TO SEE IT.
AH...
Phew
SLS
SLSSS
SLS
Eeek!!
WMP
T- TAKA-SHI?! WHAT'S WRONG?
!
NOTHING... CAN I USE YOUR RESTROOM ...?

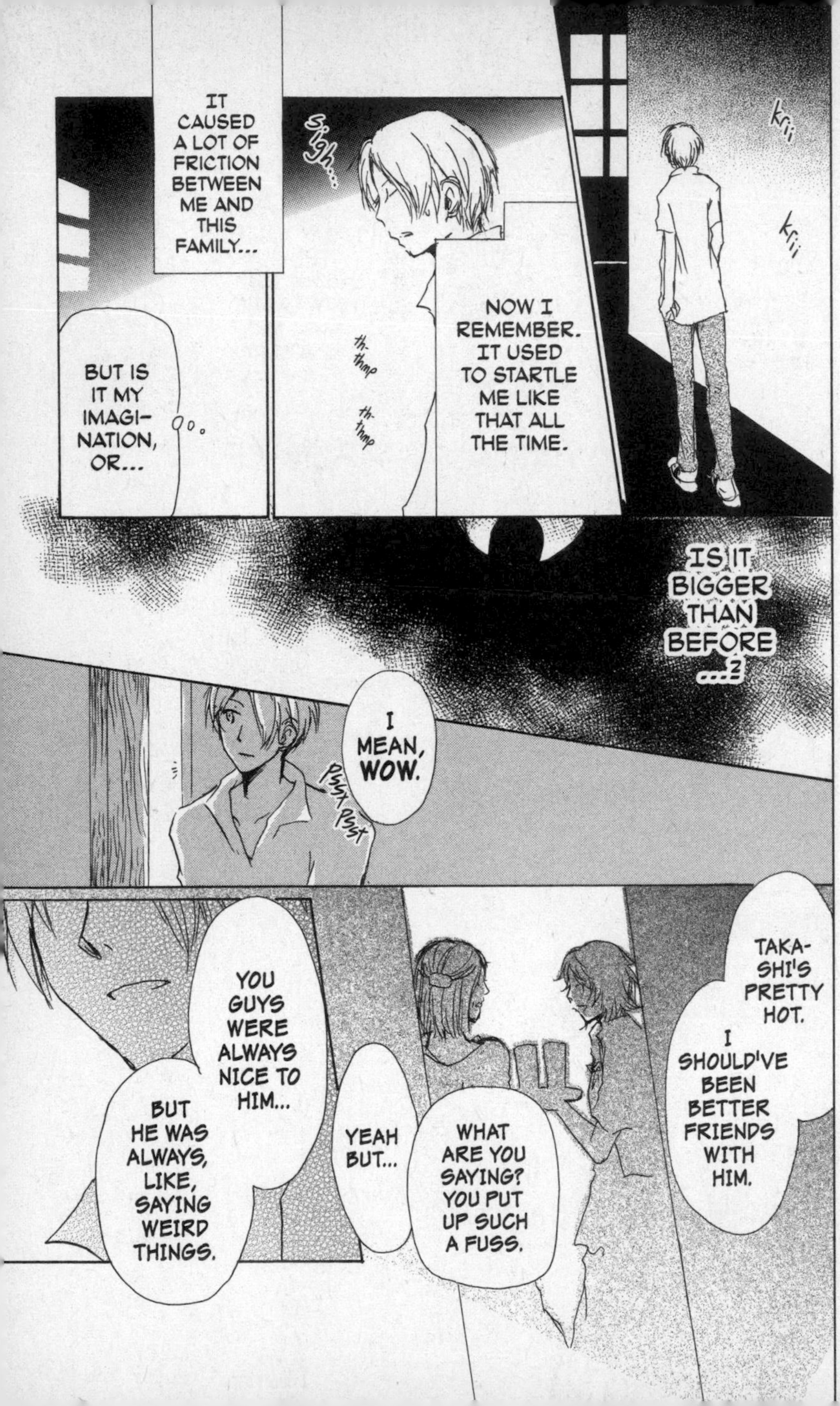
krii
krii
IT CAUSED A LOT OF FRICTION BETWEEN ME AND THIS FAMILY...
sigh...
NOW I REMEMBER. IT USED TO STARTLE ME LIKE THAT ALL THE TIME.
th-thmp
th-thmp
BUT IS IT MY IMAGINATION, OR...
IS IT BIGGER THAN BEFORE...?
I MEAN, **WOW.**
Pssst Pssst
TAKASHI'S PRETTY HOT.
I SHOULD'VE BEEN BETTER FRIENDS WITH HIM.
WHAT ARE YOU SAYING? YOU PUT UP SUCH A FUSS.
YEAH BUT...
YOU GUYS WERE ALWAYS NICE TO HIM...
BUT HE WAS ALWAYS, LIKE, SAYING WEIRD THINGS.

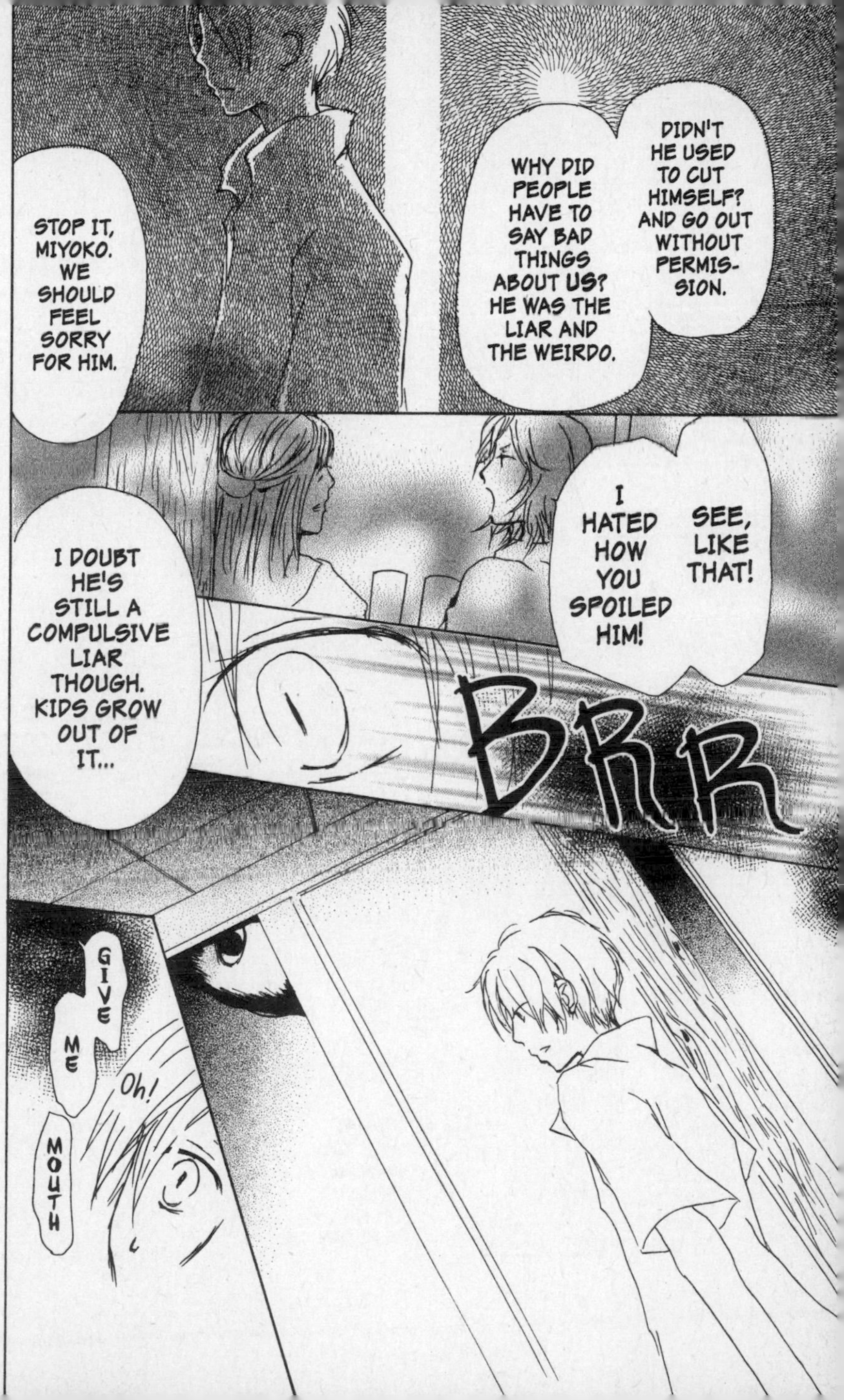
DIDN'T HE USED TO CUT HIMSELF? AND GO OUT WITHOUT PERMIS-SION.
WHY DID PEOPLE HAVE TO SAY BAD THINGS ABOUT US? HE WAS THE LIAR AND THE WEIRDO.
STOP IT, MIYOKO. WE SHOULD FEEL SORRY FOR HIM.
SEE, LIKE THAT!
I HATED HOW YOU SPOILED HIM!
I DOUBT HE'S STILL A COMPULSIVE LIAR THOUGH. KIDS GROW OUT OF IT...
BRR
GIVE ME MOUTH
Oh!

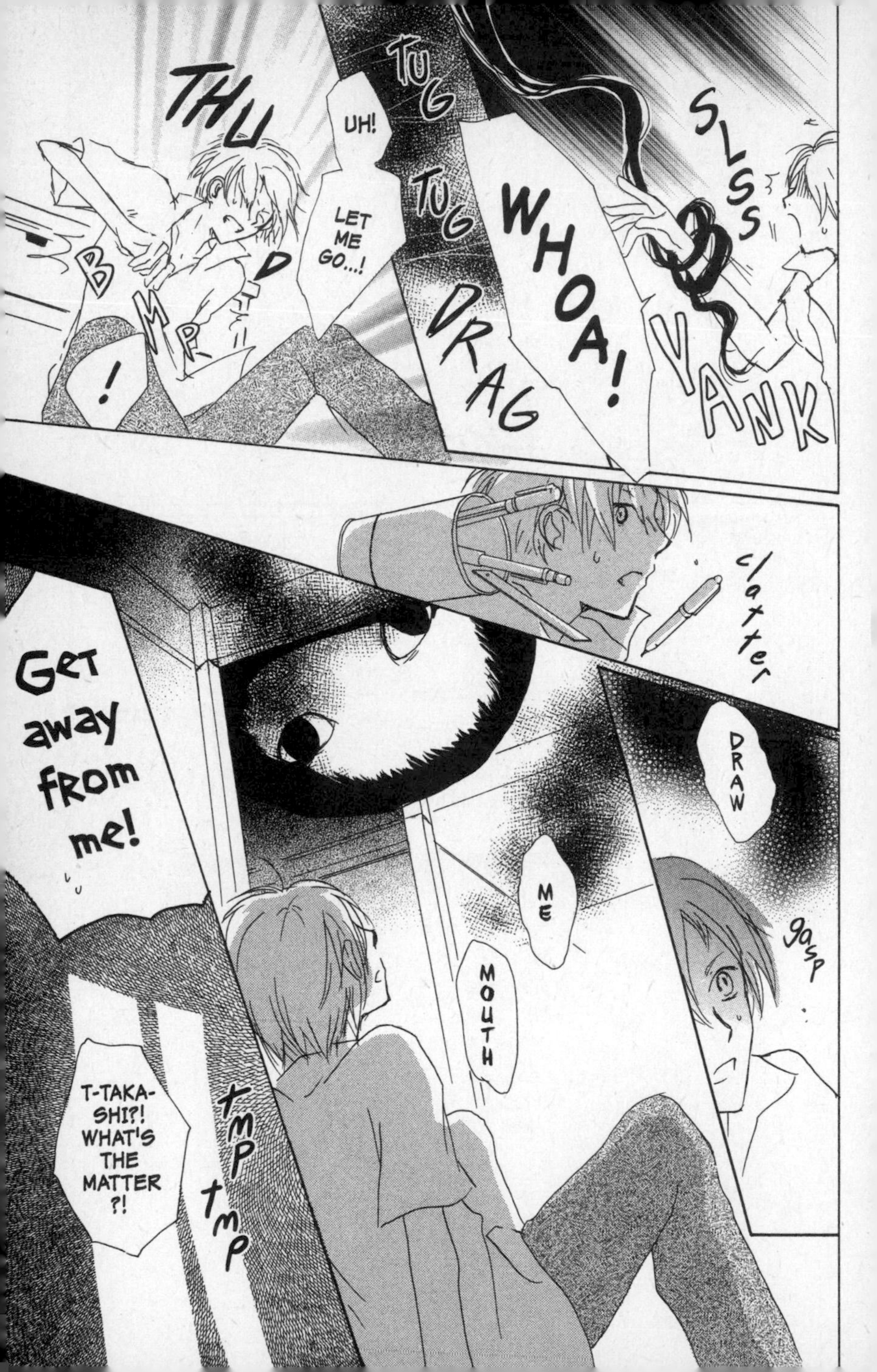
SLSS
YANK
WHOA!
DRAG
TUG TUG
LET ME GO...!
UH!
THUD
BUMP
!
clatter
DRAW
gasp
ME
MOUTH
Get away from me!
tmp tmp
T-TAKASHI?! WHAT'S THE MATTER?!

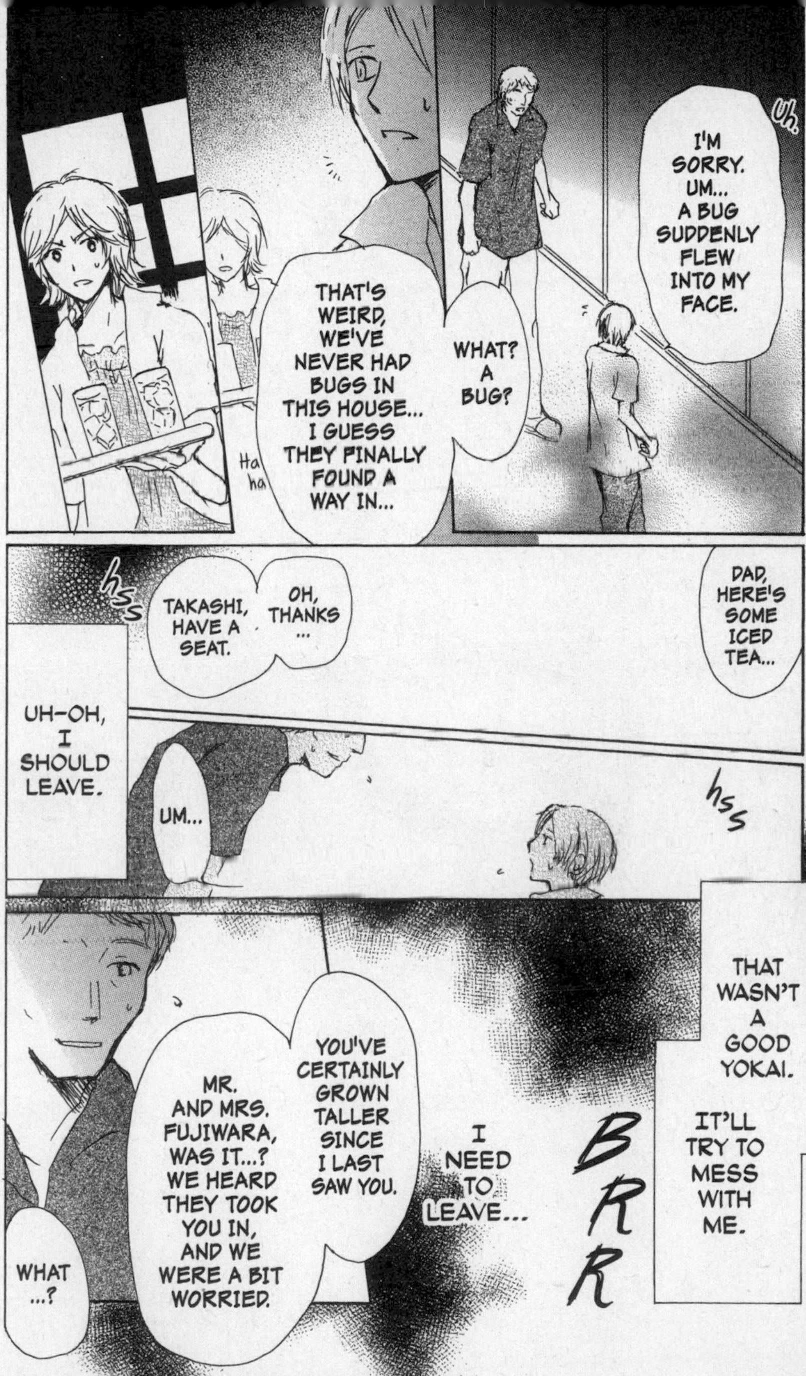
Uh.
I'M SORRY. UM... A BUG SUDDENLY FLEW INTO MY FACE.
WHAT? A BUG?
THAT'S WEIRD, WE'VE NEVER HAD BUGS IN THIS HOUSE... I GUESS THEY FINALLY FOUND A WAY IN...
Ha ha
DAD, HERE'S SOME ICED TEA...
OH, THANKS ...
TAKASHI, HAVE A SEAT.
hss
hss
UM...
UH-OH, I SHOULD LEAVE.
THAT WASN'T A GOOD YOKAI.
IT'LL TRY TO MESS WITH ME.
BRR
I NEED TO LEAVE...
YOU'VE CERTAINLY GROWN TALLER SINCE I LAST SAW YOU.
MR. AND MRS. FUJIWARA, WAS IT...? WE HEARD THEY TOOK YOU IN, AND WE WERE A BIT WORRIED.
WHAT ...?

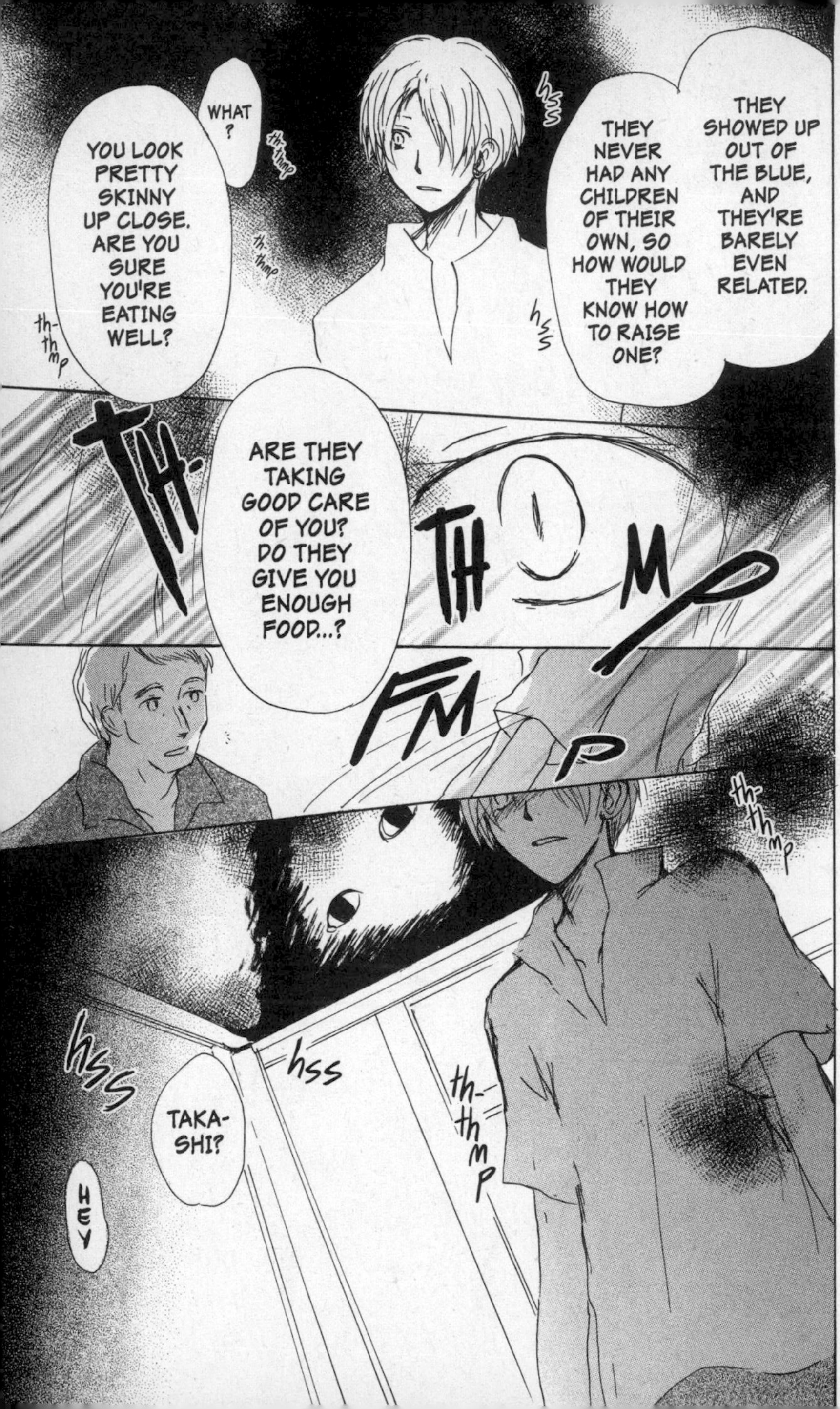
THEY SHOWED UP OUT OF THE BLUE, AND THEY'RE BARELY EVEN RELATED.
THEY NEVER HAD ANY CHILDREN OF THEIR OWN, SO HOW WOULD THEY KNOW HOW TO RAISE ONE?
hss
hss
WHAT?
th-thmp
th-thmp
YOU LOOK PRETTY SKINNY UP CLOSE. ARE YOU SURE YOU'RE EATING WELL?
th-thmp
TH-THUMP
ARE THEY TAKING GOOD CARE OF YOU? DO THEY GIVE YOU ENOUGH FOOD...?
TH-
FMP
th-thmp
th-thmp
hss
TAKASHI?
hss
HEY

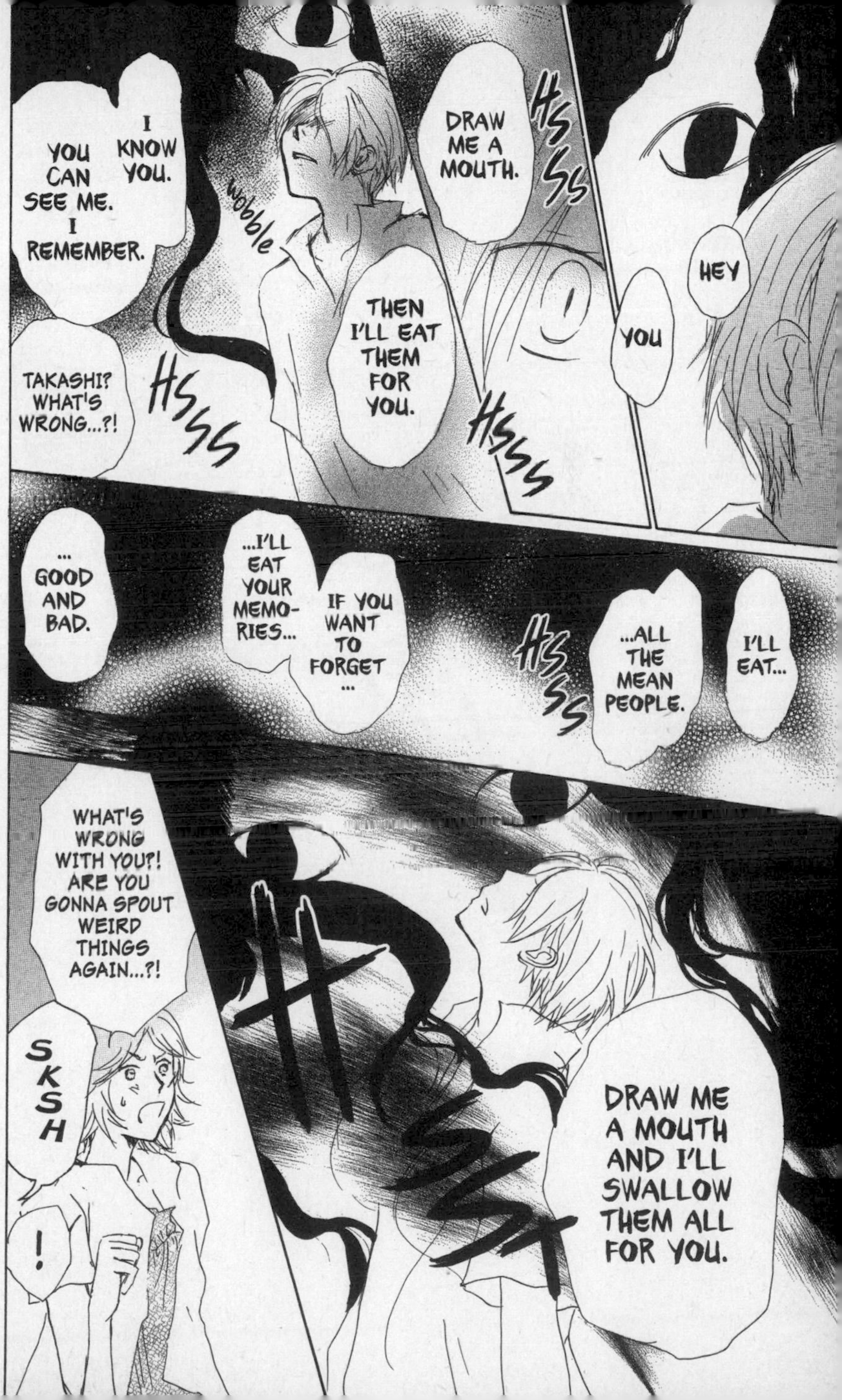
HEY
YOU
DRAW ME A MOUTH.
HSSS
HSSS
I KNOW YOU. YOU CAN SEE ME. I REMEMBER.
wobble
THEN I'LL EAT THEM FOR YOU.
HSSS
TAKASHI? WHAT'S WRONG...?!
I'LL EAT...
...ALL THE MEAN PEOPLE.
HSSS
IF YOU WANT TO FORGET...
...I'LL EAT YOUR MEMORIES...
... GOOD AND BAD.
DRAW ME A MOUTH AND I'LL SWALLOW THEM ALL FOR YOU.
HSSST
WHAT'S WRONG WITH YOU?! ARE YOU GONNA SPOUT WEIRD THINGS AGAIN...?!
SKSH
!

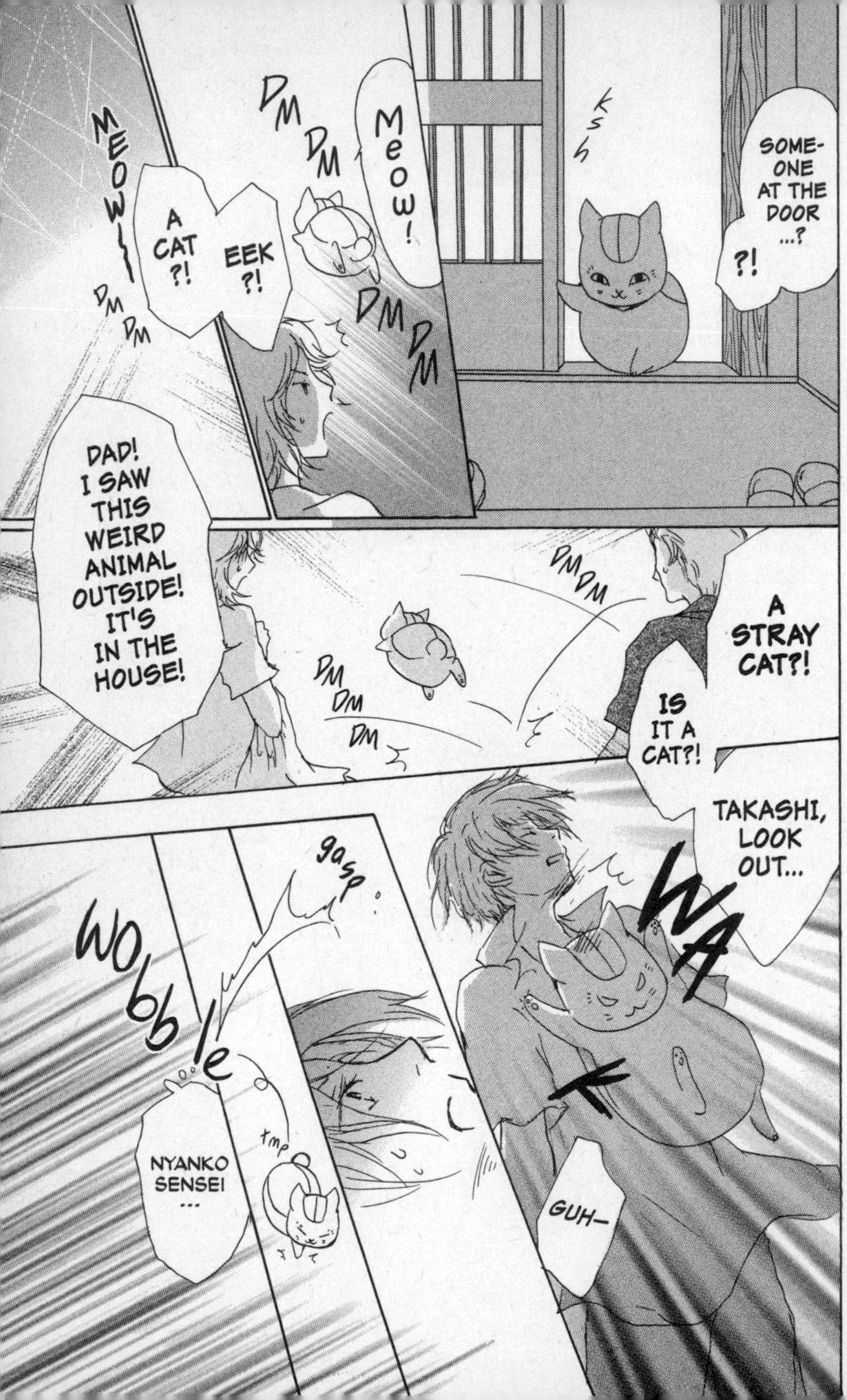
ksh
SOME-ONE AT THE DOOR ...?
?!
Meow!
DM DM DM DM DM
EEK ?!
A CAT ?!
MEOW~~
DM DM
A STRAY CAT?!
IS IT A CAT?!
DMDM
DM DM DM
DAD! I SAW THIS WEIRD ANIMAL OUTSIDE! IT'S IN THE HOUSE!
TAKASHI, LOOK OUT...
WAK
GUH–
gasp
wobble
NYANKO SENSEI ...
tmp

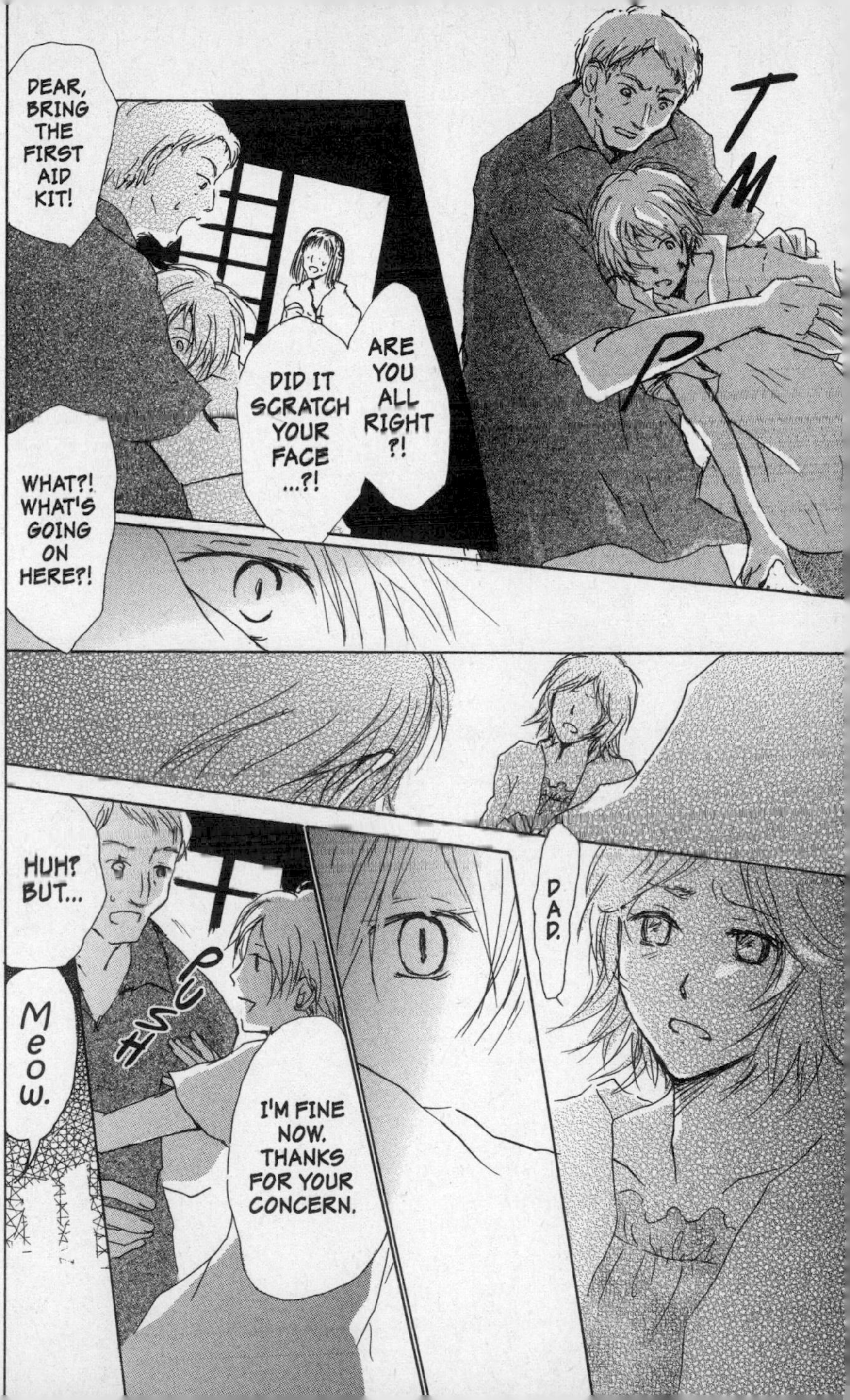
TMP
ARE YOU ALL RIGHT?!
DID IT SCRATCH YOUR FACE ...?!
DEAR, BRING THE FIRST AID KIT!
WHAT?! WHAT'S GOING ON HERE?!
DAD.
I'M FINE NOW. THANKS FOR YOUR CONCERN.
PUSH
HUH? BUT...
Meow.

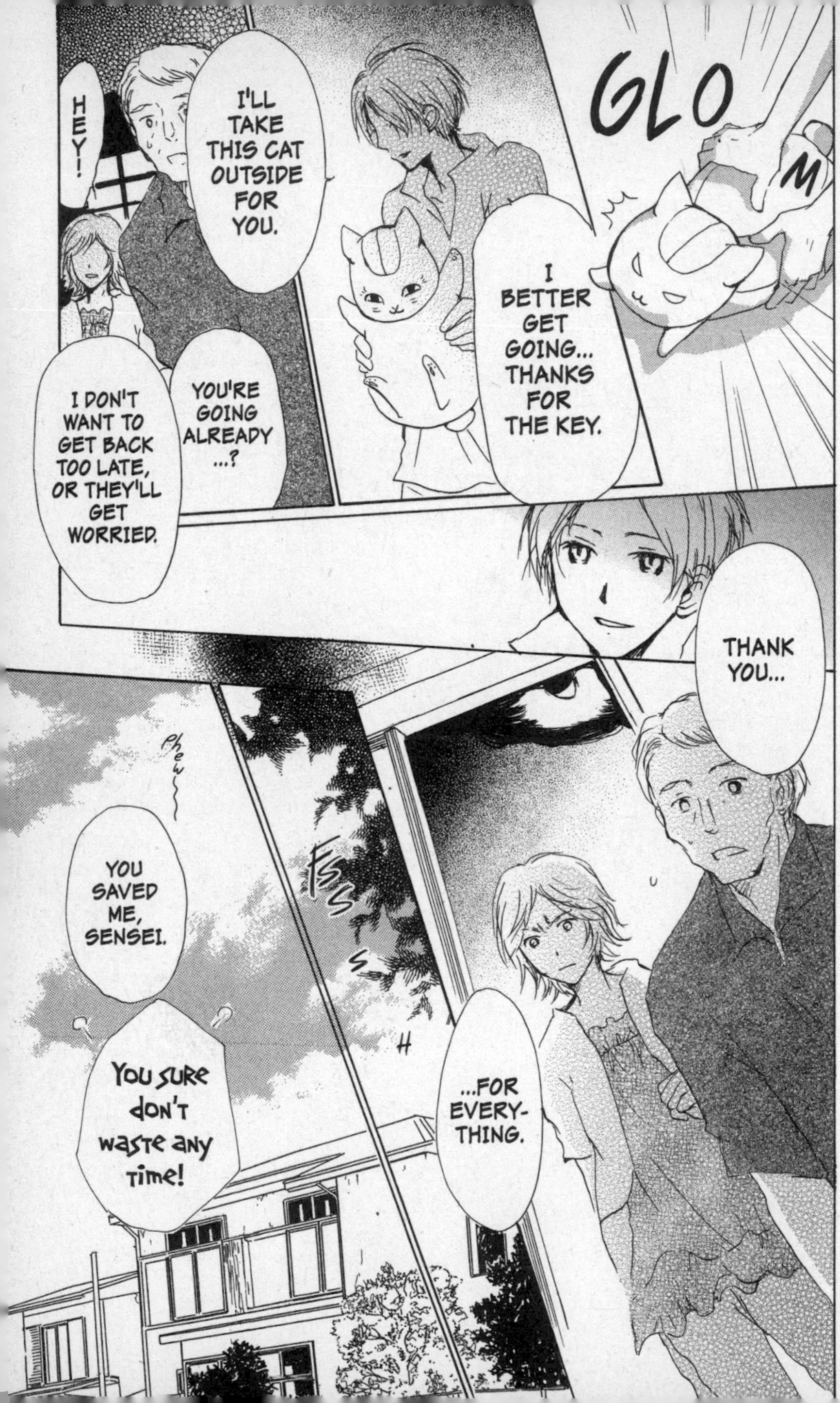
GLOM
I'LL TAKE THIS CAT OUTSIDE FOR YOU.
HEY!
I BETTER GET GOING... THANKS FOR THE KEY.
YOU'RE GOING ALREADY ...?
I DON'T WANT TO GET BACK TOO LATE, OR THEY'LL GET WORRIED.
THANK YOU...
...FOR EVERYTHING.
FSSSH
Phew~
YOU SAVED ME, SENSEI.
You sure don't waste any time!

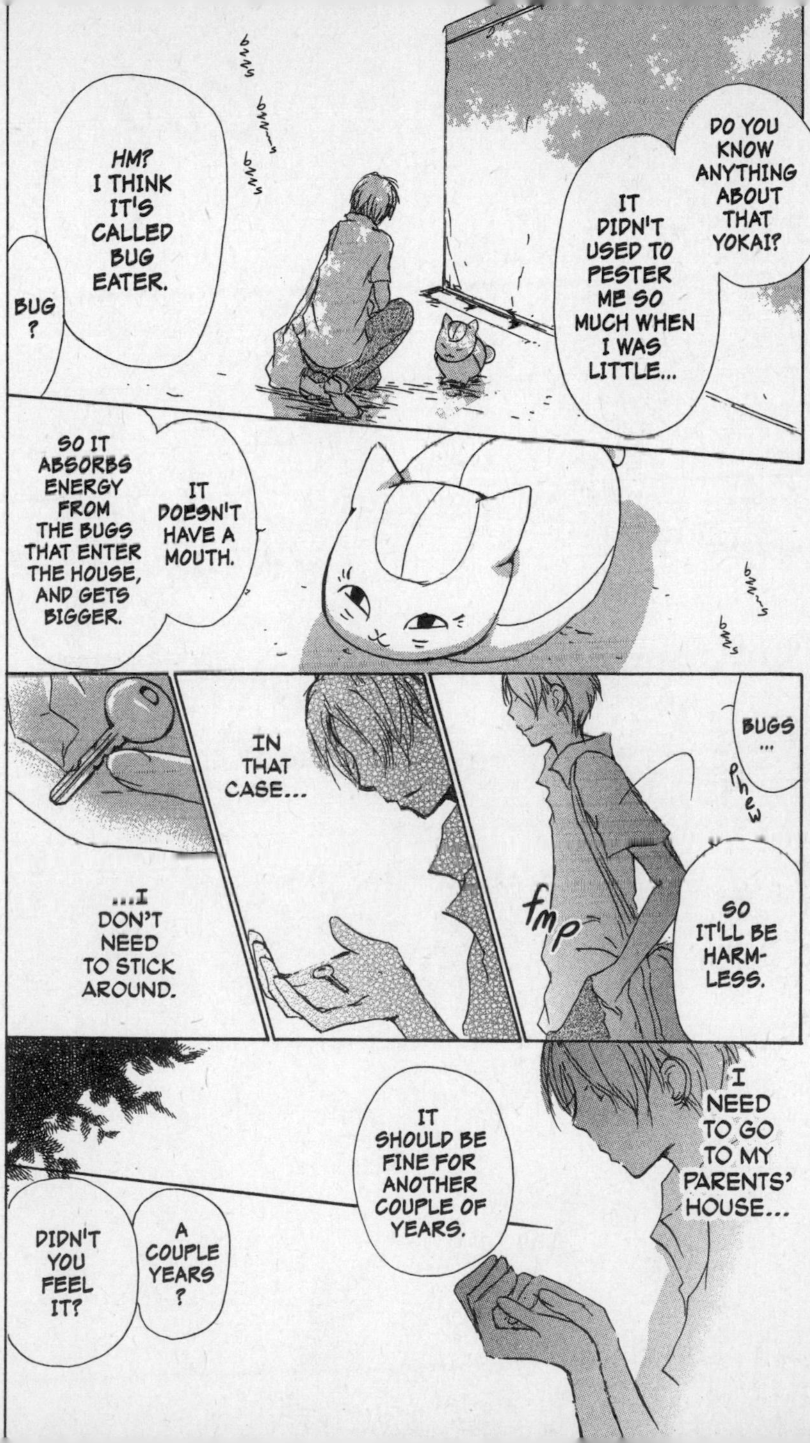
DO YOU KNOW ANYTHING ABOUT THAT YOKAI?
IT DIDN'T USED TO PESTER ME SO MUCH WHEN I WAS LITTLE...
bzzs
bzzs
bzzs
HM? I THINK IT'S CALLED BUG EATER.
BUG?
bzzs
bzzs
IT DOESN'T HAVE A MOUTH.
SO IT ABSORBS ENERGY FROM THE BUGS THAT ENTER THE HOUSE, AND GETS BIGGER.
BUGS...
phew
SO IT'LL BE HARMLESS.
fmp
IN THAT CASE...
...I DON'T NEED TO STICK AROUND.
I NEED TO GO TO MY PARENTS' HOUSE...
IT SHOULD BE FINE FOR ANOTHER COUPLE OF YEARS.
A COUPLE YEARS?
DIDN'T YOU FEEL IT?

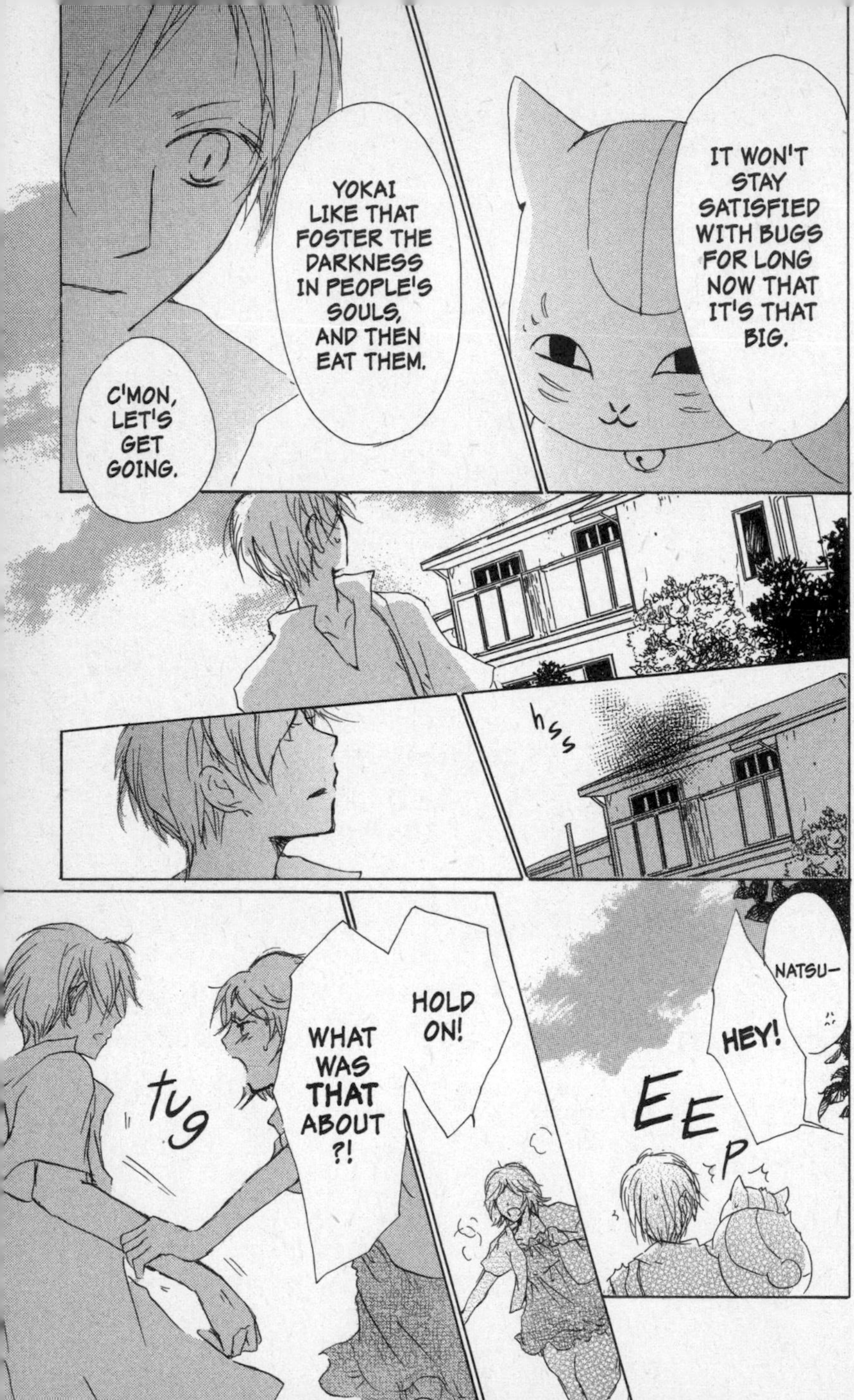
IT WON'T STAY SATISFIED WITH BUGS FOR LONG NOW THAT IT'S THAT BIG.
YOKAI LIKE THAT FOSTER THE DARKNESS IN PEOPLE'S SOULS, AND THEN EAT THEM.
C'MON, LET'S GET GOING.
hss
NATSU—
HEY!
EEP
HOLD ON!
WHAT WAS THAT ABOUT?!
tug

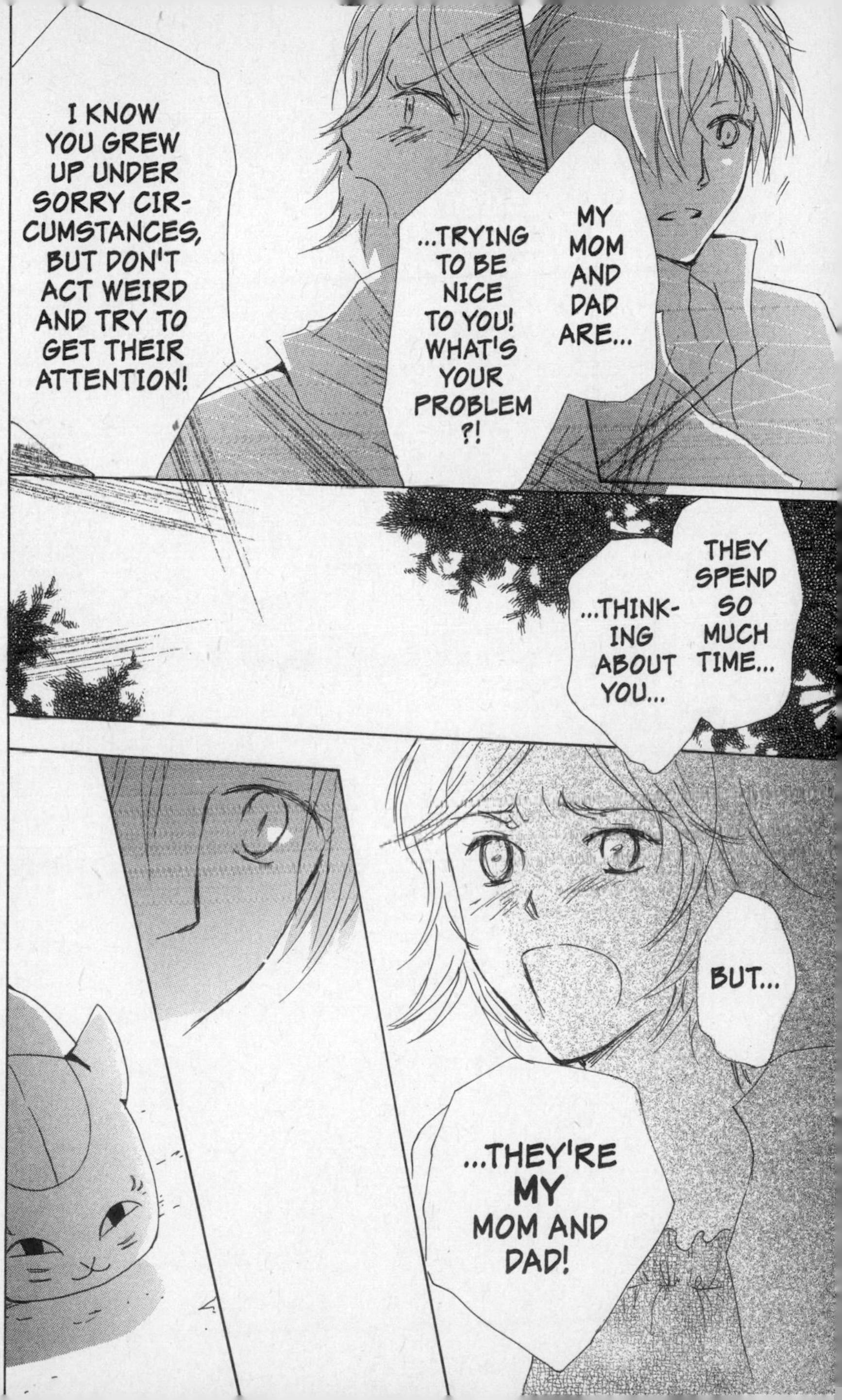
MY MOM AND DAD ARE...
...TRYING TO BE NICE TO YOU! WHAT'S YOUR PROBLEM?!
I KNOW YOU GREW UP UNDER SORRY CIR-CUMSTANCES, BUT DON'T ACT WEIRD AND TRY TO GET THEIR ATTENTION!
THEY SPEND SO MUCH TIME...
...THINK-ING ABOUT YOU...
BUT...
...THEY'RE **MY** MOM AND DAD!

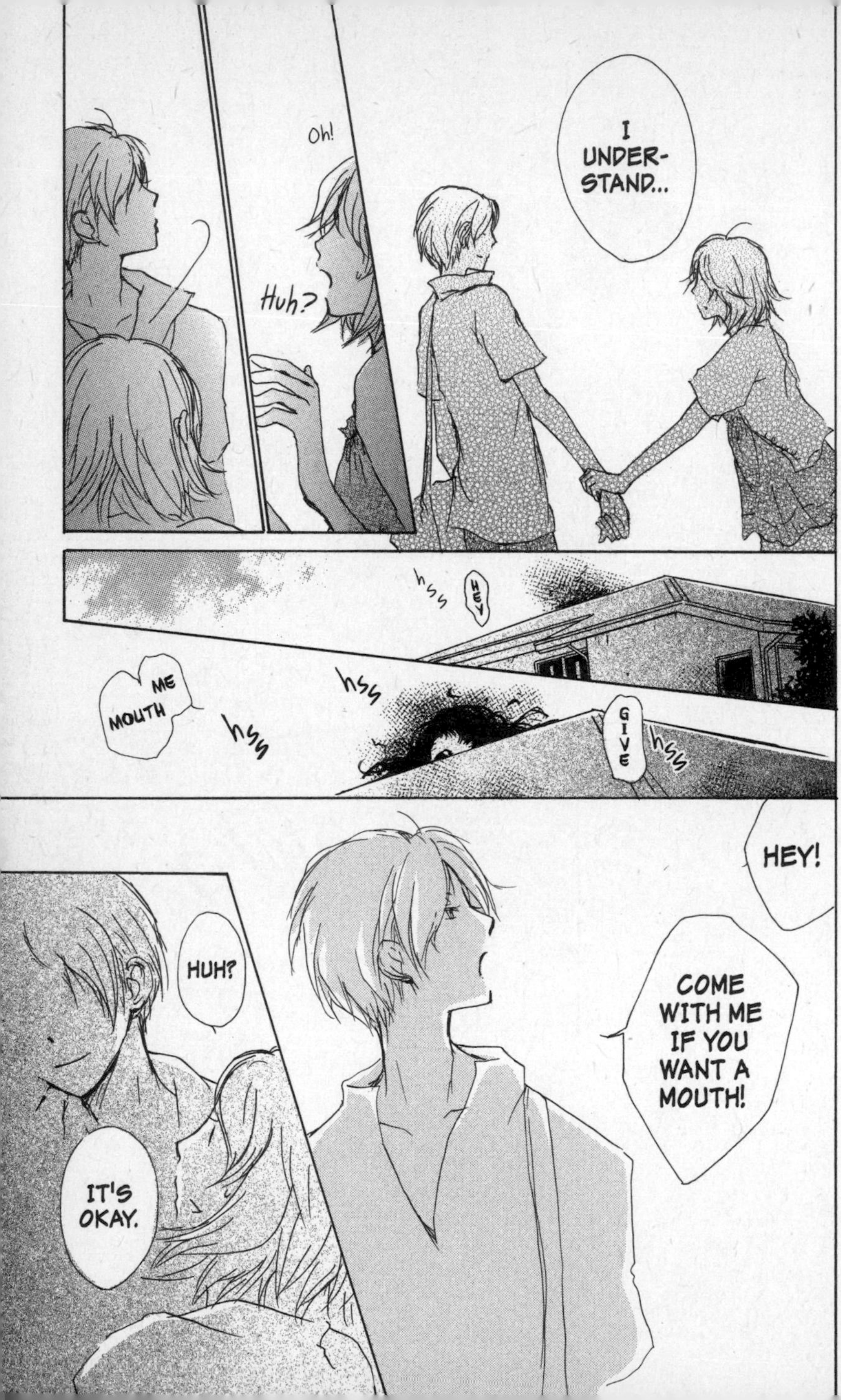
I UNDER-STAND...
Oh!
Huh?
HEY
hss
hss
GIVE
hss
ME MOUTH
hss
HEY!
COME WITH ME IF YOU WANT A MOUTH!
HUH?
IT'S OKAY.

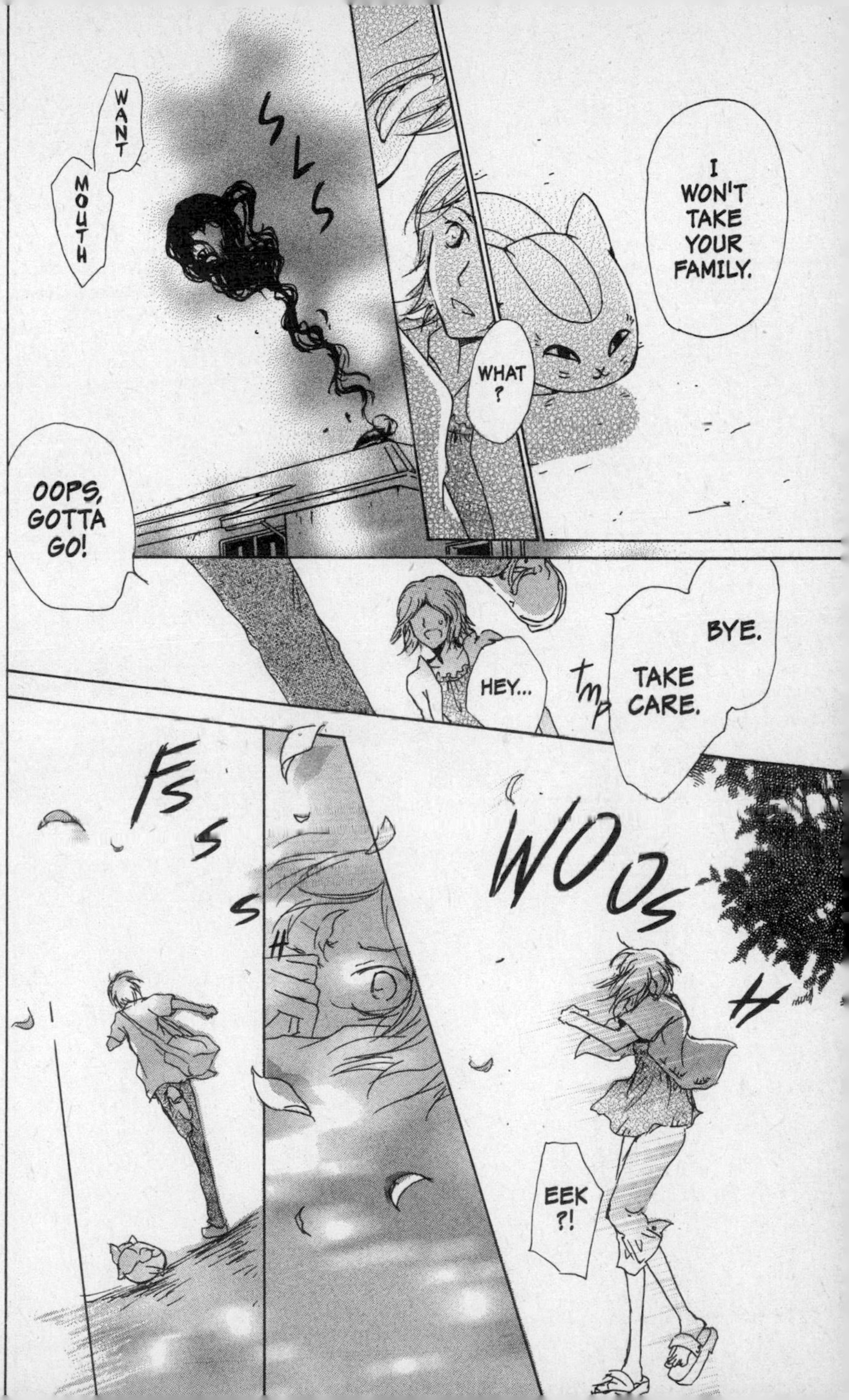
I WON'T TAKE YOUR FAMILY.
WHAT?
SLS
WANT
MOUTH
OOPS, GOTTA GO!
BYE.
TAKE CARE.
tmp
HEY...
WOOSH
EEK?!
FSSSH

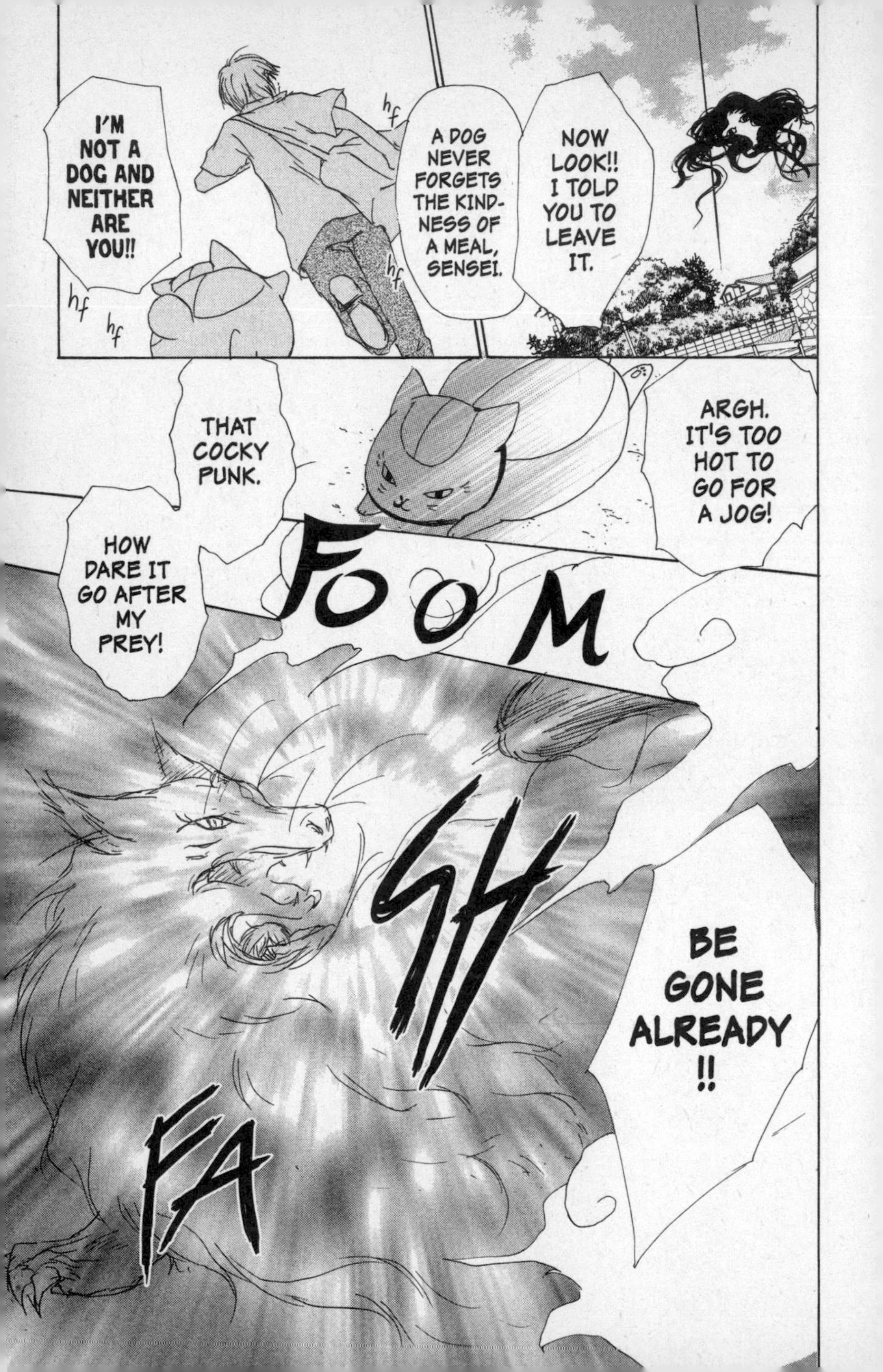
NOW LOOK!! I TOLD YOU TO LEAVE IT.
A DOG NEVER FORGETS THE KIND-NESS OF A MEAL, SENSEI.
hf
hf
I'M NOT A DOG AND NEITHER ARE YOU!!
hf
hf
ARGH. IT'S TOO HOT TO GO FOR A JOG!
THAT COCKY PUNK.
HOW DARE IT GO AFTER MY PREY!
FOOM
BE GONE ALREADY !!
SH
FA

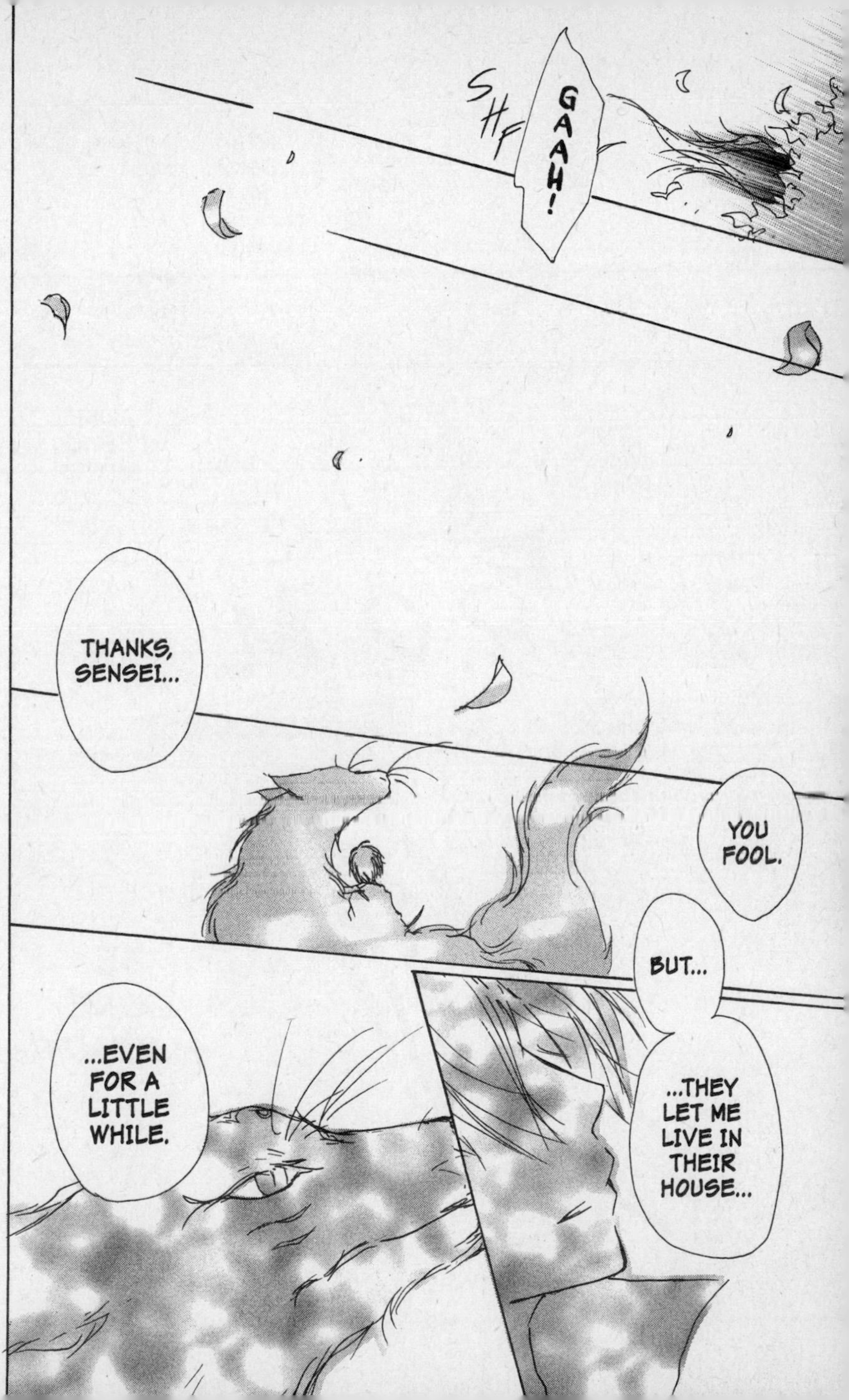
GAAH!
SHF
THANKS, SENSEI...
YOU FOOL.
BUT...
...THEY LET ME LIVE IN THEIR HOUSE...
...EVEN FOR A LITTLE WHILE.

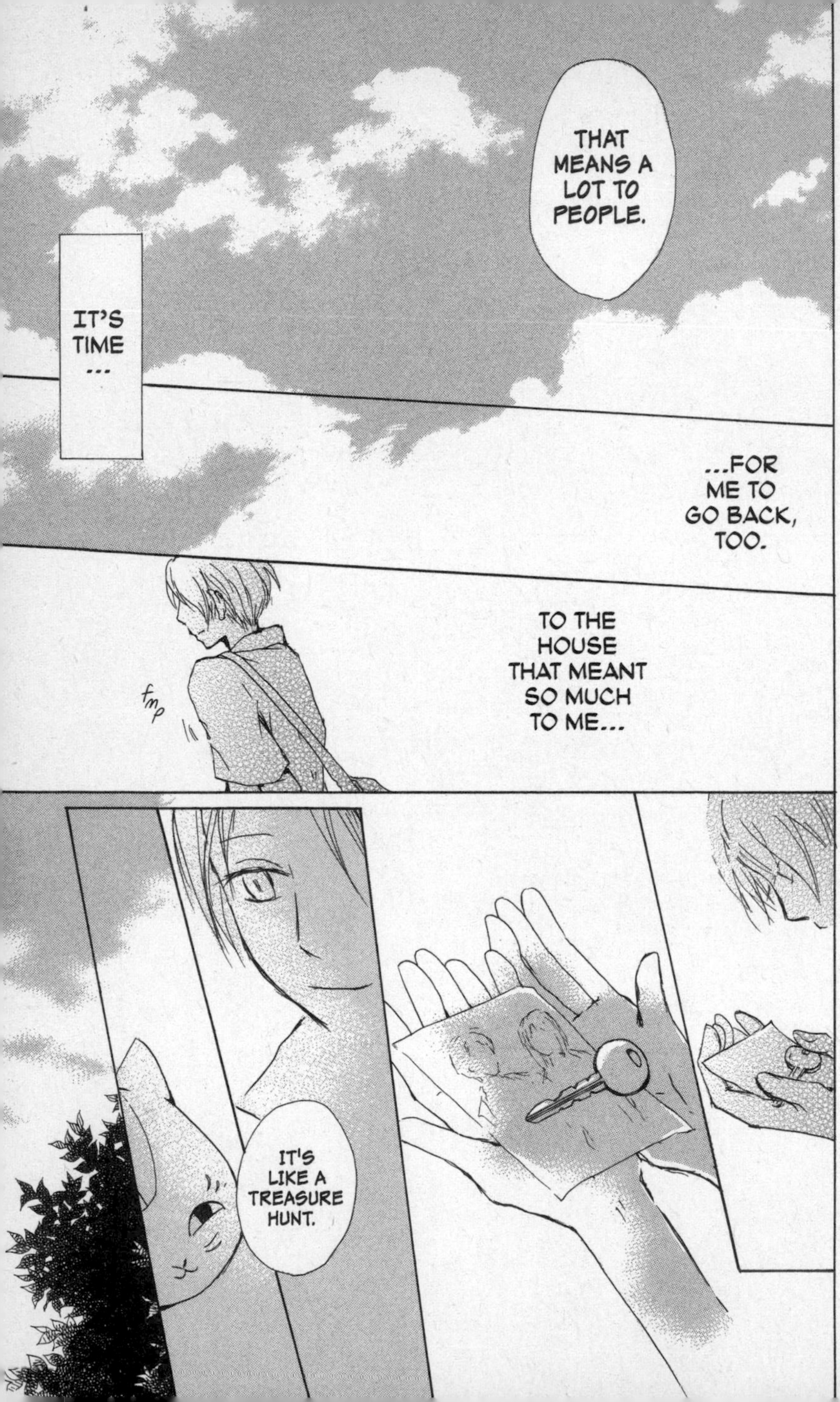
THAT MEANS A LOT TO PEOPLE.
IT'S TIME...
...FOR ME TO GO BACK, TOO.
TO THE HOUSE THAT MEANT SO MUCH TO ME...
fmp
IT'S LIKE A TREASURE HUNT.

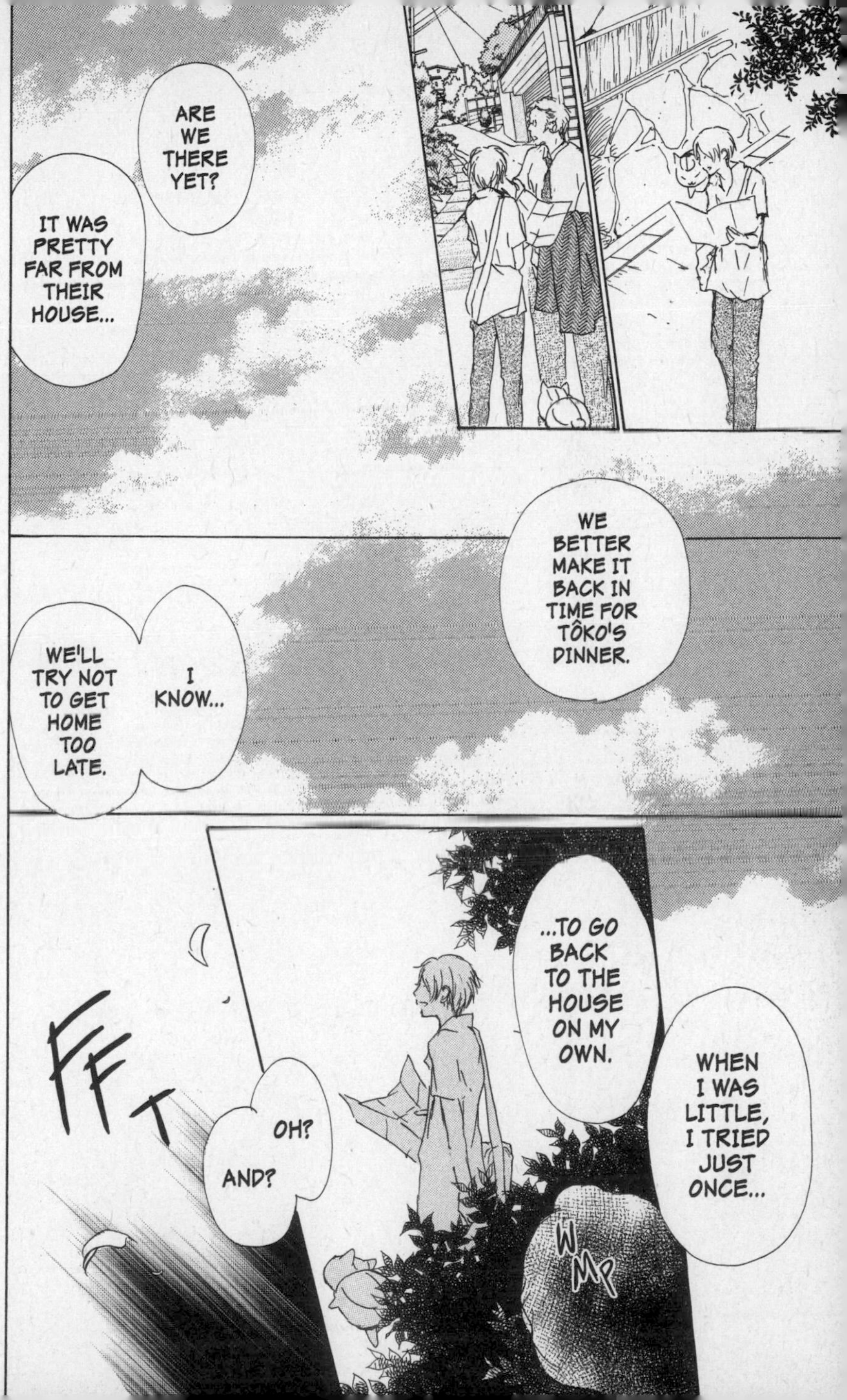
ARE WE THERE YET?
IT WAS PRETTY FAR FROM THEIR HOUSE...
WE BETTER MAKE IT BACK IN TIME FOR TÔKO'S DINNER.
I KNOW...
WE'LL TRY NOT TO GET HOME TOO LATE.
WHEN I WAS LITTLE, I TRIED JUST ONCE...
...TO GO BACK TO THE HOUSE ON MY OWN.
OH?
AND?
WMP
FFT

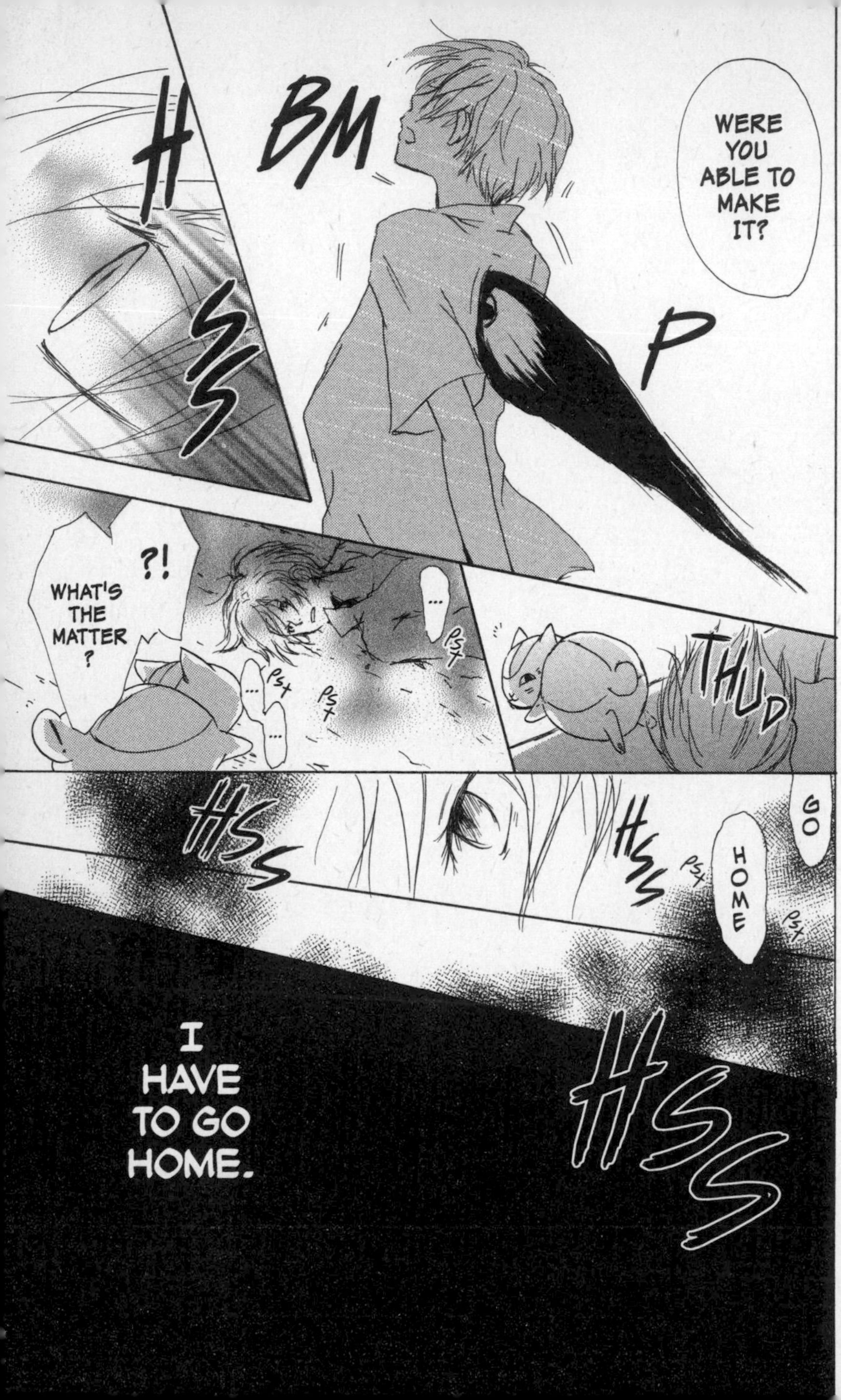
WERE YOU ABLE TO MAKE IT?
BM
P
HSS
THUD
PST
...
?!
WHAT'S THE MATTER ?
PST
...
PST
...
GO
HOME
PST
PST
HSS
HSS
HSS
I HAVE TO GO HOME.

Kaname Tanuma,
as a child

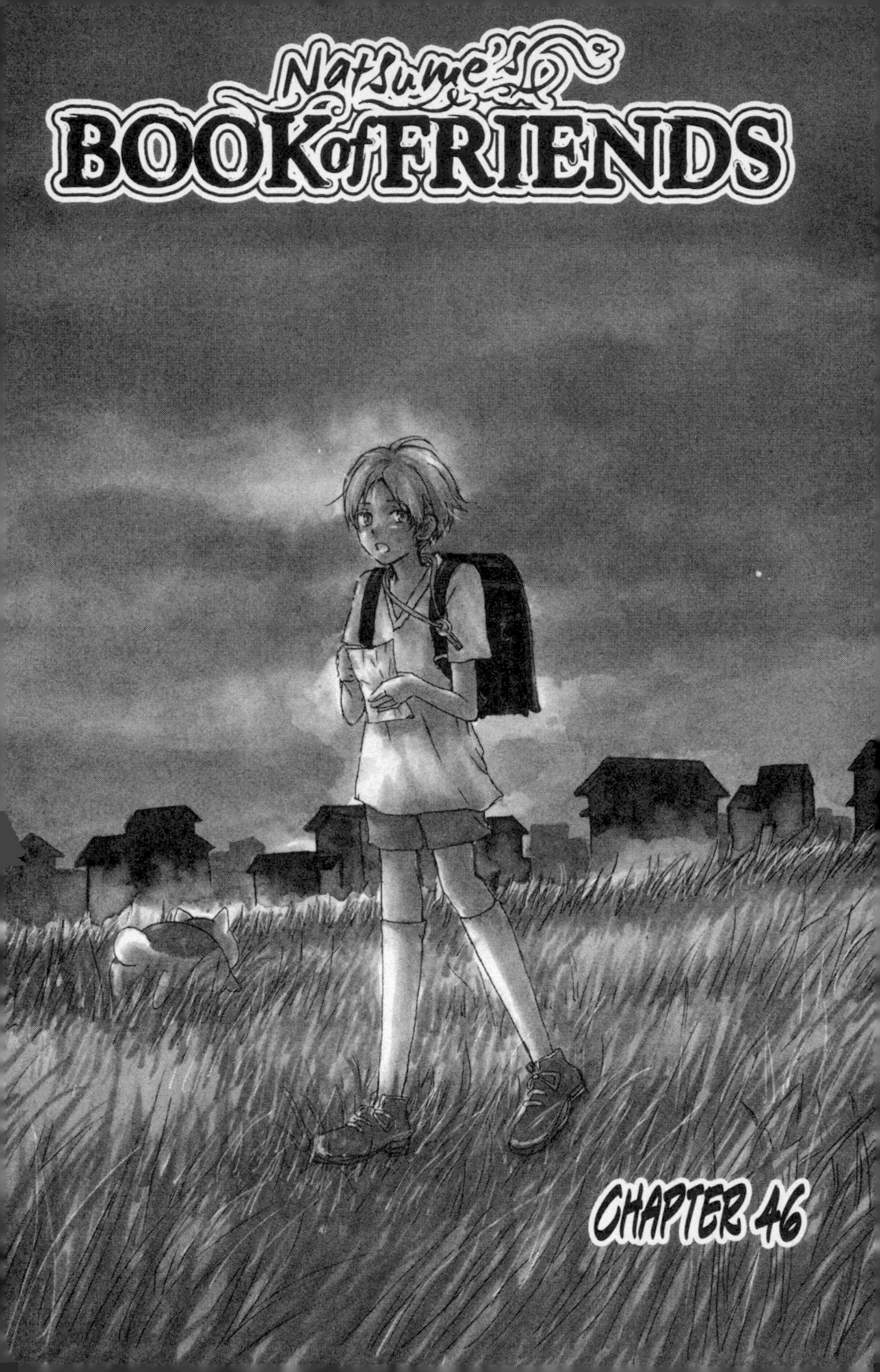
Natsume's
BOOK of FRIENDS
CHAPTER 46

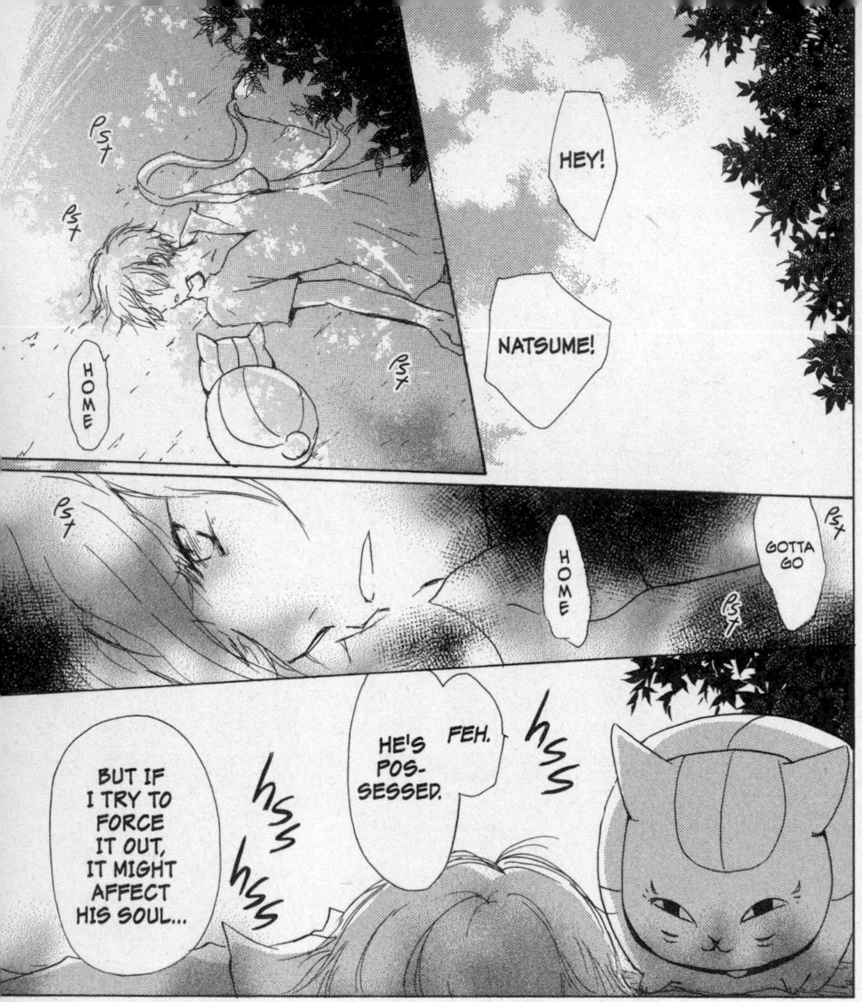
HEY!
NATSUME!
pst
pst
HOME
pst
pst
GOTTA GO
pst
HOME
pst
FEH.
HE'S POS-SESSED.
hss
hss
hss
BUT IF I TRY TO FORCE IT OUT, IT MIGHT AFFECT HIS SOUL...

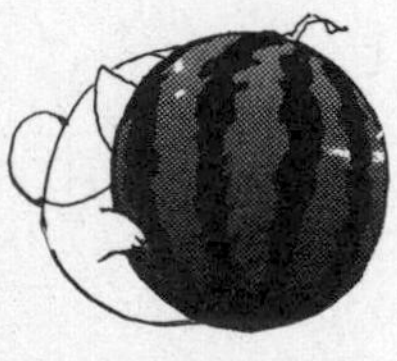

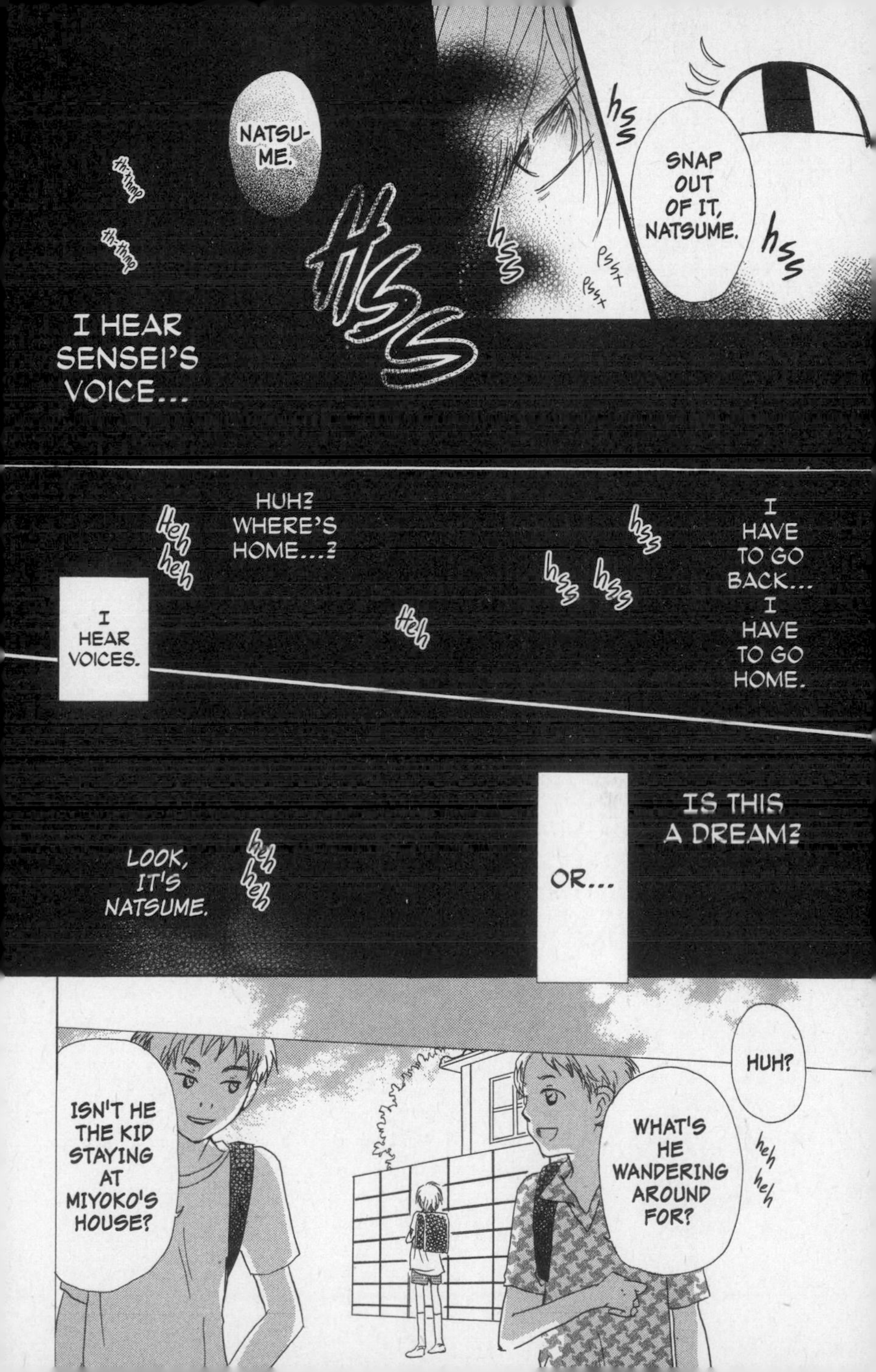
hss
SNAP OUT OF IT, NATSUME.
hss
pssx pssx
hss
NATSU-ME.
HSS
th-thump th-thump
I HEAR SENSEI'S VOICE...
I HAVE TO GO BACK... I HAVE TO GO HOME.
hss hss hss
Heh
HUH? WHERE'S HOME...?
Heh heh
I HEAR VOICES.
IS THIS A DREAM?
OR...
heh heh
LOOK, IT'S NATSUME.
HUH?
WHAT'S HE WANDERING AROUND FOR?
heh heh
ISN'T HE THE KID STAYING AT MIYOKO'S HOUSE?

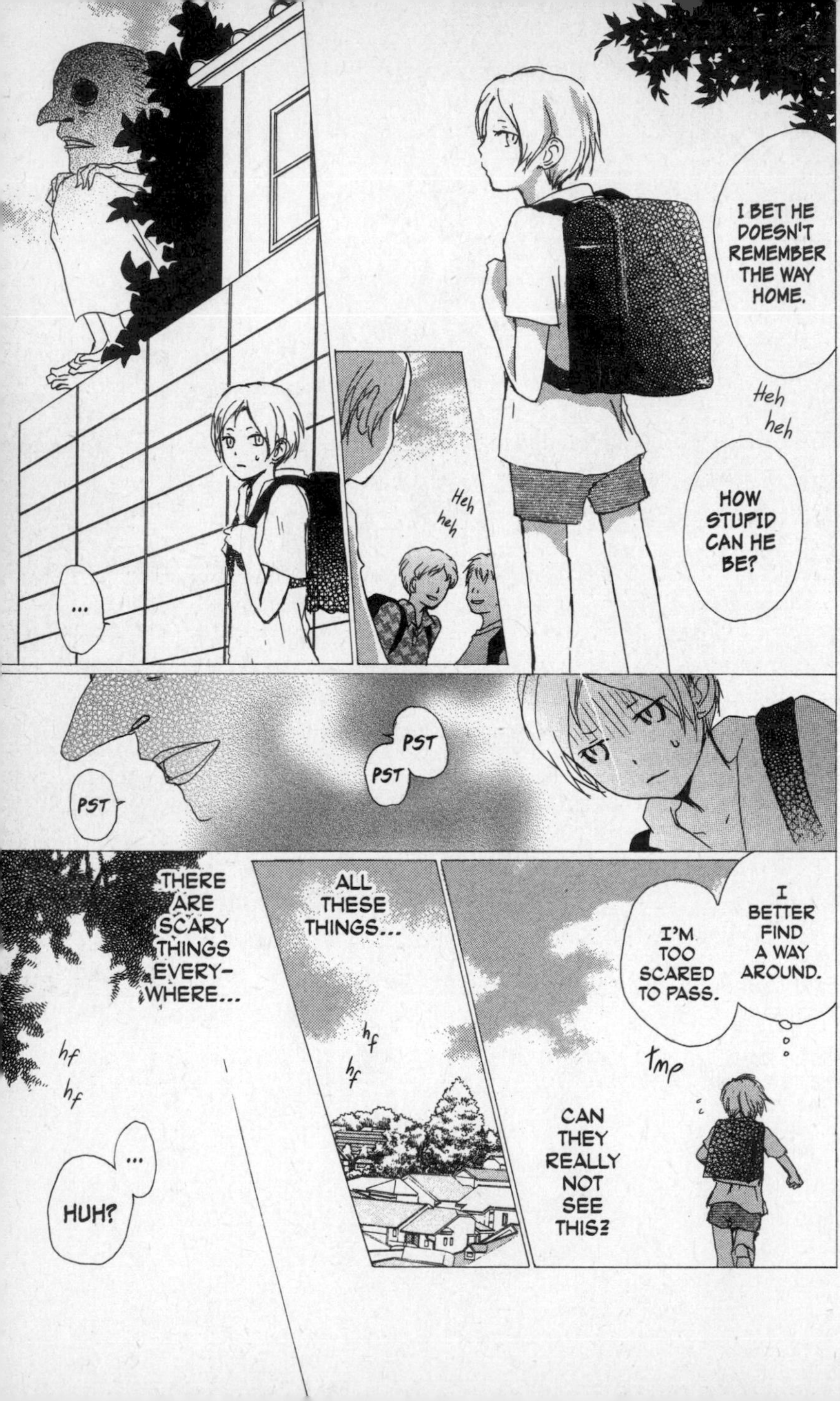
I BET HE DOESN'T REMEMBER THE WAY HOME.
Heh heh
HOW STUPID CAN HE BE?
Heh heh
...
PST
PST
PST
I BETTER FIND A WAY AROUND.
I'M TOO SCARED TO PASS.
tmp
CAN THEY REALLY NOT SEE THIS?
ALL THESE THINGS...
hf hf
THERE ARE SCARY THINGS EVERYWHERE...
hf hf
...
HUH?

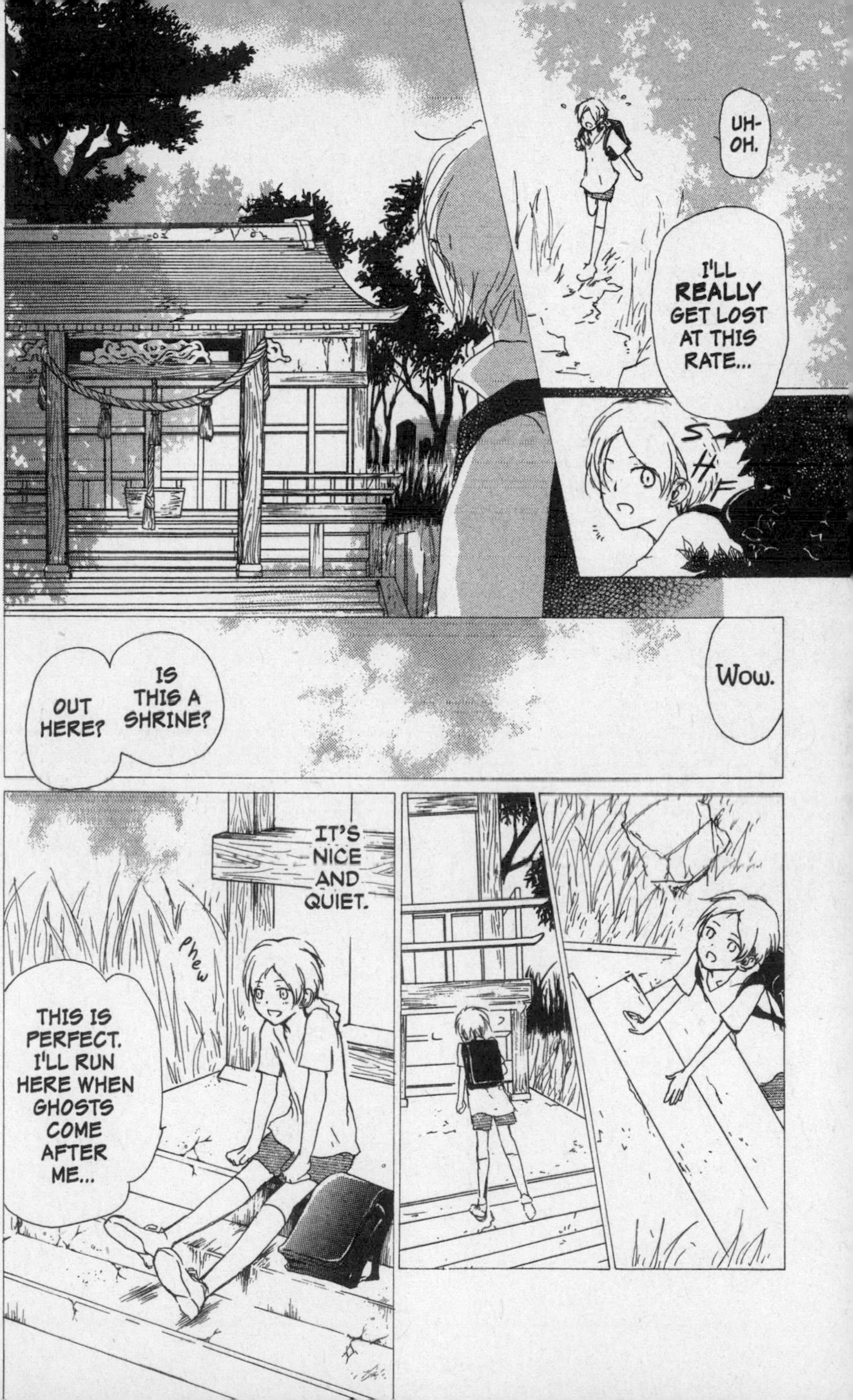
UH-OH.
I'LL REALLY GET LOST AT THIS RATE...
SHF
Wow.
IS THIS A SHRINE?
OUT HERE?
IT'S NICE AND QUIET.
Phew
THIS IS PERFECT. I'LL RUN HERE WHEN GHOSTS COME AFTER ME...

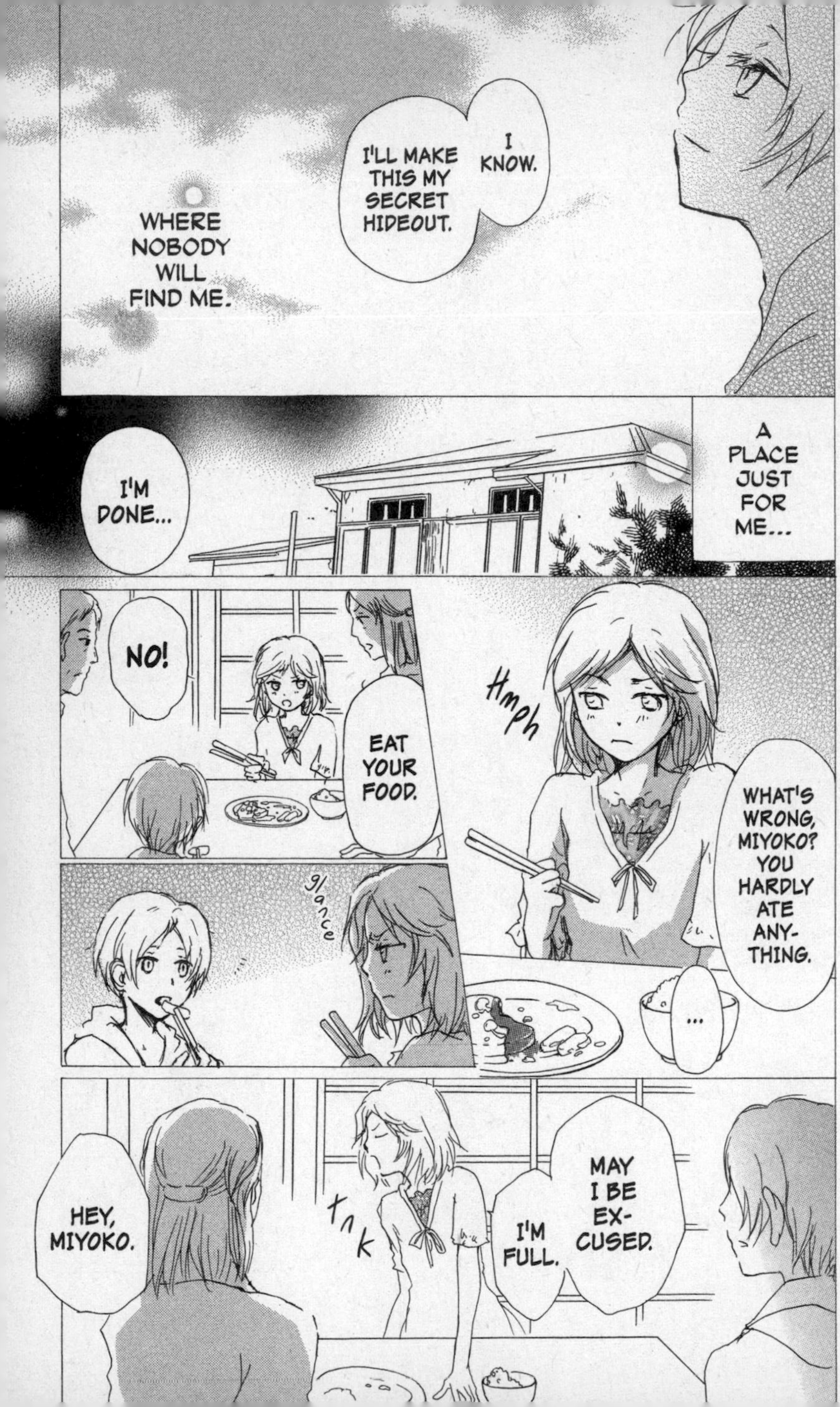
I KNOW.
I'LL MAKE THIS MY SECRET HIDEOUT.
WHERE NOBODY WILL FIND ME.
A PLACE JUST FOR ME...
I'M DONE...
WHAT'S WRONG, MIYOKO? YOU HARDLY ATE ANYTHING.
Hmph
...
EAT YOUR FOOD.
NO!
glance
MAY I BE EX-CUSED.
I'M FULL.
tnk
HEY, MIYOKO.

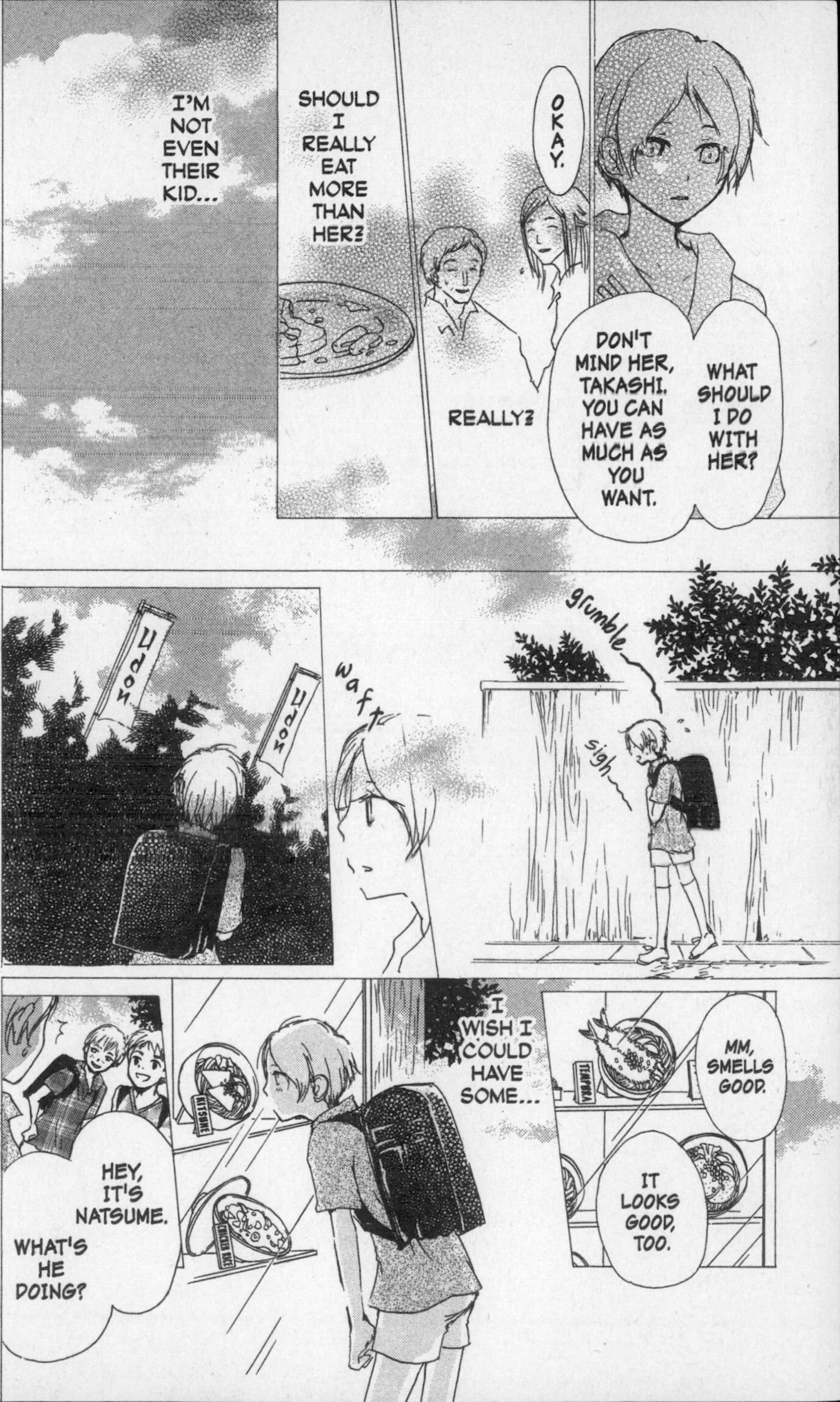
OKAY.
WHAT SHOULD I DO WITH HER?
DON'T MIND HER, TAKASHI. YOU CAN HAVE AS MUCH AS YOU WANT.
REALLY?!
SHOULD I REALLY EAT MORE THAN HER?!
I'M NOT EVEN THEIR KID...
grumble
sigh
waft
udon
udon
MM, SMELLS GOOD.
IT LOOKS GOOD, TOO.
TEMPURA
I WISH I COULD HAVE SOME...
KITSUNE
CHICKEN RICE
HEY, IT'S NATSUME.
WHAT'S HE DOING?

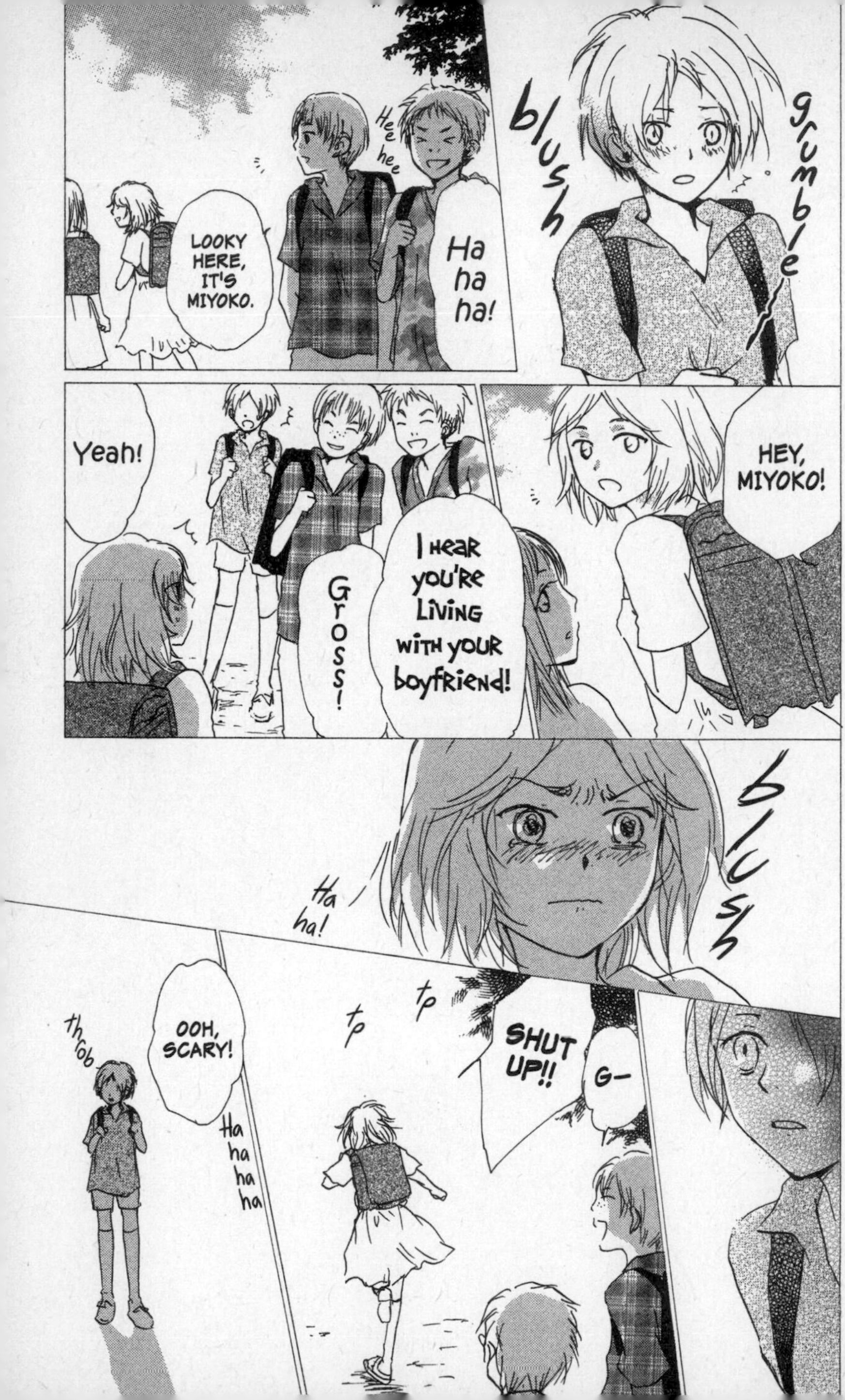
blush
grumble
Hee hee
Ha ha ha!
LOOKY HERE, IT'S MIYOKO.
HEY, MIYOKO!
I hear you're living with your boyfriend!
Gross!
Yeah!
BLUSH
Ha ha!
G—
SHUT UP!!
tp
tp
Ha ha ha ha ha
OOH, SCARY!
throb

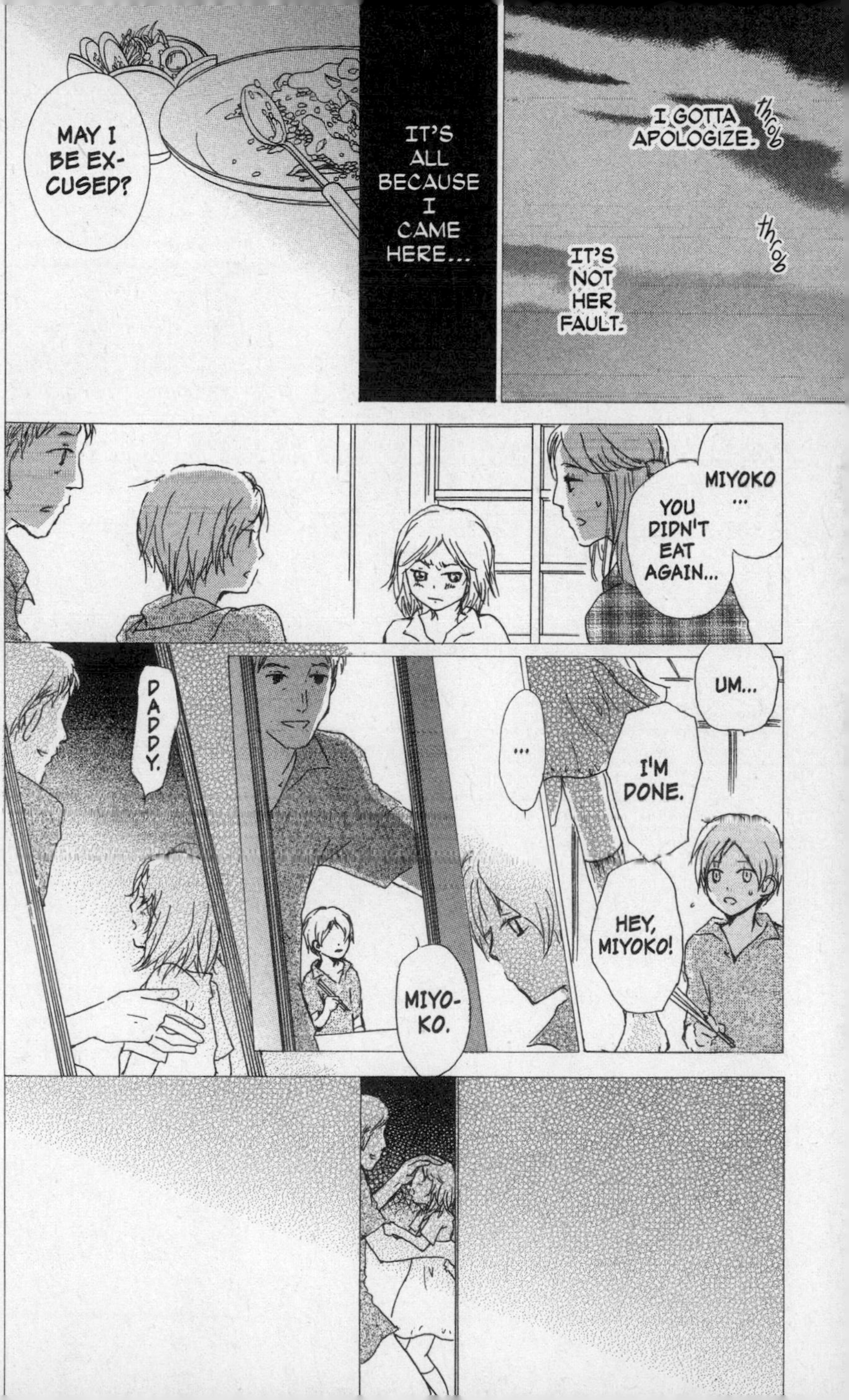
throb
I GOTTA APOLOGIZE.
throb
IT'S NOT HER FAULT.
IT'S ALL BECAUSE I CAME HERE...
MAY I BE EX-CUSED?
MIYOKO ...
YOU DIDN'T EAT AGAIN...
UM...
I'M DONE.
...
HEY, MIYOKO!
MIYO-KO.
DADDY.

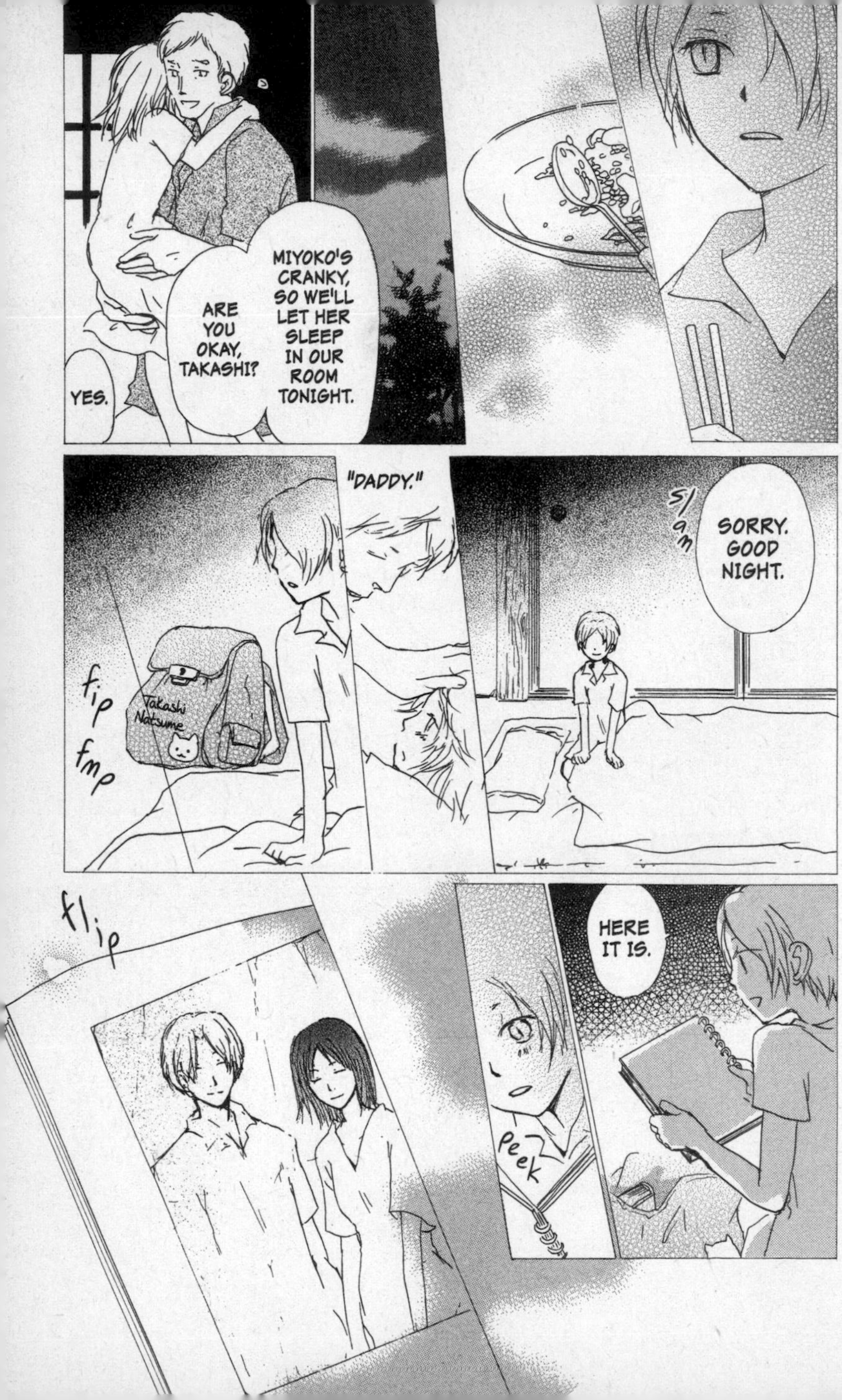
MIYOKO'S CRANKY, SO WE'LL LET HER SLEEP IN OUR ROOM TONIGHT.
ARE YOU OKAY, TAKASHI?
YES.
slam
SORRY. GOOD NIGHT.
"DADDY."
Takashi Natsume
HERE IT IS.
peek
flip

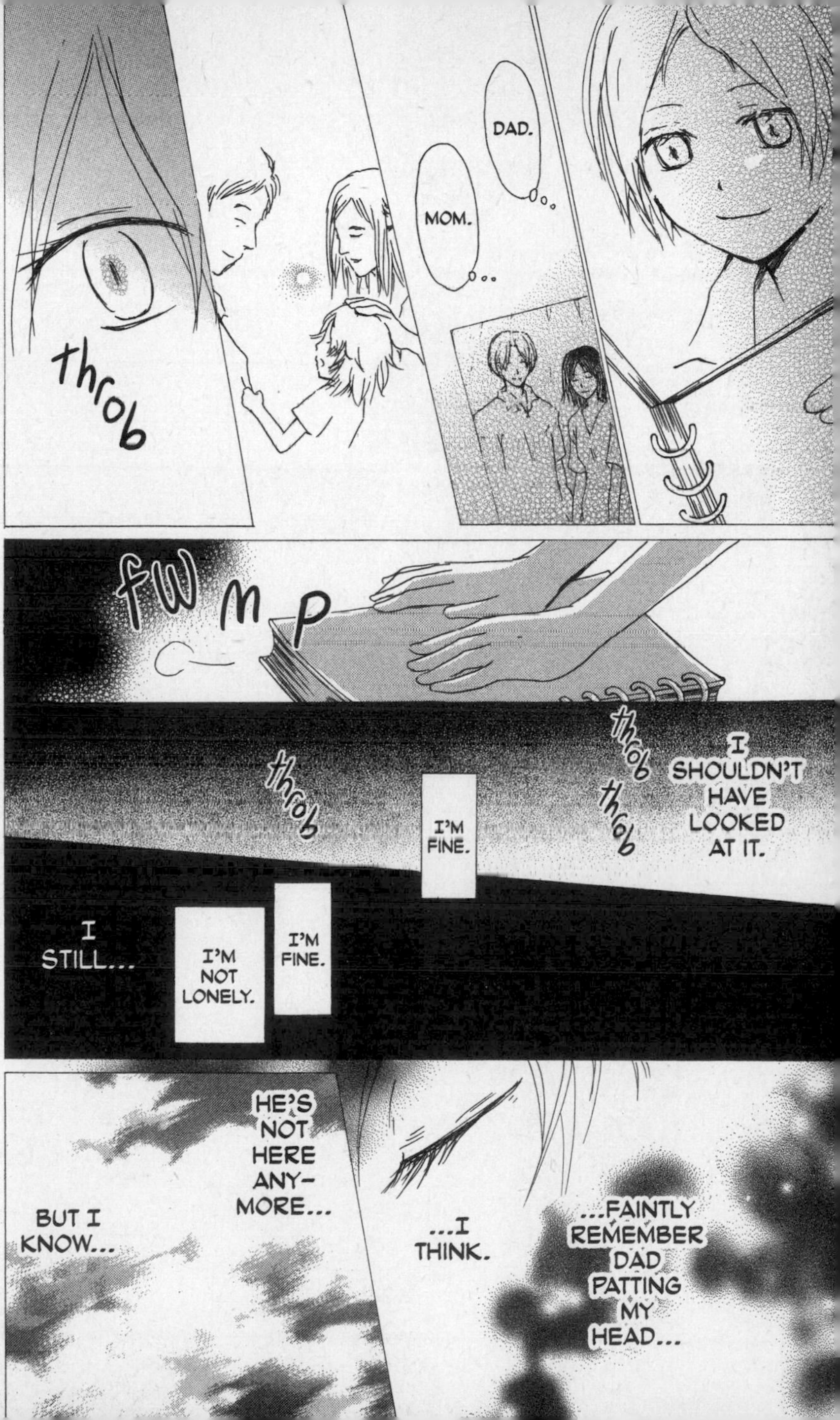
DAD.
MOM.
throb
fwmp
I SHOULDN'T HAVE LOOKED AT IT.
throb throb
I'M FINE.
throb
I'M FINE.
I'M NOT LONELY.
I STILL...
...FAINTLY REMEMBER DAD PATTING MY HEAD...
...I THINK.
HE'S NOT HERE ANY-MORE...
BUT I KNOW...

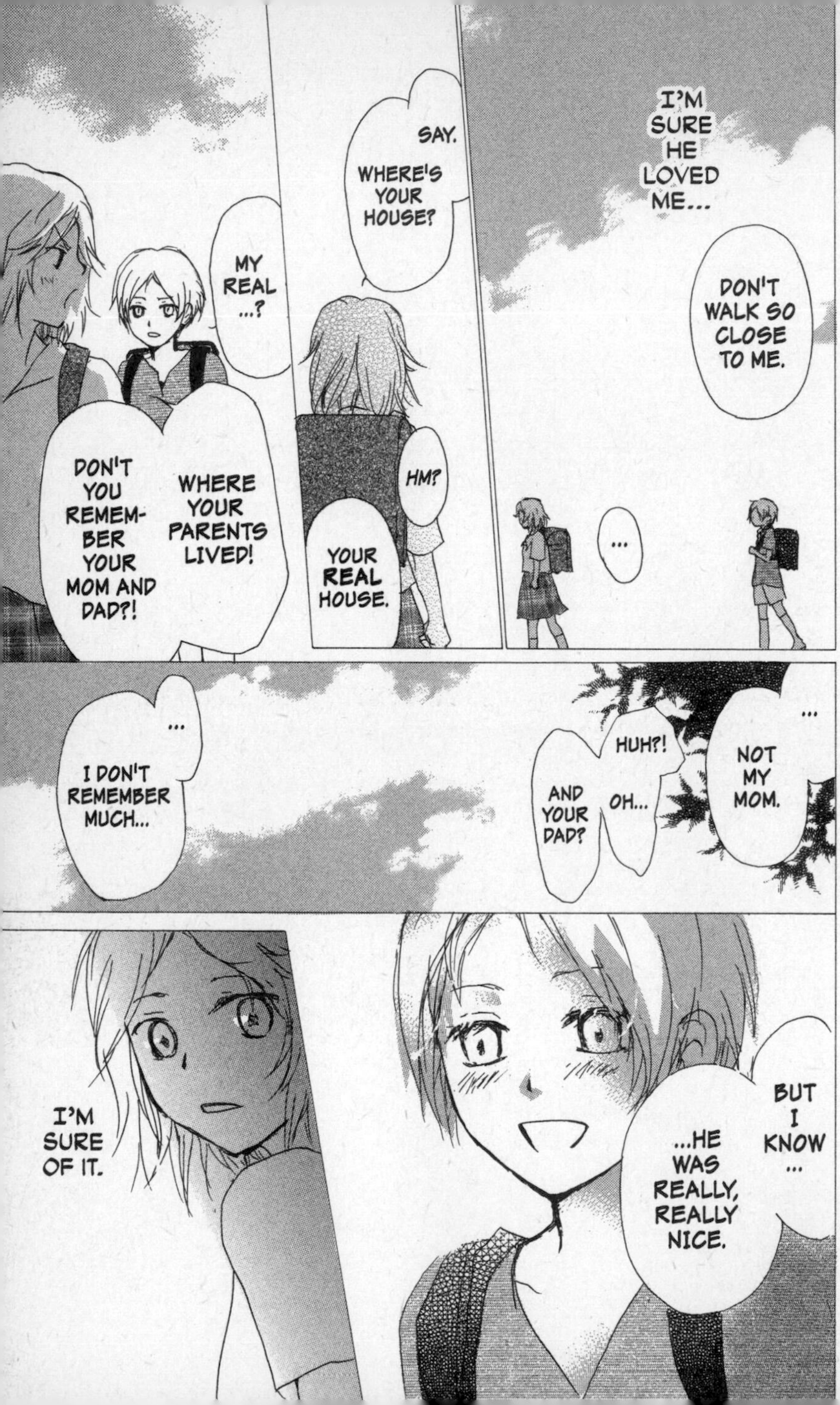
I'M SURE HE LOVED ME...
DON'T WALK SO CLOSE TO ME.
...
SAY.
WHERE'S YOUR HOUSE?
HM?
YOUR REAL HOUSE.
MY REAL ...?
WHERE YOUR PARENTS LIVED!
DON'T YOU REMEMBER YOUR MOM AND DAD?!
...
NOT MY MOM.
HUH?!
OH...
AND YOUR DAD?
...
I DON'T REMEMBER MUCH...
BUT I KNOW ...
...HE WAS REALLY, REALLY NICE.
I'M SURE OF IT.

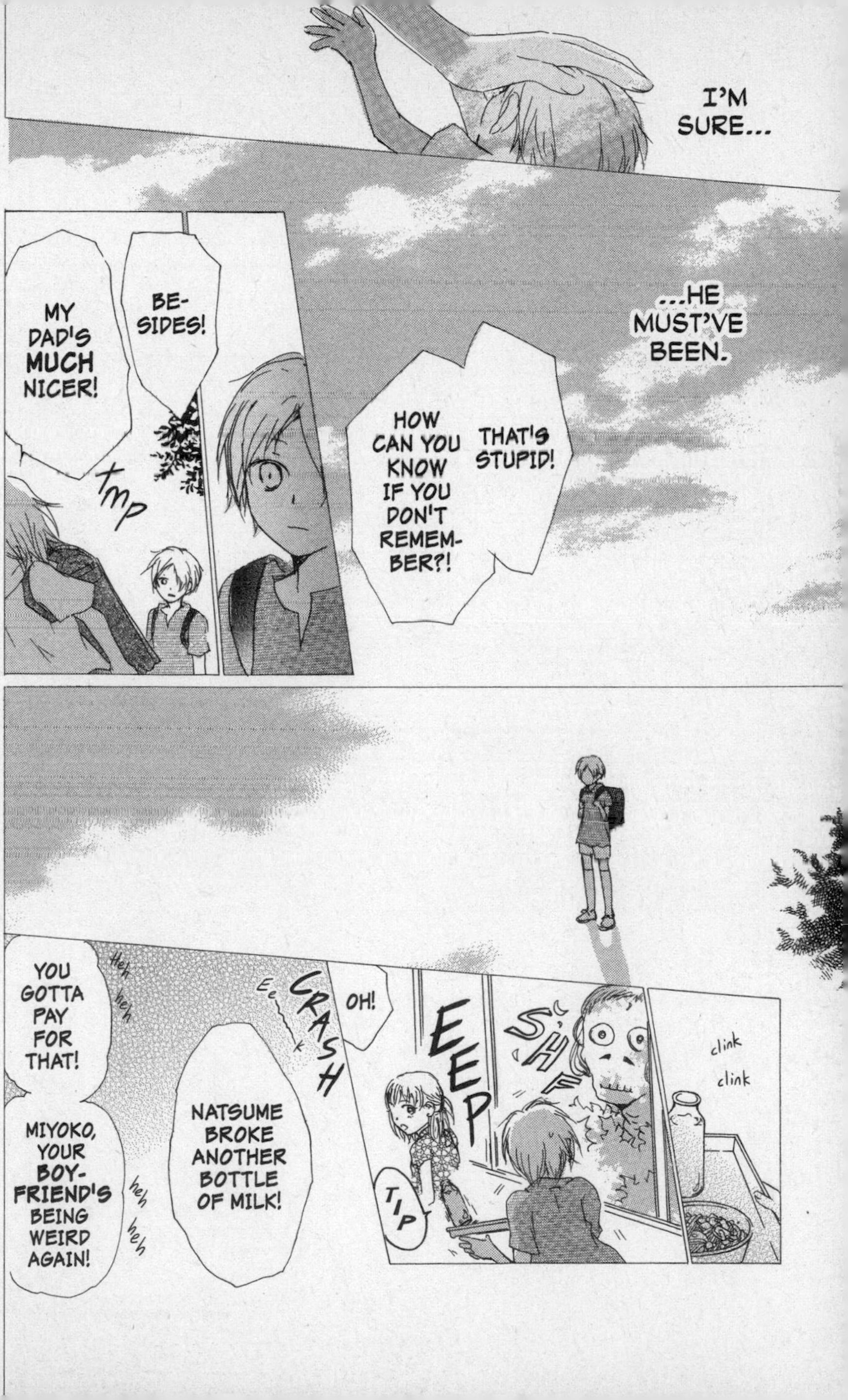
I'M SURE...
...HE MUST'VE BEEN.
THAT'S STUPID!
HOW CAN YOU KNOW IF YOU DON'T REMEM-BER?!
BE-SIDES!
MY DAD'S MUCH NICER!
tmp
clink
clink
SHF
EEP
TIP
OH!
CRASH
Eeek
NATSUME BROKE ANOTHER BOTTLE OF MILK!
YOU GOTTA PAY FOR THAT!
heh heh
MIYOKO, YOUR BOY-FRIEND'S BEING WEIRD AGAIN!
heh heh

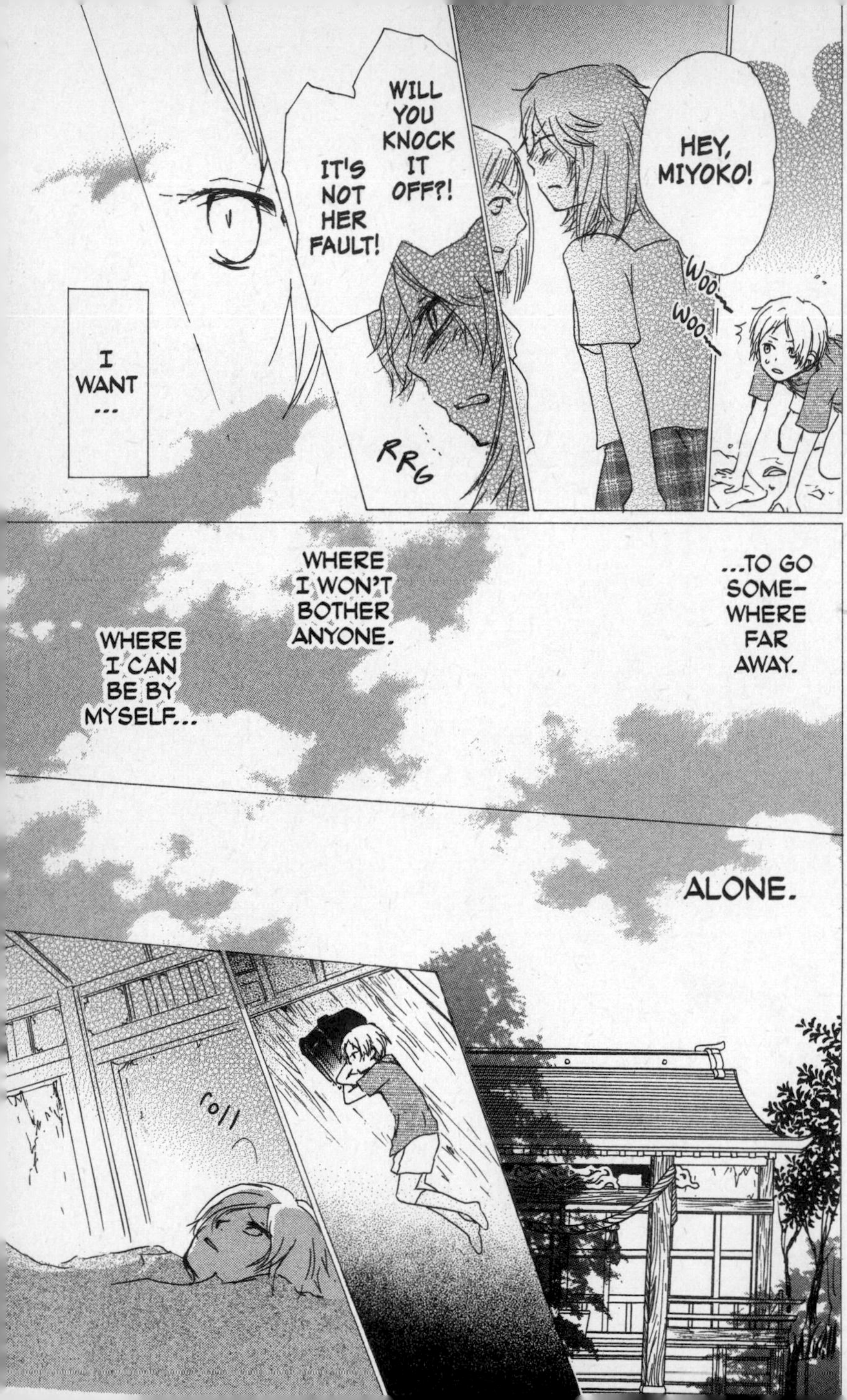
HEY, MIYOKO!
WOO~ WOO~
WILL YOU KNOCK IT OFF?!
IT'S NOT HER FAULT!
RRG
I WANT...
...TO GO SOME-WHERE FAR AWAY.
WHERE I WON'T BOTHER ANYONE.
WHERE I CAN BE BY MYSELF...
ALONE.
roll

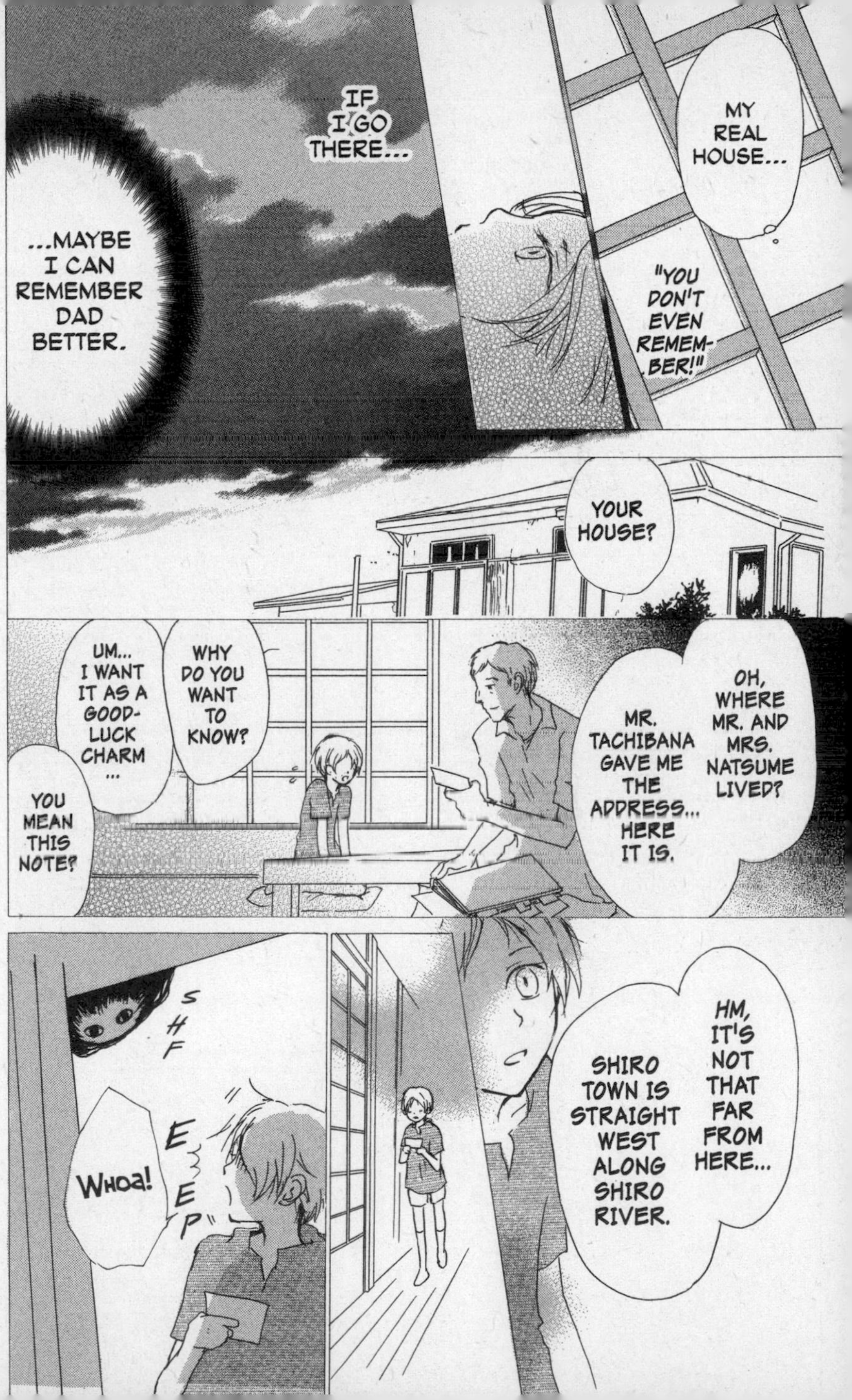
MY REAL HOUSE...
"YOU DON'T EVEN REMEMBER!"
IF I GO THERE...
...MAYBE I CAN REMEMBER DAD BETTER.
YOUR HOUSE?
OH, WHERE MR. AND MRS. NATSUME LIVED?
MR. TACHIBANA GAVE ME THE ADDRESS... HERE IT IS.
WHY DO YOU WANT TO KNOW?
UM... I WANT IT AS A GOOD-LUCK CHARM...
YOU MEAN THIS NOTE?
HM, IT'S NOT THAT FAR FROM HERE...
SHIRO TOWN IS STRAIGHT WEST ALONG SHIRO RIVER.
SHF
EEEP
Whoa!

05

❋ Giveaways

The monthly magazine LaLa, where Natsume is serialized, often includes Natsume-themed gifts and giveaways. There usually isn't enough lead time for me to advertise for them in the graphic novels, so please check the magazine out once in a while.

❋ Deep Gratitude

So many people work hard to make these quality products. And it's all thanks to the support of my readers. I'll keep giving all I've got to make manga worthy of your interest.

End of $\frac{1}{4}$ columns.

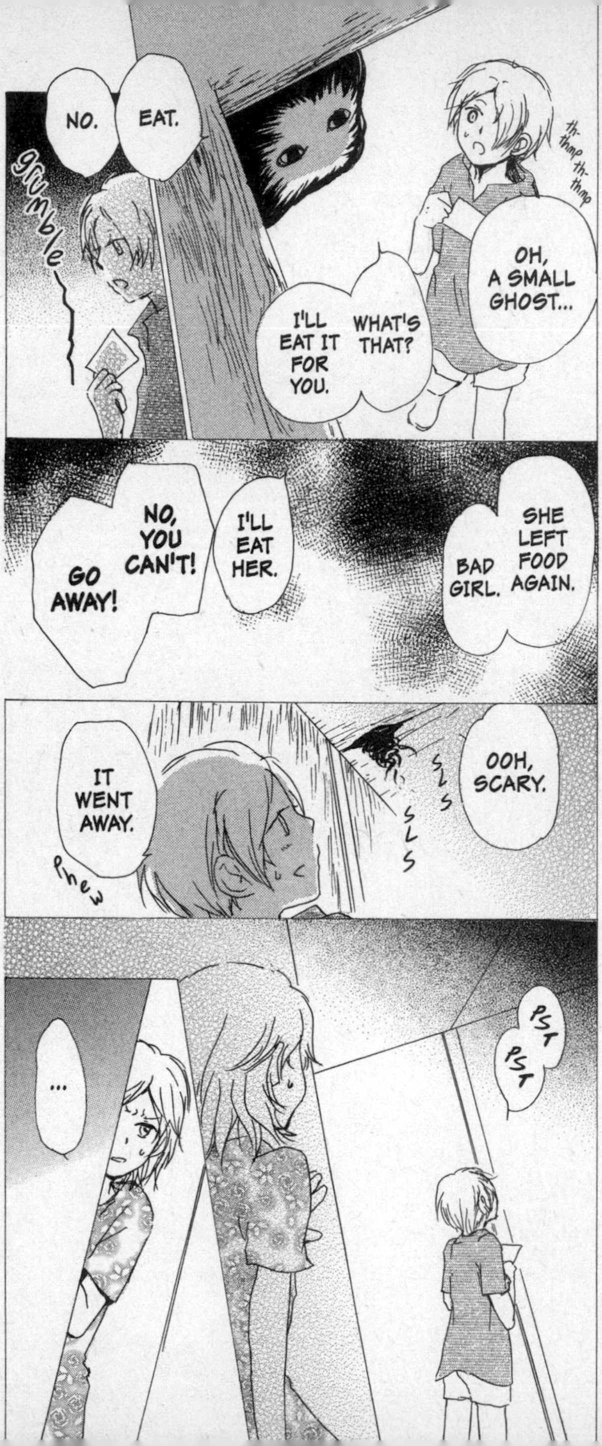
th-thmp th-thmp
OH, A SMALL GHOST...
WHAT'S THAT?
I'LL EAT IT FOR YOU.
EAT.
NO.
grumble
SHE LEFT FOOD AGAIN.
BAD GIRL.
I'LL EAT HER.
NO, YOU CAN'T!
GO AWAY!
OOH, SCARY.
SLS SLS
IT WENT AWAY.
phew
PST PST
...

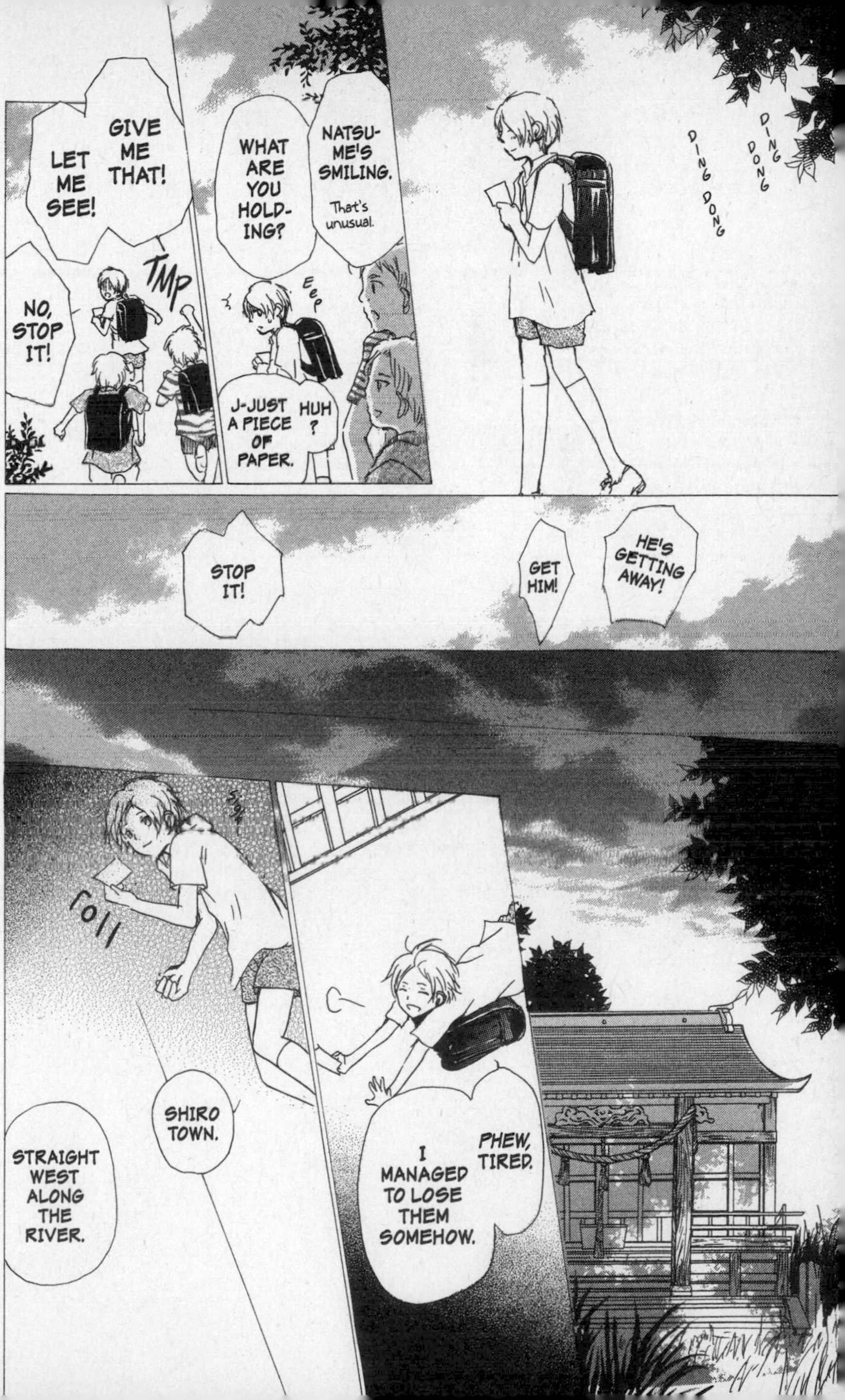
DING DONG
DING DONG
NATSUME'S SMILING.
That's unusual.
WHAT ARE YOU HOLDING?
Eep
HUH?
J-JUST A PIECE OF PAPER.
GIVE ME THAT!
LET ME SEE!
TMP
NO, STOP IT!
HE'S GETTING AWAY!
GET HIM!
STOP IT!
PHEW, TIRED.
I MANAGED TO LOSE THEM SOMEHOW.
roll
SHIRO TOWN.
STRAIGHT WEST ALONG THE RIVER.

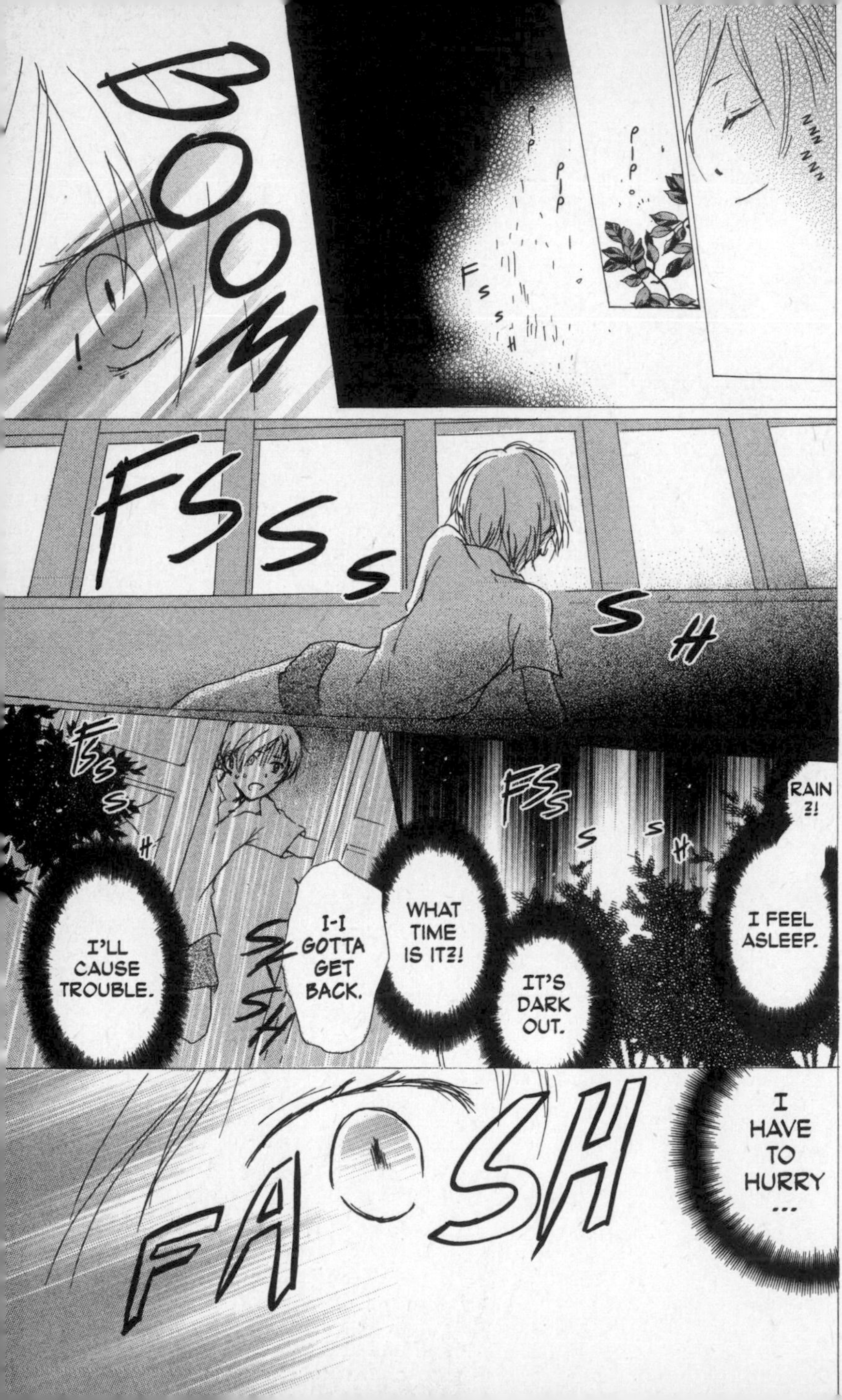
NNN NNN
PIP PIP PIP
FSSH
BOOM
!
FSSSSH
RAIN?!
I FEEL ASLEEP.
FSSSH
IT'S DARK OUT.
WHAT TIME IS IT?!
I-I GOTTA GET BACK.
SKSH
FSSH
I'LL CAUSE TROUBLE.
I HAVE TO HURRY...
FASH

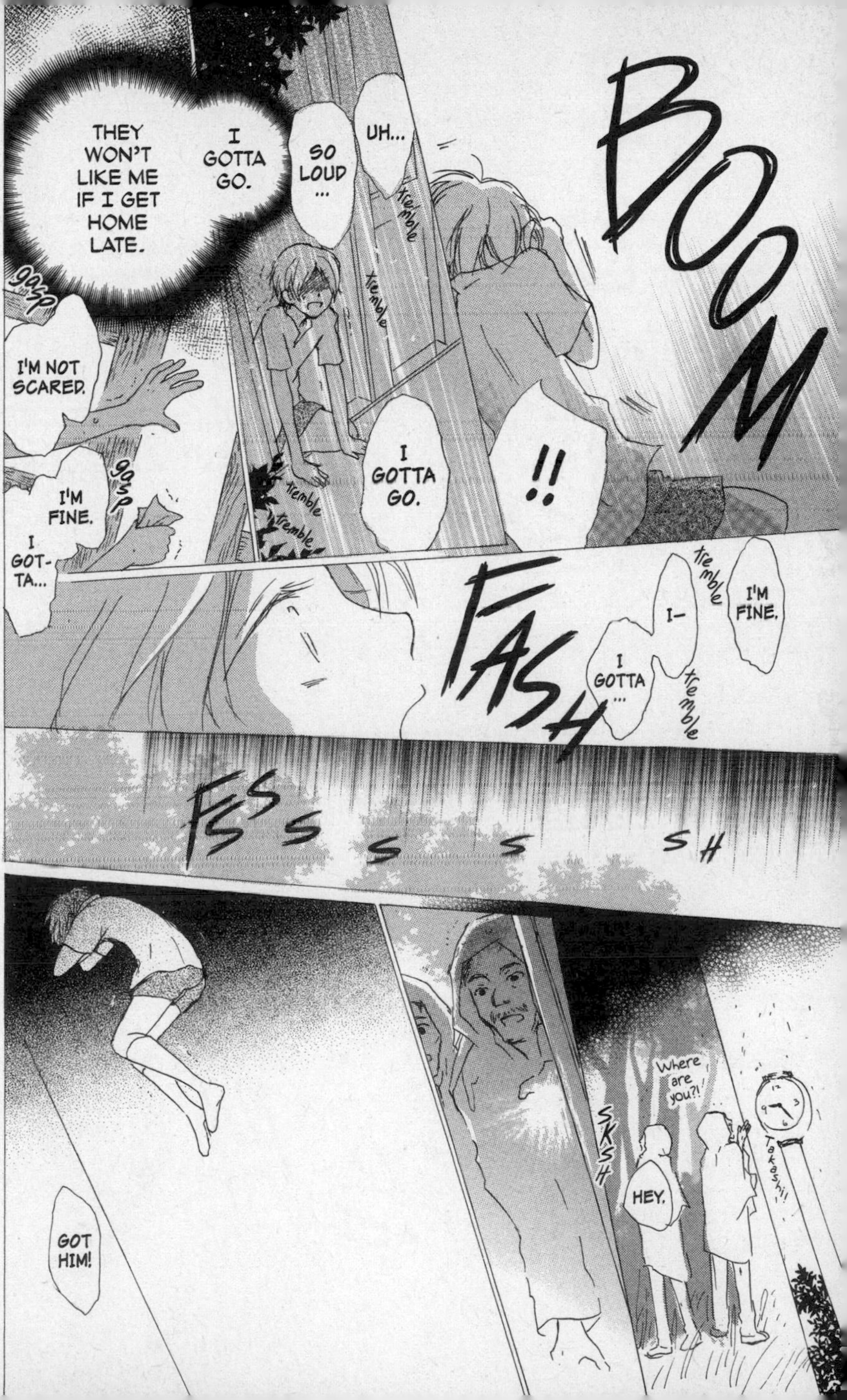
BOOM
UH...
tremble
SO LOUD ...
tremble
I GOTTA GO.
THEY WON'T LIKE ME IF I GET HOME LATE.
!!
I GOTTA GO.
tremble
tremble
gasp
I'M NOT SCARED.
gasp
I'M FINE.
I GOT-TA...
I'M FINE.
tremble
I-
I GOTTA ...
tremble
FASH
FSSSSSSH
Where are you?!
Takashi!
SKSH
HEY.
GOT HIM!

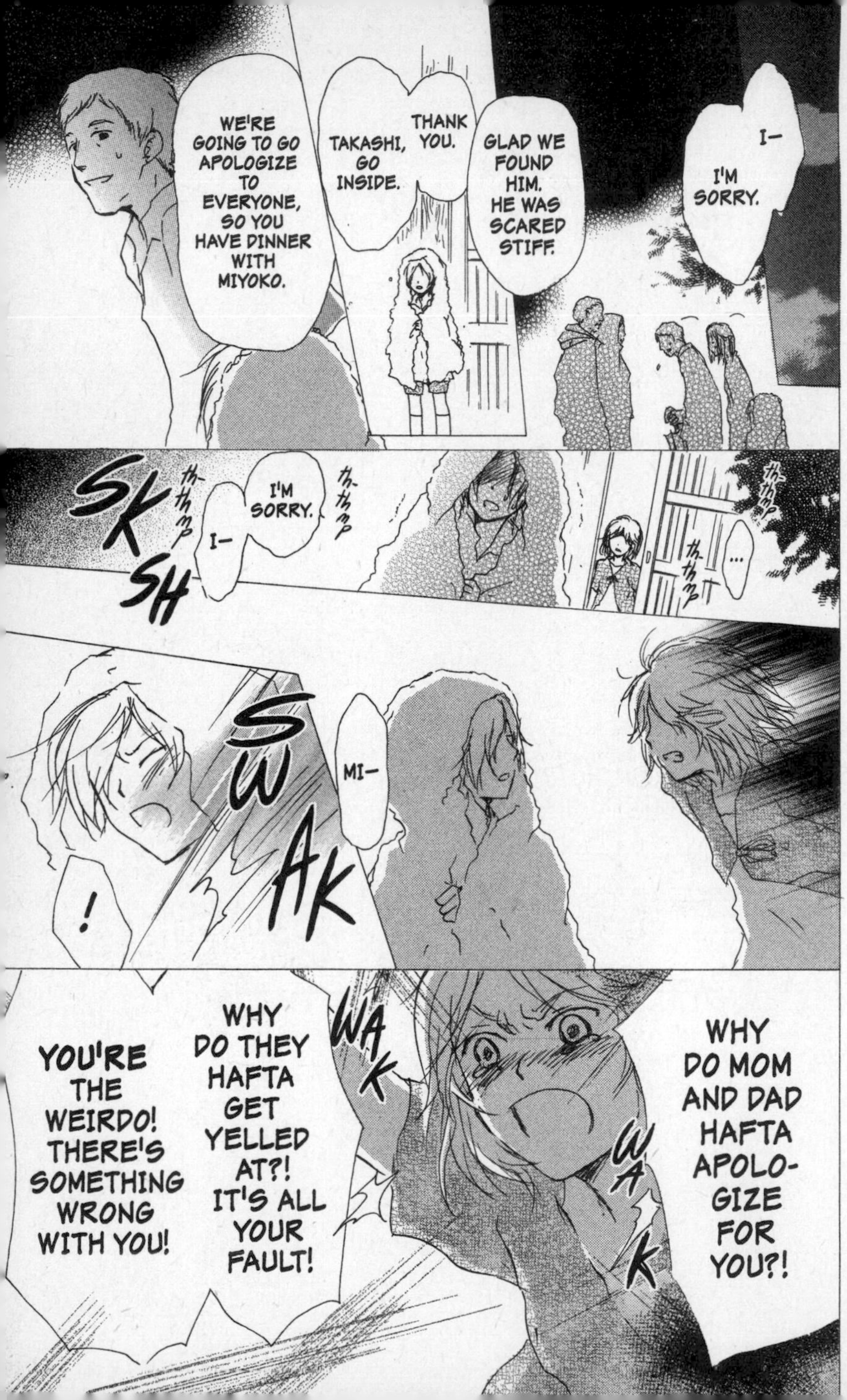

I— I'M SORRY.
GLAD WE FOUND HIM. HE WAS SCARED STIFF.
THANK YOU.
TAKASHI, GO INSIDE.
WE'RE GOING TO GO APOLOGIZE TO EVERYONE, SO YOU HAVE DINNER WITH MIYOKO.
th-thmp
...
th-thmp
th-thmp
th-thmp
I'M SORRY.
I—
SKSH
MI—
SWAK
!
WHY DO MOM AND DAD HAFTA APOLO-GIZE FOR YOU?!
WAK
WAK
WHY DO THEY HAFTA GET YELLED AT?! IT'S ALL YOUR FAULT!
YOU'RE THE WEIRDO! THERE'S SOMETHING WRONG WITH YOU!

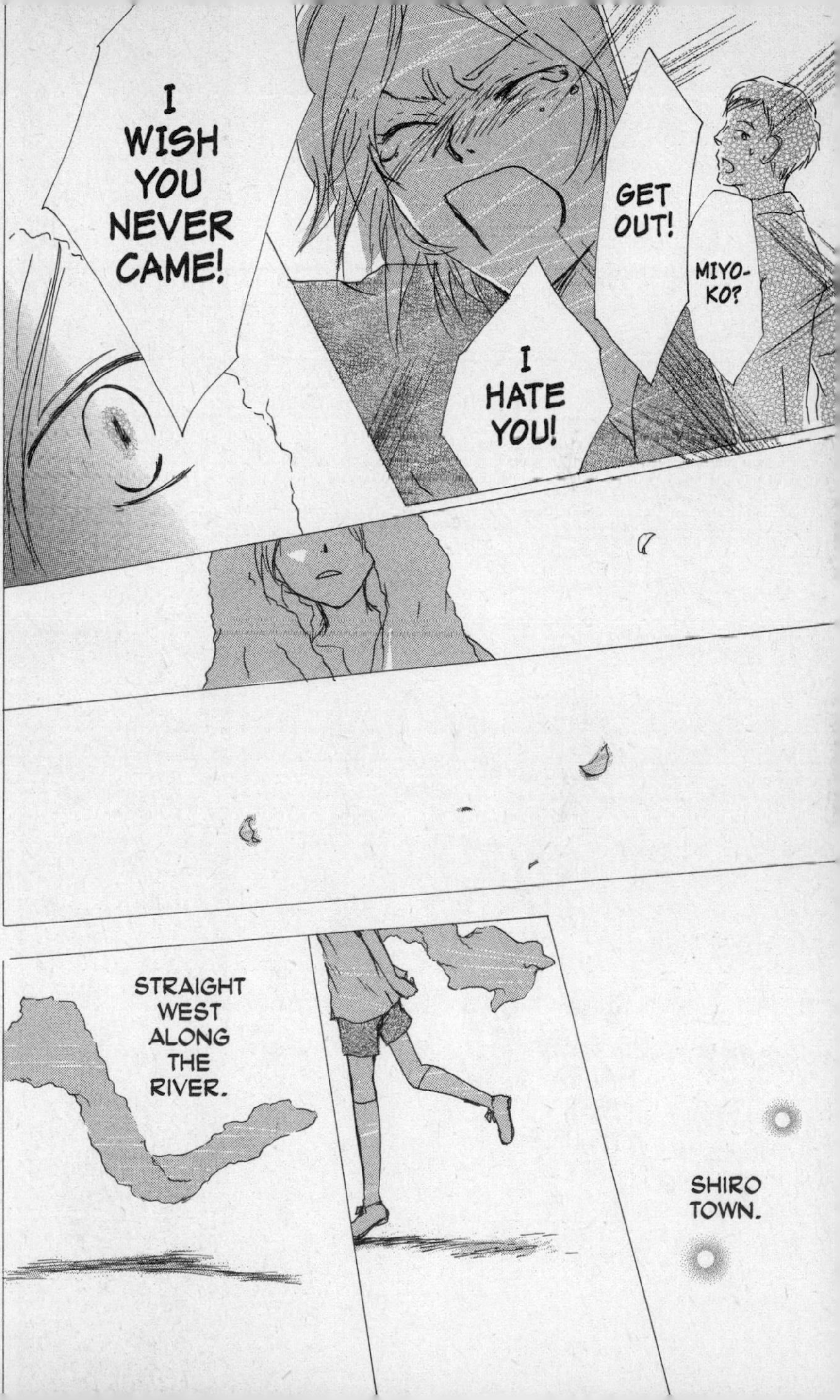
MIYO-KO?
GET OUT!
I HATE YOU!
I WISH YOU NEVER CAME!
SHIRO TOWN.
STRAIGHT WEST ALONG THE RIVER.

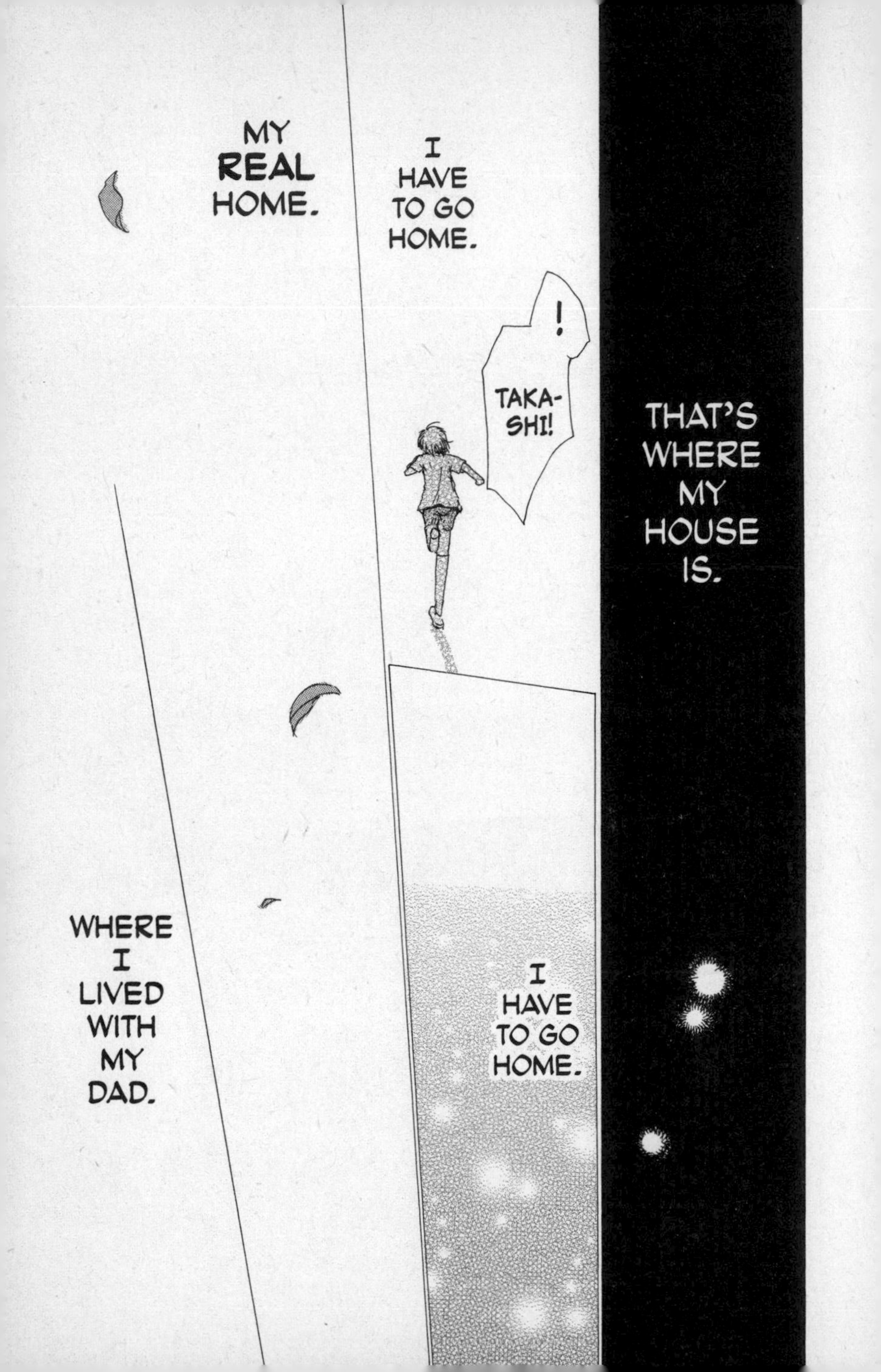
THAT'S WHERE MY HOUSE IS.
I HAVE TO GO HOME.
!
TAKA-SHI!
I HAVE TO GO HOME.
MY REAL HOME.
WHERE I LIVED WITH MY DAD.

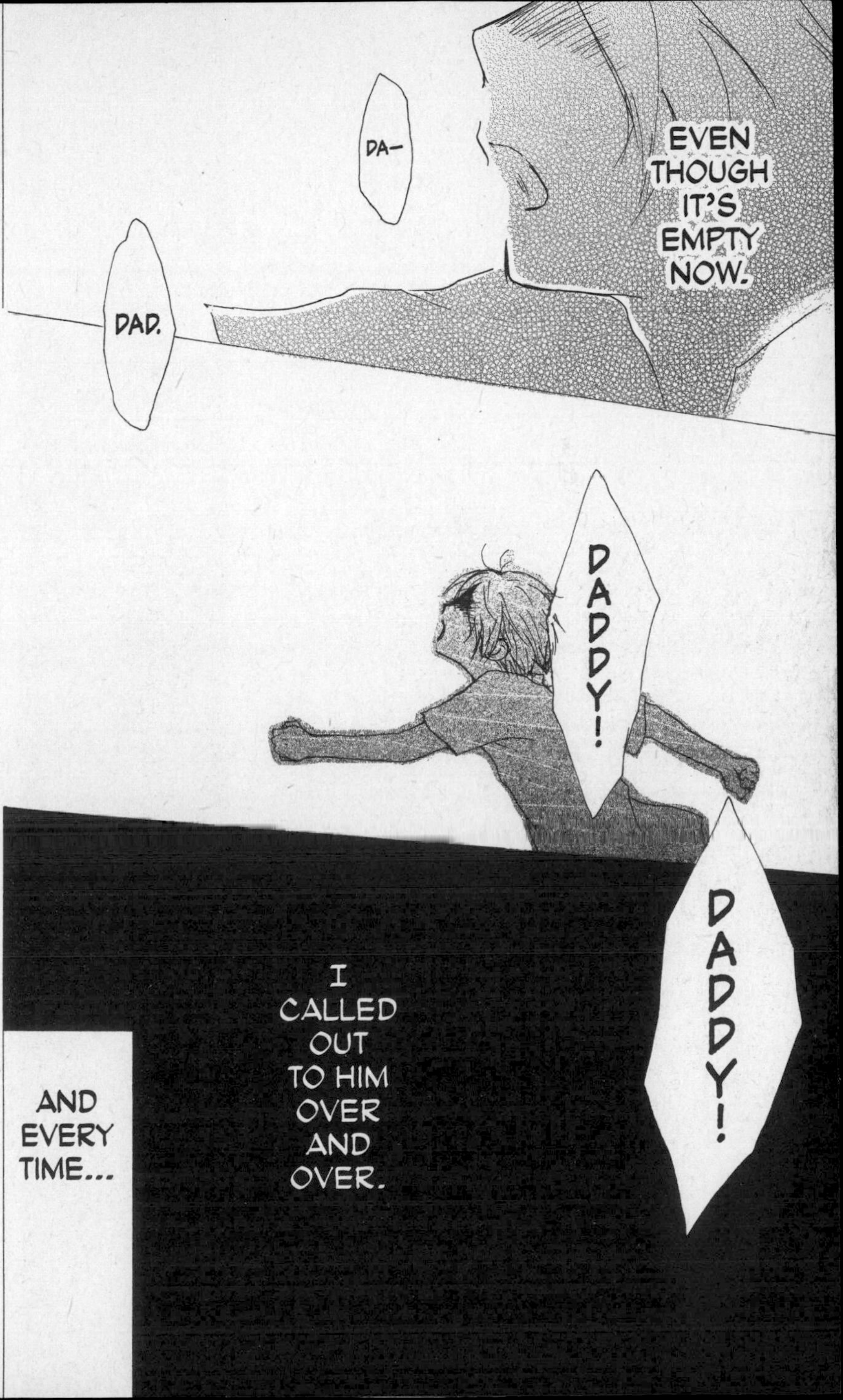
EVEN THOUGH IT'S EMPTY NOW.
DA—
DAD.
DADDY!
DADDY!
I CALLED OUT TO HIM OVER AND OVER.
AND EVERY TIME...

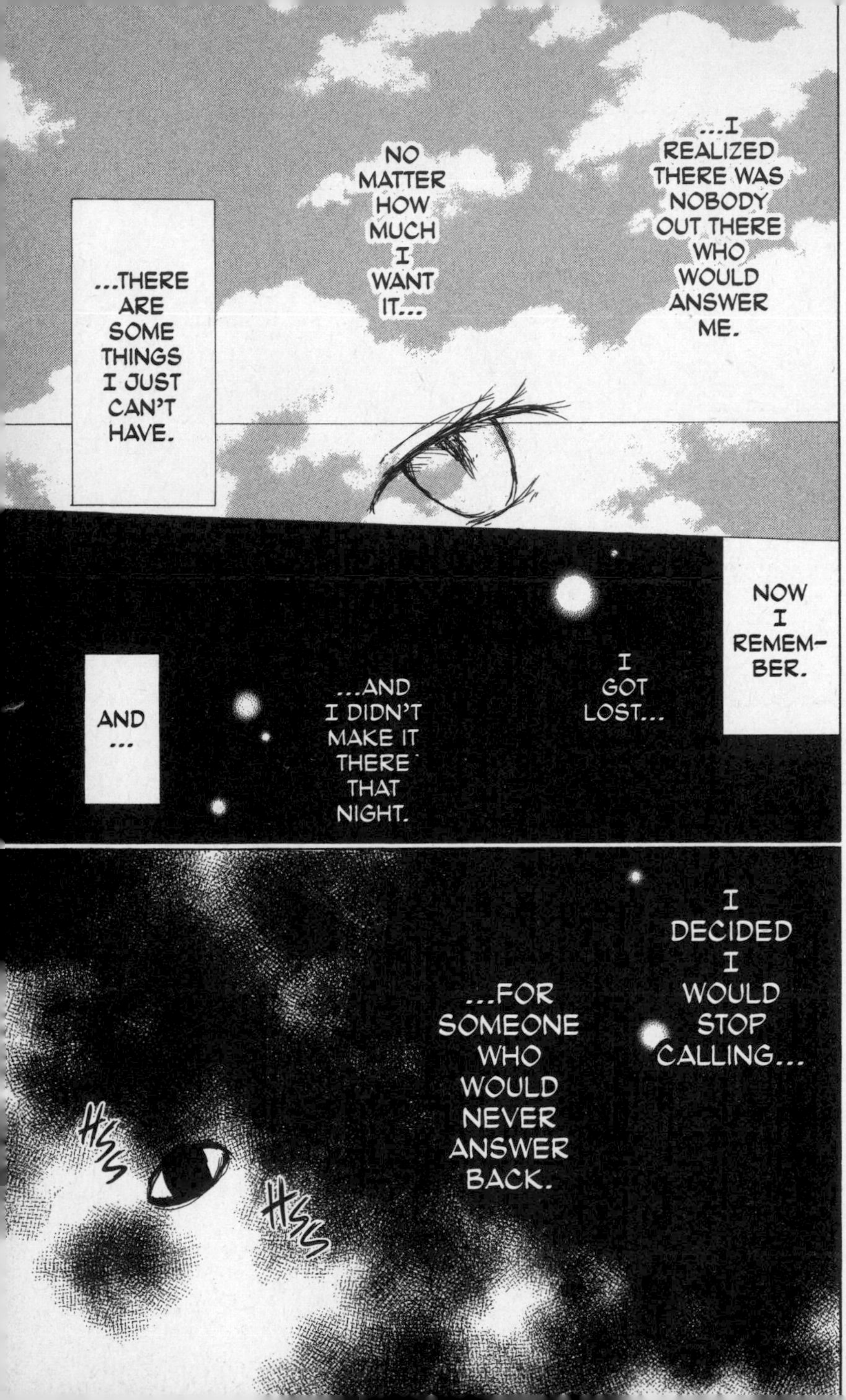
...I REALIZED THERE WAS NOBODY OUT THERE WHO WOULD ANSWER ME.
NO MATTER HOW MUCH I WANT IT...
...THERE ARE SOME THINGS I JUST CAN'T HAVE.
NOW I REMEMBER.
I GOT LOST...
...AND I DIDN'T MAKE IT THERE THAT NIGHT.
AND ...
I DECIDED I WOULD STOP CALLING...
...FOR SOMEONE WHO WOULD NEVER ANSWER BACK.

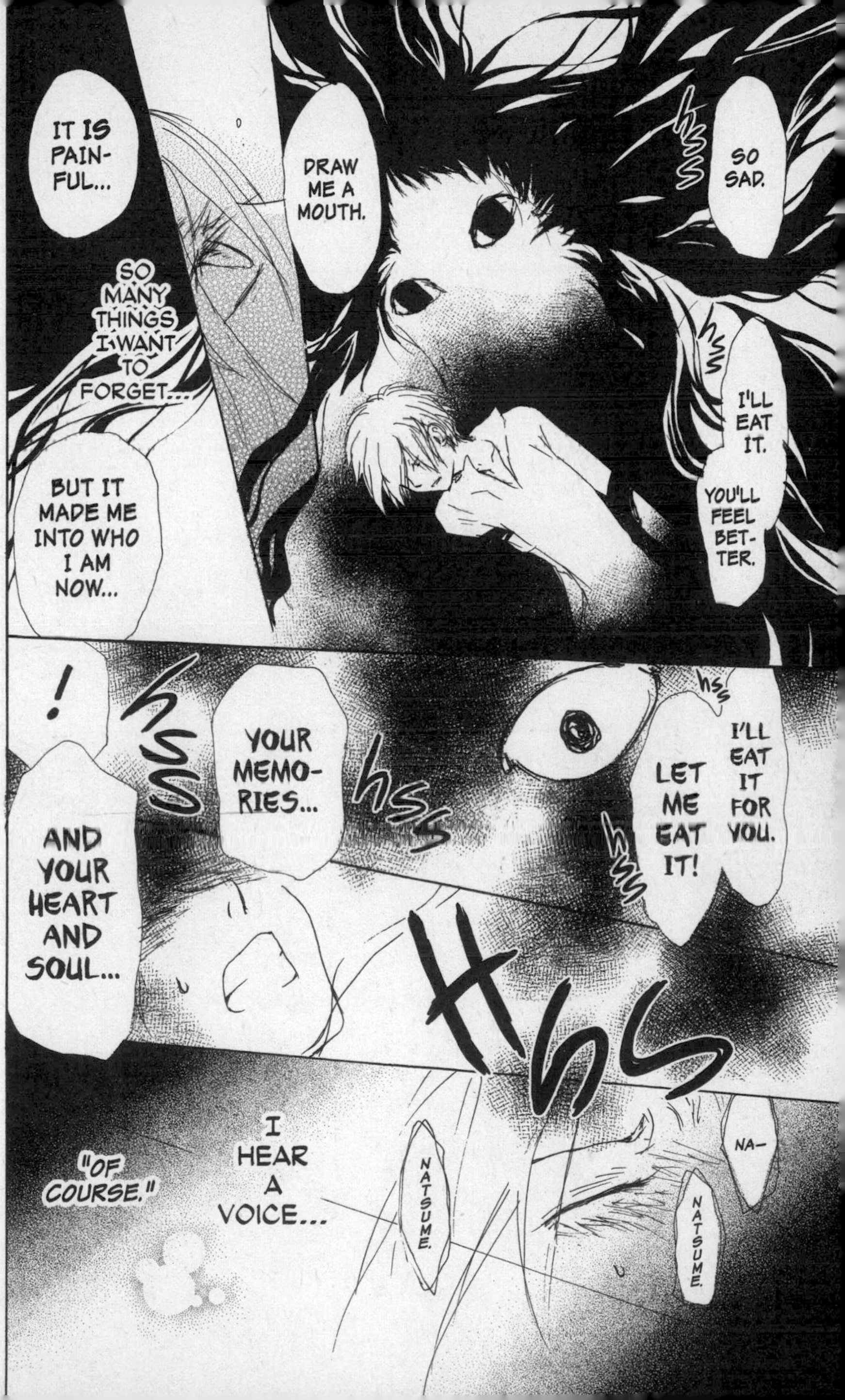
hss
SO SAD.
hss
I'LL EAT IT.
YOU'LL FEEL BETTER.
DRAW ME A MOUTH.
IT IS PAINFUL...
SO MANY THINGS I WANT TO FORGET...
BUT IT MADE ME INTO WHO I AM NOW...
hss
I'LL EAT IT FOR YOU.
LET ME EAT IT!
hss
hss
YOUR MEMORIES...
hss
!
AND YOUR HEART AND SOUL...
Hss
NA—
NATSUME.
NATSUME.
I HEAR A VOICE...
"OF COURSE."

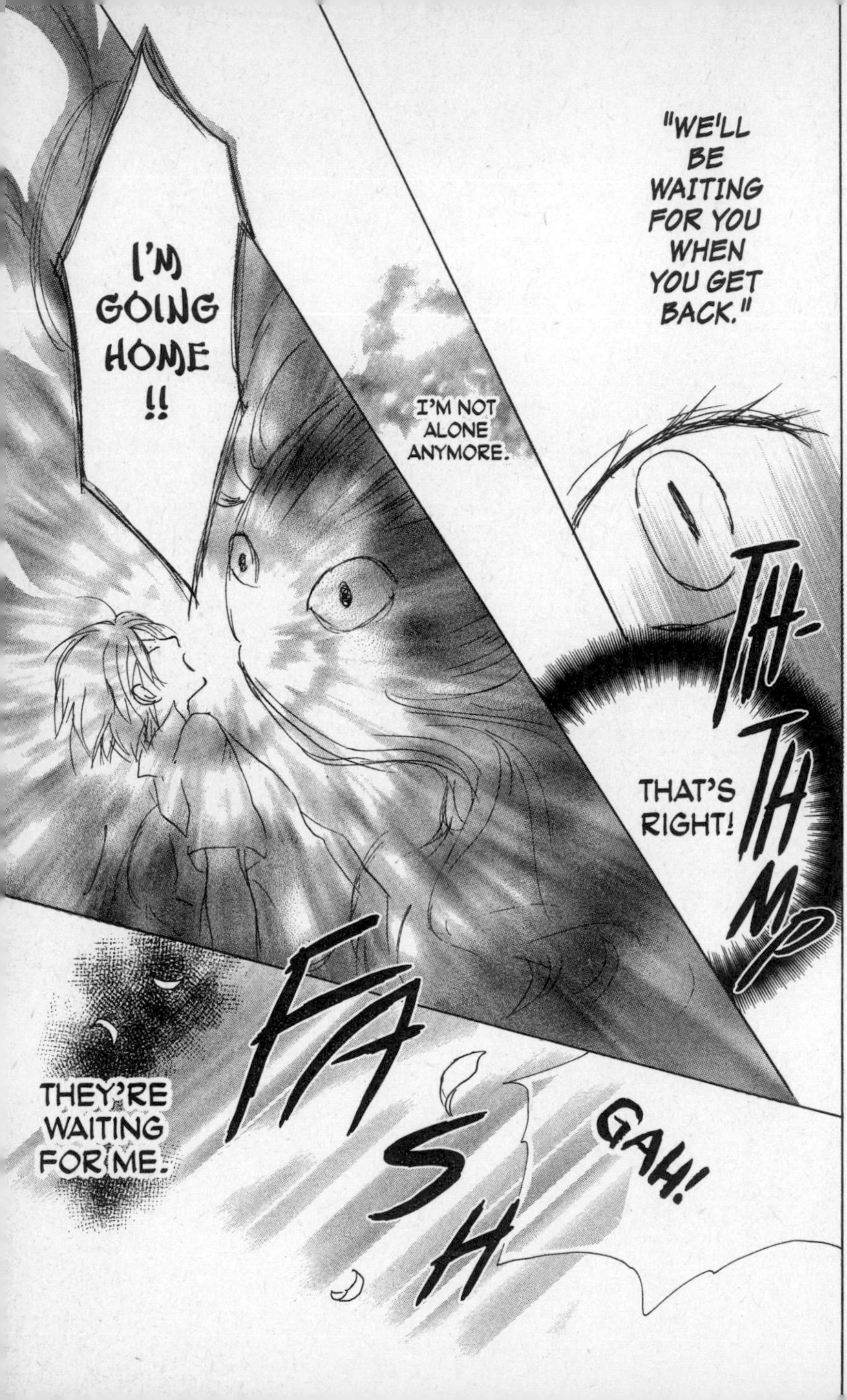
"WE'LL BE WAITING FOR YOU WHEN YOU GET BACK."
TH-THMP
THAT'S RIGHT!
I'M NOT ALONE ANYMORE.
I'M GOING HOME!!
GAH!
FASH
THEY'RE WAITING FOR ME.

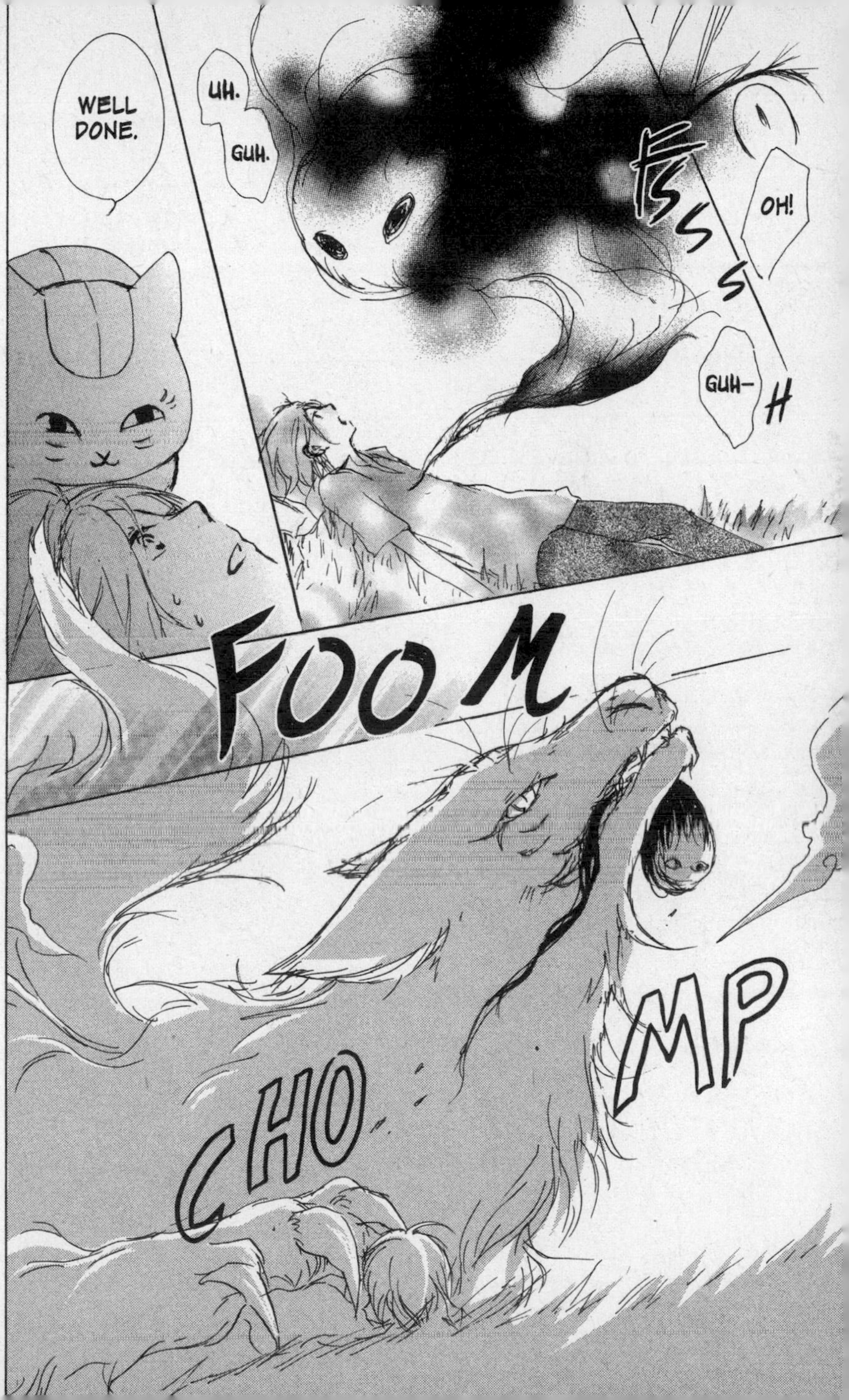
OH!
FSSSH
GUH-
UH.
GUH.
WELL DONE.
FOOM
CHOMP

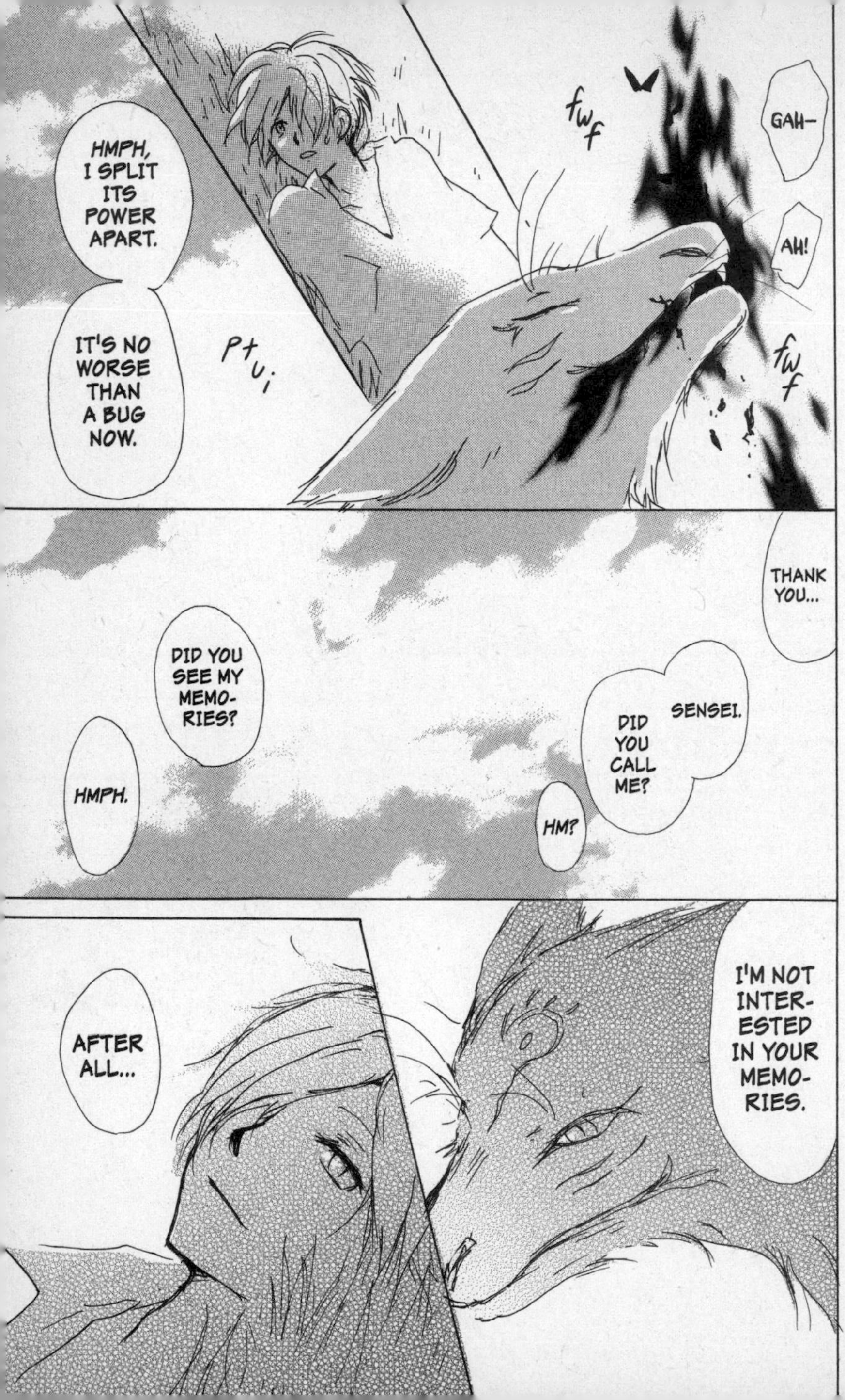
GAH-
AH!
fwf
fwf
Ptui
HMPH, I SPLIT ITS POWER APART.
IT'S NO WORSE THAN A BUG NOW.
THANK YOU...
SENSEI.
DID YOU CALL ME?
HM?
DID YOU SEE MY MEMO-RIES?
HMPH.
I'M NOT INTER-ESTED IN YOUR MEMO-RIES.
AFTER ALL...

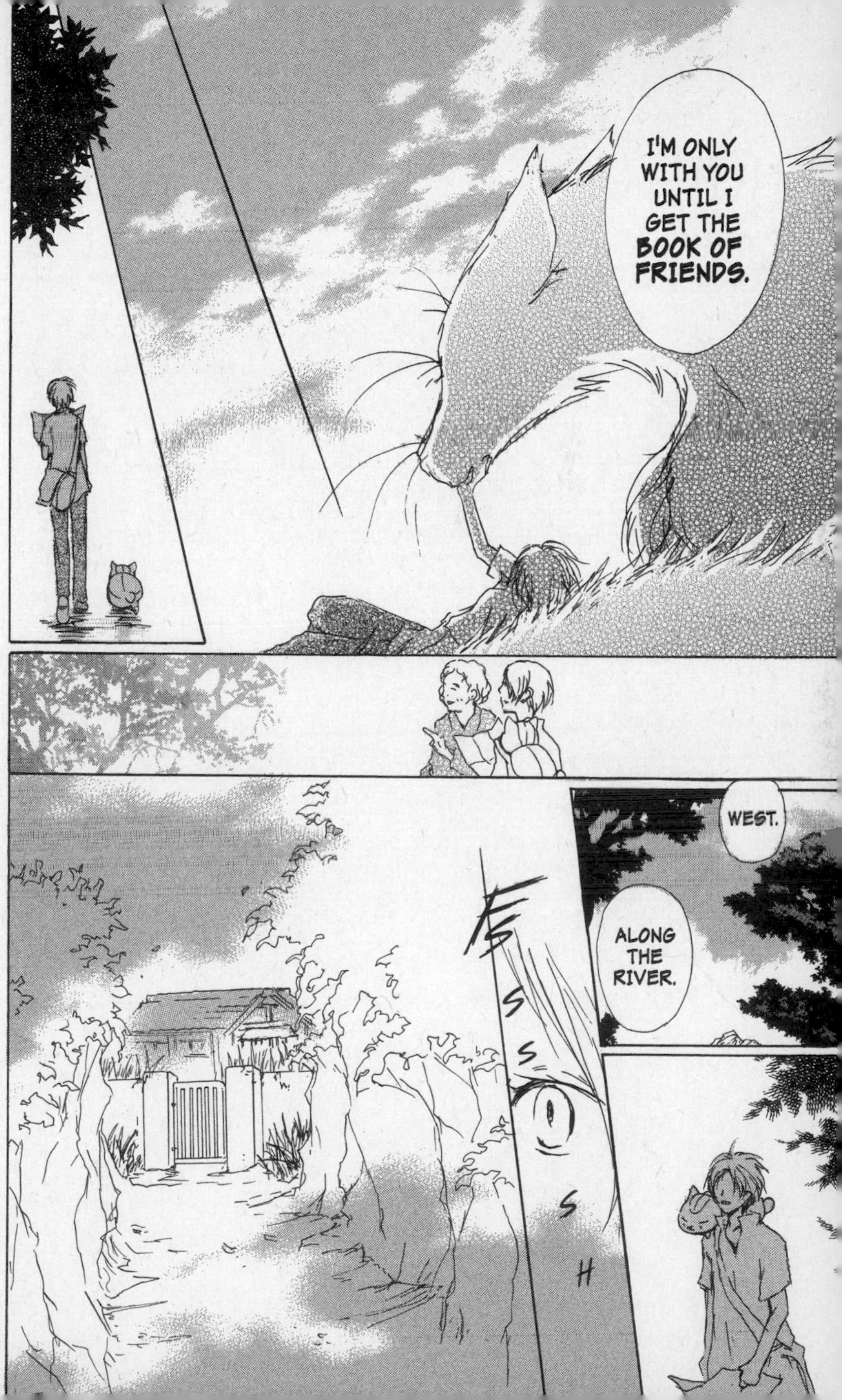
I'M ONLY WITH YOU UNTIL I GET THE BOOK OF FRIENDS.
WEST.
ALONG THE RIVER.
SSSSH

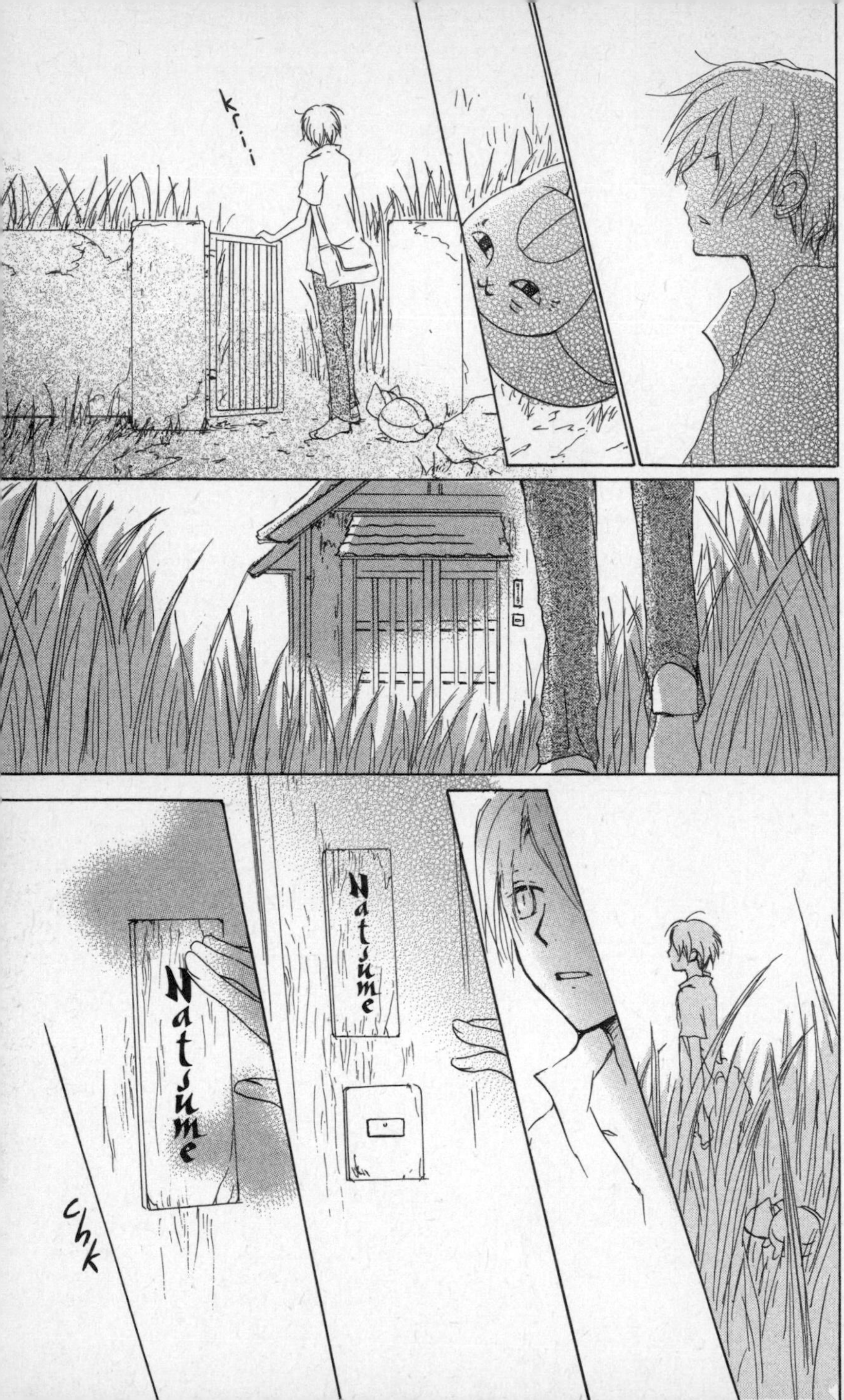
kr...i
Natsume
Natsume
chk

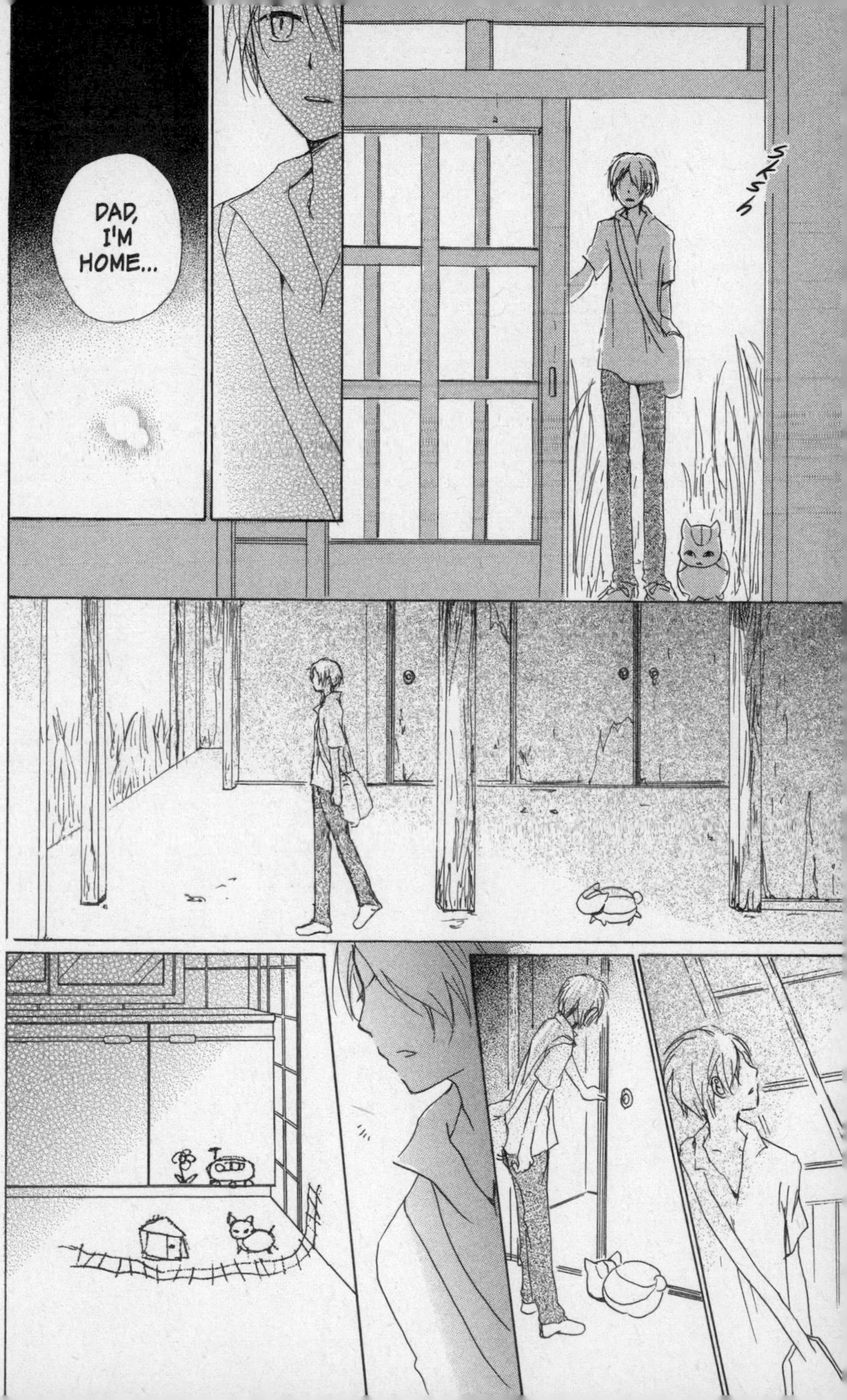
SKSH
DAD, I'M HOME...

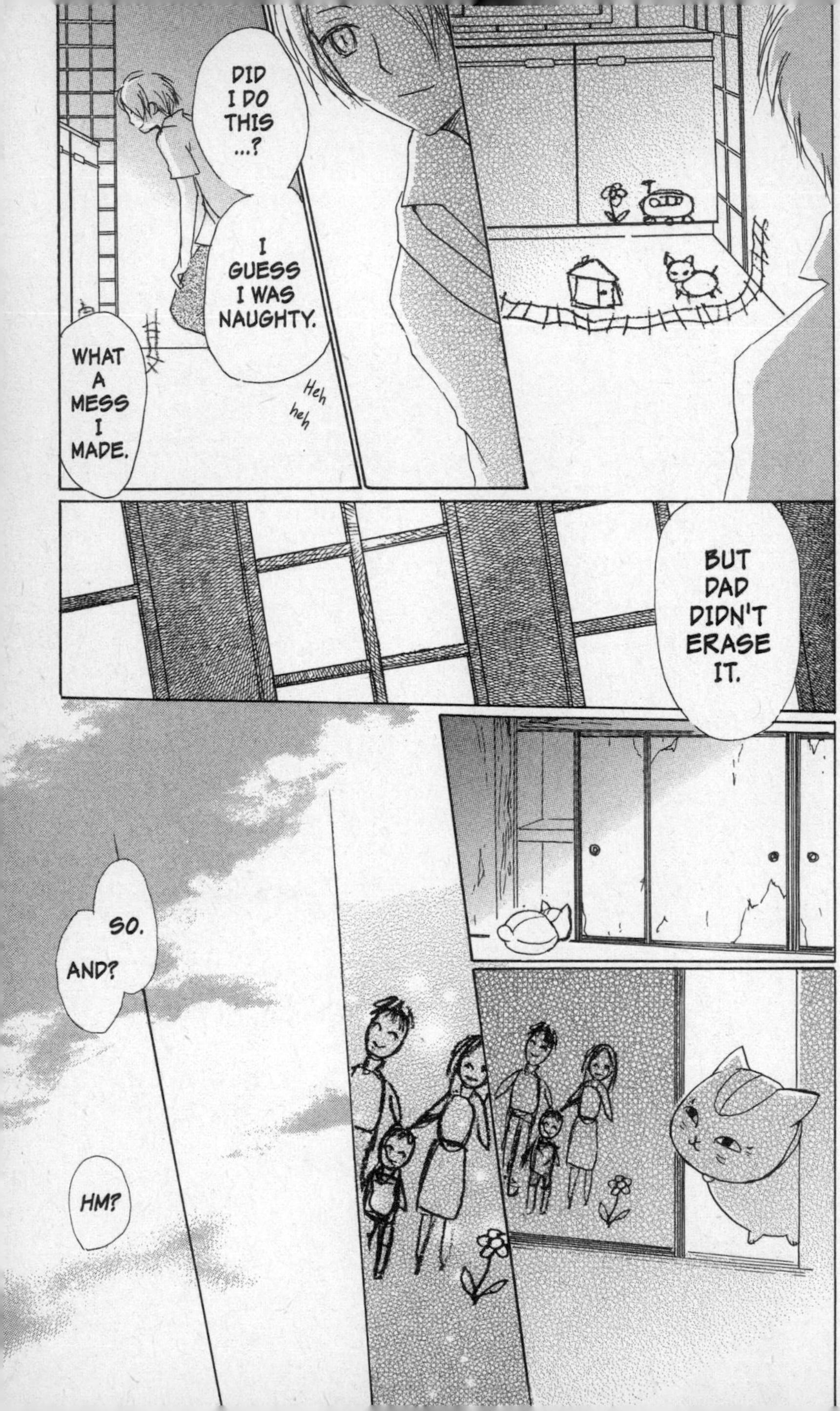
DID I DO THIS ...?
I GUESS I WAS NAUGHTY.
Heh heh
WHAT A MESS I MADE.
BUT DAD DIDN'T ERASE IT.
SO. AND?
HM?

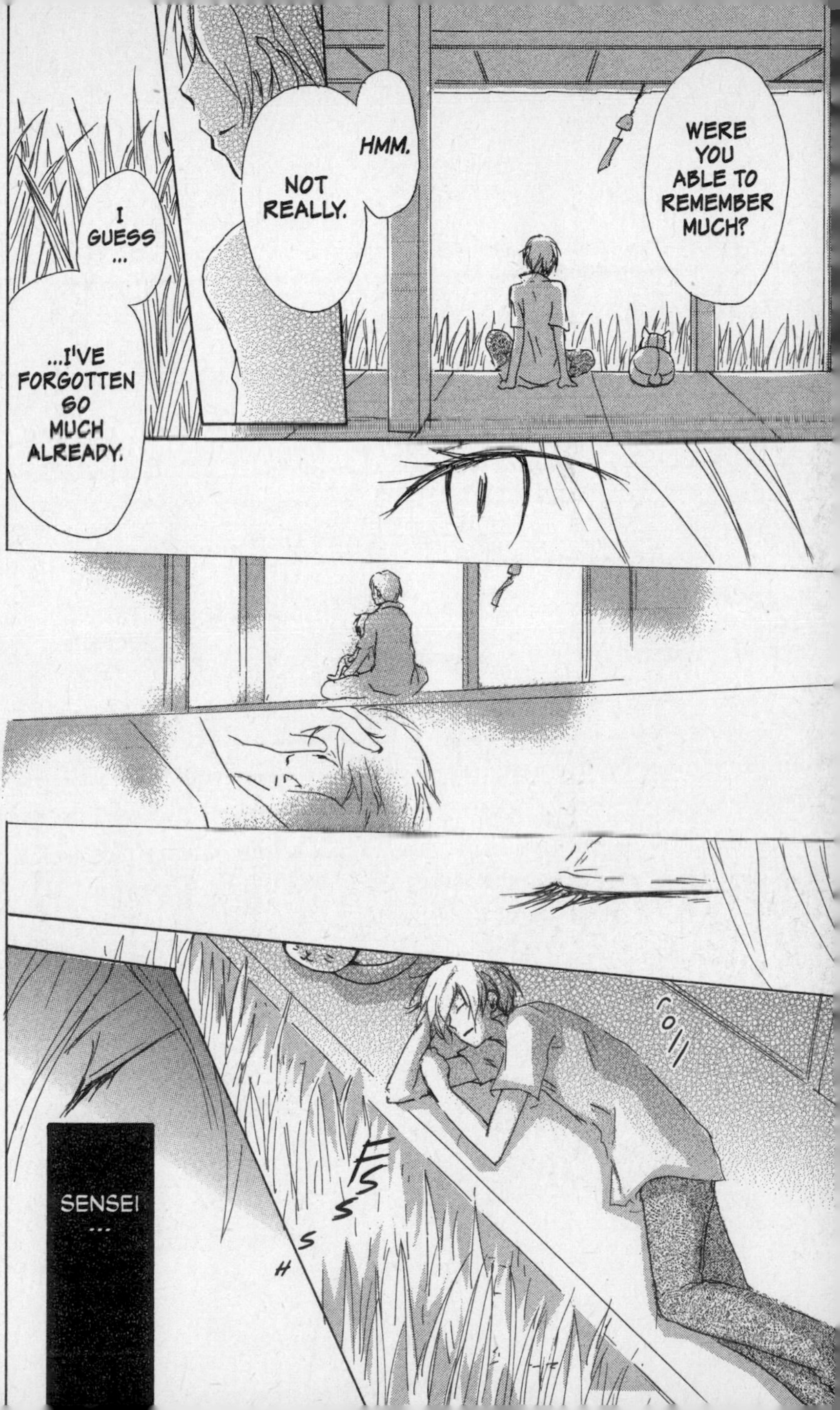
WERE YOU ABLE TO REMEMBER MUCH?
HMM.
NOT REALLY.
I GUESS...
...I'VE FORGOTTEN SO MUCH ALREADY.
roll
FSSSH
SENSEI...

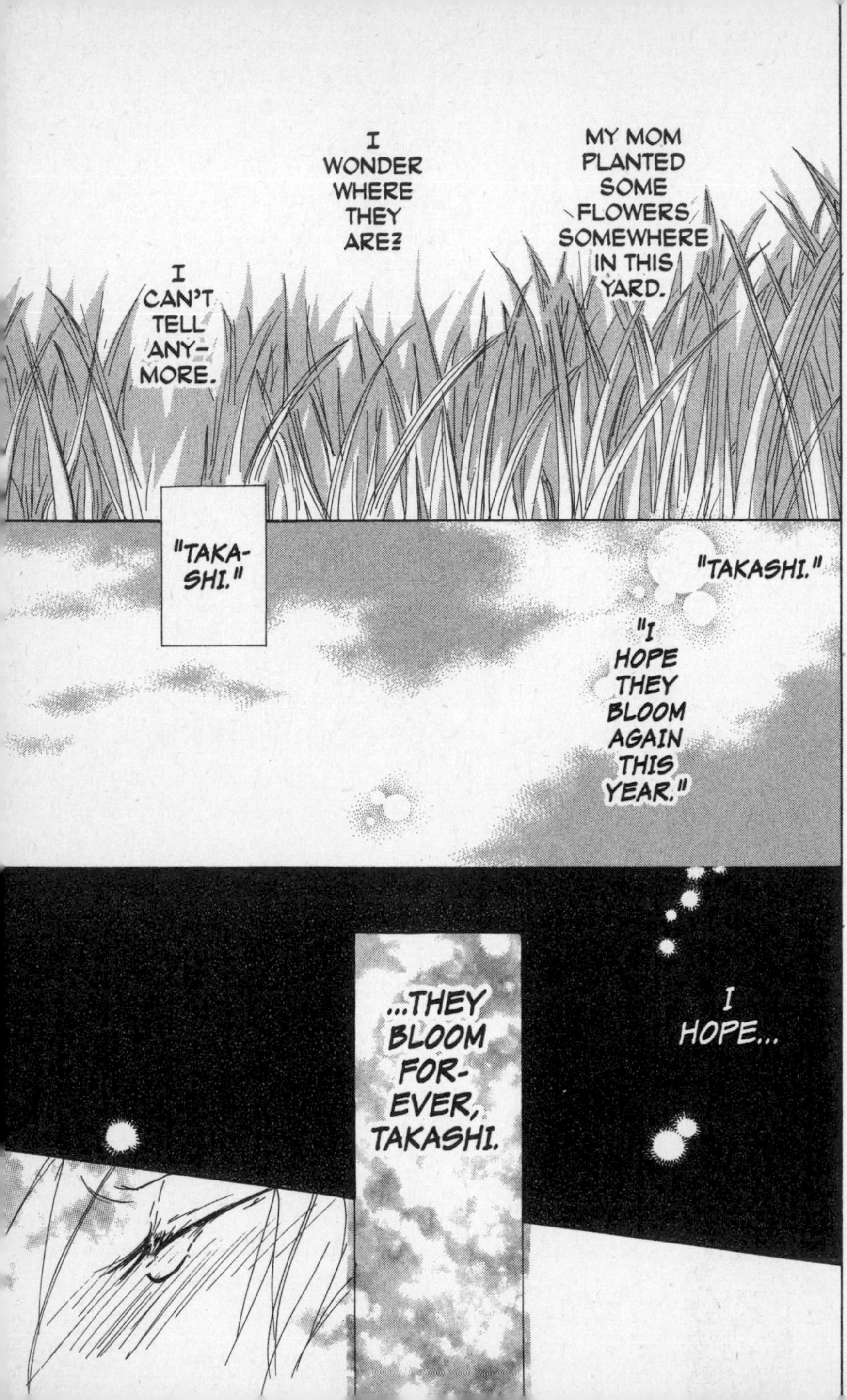
MY MOM PLANTED SOME FLOWERS SOMEWHERE IN THIS YARD.
I WONDER WHERE THEY ARE?
I CAN'T TELL ANY-MORE.
"TAKASHI."
"I HOPE THEY BLOOM AGAIN THIS YEAR."
"TAKA-SHI."
I HOPE...
...THEY BLOOM FOR-EVER, TAKASHI.

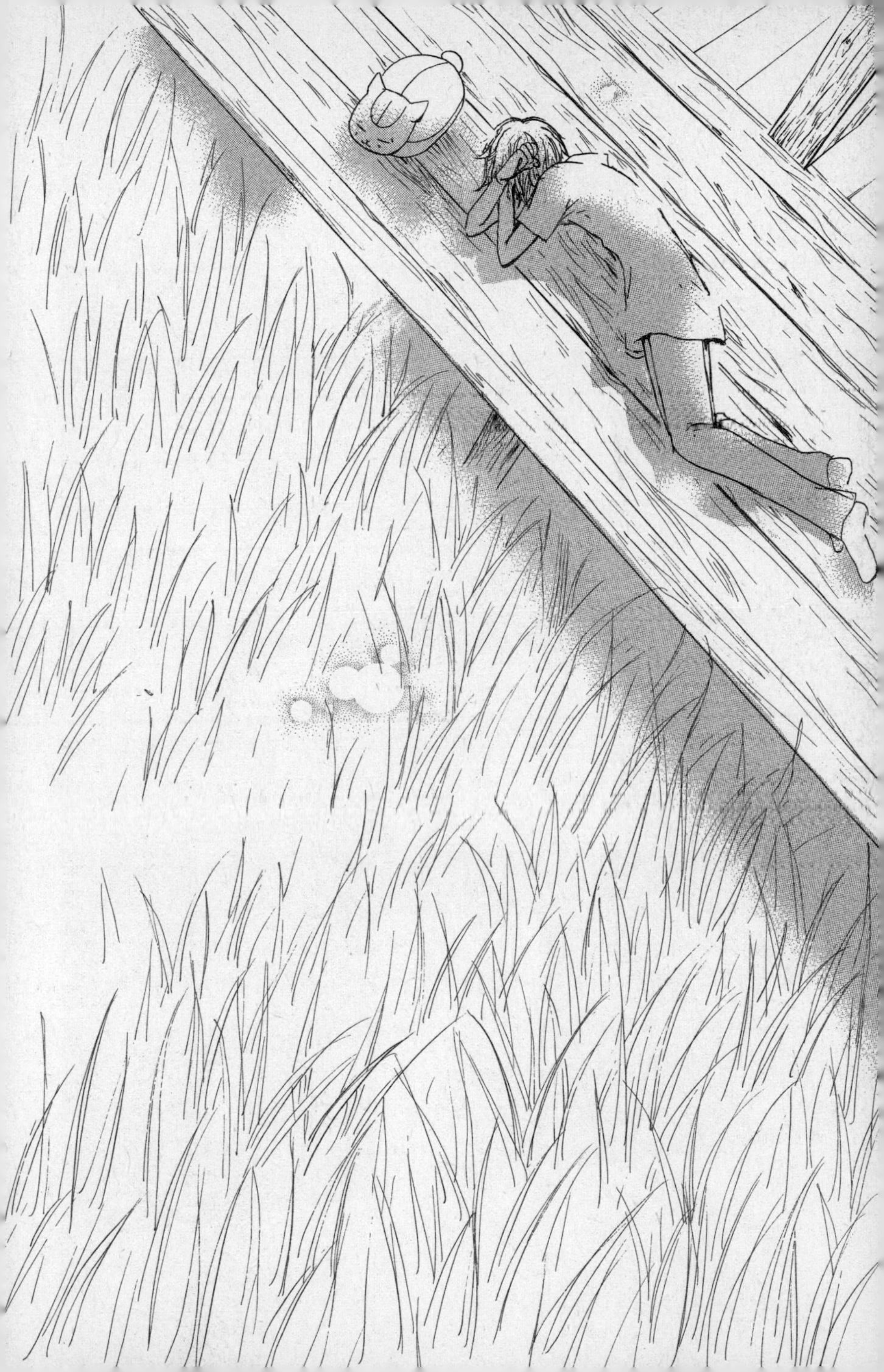

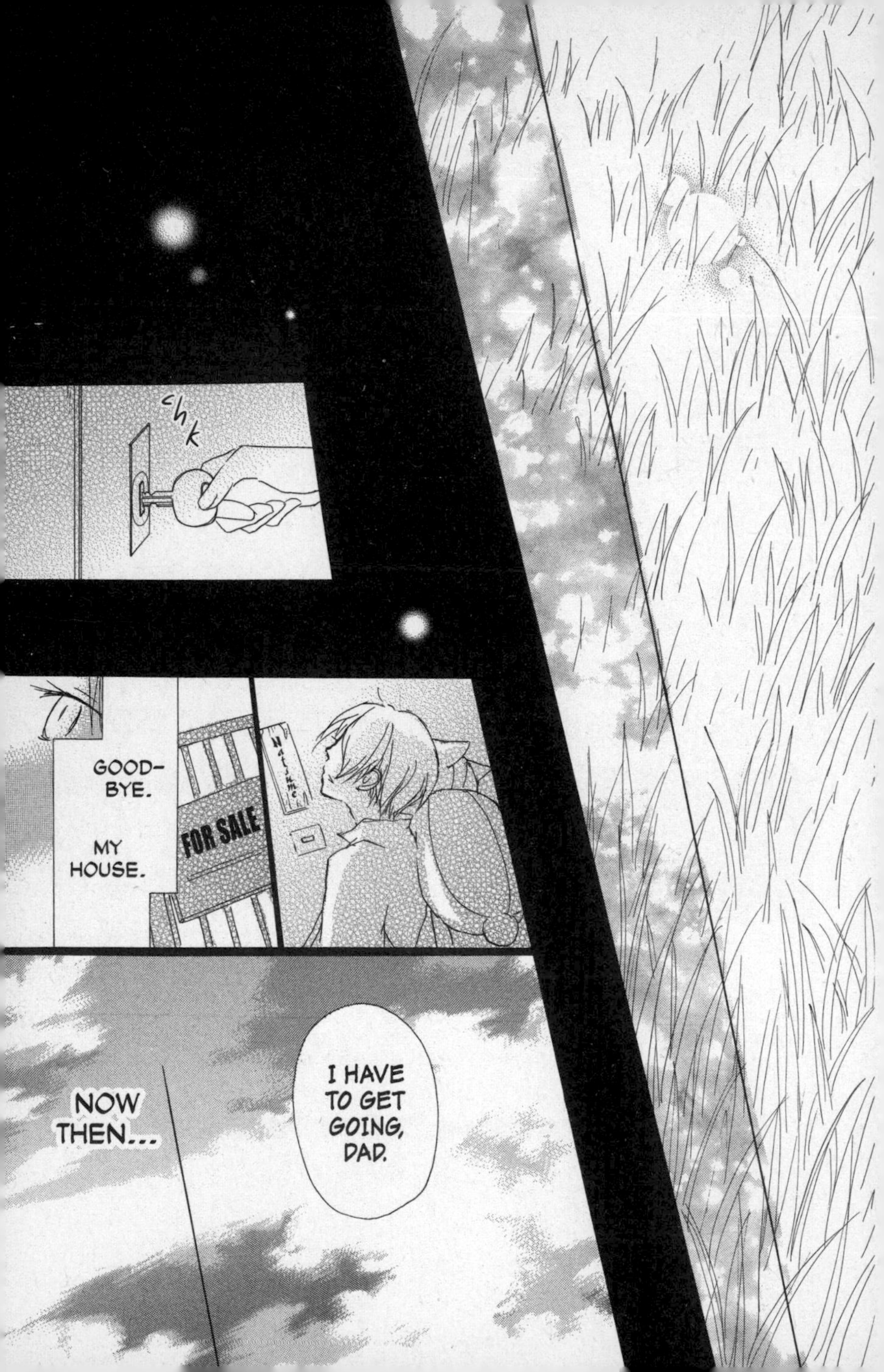
chk
GOOD-BYE.
MY HOUSE.
FOR SALE
I HAVE TO GET GOING, DAD.
NOW THEN...

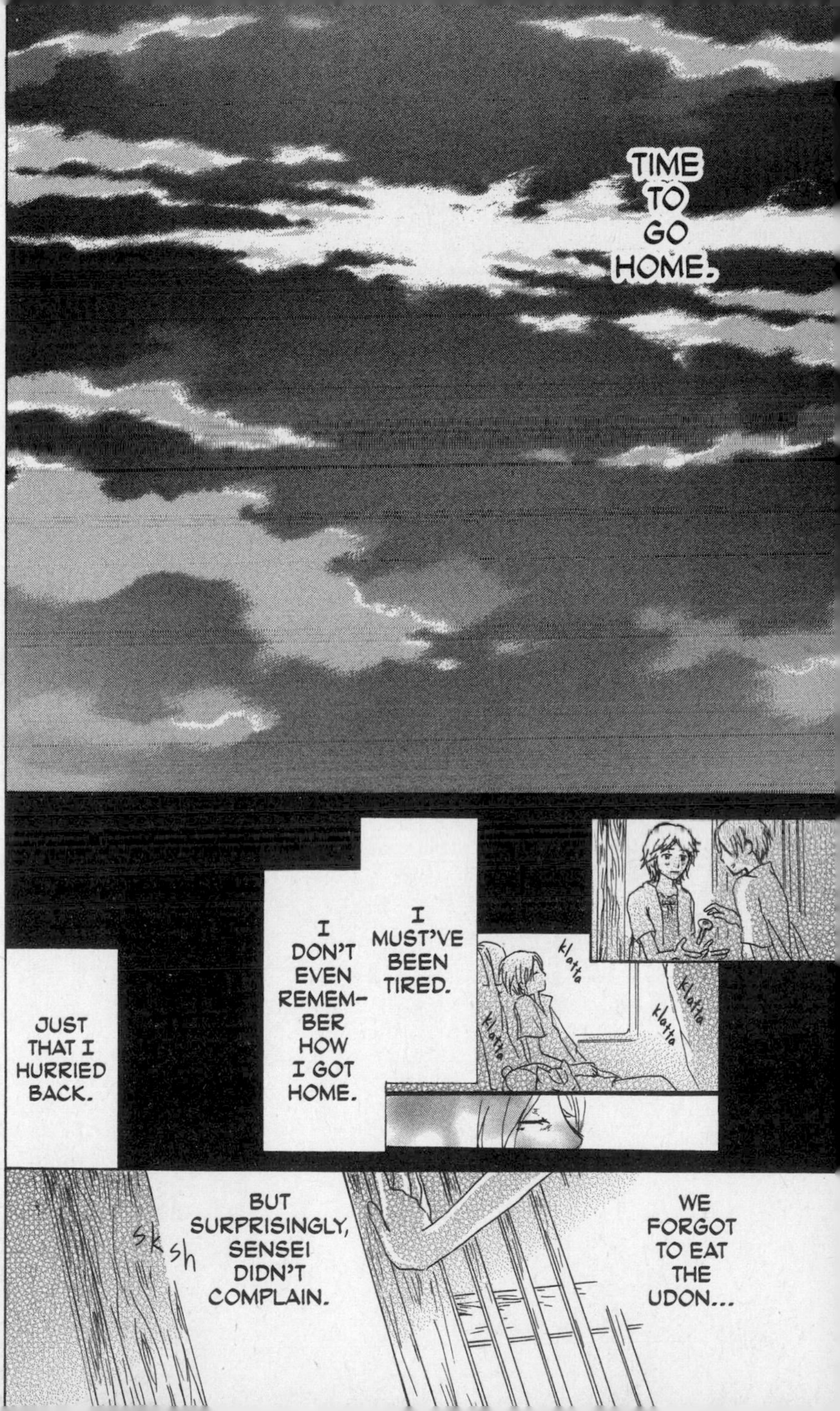
TIME TO GO HOME.
klatta
klatta
klatta
klatta
I MUST'VE BEEN TIRED.
I DON'T EVEN REMEMBER HOW I GOT HOME.
JUST THAT I HURRIED BACK.
WE FORGOT TO EAT THE UDON...
BUT SURPRISINGLY, SENSEI DIDN'T COMPLAIN.
sk sh

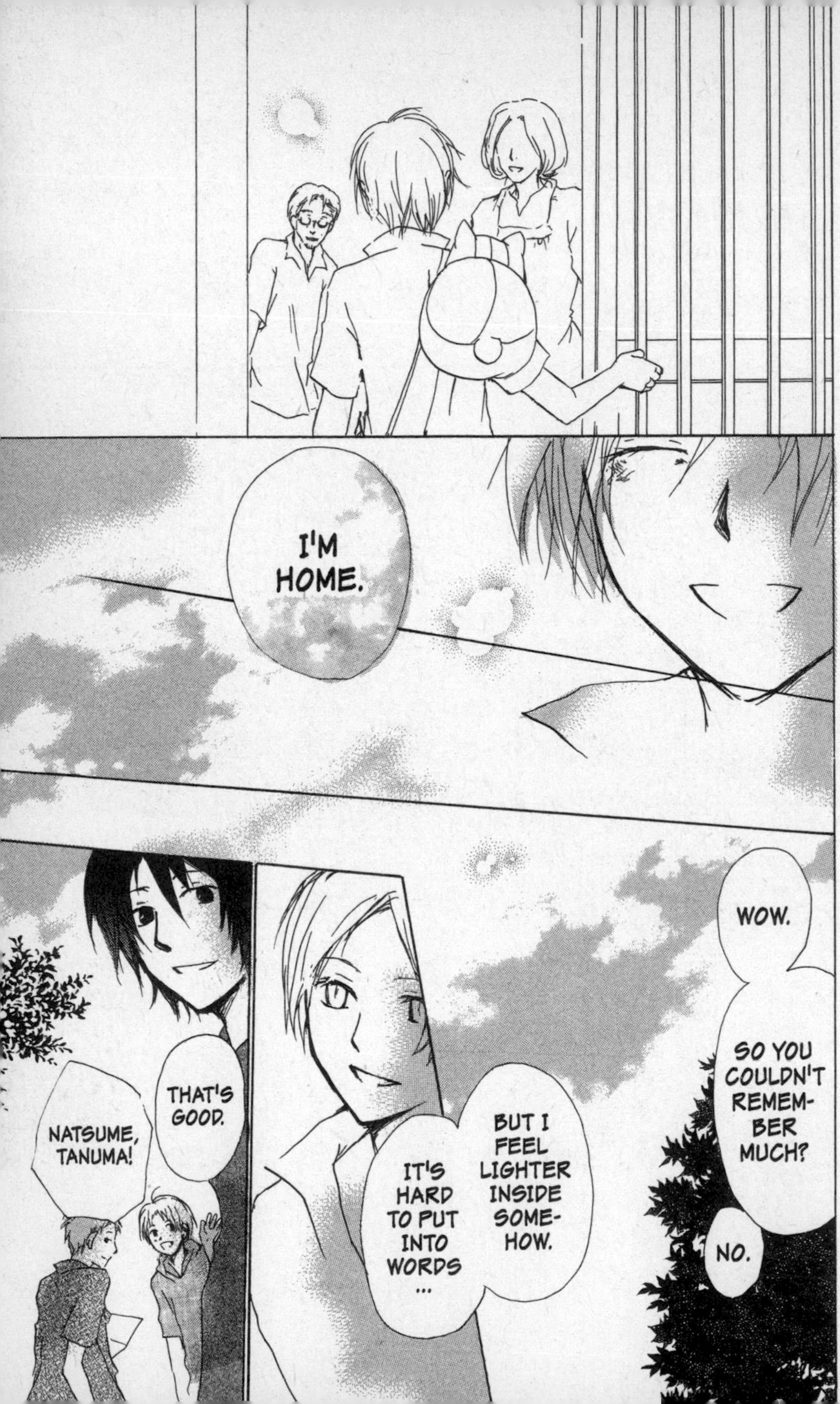
I'M HOME.
WOW.
SO YOU COULDN'T REMEMBER MUCH?
NO.
BUT I FEEL LIGHTER INSIDE SOMEHOW.
IT'S HARD TO PUT INTO WORDS...
THAT'S GOOD.
NATSUME, TANUMA!

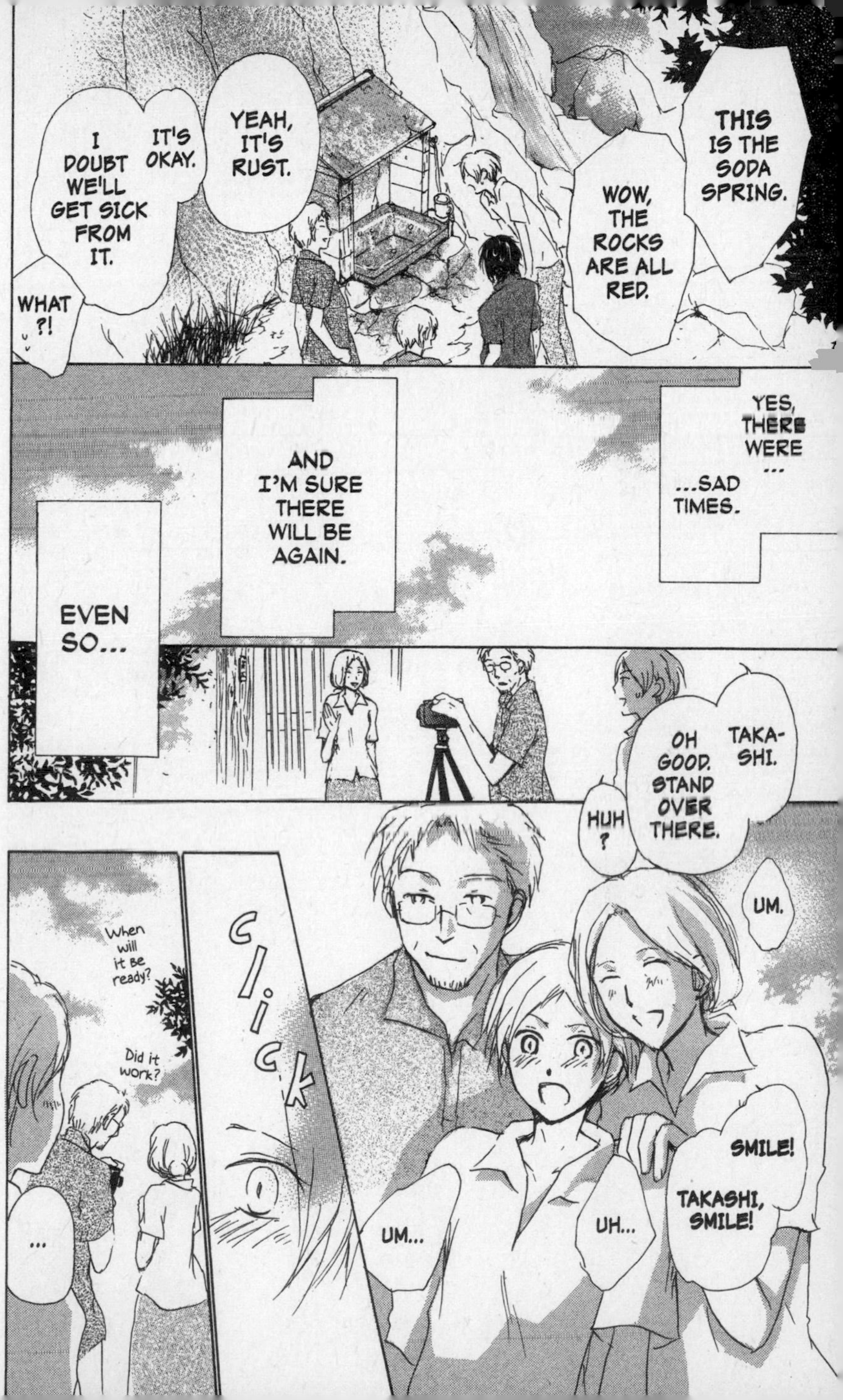
THIS IS THE SODA SPRING.
WOW, THE ROCKS ARE ALL RED.
YEAH, IT'S RUST.
IT'S OKAY.
I DOUBT WE'LL GET SICK FROM IT.
WHAT?!
YES, THERE WERE...
...SAD TIMES.
AND I'M SURE THERE WILL BE AGAIN.
EVEN SO...
TAKASHI.
OH GOOD. STAND OVER THERE.
HUH?
UM.
SMILE!
TAKASHI, SMILE!
UH...
UM...
CLICK
When will it be ready?
Did it work?
...

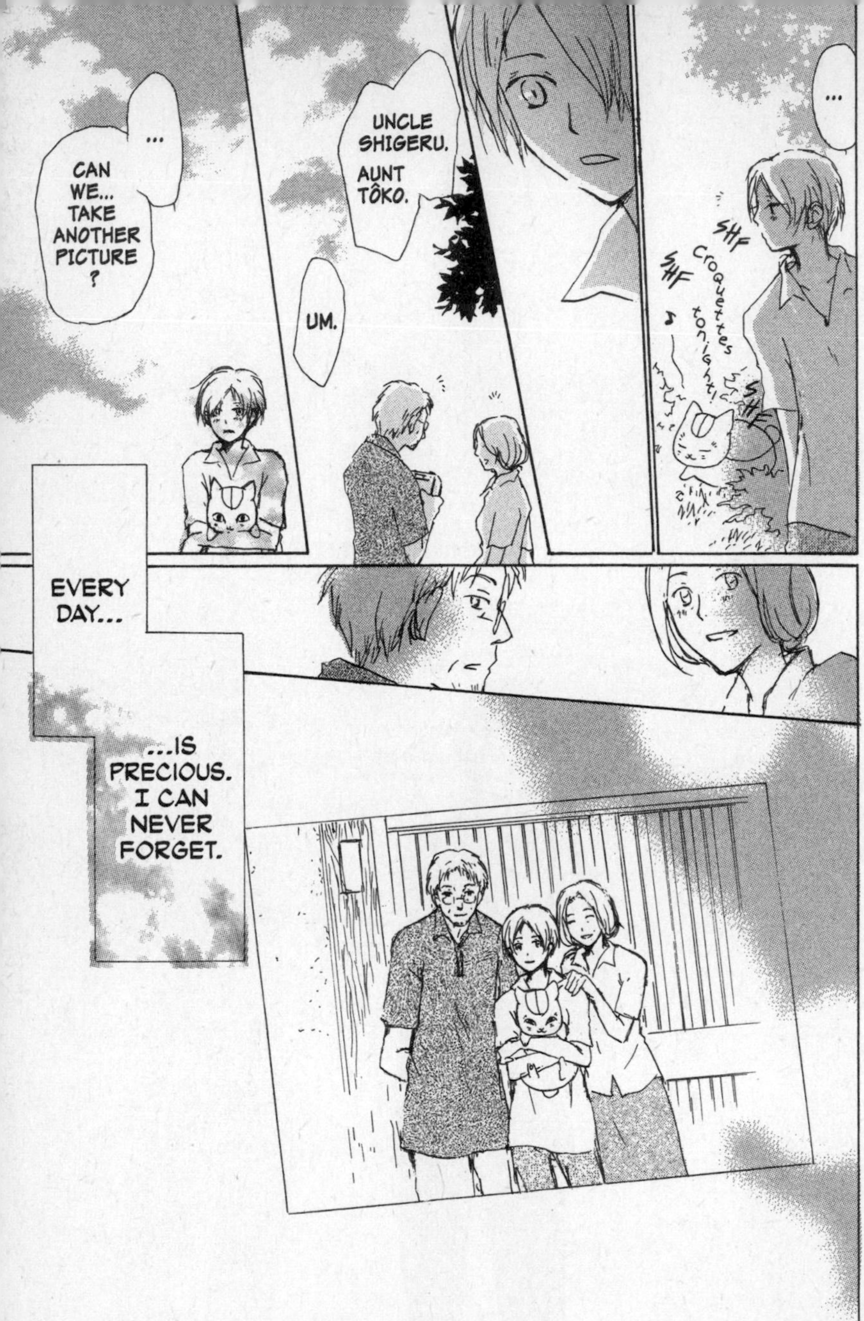
...
SHF
SHF
SHF
Croquettes tonight!
SHF
UNCLE SHIGERU.
AUNT TÔKO.
UM.
...
CAN WE... TAKE ANOTHER PICTURE?
EVERY DAY...
...IS PRECIOUS. I CAN NEVER FORGET.

NATSUME'S BOOK OF FRIENDS, VOL. 11: END

Seiji Matoba and Shuichi Natori
in high school.

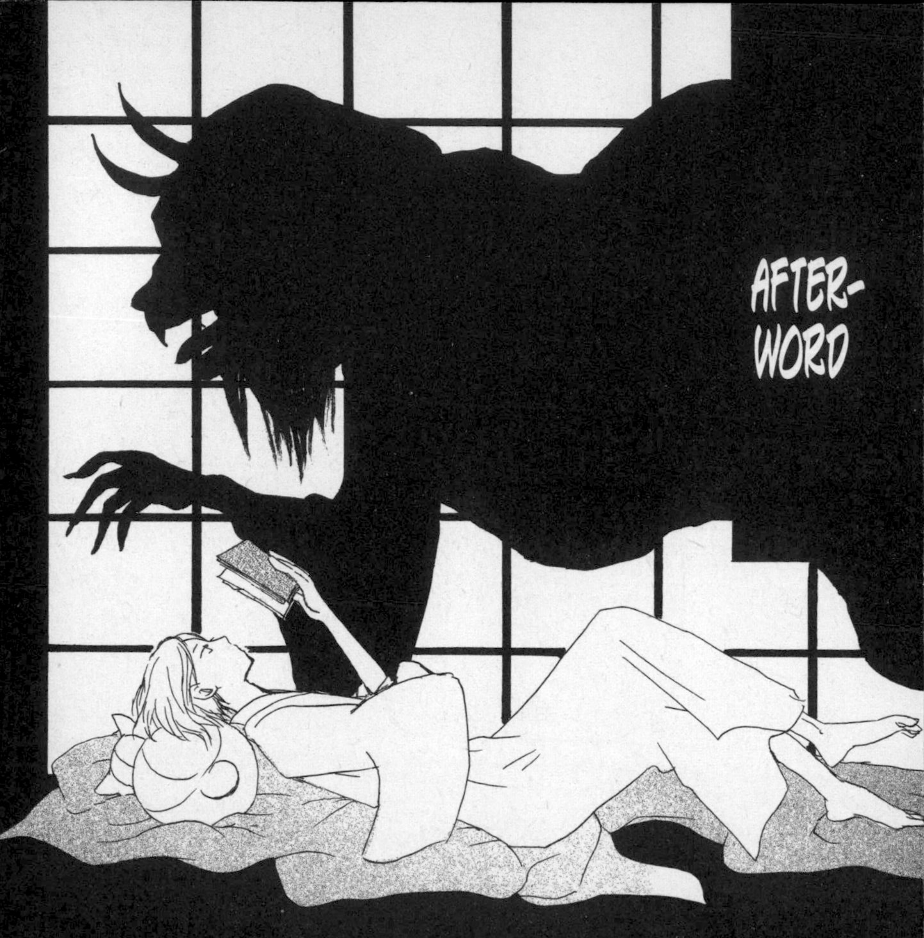
AFTER-
WORD

Thank you for reading.

Natsume finally discovers the joys of being accepted by those around him, and begins to want to open up about himself. But there are still some things he can't divulge in order to preserve his current living situation. He wants to at least convey his feelings, but he hasn't really come to terms with them himself. He's going to have to face things he's kept bottled up.

I enjoyed working on this volume, since I got to write episodes I've been dying to include, about Taki's grandfather, and Natsume's visit to his old home. Please read the rest of this afterword only after reading the entire volume to avoid spoilers.

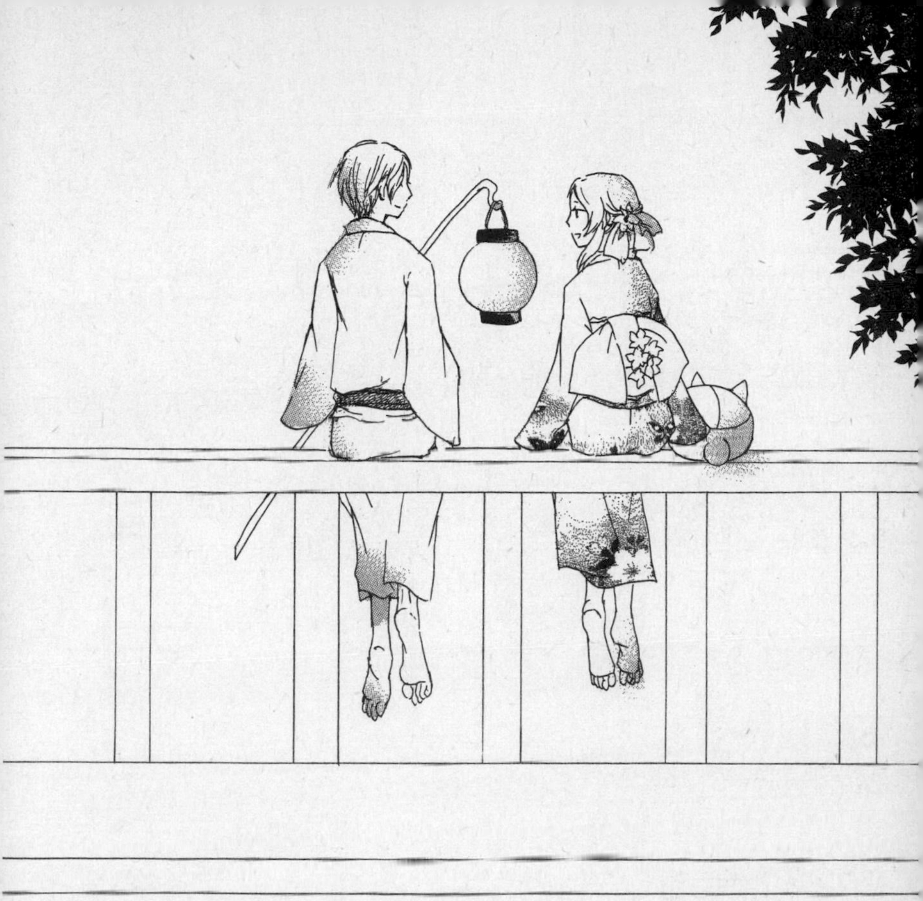

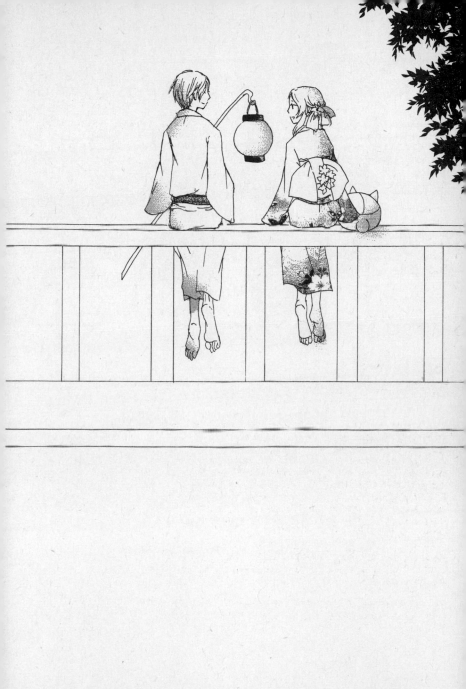

CHAPTERS 42, 43

Sealed

I've always wanted to draw the trio of Natsume, Tanuma and Taki hanging out. Before, Tanuma thought he might be a little crazy, but Natsume affirmed what used to be an unstable world for him. Natsume's existence was basically his salvation, but he realizes that he can't be much help to Natsume. It's a dilemma he'll have to keep facing as his friend. On the other hand, I've discovered that Taki, who also can't see but knows Natsume's circumstances, is delighted at the things she discovers. It's difficult but fun to draw these three together. I was also happy drawing Taki's empty house, images of a white ghost flapping in the darkness, and small yokai hopping and frolicking about.

CHAPTERS 44-46

Long Way Home

This is another story I've wanted to write for a long time. Even Natsume had to have memories of happy moments from his childhood. But he's had to move from place to place, relying on one family after another to take him under their wing. He feels guilty whether he clings to the memories of people who loved him, or whether he forgets them and moves on. This time, he was finally able to do something for himself. I loved being able to draw Natsume when he was young and more expressive, his parents, and Miyoko.

He finally touched upon the memories he was avoiding because the pain was too great. I feel some of the weight has been lifted from him.

So this makes eleven volumes of Natsume. The environment surrounding Natsume is changing, in both good and ominous ways.

I'm so grateful that they're making a third season of the anime. Thanks so much to all the fans, Director Omori, the voice actors, the animation staff, and everyone who made the first two seasons so nostalgically beautiful.

The manga is like the sheet music with the melody I want to convey, and it gets arranged in various ways in the readers' heads. Then Director Omori calls out to the various musicians and conducts a heartwarming and vivid orchestra expressed by many people. I feel so blessed that I was able to participate as the manga artist. It brings tears to my eyes even as I write.

To everyone who lovingly worked on the first two seasons, the people who newly joined for the third season, the viewers looking forward to the new season, the editors, and my dear readers, I'll keep working hard, so please continue with your support.

Thanks to:
Tamao Ohki
Chika
Mika
Mr. Sato
My sister
Hoen Kikaku, Ltd.
Thank you.

AFTERWORD: END

Natsume's
BOOK of FRIENDS
VOLUME 11 END NOTES

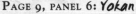

PAGE 9, PANEL 6: Yokan
A traditional Japanese dessert made from sweet bean paste jellied with agar (a seaweed that acts like gelatin).

PAGE 13, PANEL 1: Kokeshi
Simple wooden dolls with a cylindrical body, round head and painted features. Originally a toy for children, it has since evolved into a traditional art form.

PAGE 15, PANEL 1: Kappa
Child-sized water goblins that are usually green with webbed hands and feet, a turtle-like shell, and a plate-like water reservoir in the top of their heads. If their reservoir runs dry, kappa become weak and may even die, so the water level must be maintained. They are also fond of cucumbers, which is why cucumber sushi rolls are called *kappa-maki*.

PAGE 18, PANEL 4: Yakisoba
Noodles commonly stir-fried with vegetables (often cabbage, carrots and onions) and pork, and flavored with a thick variation of Worcestershire sauce. Although called "soba," it is not made from buckwheat.

PAGE 91, SIDEBAR: Kumamoto
A prefecture in western Kyushu Island.

PAGE 115, PANEL 5: Ekiben
Ekiben are a type of bento (boxed lunches) that can be bought at train stations and also on the train itself. These lunches often showcase local or seasonal cuisine.

PAGE 117, PANEL 4: Udon
A thick wheat noodle, usually served hot or cold in broth with various toppings.